ASCEND
THE
MOUNTAIN

A Guide To Judaism

VOLUME ONE

From Bar/Bat-Mitzvah
to Pre-Marriage

by

Rabbi E. S. Rabinowitz

First published in Great Britain in 1984 by Anthony Blond

Anthony Blond is an imprint of Muller, Blond & White Limited,
55/57 Great Ormond Street, London WC1N 3HZ

British Library Cataloguing in Publication Data
Rabinowitz, E.S.
  Ascend the mountain.
  1. Judaism
  I. Title
  296'024055   BM561
  ISBN 0-85634-174-6

Typeset and printed in Great Britain by The Pitman Press, Bath

CONTENTS

PREFACE

Whether its compiler was king Solomon, as Jewish tradition maintains, or an anonymous scribe many centuries later, during the reign of king Herod, as the historian Graetz opines; the scroll of *Ecclesiastes* first appeared in an age when all literary works were laboriously penned by hand on parchment. Yet even in those circumstances the author informs us: "Of making many books there is no end."

How much more true is this in our own times, when books in almost every language, on every conceivable subject, roll smoothly off the printing-presses in their thousands year by year! In the sphere of Jewish literature, moreover, there is an ample supply of excellent volumes on Jewish life, law and custom, with no need for it to be supplemented.

Yet, to the knowledge of this author, there is nothing available like this work which, while its contents are applicable and should therefore be of use to readers of all ages, has three distinctive features:

It is addressed primarily to the teenager, devoting particular attention to the problems which confront, and the questions which are likely to be asked by him or her in modern times. From the moment night falls at the very commencement of the day on which commitment to the Jewish way of life becomes mandatory, the reader is taken chronologically, step by step, first through a complete weekday and then a complete Shabbat — which together collectively comprise the whole of the year, apart from a score-or-so of days; and

At every stage due regard is given to the duties of the lady in Judaism, and the prominent role she plays in the community. Other features are the emphasis laid on the ethics of Judaism, and the precedence they have in the totality of our religion; the correct definition of the term "Torah"; the true meaning of the commandment popularly rendered "Thou shalt love thy neighbour as thyself" – and many other clarifications of inadequately translated Hebrew terms.

It is stressed, and will be reiterated again, that the treatment of the commandments dealt with in this volume is, in the main, superficial, intended as an incentive to the reader to study them in depth in one of the many books available specifically devoted to the codification of Jewish laws and customs.

This volume is dedicated to my dear wife, Gienia, for her life-long devotion, and her patience and help during the years of its composition – may she live to 120! And to the memory of a dear friend, the late Gordon L. Davies, *alav hashalom*, who urged me on to write it, but did not realise his hope, alas, to live to see it in print.

My sincere thanks are expressed to Dr. Alan Unterman for undertaking the arduous task of reading the manuscript, correcting its faults and suggesting improvements – and the painful one of advising where demanded excisions should be made; to Mr. Sidney Friedland, for his encouragement and introduction to the publishers; to Mark (Monty) Raviden, for his material assistance; and, above all, to my publisher, Mr Anthony Blond, for the confidence he has shown in accepting the work for publication.

E. S. Rabinowitz

Annotation: In order not to distract the reader's attention with numbered note-references, these are indicated by being quoted in double quotation-marks. The notes are appended to the chapters, which are divided into sections for easy reference.

INTRODUCTION

Section 1. **From Seven Commandments**
As everyone who has a whit of Bible-knowledge knows, only one commandment was explicitly given to Adam, to be observed by him and his wife alone: "From the tree of the knowledge of good and evil, thou shalt not eat of it." But according to the Jewish doctors of law, the verse immediately preceding this one, implicitly contains "six commandments divinely given to him", binding upon him and all his descendants – the whole of mankind. They are: prohibitions against (i) idolatry, (ii) blasphemy, (iii) bloodshed, (iv) incest, and (v) theft; and (vi) the duty to establish courts for the administration of social justice.

By the time of the Flood, they had all been universally violated, except by Noah and his family; and after that deluge, when for the first time "flesh was permitted as man's food", a seventh universal commandment was added – (vii) not to eat a limb torn from a living animal, deduced from "flesh with the life thereof . . . you shall not eat;" and they thus became known as 'The Seven Commandments for the descendants of Noah', a term which includes all mankind.

Section 2. **To Ten Commandments**
Ten generations later, Abram (afterwards Abraham) was born, the first man of whom G–d said: "he hearkened to My voice, and kept My charge," and to his descendants, the children of Israel his grandson, the "Ten Commandments" were divinely given – and within two months of receiving them they were violating the first and most important of the Ten! Fortunately however, as a result of the entreaties of their leader Moses, they were given 'a second chance'.

Largely through the media of Judaism's two daughter-religions, hundreds of millions of mankind acknowledge the divine origin of the Ten Commandments, nominally accept them as such, and teach them

ix

to their children from an early age – which is not a very difficult thing
to do. For the average five-to-six year old child knows 'how many
make ten', can count that number on the fingers of both hands: and if
told that, besides the father he knows and obeys, there is also a
'Father of all people in heaven' Who tells us we must, or must not, do
ten things, he will understand in a general way.

Of course, as they grow older, those children will undoubtedly ask
many questions about the nature of this universal Father, and enquire
about the meaning of the individual commandments. But if the
explanation is given them by a judicious parent or trained teacher,
they should not find it too difficult to grasp the import of just ten
precepts.

Section 3.   **To Six Hundred and Thirteen!**
But that is not what the growing *Jewish* child is taught: he is told that
not ten, but "six hundred and thirteen commandments were communicated to Moses" by G–d on mount Sinai, and transmitted to us
in writing in the 'Five Books of Moses'; and that he should know
them all "by the age of ten, and fulfil them from the age of thirteen" –
and a girl from even an earlier age than that, as we shall see! Who
could blame them for feeling deeply anxious about the possibility of
mentally digesting, let alone practically fulfilling, so huge a number of
divine commandments at so early an age?

But of course it is not so! As will be explained in chapter five, only
some 270 of them come the way of the average Jewish man or woman
today; and the number of commandments calling for fulfilment by the
teenager, employing that term loosely to mean the years from
Bar/Bat-Mitzvah (in future BM for short), is very much less. In this
book I have selected and numbered one hundred of them, the most
important and comprehensive, which have to be fulfilled from the
very day BM age is reached. Those applicable on weekdays and
Shabbatot, of which all but a score or so of our lives are comprised,
are treated chronologically, from the moment the stars usher in the
BM day onwards.

I have been talking of the practical fulfilment of the commandments: but it is important to stress that *knowledge* of *all* the 613
should be acquired as soon as possible: for all of them – no more and
no less – make up the grand divine design, G–d's ideal constitution,
for the Jewish people as a whole, living in tranquility within the
boundaries of their ancestral Land, with the rebuilt Temple in
Jerusalem as its crown. And it is towards the achievement of this
Messianic goal that you and I, and every Jew and Jewess should ever
aspire.

"ASCEND THE MOUNTAIN"

Section 4. The title of this book is adapted from the verse: "And the Eternal said unto Moses: 'Come up to Me into the mount, and be there; and I will give thee the tablets of stone, the Torah and the commandment, which I have written that thou mayest teach them.'" The conscientious observance of the hundred Torah commandments expounded in this volume will take the teenager as high as he or she can "ascend the mountain of the Eternal, and stand in His holy place."

Interpreting the above verse, Rashi says: "All the 613 commandments are implicitly contained in the Ten Commandments;" while Resh Lakish says that "'the commandment' refers to the Mishnah" – about which more in the above-mentioned Chapter. I only mention these two interpretations here to explain how it is that within the 100 numbered commandments, quite a few other Torah commandments will be mentioned but not numbered, because they are either implicit in the listed commandment, or because they are unlikely to be encountered. Again, much recourse is had to the Mishnah and Gemara – to which Resh Lakish there says the phrase 'that thou mayest teach them' refers – in our discussion of the 100.

Section 5.   **To The Older And Scholarly Reader**
Though selected because they have immediate applicability for the BM, the 100 Torah commandments in this book apply also, of course, to *every* Jew and Jewess over that age: indeed, they comprise the greater part of practical, everyday Jewish life. A companion volume to this, taking the adult through the century or so between marriage and eternal bliss, is almost ready for publication – with the Almighty's help!

Any scholar who may by chance peruse this work may well, at first glance, question the inclusion of this, or the omission of that, commandment from those listed, and the particular prominence given to some of them. Reflection will however prove, I trust, that selection and place are in accord with the time and environment in which the modern teenager lives.

What was taken for granted yesteryear, and still *is* in the minority very religious community, is questioned among the majority of youth today; what were once thrilling religious experiences for all, are now mere conventions, apathetically and reluctantly observed by most – if observed at all. The aim of this book is to answer the questions the modern teenager asks, and to restore the thrill which the full Jewish life brings to those who walk in its paths. "He who causes others to

do good," said R. Eleazar, "is greater than the doer" — and that is the
only greatness I pray for from this effort.

Section 6.   **The Ladder of Ascent**
The contents are divided into two parts: the first lays down a firm
foundation on which a very tall and strong ladder can safely stand;
and the second fashions that ladder, consisting of two sturdy
uprights, each formed of five commandments which must constantly
be borne in mind, and the ninety rungs which they support. So, young
reader: let us set the foundation, then — ascend!

Section   **Notes**
1   Genesis 2.17; Sanhedrin 56b; Genesis 9.3; Genesis 9.4.
2   Genesis 26.5; Exodus 20.1–14.
3   Makkot 23b; Ethics 5.24.
4   Exodus 24.12; Psalms 24.3; on first note here; Berachot 5a.
5   B. Batra 9a.

One

"THE RIGHTEOUS SHALL LIVE BY HIS FAITH"

Section 1. Judaism is a 'Faith'. What is 'faith'? To have faith is to accept unquestioningly as absolute fact a theory which cannot demonstrably be proven to be true by scientific evidence.

At the very outset, Judaism asks of us that we have such faith in – the authenticity of a Book, and in the existence of its Author as the sole and supreme, spiritual and eternal Divine Being Who created the universe, with Man as the predetermined goal of that Creation. For the present we will use the English Name, G–d, for this Supreme Being, to be followed later by a more detailed study of the various Hebrew Names and their respective significance.

The 'Book' is called the 'Torah' in Hebrew, 'The Five Books of Moses' or the 'Pentateuch' (meaning 'five books' in Greek) in English. It is ascribed to Moses because it was to him, the greatest of the Prophets, that G–d directly conveyed its contents, to be transmitted in writing to the ancestors of the Jewish people, in trust for the whole of humanity.

It will be shown in the next chapter that for the Jew the term 'Torah', in its widest connotation, includes the totality of Jewish law and practice as it has developed from Moses' time to this day. Any references in this chapter, therefore, to texts post-dating Moses should be accepted in good faith until proof has been proffered showing how this wider interpretation is inherent in the Pentateuch itself.

Since none but Moses was present when the Torah was given him – for he was commanded "And no man shall come up with thee, neither shall any man be seen throughout all the mount"; and since G–d is wholly spiritual and incorporeal, whilst science can only prove the existence of *matter*; acceptance of the divine origin of the Torah and the existence of its Author can only be through faith, and are the basic elements of the Jewish Faith.

1

It is true that some great Jewish thinkers attempted to prove G–d's existence by logical argument, most of them employing the syllogism: everything that exists must have had a cause, an origin; the universe exists; therefore the universe had an originator – Who is G–d, "the First Being, Who brought every existing thing into being." But they only did so in response to the challenges of Greek and Moslem philosophers, their own belief in G–d and the Torah remaining firmly rooted in faith, not philosophy.

The order in which these two basic elements of Judaism have been stated – first the Book and then G–d, was chosen with deliberation, for two reasons:

First: Though an instinctive intimation of the existence of a Divine Being is inborn in man, as will be affirmed later, *knowledge* of G–d's nature, attributes and ways, so far as it is in man's intellectual capacity to understand them, can only be acquired through the medium of Torah study;

Secondly: To Judaism, abstract faith, unsupported by the practices it enjoins, has little, if any, meaning. Of necessity, as far as the Jew is concerned, faith in G–d demands that one should conduct one's life according to the detailed guide-lines laid down in the divine Book – the Torah; and *they* cannot be followed until they are known.

Section 2.   **Faith – Despite Challenges**

Judaism begins with faith – but it also ends with faith: for daily life around us seems so often to disprove the teachings of the Torah that, unless you firmly resolve to face these apparent inconsistencies with a categorical 'nevertheless, I have absolute faith in the words of the Torah and its divine Author,' you could easily become prey to doubt and uncertainty. It is in the sphere of moral justice, with which the Torah is so much concerned, that most of the challenges arise, so let us take a brief glance into it.

King David said "Righteousness and justice are the foundation" of G–d's throne; yet elsewhere he himself asks: "Why standest Thou afar off, O Eternal? Why hidest Thou Thyself in times of trouble? Through the pride of the wicked, the poor is hotly pursued. . . ." In similar vein, his son king Solomon, traditionally considered to be the author of *Ecclesiastes*, bemoans: "I have considered all the oppressions that are done under the sun, and behold the tears of the oppressed, and they had no comforter; and on the side of their oppressors there was power."

But we can go back to the father of our people and see how he boldly put the question directly to G–d: "Shall not the Judge of all the earth do justly?" when told that the cities of the plain, together with their inhabitants, were to be destroyed. That, however, had been a rhetorical question, for the asking of which "Abraham was rewarded," since it showed he had compassion on his fellow-men, "desiring that judgment against the wicked should be suspended for the sake of the righteous."

Section 3. **Faith Unswerving!**
So far as he himself was concerned, Abraham's faith in G–d was unswerving, absolute. When given what to others would be the incredulous information that he, at the age of one hundred, and his erstwhile barren wife Sarah at the age of ninety, were to have a son, he "fell upon his face and rejoiced . . . and he believed" in G–d, Who assured him that his descendants from that son would be as numerous as the stars of the heaven. Again, when he was commanded to offer up that son, still unmarried, as a sacrifice, he obeyed with alacrity and without questioning as to how the earlier promise could thereafter be fulfilled. That was a demonstration of faith!

The whole book of Job is a profound thesis on the sufferings of the righteous, meriting deep study. That prophet's avowal, after having been bereft of his children, deprived of all his material possessions, and smitten with horrible disease, that "Though He slay me, yet will I trust in Him," has justifiably been described as "the quintessence of the Hebraic spirit of magnificent faith."

The prophet Habakkuk declared: "Though the fig-tree shall not blossom, neither shall fruit be in the vine . . . the fields shall yield no food, the flock shall be cut off from the fold, and there be no herd in the stalls – yet I will *rejoice* in the Eternal, I will *exult* in the G–d of my salvation"! To rejoice and exult in "the Giver of food to all flesh" as the G–d of one's salvation, when deprived of every kind of sustenance – that is also a display of sublime faith!

Section 4. **The Initial And The Sublime**
But it is a long, up-mountain climb from the initial faith in the authenticity of the closed Book and the existence of a Supreme Being to the death-defying and sublime faith of the Patriarchs and the Prophets towards which we must ever aspire. The Book has to be opened and assiduously studied from cover to cover with the aid of all its complements and commentaries mentioned in the next chapter, and its ordained duties towards G–d and your fellow-beings integrated scrupulously and willingly into your everyday life as each is learnt.

When we come to consider the word *yir'ah* (in chapter eight) we will see that it has two meanings: 'fear' of punishment, like that which deters a child from disobeying his father; and 'reverence', which makes any thought of disobeying one who is loved inconceivable. And so it is with *emunah*, faith: there is the simple faith of a child, which can be shaken by the slightest setback; and the cultivated, mature faith of the man of knowledge and experience, which is so deeply rooted that the most violent tempest cannot shake it.

It was undoubtedly to this latter kind of sublime faith in G–d that R. Nachman b. Isaac was referring when he said that "Habakkuk came and based all the six hundred and thirteen commandments of the Torah on one principle" when that prophet declared: "The righteous man shall live by his faith," the faith which is the mature fruit of Torah study – the "Tree of Life to those who uphold it, and makes happy those who support it."

Assuming that you have now accepted these two basic elements of Judaism, we will now proceed to a detailed consideration of what Torah is; Who G–d is – so far as it is possible for man to understand; what Man is; and what the relationship between man and G–d should be, especially for the Jew.

Section   **Notes**
1 Exodus 34.3; Yad 1.1.
2 Psalms 97.2 & 10.1; Eccles. 4.1; Genesis 18.25; MR. Genesis 49.9.
3 Genesis 17.17 (see Rashi), 15.5–6 and 22.3; Job 13.15 and SBB comment; Habakkuk 3.17–18; Psalms 136.25.
4 Makkot 23b; Habakkuk 2.4; Proverbs 3.18.

Two

WHAT IS "TORAH"?

Section 1. The noun 'torah' is derived from the Hebrew verb *lehorot*, the meaning of which is clearly indicated in the verse telling us that Jacob "had sent Judah in advance unto Joseph, *to show the way* before him unto Goshen", the best area in the land of Egypt in which Pharaoh had agreed the Patriarch's family should settle.

The verb also means 'to teach' – for to teach is to show the way in which something should be done. Thus, after the children of Israel had promised to obey all of G–d's words, Moses was commanded: "Come up to Me into the mount, and be there; and I will give thee the tables of stone, and the Torah and the commandment, which I have written, that thou mayest teach (*lehorot*) them."

The Torah, then, is the divine route-map for man, a guide and a teacher. "I am the Eternal thy G–d, Who teacheth thee to progress, Who leadeth thee in the way that thou shouldest go."

Section 2.   **Strict Meaning**
In its narrowest connotation, Torah refers to the "Five Books of Moses", the contents of which were directly transmitted to him by G–d, and are termed the "Written Torah". They form, as it were, a mosaic in which are intertwined two threads, historical narrative and legislation.

The first commences with a thumb-nail account of the creation of the universe, not intended as a thesis on cosmogony, but as a brief introduction to the climax of that creation, the emergence of Man, his genealogy and moral development, the prime theme of the Torah. There follow the story of the Flood; the lives of the Patriarchs, Abraham, Isaac and Jacob; the bondage of their descendants is Egypt their deliverance and wanderings in the wilderness.

The narrative ends with the children of Israel's encampment on the eastern bank of the river Jordan, within sight of the land of Canaan

5

which G–d had promised to each of the Patriarchs in turn as the inalienable inheritance of their descendants; and the death of Moses there, after having been permitted to see, but barred from entering, the Promised Land.

The legislative strand of the divine mosaic comprises G–d's commandments, directives to man, and specifically to the Israelites, as to what they must and must not do, if they were to honour their promise to obey all G–d's words. "You shall not add unto the word which I command you, neither shall you diminish from it, that you may keep the commandments of the Eternal your G–d which I command you."

It should now be apparent to you why it is misleading to refer to the Five Books of Moses as 'The Law', which is the common practice. There is much vital and practical 'Torah' – guidance to moral living, in the narrative chapters of those Books as well, which will be amply illustrated as we proceed.

Being the word of G–d, all the contents of the Torah are sacrosanct. Some of its commandments may temporarily become inapplicable at times, short or long; at others, the Sages found it necessary, with Torah sanction, to "erect a fence around the Torah" commandments, in order to protect them from violation.

Some of those which have been in abeyance for almost two thousand years are already being revived in modern Israel, and the others eventually will be, for "the word of our G–d shall stand for ever". And it may be that some of the stakes in the rabbinic fence will gradually be removed, should the reason for their enactment no longer apply. But the main consideration will always be to protect the precious word of G–d from inadvertent violation.

Section 3.   **Wider Meaning Of Torah**
The need for divine guidance did not cease with the death of Moses, however: on the contrary, it increased. For whereas a large part of Moses' teaching in the wilderness and the plains of Moab was theoretic – instructions as to how the people should live and govern themselves once they had conquered and settled in the Land of Promise; that achieved, they would have to put that theory into practice, which is a difficult task in any sphere of life, as you will no doubt have already experienced yourself in implementing your post-BM duties.

Moses had prepared the people for that eventuality, informing them that after his death, "A prophet will the Eternal thy G–d raise up for thee, from the midst of thee of thy brethren like me; unto him you shall hearken." And G–d confirmed this, saying of such a prophet: "And I will put My words in his mouth, and he shall speak unto them all that I shall command him."

It can therefore justifiably be said that the Nevi'im, "The Prophets", from *Joshua* through to *Malachi*, all of which contain messages from 'inspired spokesmen of G–d's will', which is what the word 'prophet' means (see Hertz' *Pentateuch And Haftorahs* – HPH in future – p. 235), are an extention of the Torah proper.

The same can be said of the authors of the *Ketuvim*, "The Writings", whose works approximately span the same seven centuries as do the Prophets, and who were also considered to be inspired by G–d. The Writings commence with the poetical *Psalms*, and conclude with the historical *Chronicles*, those between them being of similar content, containing a wealth of guidance to human conduct. But there is this important difference between the Torah proper, on the one hand, and the Prophets and Writings on the other. While the latter are considered to be an extension of the former, because they illustrate the consequences of adherence or disobedience to G–d's command-ments by both individuals and nations, they do not add one command-ment to the 613 given to Moses.

These three, *Torah, Nevi'im* and *Ketuvim*, are the complete Jewish 'Bible', to which we give the name *Tenach*, an acronym formed from the first letter of each part; and that is what it will be called from now onwards.

Section 4.   **The Widest Meaning Of Torah**

But what of the centuries after the closure of the period of the Prophets and the Writers, and especially after the destruction of the Second Temple? If the Jewish people needed divine guidance while still in their own land, with their national and religious institutions functioning, even if restrictively under Roman domination; how much more so did they, *do* they, require such guidance in the lands of their dispersion, having to maintain their identity as minorities, often minute, among nations professing other religions – or none!

The Torah provides for this contingency also. It tells us: "If there arise a matter too difficult for thee for judgment . . . matters of controversy within thy gates . . . thou shalt come to the priests the Levites, or to the judge that shall be in those days; and thou shalt enquire, and they shall declare unto thee the word of judgment. . . . According to the Torah which they shall teach thee, and according to the judgment which they shall tell thee, thou shalt do; thou shalt not depart from the word they shall tell thee, to the right or to the left."

In context these verses refer to Israel settled in their land, the 'priests the Levites' to those who served in the Temple and were the final authority in all ritual matters, and to the courts of law that sat in Jerusalem. But the qualification contained in the phrase 'or the judge that shall be *in those days*' extends authority to declare and administer Jewish religious law to *any* judge, or court of judges (*Beth-Din*), expert in Torah legislation and ruling in accordance with it, anywhere.

Section 5.   **The Oral Torah As Well**

Those judges have to be well-versed not only in the legislation of the Torah proper, the Written Torah, but also in that of the Oral Torah, the interpretation of it which was given to Moses by G–d orally, and which he, in turn, orally "handed down to Joshua, and Joshua to the elders. . . ." and so on (see Hertz commentary on the Prayer-Book – in future HPB – p. 613), until it was committed to writing in the *Mishnah*, discussed at length in the *Gemara* – these two together comprising the *Talmud*, and the consensus conclusions finally encoded in the *Shulchan Aruch* (Sh.Ar.), first published in the second half of the sixteenth century.

From that time to this, whenever a matter of difficulty has arisen, the recognised religious authorities of every age and in every place, have resorted to this compendium of the Talmud, and the many learned commentaries on it that have since been compiled, in order to find the solution. And they have succeeded, even with the numerous problems which our own age of swift advances in science and technology pose.

They do so by dint of deep and patient research, and by consultation amongst themselves and with experts in the subjects involved in the particular problem. Their success must be admired – but should not be considered wondrous: for the original source of the Sh.Ar. is the Torah, divinely given to man for his guidance in all ages.

There are two Talmuds, the more comprehensive and widely studied Talmud *Bavli*, containing the discussions of the Babylonian Sages, and the Talmud *Yerushalmi*, those of the Sages of the Holy Land. (Reference to any tractate in the latter is preceded by the letter Y, e.g. Y. Berachot.) They both have profuse homiletical passages, collectively called *Aggadah*, as distinct from *Halachah*, their legislative content.

The Aggadah explains and illustrates the narrative strand of the Torah, in the main, elucidating many a biblical text which would otherwise be incomprehensible. It has been extracted from the Talmud, and supplemented from other sources in various works, notably the *Midrash Rabba* (MR) on the Torah and Five Megillot, and the *Yalkut Shimoni* (YSh) on the whole of the Tenach.

All the sources mentioned in this chapter are Torah in the widest sense of that term, and it is upon them that this volume mainly draws. However, since our subject-matter is the explicit commandments of the Written Torah, liberal recourse will also be had to the most authoritative classifier of them, and his commentaries on them – to be named when we consider the answer to the question, "Which are the commandments?".

Section 6.   **Civil Law**
Hitherto we have been talking of Jewish religious law, which must reign supreme in our lives. As for the civil law, it was long ago laid down that "the law of the country is the law" wherever you live. Problems have arisen in the past, and still arise today, when such legislation involves violation of religious law – as when, for instance, compulsory Shabbat schooling was enacted in Eastern Europe, or when Governments today insist on electrically stunning cattle before slaughter. But solutions have been found, within the framework of halacha, or exemptions obtained, in most cases, especially in democratic countries, which have regard for the religious beliefs of all minorities.

Section   **Notes**
1   Genesis 46.28 & 47.6; Exodus 24.12; Isaiah 48.17.
2   Deuter. 4.2; Ethics 1.1; Isaiah 40.8.
3   Deuter. 18.15 & 18.
4   Deuter. 17.8–12.
5   See chapter 5.
6   B. Kama 113b.

Three

THE ETERNAL, *HE* IS G–D

Is G–d A Male?

Much inelegance of syntax must have been apparent to you in the previous chapters, made necessary by a determination not to anticipate the answer to this question until we have discussed it here – except in biblical quotations. An explanation for ascribing masculinity to G–d is certainly called for, since the absolutely spiritual nature of the Supreme Being had been posited as a very basic principle of Judaism.

A tentative reason may be this: the Hebrew language, like some others, has no neuter gender; everything, living and inanimate, is either masculine or feminine. When, then, Hebrew is translated into a language like English which *does* have a neuter gender, 'it' is employed wherever the text requires it, whether the original Hebrew is masculine or feminine. It would, however, sound and appear very irreverent to refer to G–d as "It" – even with a capital I: and so the masculine pronoun used for G–d in the original Hebrew is rendered as such into English.

But this poses another question: Why *does* Hebrew use the masculine? Why do we call on G–d as "our Father, our King" (SPB 57–9), rather than "our Mother, our Queen"? It is, I would suggest, because one of the main attributes we ascribe to G–d, supreme power, 'almighty-ness', is normally the characteristic of the male in animal and human life – though to a much lesser degree, of course; and therefore attributing supposed masculinity to G–d is an indication of His omnipotence. Furthermore, it is generally the father who sustains his family, and G–d is the universal Provider.

It was no doubt for this reason that, when G–d gave signal proof of His omnipotence by sending down fire from heaven to consume Elijah's water-drenched offering, all the people fell on their faces and emphatically exclaimed: "The Eternal, *He* is G–d! The Eternal, *He* is

G–d!" – just as we do, not twice but seven times, (SPB 366) as the Day of Atonement ends.

It is not to be assumed from this that G–d lacks those attributes in which the female excels, such as grace, compassion, and steadfastness. I will have more to say on this subject later, but to give just one example: "As one whom his *mother* comforteth, so will I comfort you," says the Eternal. G–d is the sum of all the virtues, to perfection and in excellence.

Section 2.   **Anthropomorphisms**
For a somewhat similar reason, in order to make His ways more intelligible to mortals, the Torah – and even G–d Himself, often "speaks in the language of men" by attributing imaginary human limbs, like face and eyes, ears and eyes, arms and feet; and human emotions like love and hatred, anger and pleasure, and so on, to the supremely spiritual Being.

But it must be stressed again that G–d is *not* corporeal. About their unique meeting with G–d at mount Sinai, Moses warned the children of Israel: "Take great heed to yourselves – for you saw no manner of form on the day the Eternal spoke unto you. . . . You heard the voice of words – only a voice." Yet a little later he refers to that occasion as a "face to face" meeting with the Eternal, which only means a direct communication from Him.

That divine revelation took place amid thunderings, lightning and fire – "The voice of the Eternal in power (that) . . . breaketh in pieces the cedars of Lebanon . . . cleaveth flames of fire . . . maketh the wilderness to tremble" (SPB 145). But its most potent effect is when it speaks in "a still small voice" to man's conscience.

Section 3.   **His Names**
The Divine Name with which the Torah opens is E-L-O-H-I-M, a 'plural of Majesty' translated 'G–d' into English, which conveys two aspects of His Being: as the Creator of the Universe, with man as the climax, as the first two chapters of Genesis show; and as the Supreme Judge of mankind. In its profane form, the term is used for human judges, as in: "both parties shall come before the judges (*elohim*)", so called because if they administer true justice, they are acting on behalf of G–d, "the Judge of the whole earth" Who says of Himself "I will not justify the wicked".

There is an interesting verse which not only includes both the holy and profane meanings of the term, but also an abbreviated form of it which has the same meaning. "G–d (E-L-O-H-I-M) stands in the congregation of G–d (E-L); He judgeth among the judges (elohim)".

(From the first part of this verse it is deduced that "if ten people pray together, the Divine Presence is with them".)

The most frequently *written* Name of the Supreme Being in Holy Writ is one which is never now read as it is written, so holy is it considered to be. It is formed from the four Hebrew letters corresponding to the English Y H V H, from which all three tenses of the Hebrew verb 'to be' can be derived, pointing to the Name's first significance – His eternity, and therefore rendered in this book 'The Eternal' who was, is, and ever will be.

Its other significance is His attribute of mercy, as He Himself informed Moses: "The Eternal – the Eternal is a merciful and gracious G–d, long-suffering, and abundant in kindness and truth". (This Name also has its abbreviated form, Ya-H, most popularly known through its occurrence in the second part of the compound word *Hallelu-yah* commonly translated 'Praise ye the Lord'.)

But the most frequently *heard* Name is A-D-O-N-AY: for though it occurs only sixteen times in the whole Torah, if you go to a synagogue whenever the Torah is read – as I trust you do, you will *hear* it pronounced hundreds of times – for it is read in place of the Ineffable Name. It also, like the full Name for G–d, is a 'plural of Majesty' form in which we address Him – of the Hebrew *Adon*, and means, 'my Lord', though it is usually rendered 'The Lord', as most versions also render the unpronounced Name. This Name conveys its own significance – the Lord-liege, Master-servant relationship between Creator and Benefactor, and man, the recipient of His favours.

Section 4.   **Epithets And Attributes**

All these Names for the Supreme Being, and others, are holy, and while they are used profusely in prayer and in public reading of the Torah, not only is it "forbidden to erase them", but it is customary not to pronounce them in secular conversation, or even when privately studying the Torah and other religious literature. The methods we employ to avoid doing this will be given in chapter 31.

The Talmud, Midrash and other rabbinic writings use epithets descriptive of the attributes of G–d, the most recurrent of them being "The Holy One, blessed be He", sometimes preceded in prayer by "the supreme King of kings" (SPB 203 &221); and "the Merciful One" (Ibid 381), though usually in its Aramaic form, *Rachmana*. We have had one example above of the term *Shechinah*, the "Divine Presence", being present when a *minyan* (at least ten adult males) pray together; and that Presence also "abides among ten people who sit and occupy themselves with Torah".

The origin and significance of another Appellation – *HaMakom*,

'The Place' (SPB 147, but there rendered 'The Almighty') are interesting. R. Ammi interprets the phrase "And he lighted upon the place" to mean that Jacob met with G–d there – as he did in his dream, and asks: "Why is the Name of the Holy One, blessed be He here changed to 'The Place'?" And he answers: "Because He is the Place of the World", i.e. He is limitless, the universe, however extensive, being His creation, and not He identified and equated with it, as the theory of Pantheism posits.

It was stated above that His omnipotence is inherent in the Name "G–d", and an example of this attribute was given there. He is also omnipresent – everywhere. King David opens a beautiful passage on the subject with the rhetorical question: "Whither shall I go from Thy spirit, or whither shall I flee from Thy presence?" And He Himself asks: "Can any hide himself in secret places that I shall not see him? saith the Eternal; Do I not fill the heavens and the earth, saith the Eternal?"

He is also omniscient, knowing everything. "They say . . . the G–d of Jacob will not understand . . . The Eternal knoweth the thoughts of men. . . ." "The refining pot is for silver and the furnace for gold; so doth the Eternal try hearts". And He is just. In his farewell song Moses declared: "The Rock, His work is perfect, for all His ways are justice . . . Just and upright is He". And David said (SPB 31): "The Eternal is just in all His ways. . . . He guardeth all that love Him, but will destroy all the wicked". Yet who has not witnessed, or at least heard of, the apparently "righteous man for whom things go ill, and the wicked man who prospers"? Can this be harmonised with the assertion that "Righteousness and justice are the foundation of Thy throne"?

Section 5.   **Earthly Life Intermediate Stage**
When Moses requested of the Eternal, "Make known to me Thy ways, that I may know Thee," an answer to the above question was the essence of that request – but he received no answer to it, said R. Meir. When replying "I will do this thing also that thou hast spoken," the Eternal, said R. Meir, was granting another request, and not promising to answer our question. As for *that*, He forewarned Moses that "I will be gracious to whom I will be gracious", although he may not deserve it, "and I will show mercy to whom I will show mercy", although he may not deserve it! In other words, even Moses could not have *all* G–d's ways made known to him.

But attempts have been made to reconcile G–d's perfect justice with the apparent unfair punishment and reward some receive; and the most cogent of them rests upon another fundamental belief of

Judaism: that life does not begin or end on earth, our existence here being an intermediary stage between the eternal soul's entry into the human body at birth, and its return to its Maker at the body's demise. "This world is like an ante-chamber to the world-to-come; prepare thyself in the antechamber, that thou mayest enter into the reception-hall": and on arrival there, "thou wilt perforce have to give account before the supreme King of kings, the Holy One, blessed be He" on the extent to which, in your earthly existence, you contributed towards realising your Creator's purpose for you.

Seen in this light, life on earth, with all its vicissitudes is nothing less than a challenge to our moral fibre, a trial of our spiritual stamina. Just as, in other spheres, like sport and military training, the greater our success, the higher the hurdles and obstacles placed in our path; so, the more trials and ordeals the righteous have to endure, the greater is the divine Examiner's interest in them. "The Holy One, blessed be He, deals strictly with those around Him, even to a hair's breadth": i.e. those who come closest to achieving His highest expectations of them, are most severely tested – like Abraham, who "was tried with ten trials, and he stood firm in them all, to make known how great was his love" for G–d – "and G–d's for him."

Section 6.   **Interim Settlement Here**
Another possible solution, based on this same theory, takes into consideration the nature of the human rank-and-file. On the one hand, "There is no man on earth who doeth only good and sinneth not"; while on the other, "there is none so wicked that he does not possess some good deeds." "Every man," says Maimonides, "has merits and demerits. One whose merits outweigh his demerits, is considered a righteous man; and he whose demerits out-balance his merits, is wicked."

However, if one's deeds come close to one extreme or the other, so this theory goes, the almost wholly righteous are punished for their few sins in this existence – which explains their suffering – so that they might immediately enter the bliss of the Hereafter at their death; and the very wicked are here given the reward for their good deeds – hence their prosperity – so that they can pay for their wickedness immediately after their earthly demise. (Due note, however, should be taken of the power of repentance – which will be dealt with in the section on the commandments – to avert an evil decree.)

Section 7.   **But – Caution!**
But we must always bear in mind the lesson G–d taught Samuel when he was seeking Saul's successor among the sons of Jesse: "Look not

on his (David's brother, Eliab's) countenance, or on the height of his stature; for it is not as man seeth; for man looketh on the outward appearance, while the Eternal looketh to the heart." True, *generally speaking*, "All in whom the spirit of his fellow-creatures takes delight, the spirit of the all-Present takes delight": but, as with most general rules, it has its exceptions.

A very astute person *can* fool *all* the people *all* of the time – despite the popular adage to the contrary. *We* might consider a certain person a veritable saint, and be appalled at what seems to be unjust sufferings brought upon him. But *G–d* knows his innermost motivation and secret acts, and may be dealing with him accordingly. Contrariwise, the outwardly gruff and apparently impious man may have a heart of gold, many hidden virtues, and may unostentatiously, without our knowledge, perform a multitude of acts of loving kindness and prayer. "Even the 'empty ones' of Israel are as full of good deeds as a pomegranate is of seeds."

Another example of an exception to the rule 'Whom man likes, G–d likes' is the almost nation-wide following the false prophets of Baal had in Elijah's time, whereas he and the other true prophets of G–d were rejected and reviled – just as, in our own age, the advocates of 'less restrictive' Judaism, hedonism, and permissiveness score heavily against the preachers of moral and religious discipline, of Torah-true Judaism.

With regard to the individual who genuinely feels he is not receiving his just deserts, is passing through undeserved ordeals, the Sages advise: "If one experiences painful sufferings, let him examine his actions, as it is said, 'Let us search and try our ways, and return unto the Eternal'; if, having so examined his actions, he is convinced he has done no wrong, he can be sure that his are the sufferings of love, for it is said:

'For whom the Eternal loveth He chastiseth, even as a father the son in whom he delighteth'." The Talmud proceeds to give some examples of such "sufferings of love", including the most poignant account of how R. Yochanan who – presumably whenever he went to comfort those who had lost a child – showed them a tooth, explaining that it had come from the tenth of his sons to die in his lifetime!

Section 8.   **Suffering Of Innocents**
This chapter cannot close without some mention of the most difficult question this problem poses – the suffering of the obvious innocent, such as the congenital malformed, or the death of little children. Some aspects of it will be dealt with in the section on the commandments;

but, ideally, the works of learned Jewish moralists, who have given much thought to the subject, should be consulted.

All that can, and must, be said here is this: since G–d *is* just, there must be some essential place in the overall divine pattern for mankind for such heart-rending phenomena. Indeed, it has been suggested, as a not very tenable theory, that the very heart-ache such sufferings cause the able-bodied *is* their purpose: to make the healthy and whole thankful for their fortunate state every moment of their lives; and to arouse in them emotions of compassion towards *all* forms of suffering, among all G–d's creatures.

Who knows? All we can answer of a certainty is – G–d knows!

Inevitably in discussing a little of the nature of G–d and some of His attributes, incidental reference has occasionally been made to man, the Creator's goal, the ultimate creation, for whose guidance the Torah was written. Now we must consider what man is, what is his purpose.

Section   **Notes**

1   I. Kings 18.16–39; Isaiah 66.11.

2   Berachot 31b; Deuter. 4.12 & 15; Ibid. 5.4; I. Kings 19.12.

3   Exodus 22.7–8; Genesis 18.25; Exodus 23.7; Psalms 82.1; Berachot 6a; Exodus 34.6.

4   Y De'ah 276.9–10; Ethics 3.7; Genesis 28.11; MR. Genesis 68.9; Psalms 139.7–12; Jeremiah 23.24; Psalms 94.7ff; Proverbs 17.3; Deuter. 32.4; Berachot 7a; Psalms 89.15.

5   Exodus 34.13–19; Ethics 4.21; Ibid 4.29; Yevamot 121b; Ethics 5.4; Isaiah 41.8.

6   Eccles. 7.20; MR. Cant. 4.4; Yad. Teshuva 3.1.

7   I. Samuel 16.7; Ethics 3.13; MR. Cant. 4.3; Berachot 5b; Lamentations 3.40; Proverbs 3.12.

Four

WHAT IS MAN?

Introduction

Man was the final creature fashioned by G–d, from the dust of the earth at the end of six days in which the whole universe was created – as we are told in a thumb-nail sketch of the Creation in the opening chapters of the Torah. Furthermore, if we carefully study the chronology of the Torah, we must come to the conclusion that this six-day Creation took place 5,744-or-so years ago.

If anything which is to be said hereafter is to be given any credence at all, these two statements must obviously be explained first. For even the youngest reader, with the merest smattering of the sciences of natural history and archaeology 'knows' that man evoved through eons of time from the amoeba, and that the universe has existed for billions of years, and man for millions!

Though the Torah is not, *explicitly*, a text-book on cosmogony and natural history, it is nevertheless 'a law of truth'. Science, also, professes to determine the true laws of Nature. How then can these two truths, varying so widely, be harmonised – if, indeed, they can at all be?

Section 1. **How Old *Is* The Universe – Man?**

Many learned articles and books have been written in attempts to establish harmony between the biblical and scientific accounts of the universe's creation, or coming into being; and these should be studied in order to attain a comprehensive knowledge of the various theories. Suffice it to quote here just one sentence from Hertz's excursus on the subject: "There is, therefore, nothing inherently un-Jewish in the evolutionary conception of the origin and growth of forms of existence from the simple to the complex, and from the lowest to the highest." (HPH 194).

Implicitly, however, the Torah itself affords ways of harmonising

17

its views of the Creation with the scientific – if we make a deeper
study of its very words, its idiomatic usages and grammatical
nuances. For example: from the additional words in the phrase at the
end of the story of Creation, "and *behold* it was *very* good", instead
of the mere five-times previously stated "it was good", it is deduced:
"This proves that the Holy One, blessed be He, went on creating
worlds (i.e. civilisations) and destroying them, until He had created
this one, declaring 'This one pleases Me; the others did not please
Me.'"

In other words: there were many other civilisations before ours,
extending over millions of years, which were destroyed either by their
Creator because of their wickedness, or by their own abuse of the
scientific talents gifted them for man's good. And the discoveries of
the modern archaeologists are the remains of the creatures of these
previous civilisations.

Impressive support for such a theory is given by Sir James
Hopwood Jeans, Professor of Astronomy, at the end of his article on
Cosmogony in the authoritative *Encyclopaedia Britannica*: "Thus
our solar system, with its age of only a few thousand million years, is
very probably the youngest planetary system in the whole colony.
Our terrestrial civilisation, *with only some six thousand years of
existence behind it, is almost certainly the youngest civilisation*."

But for the man of faith, such harmonisation is not really necessary: for, if a Supreme Being could create from nothing so wondrous a
Universe as that which surrounds us; surely He was able to create it to
give the *appearance* that it has existed for billions of years. After all, if
mere man can so skilfully reproduce 'antique' furniture, paintings,
diamonds and even skeletons, often deceiving even experts; surely the
original Creator could have genuinely created the Universe some
5,744 years ago, to give the *impression* of vastly greater antiquity, *as
a test of our faith in Him and His Torah* – the acquisition of which,
you will recall, was considered to be a pre-requisite to our ascent of
the mountain towards G–d!

As for the Darwinian theory of man's descent from the ape: though
its validity is being increasingly questioned today, let us assume, for
argument's sake, that it is true. But it is also true that, despite all
man's attempts to civilise the ape, it still remains – an ape! Whereas
man is ever-developing, with a highly sophisticated civilisation to his
credit. Whence came this excellence of man over his closest animal
'relative', if not from G–d?

Judaism avers that man was a separate, especial being, created by
G–d with deliberate aforethought, for some sublime divine purpose.
The question can now be posed: What was that purpose?

Section 2. **The Reason For Man's Creation**

When He came to this last stage of the Creation, G–d said: "Let *us* make man in *our* image, after *our* form." To whom, or what, was He speaking? The use of the plural here even worried His amanuensis! Said R. Yochanan: "When, Moses, in writing the Torah, came to this verse he exclaimed, 'Sovereign of the Universe! Why do You furnish an excuse for the heretics (to assume that the universe has more than one Creator)? And G–d replied: 'Write it! and let whoever wishes to err, err!'" – another test of faith!

Nevertheless, it is recounted, when the Egyptian King Ptolemy Philadelphus summoned seventy-two elderly scholars from Jerusalem, put each of them incommunicado in a separate cell, provided them with writing materials, and only then revealed his purpose – that they were each to translate the Torah into Greek; every single one of them altered the above test to read, "*I* will make man in *my* image and likeness", so that the polytheistic Greeks should *not* err in thinking that Judaism also had more than one G–d.

The plural *is* used, however, and the Sages offer *us* various suggestions whom or what G–d consulted before forming His ultimate creature, man. The most likely answer – as is so often the case! – is the simplest one, the one contained within the actual text, if we follow the normal grammatical rule that a pronoun refers to the last noun mentioned.

The verse "Let us make man . . ." follows immediately upon that describing the creation of the earth-bound animals, which is itself preceded by that describing the swarming forth of the denizens of sea and sky. It was to *them*, the rest of the animate world, that G–d said "Let *us* make man in *our* image, after *our* form." That is to say: the new creature should be a synthesis of divine and animal qualities, possessing the earthly propensities of the animal, together with an inherent measure of the divine virtues.

And so it was: "And the Eternal G–d formed man of the dust of the ground" – almost the *exact* words used when creating the animals; "and man became a living soul" – *the* exact words used of the animals; the one and only difference between the two being that into *man*, in addition to giving im a living soul (*nefesh*) like all the other animals, "He breathed into his nostrils the *neshamah* (breath) of life" – *His* spirit.

The animals, for their part, each contributed of its own forte: Indeed, from the verse "He (i.e. G–d) teaches us from the beasts of the earth, and makes us wise from the fowl of the heaven", R. Yochanan draws the remarkable lesson: "Had the Torah not been given, we would have learnt modesty from the cat, honesty from the ant,

chastity from the dove, and good marital manners from the rooster."
The "industry of the ant" is cited as an example to the sluggard; and
I'm sure you can yourself think of more animal qualities, like the
loyalty of man's 'best friend', the dog, which man can emulate.

This theory might well suggest a deeper than the literal meaning of
the prophetic vision of the Messianic Era when "the wolf shall dwell
with the lamb, and the leopard shall lie down with the kid, and the
calf and the young lion and the fatling together, and a child shall lead
them." That is to say: all the conflicting animal instincts within man
will function harmoniously together, in the service of the divine spirit,
reaching towards G–d in all their actions, with the innocence of a
child.

Section 3.   **Animal and Divine Impulses**
Thus man is an amalgam of the spiritual and moral 'image' or
reflection of G–d, and the physical 'form' or 'likeness' of his
fellow-animals. The former is termed by our Sages the *yetzer hatov*,
the divine urge, and the latter the *yetzer hara*, the animal instinct –
which are better renderings of these two Hebrew terms than the
customary 'good and evil inclinations'.

This contention is remarkably borne out by the comment of R.
Samuel on another aspect of a verse already quoted. Had the Torah
said, "Behold, it was very good" it would have been referring (only)
to the *yetzer hatov*, he says; but adding the word "*And* behold it was
very good" it describes the *yetzer hara* as also being good! The
Midrash then asks in wonderment, "Can the '*evil*' instinct be *good*?"
And it answers, "Yes! for were it not for the *yetzer hara* (i.e. the
animal, or lower, instincts in man), none would build a house, none
would take a wife and have children, none would engage in business!
'For all labour springs from man's rivalry with his neighbour'" –
which is an animal impulse.

Section 4.   **Man's Purpose And Free-Will**
But why was man created at all? This is the question which the
Psalmist so beautifully asks – and the Sages attribute to the envious
angels, addressing G–d: "What is man, that Thou art mindful of him,
and the earth-born creature that Thou thinkest of him? Whom Thou
hast made but a little lower than the angels, hast crowned him with
glory and honour, hast given him dominion over the works of Thy
hands!"

R. Aibu opines that G–d's answer was: "I can be compared to a
king who has a palace full of good things – and no guests! What
pleasure has the king in having filled it?" And this parable is cited to

prove that man was created only after due deliberation, and preparation for his advent. But a question still remains: why make the preparations at all, why did G–d *want* the guests, that He should have to make preparations for receiving them?

And the answer? Man's creation was nothing less than a grand divine experiment – to see whether this new kind of creature, a synthesis of the animal and the divine, could so successfully blend the two elements in his nature as to become an earth-bound servant of G–d, *higher* than the angels – for they have no *yetzer hara* to contend with! – *of his own free will!*

That last phrase is of vital importance, fundamental to Judaism. The first sixteen chapters of Genesis, primarily narrative, containing only one actual commandment for all mankind, are intended to, and do, forcefully teach the lesson that man has absolute freedom to choose his own path in life, for good or ill – and, of course, suffer or benefit from the consequences of his actions. How is this lesson taught?

Imagine, for a moment, a highly-experienced scientist, who has painstakingly and laboriously put together, after long preparation, an intricate electronic computer of which he has great expectations. He switches it on, watches its functioning closely and constantly – and suddenly detects that something has gone wrong. If he does not correct it immediately, the whole experiment will collapse in ruin. Need one ask what he does? He exerts all his skill and effort in rectifying the fault, so that the experiment can proceed!

Yet G–d, Who "knows all the thoughts of man," Who can turn even "the heart of a king . . . whithersoever He will," refrained from interfering when He saw Eve and Adam about to violate the *one and only* commandment He had given them, which violation would bring *His* experiment to ruin at its very outset! He could have diverted the heart or hand of Eve from temptation – but did not: in order to emphasise man's freedom of will. They were punished, of course, according to their deserts – and the experiment continued!

It continued without divine interference for ten generations, for 1,656 years, things going from bad to worse until a stage was reached when, so deep and widespread was the wickedness of man, that "The Eternal repented that He had made man on the earth, and it pained His heart"! Such are the human terms employed to express the Creator's bitter disappointment at the dismal result of His experiment, leading to His decision to "blot out man whom I have created from the face of the earth . . ." They had had their freedom to choose; they had opted for gross evil, earning condign destruction in the Great Flood. But . . .

G–d went back to square one, graciously allowing the survival of the most righteous – or least tainted? – single human family, and the minimal representation of all other living creatures. For yet another ten, much shorter, generations, comprising a period of 340 years, man was left to exercise his own will, gradually becoming more civilised, more cultivated, thanks to his G–d-given superior intelligence – part of the *neshamah* that had been divinely breathed into him, but not recognising its Donor, until, at the end of that period, just one man, Abraham, did; and with him, the divine experiment at last showed a glimmer of possible success.

Could any greater proof than this divine forbearance from interference with the options of man, individual and collective, be given to establish the fact that man has freedom of will?

Section 5.   The Seeds Sprout – Harvest Yet To Come!

But one solitary, as-yet untried believer in G–d could not ensure the success of the grand divine experiment. "Two are better than one . . . and a threefold cord is not quickly broken." First the one thread, Abraham, had to be thoroughly tested to prove the strength of his faith – and he was, no less than ten times, each trial progressively more difficult; and he passed them all with flying colours. Then came the turn of his son, Isaac, and his grandson, Jacob – and the threefold cord held firm. Then the descendants of the last of these three Patriarchs were tried for three generations in the 'iron furnace', in body-and-soul-racking bondage in Egypt; and *this* threefold cord remained unbroken also – though not unsinged.

Thus came into being "the people of Israel", descendants of Jacob whose name was changed to Israel because he had "striven with (an angel) of G–d, and with men, and prevailed." And to them, seven weeks after their miraculous redemption from that bondage, and equally miraculous crossing of the Red Sea, was given the Torah, a guide and an aid to free men to exercise their free will in choosing their path in life, as individuals, and as a nation – up to a point (see chapter 6).

And the experiment is still a very much on-going one, far from fulfilment of the great expectations divinely hoped for it, when "The earth shall be full of the knowledge of the Eternal as the waters cover the sea"; and when "The Eternal shall be King over all the earth."

To help in achieving this goal, to become a partner with the Creator in the successful outcome of His experiment, is man's purpose on earth. And the Jew, a thread in the twice threefold cord remaining firmly entwined to this day, who, alone among all the peoples and religions on earth, has retained his faith in the Torah, the

whole Torah, and nothing but the Torah; is destined to take the lead
in this achievement. What more noble, more sublime, more challenging aspiration can one possibly have?

G–d Himself is a Partner in this task – not a 'sleeping Partner', for
"Behold, the Guardian of Israel neither slumbers nor sleeps"; and "If
it had not been for the Eternal Who was on our side when men rose
up against us, then they had swallowed us up alive when their wrath
was kindled against us." Neither is He a disinterested Partner:
through the mouth of His faithful servant, Moses, He pleads with us
to opt for the *right* path. "I set before thee life or death, blessing or
curse; therefore *choose life*, that thou mayest live, thou and thy seed."

And His concern that we choose the right path is not confined to
mere appeal. From the verse "If it concerneth the scorners, He
scorneth them; but unto the humble He giveth grace", the moral is
drawn: "If a person wants to defile himself, the doors are (reluctantly)
opened for him – for he *does* have freedom of choice; but if he desires
to purify himself, *he is helped*", i.e. the doors are opened for him
eagerly, even before he knocks!

But for those in this latter category, those who seek G–d continually, His relationship with man becomes a much closer one. And it is
now time, as promised earlier, to return to a more detailed consideration of that relationship.

Section   **Notes**
1   Genesis 1.31; MR. Genesis 9.2.
2   Genesis 1.26; MR. Genesis 8.8; Megillah 9a; Genesis 2. 7 & 9; Job 35.11;
    Eruvin 100b; Proverbs 6.6; Isaiah 11.6.
3   MR. Genesis 9.7, Eccles. 4.4.
4   Psalms 8.5–7; MR. Genesis 8.6; Psalms 94.11; Proverbs 21.1; Genesis 6.6–7.
5   Eccles. 4. 9 & 12; Genesis 32.29; Isaiah 11.9; Zechariah 14.9; Psalms 121.4;
    Ibid 124.2–3; Deuter. 30.19; Proverbs 3.34; Yoma 38b.

Five

MAN'S RELATIONS WITH G–D

Section 1. **The Commandments: Which Are They?**
The ladder which enables man to ascend the mountain of the Eternal,
so near to Him that he can become "but little less than the angels", is
fashioned out of the commandments contained in His guide to life –
the Torah. But which of His words are actual commandments: what
constitutes a 'commandment'?

R. Simlai's dictum that "six hundred and thirteen commandments
were dictated to Moses" on mount Sinai is universally recognised by
those who classify them, so far as their total number is concerned: but
there are variances of opinion as to which divine utterances should be
included as such – one authority going so far as to exclude from them
the very First Commandment – "I am the Eternal thy G–d . . ."!

By far the most widely accepted classification of the 613 is that of
the 12th. century Maimonides (popularly known as 'the RaMBaM';
an acronym of his name, *Rabbi Moshe Ben Maimon*, and henceforth
referred to briefly in this work as RM), and it is from his shorter work
on the subject, the *Sefer Hamitzvot* (SM) that all but one of the
commandments singled out in this volume are taken.

The exception comes from RM's main critic, the 13th. century
Nachmanides (the RaMBaN, from *Rabbi Mosche Ben Nachman* –
RN for short), for the reason given there (no. 90). Frequent reference
will be made to his views on the other commandments, as well as,
occasionally, to those of other classifiers of the 613.

Just to fulfil any of G–d's precepts as "a commandment of men
learned by rote", however, will not get us very far up the ladder. In
order to make possible our reaching its top, each part of that ladder
must be soundly and purposefully wrought: that is, every commandment must be observed for the right motive, in the right way, at the
right time. Let us consider these three requirements in turn.

Section 2 Motivation, Manner And Timing Of Observance

To whatever extent the average Jew conforms with the commandments, he usually does so for one or both of two motives: either to
reap the rewards for the positive, and avoid the punishment for
violating the negative, "which the Torah promises or threatens,"
either explicitly or implicitly; and/or out of habit or for convention's
sake, not to fall out with parents or community.

Both of these are legitimate motives, and though inferior to the
ideal, they keep the path clear towards its achievement. "A man
should always occupy himself with Torah and good deeds even
though not for their own sake (i.e. the ideal motive); for as a result of
doing so with an ulterior motive, he can come to do so for their own
sake".

What then is the ideal motive for observing the commandments? It
is dealt with at length in commandments 6 and 11 later on, but briefly
stated it is: to perform them solely because it is G—d Who commands
you to do so; and to exert your divinely-endowed brains to their
maximum in discovering the reasons *why* He commanded them.

Referring, according to Rashi, to the manner in which we should
fulfil the will of our Maker, there is a half-verse in *Kohelet*, the
translation of which in the Authorised Christian Version (CAV)
follows that of the Aramaic *Targum* — perhaps the very first rendering
of the Hebrew original into another language, has become almost
proverbial. It reads: "Whatsoever thy hand findeth to do, do it with
thy might".

It was not until 1916, surprisingly enough, that the first English
translation of the Tenach by a group of Jewish scholars appeared,
under the auspices of the Jewish Publication Society of America, was
adopted by Hertz in the HPH and by the publishers of the SBB, and
can therefore virtually be considered to be the Authorised Jewish
Version (JAV) of the Book of books. Its rendering of this half-verse,
following Rashi's interpretation of it is: "Whatsoever thy hand
attaineth to do by thy strength, that do;" and the *Soncino*'s commentator on it presumes to conclude that the Targum's rendering is
'incorrect', while Rashi's 'gives the true sense'. However, "the Torah
can be expounded in forty-nine different ways", and numerous
important lessons are drawn by the Talmudic Sages through slight
variations of a vowel here and a punctuation mark there in many
texts of the Tenach — which was not vocalised or punctuated in
writing in their time.

And so, like the opposing views of the Schools of Hillel and
Shammai, both the Targum's and Rashi's interpretations may be
right, "inspired by the living G—d;" and jointly they ideally convey,

particularly to those just about to set out on the path of responsible
adult Jewish living, the manner in which they should fulfil the will of
their Guide along the road of life.

Concentrate all your strength, physical and material, intellectual
and spiritual, when performing any positive commandment, and in
resisting the temptation to violate any prohibition, throughout your
life, the Targum reads into those words: but do so especially in your
prime, when that strength is at its peak, when the temptations are
really challenges, adds Rashi – before old age and feebleness set in,
before "the years draw nigh when thou shalt say 'I have no pleasure in
them'".

It is from one of those alternative readings into a Torah text
mentioned above that a comprehensive rule embracing the performance of all the commandments is drawn. In the chapter concerning the
preparations for Passover occurs the phrase "and you shall observe
the *matzot* . . .". Both CAV and JAV insert 'the feast of' – which is not
in the Hebrew text – between verb and object, the latter surprisingly
so, since the Talmud renders it literally.

It means, say the Sages, "you shall guard the *matzot*" while baking
them, not allowing the dough to become leaven, or sour, by standing
idle for any length of time between kneading it and putting it into the
oven.

Now, with no vowel-signs, as you must know, in the Torah, the
consonants which read *matzot* can also be read as *mitzvot*, from
which possible alternative reading the additional lesson is deduced:
"Just as the *matzot* must not be left idle to become leaven, so there
must be no delay in the performance of the *mitzvot* once the time for
it has arrived. If a *mitzvah* comes to hand, fulfil it immediately!" Do
not say "I am tired, busy – it can wait!" It is the will of your Maker –
so fulfil it at once, with enthusiasm and joy!

Abraham rose especially early in the morning, saddling his ass
himself in order to avoid delay – to fulfil the divine commandment to
offer up his beloved son as a sacrifice!

Section 3.   **Three Two-Way Divisions**
The Torah commandments can be divided into two categories in three
different ways: into positives and negatives; into 'judgments and
statutes'; and into those representing our duties towards G–d and our
fellow-men respectively. Let us consider each division and its categories separately.

(a)   The total 613, R. Simlai tells us, are made up of "365 negative
commandments, corresponding to the number of days in the solar

year; and 248 positive, corresponding to the number of parts in the human body."

(b) 'Judgments' – *mishpatim*, are more or less the social ordinances of the Torah which, had they not been included therein, mankind would have had to institute themselves, as best they could, for the protection of society, such as laws against murder and robbery. 'Statutes' – *chukkim*, on the other hand, are primarily of a ritual nature, "against which the evil inclination rebels, and at which other nations scoff, and are the King's decrees on His subjects", having no rational explanation.

(c) Our duties towards G–d in one category, and those towards our fellow-men in the other.

It is being assumed that you are, initially at least, one of the vast majority of Jews who, though their *sole* motive for fulfilling the commandments they do observe may not be expectation of reward and fear of punishment, nevertheless are influenced by these considerations when performing the positive and refraining from the prohibitions.

All the commandments should be observed with equal devotion and promptitude, whatever you and others may consider to be their relative importance: for, says R. Judah the Prince, "Be heedful of a light commandment as of a grave one – for *you* do not know the grant of reward for each commandment." Indeed, it may be that the 'light' ones are the more important and rewarding!

Section 4.　　　**Any Priorities – Self-Exempting?**

Nevertheless, as regards division I above, it seems more urgent to avoid violating a negative command than fulfilling a positive one – not only because there are many more of the former, but also because they act as a discipline, most of them reins upon the *yetzer hara*, the animal instinct in man, restraining him from 'doing what comes naturally'. Moreover, it is much easier to make amends for an act omitted than for a violation committed; very often "that which is crooked cannot be made straight". And though repentance, can atone for most of them, it cannot for some – until death.

As for division 2: The establishment of courts of justice to administer and enforce a code of social laws was one of the seven precepts given to the sons of Noah – i.e. to all mankind; and all nations, past and present have done so, however, primitive those codes may have been – and still are in some parts of the world. Much of the Torah's social legislation, as well as its ethical, has been adopted to some extent by Judaism's daughter religions indeed, though attempts to 'improve' them subtract from their divine perfection.

But it is in our loyalty to the *chukkim*, those Royal decrees without reasons which the human mind can comprehend, that makes us distinctive amongst the nations, and ensures our survival, witnesses to the truth of the *whole* of G—d's Torah, entrusted to us for the *whole* of mankind.

But the *chukkim* pose a danger as well! When the wisest of men declared: "All this I have tested by wisdom; I said 'I will get wisdom' – but *it* was far from me", 'it', say our Sages, referred to the classic, most inscrutable and paradoxical *chukkah* of them all – that concerning the red heifer, the solution of whose ashes purified the ritually unclean, yet defiled the ritually clean!

He, endowed by Heaven with wisdom above all men, realised and here admitted that there was a higher Wisdom Who *does* know the reasons for the *chukkim*, and how they will contribute to man's perfection. But there are those of lesser wisdom, who accept only what their own limited human intelligence can understand, loosen their grasp of the Tree of Life, and even lop off some of its branches as dead wood.

As examples of *chukkim* Rashi cites "the red heifer," which does not apply today; the commandment of *sha'atnez* (29) which does, but is widely ignored, alas; and the commandment (41) against eating swine-flesh. With reference to the last the Sifra counsels: "A person should not say, 'I do not eat swine-flesh beause I do not like it'; rather should he say, 'I would really love to have some – but what can I do? My Father in heaven has decreed I must not'".

And that is the spirit in which we should obey *all* the commandments, positive and negative, *chukkim* and *mishpatim*, whether we know the reason for them or not, whether we like them or not – because they are the will of our Father in heaven! "Do His will as if it were thy will," advises Rabban Gamaliel, son of R. Judah the Prince; "nullify thy will before His will".

Section 5.   **The 'Good-Bad' And 'Bad-Good'!**

But it is from the third division above, that between our duties towards G—d and those towards our fellow-men, that the most practical, yet the most profound and even remarkable, guidance to everyday Jewish living can be drawn. Needless to say, we must observe the commandments in *both* categories with equal dedication: but there are people who, either due to an inborn bent, or through the manner of their up-bringing, give higher preference to one of the two categories, and less to the other – or even neglect it completely.

Deducing it from Isaiah 3. vv. 10–11, the Talmud concludes: "A righteous man who is good to Heaven but not good to man, is a righteous man who is not good; but he that is evil to Heaven but not evil to man, is a wicked man who is not evil." In other words: there can be a 'good–bad' man, and a 'bad–good' man; but which of them is the *better* man? – the 'good–good' man being the best, of course!

In a remarkable comment, the Sages give *their* answer which reflects their consistent attitude. When the Jews were about to suffer their first double tragedy of seeing their Temple destroyed and being taken into exile, the Prophet was instructed that, should they ask why this catastrophe had overtaken them, he was to answer in G–d's Name: "Because they have forsaken Me, and have not kept My Torah." It is as if the Almighty had said, comments the Midrash: "Would that they had forsaken Me – but *kept* My Torah! Then by occupying themselves therewith, the light within it would have brought them back to the right path." That is to say: their following the guidance therein as to their duties to their fellow-men would have brought them to the realisation of the brotherhood of man under the Fatherhood of G–d – back to Him. So man comes first.

And it is logically so: for the Torah was given to man, "for *our* good always, that He might preserve us alive" – and not for *His* good! To deal ill with one's fellows and then praise Him is a contradiction, a *desecration* of His Name! Elsewhere the same Prophet declaimed: "Will you steal, murder, commit adultery and swear falsely . . . and then come and stand before Me in this House wherein My Name is called, and say 'we are delivered'"!

Section 6.   **A More Inspiring Proof**

But we have a more inspiring proof of the Sages' view on this subject in an incident in the life of our first Patriarch. Abraham had just been circumcised, and the Eternal then appeared to him – to exemplify to us the duty of visiting the sick and convalescent. As he was conversing with his divine Guest, he saw three weary travellers approach, and he said: "*Adonai!* if I have now found favour in thy sight, pass not away, I pray thee, from thy servant."

Now his first word could have been either the ordinary plural of a courtesy title to the travellers meaning "My lords!" or, as has been explained, the majestic plural "My Lord!", addressed to his Visitor. The Sages argue the point, and come to the conclusion that the word is 'holy', that is, Abraham was asking G–d kindly to wait awhile until he had provided the travellers with hospitality, as was always his wont. And from this it is deduced: "Hospitality to wayfarers is greater than entertaining the Divine Presence" – and He *did* wait!

Yet, according to RM, "giving hospitality to the wayfarer is not a commandment in its own right" – though (SPB 6) it is a very great *'mitzvah'* or good deed – but only a corollary of the comprehensive "Love thy neighbour" (36). How much more, then, would G–d agree that doing one of His explicit commandments towards one or more of His children should take precedence over one due to Him! But of course, where and whenever it is at all possible, we must strive to fulfil *both*.

Many more proofs of the importance of our duties towards our fellow-men could be adduced, but only one more will be cited. Commenting on the words "if you do that which is right in His eyes", the *Mechilta*, the oldest of the commentaries on *Exodus*, says: "This refers to our dealings with our fellow-men, and teaches us that everyone who deals honestly with them earns their goodwill and is considered as if he had kept the whole Torah".

Which brings us back to the father of our people! The Eternal promised to bless Isaac and his descendants "because Abraham . . . kept My *mitzvot*, My *chukkim*, and My *'torot'*". From this last word both Shammai and Hillel deduced that we have two Torahs, the Written and the Oral; and R. Yochanan opines that Abraham kept both of them, "even the minutiae of the Oral Torah"! All this is homiletical.

The English versions translate *torot* 'laws', but as we saw earlier, that is what *mitzvot* and *chukkim* are. In chapter two, 'Torah' was defined as Guidance to moral life contained in the narrative portions of the Tenach, and therefore *torot* can be taken to mean ideal ethical relations with one's fellow-beings, in which sphere Abraham excelled. He can thus "be considered as if he had kept the *whole* Torah"!

Section 7.   **Not Yet A Jew**
However, extracting from the Torah all the duties of man towards his neighbour, and performing them alone, does not make a person into a Jew. He might thereby become a perfect gentleman, a kindly humanist, be morally "equal in rank to a High Priest," as R. Meir was wont to aver; and as "one of the pious among the Gentiles" who, like the righteous of Israel, "have a portion in the world to come" – but it takes more than that to be a complete Jew.

For to be a complete Jew you cannot *choose* which of the commandments you will perform: you must do them *all*, without distinction, because they are *commanded* by G–d; and, as will be explained in commandment 17, it is psychologically more difficult to do something you are ordered to do, than performing the same act out of *choice*. And those commandments are in *the* Book, acceptance of the authenticity of which, and unswerving belief in its divine Author, are the two foundations of the *faith* upon which Judaism rests, and this work is based (see chapter one).

Moreover, though this volume is confined to a presentation of those Torah commandments applicable to the teenager, roughly speaking – i.e. between BM and marriage; it is essential (see introduction to commandment 16), if you are fully to appreciate the wisdom and beauty of the totality of Torah Judaism, intensely to *study all 613* of its commandments, together with the ethical . guidance contained in its narrative passages.

The Torah as a whole is, as it were, a giant intellectual and spiritual jigsaw puzzle of 613 separate pieces, deliberately so devised by its divine Compiler in order to provide us with an engrossing life-long occupation in fitting each into its proper, timely place in our lives, progressively understanding and applying each piece, and eventually revealing the full grandeur of the complete picture – that of an educated and industrious nation, planted securely in brotherly harmony in their own sovereign Land, living in accordance with the Torah of G–d.

But until that ideal is achieved, not all the 613 pieces can be fitted into their proper places; yet a smaller and more modest picture, though far less satisfying or impressive, *can* be constructed from those which still have a place in our lives. How many are they? In his introduction to his classical exposition of SM, the *Sefer Hachinuch* (in future 'the Chinuch'), R. Aaron haLevi of Barcelona has this to say:

"There are altogether 369 commandments applicable today, some of them, however, dependent on situations which may never occur throughout one's life. . . . But those which are unconditionally mandatory upon every Jew number 270, 48 positive and 222 negative."

The Chinuch stoutly defends RM's classification of the 613 against all his critics; and it is from his 270 that the pieces for our smaller picture – or, to change the metaphor, the uprights and rungs of our ladder, are taken in the main. However, as has already been said, a little alternative or supplementary use will be made of individual commandments from the selections of other classifiers of the 613.

Recourse will frequently be had, of course, to the rabbinic elucidation of the commandments, without which many of them could not be understood; and to their own enactments, "the fence they erected around the Torah" commandments to protect them from violation, in fulfilment of G–d's instruction to them, "And you shall guard My charge", i.e. the Torah, against violation.

This concludes the laying of the foundation upon which our sturdy heavenward-reaching ladder can safely stand; and so, after a brief introduction we will commence fashioning its two uprights, each consisting of five dovetailed commandments which have constant application.

Section	**Notes**

1 Psalms 8.6; Makkot 23b; see commandment 1; Isaiah 29.13.
2 E.g. Deuter. 5.16 & Levit. 17.10; Pesachim 50b; Eccles 9.10; MR. Numbers 2.3; Eruvin 13b; Eccles. 12.1; Exodus 12.17; Pesachim 48b; Mechilta on Exodus 12.17; Genesis 22.3.
3 Makkot 23b; Yoma 67b; Ethics 2.1.
4 Eccles. 1.15; Ibid 7.23; Numbers chap. 19; Genesis 26.5 & Levit. 18.4; Sifra Kedoshim 128; Ethics 2.4.
5 Kiddushin 40a; Jeremiah 16.11; MR. Lament. Proem 1.2; Deuter. 6.24; Jeremiah 7.9–11.
6 Genesis 17.26 to 18.3; Shabbat 127a; SM. Introduction 1; Exodus 15.26; Genesis 26.3–5; ADRN chap. 15; Yoma 28b & MR. Genesis 64.4.
7 B. Kama 38a; Tosefta Sanhedrin 13.2 & Yad. Teshuva 3.5; Ethics 1.1; Levit. 18.30.

Six

AN INTRODUCTION TO THE COMMANDMENTS

We have now reached the point where we can commence to study in detail the one hundred Torah commandments most likely, in modern times, to come the way of the initiate into responsible adult Judaism. He or she may imagine it feasible to skip the earlier chapters and commence here; but such a choice would entail great risks, and is very inadvisable.

For the ladder we are about to construct could then be in danger of disintegration at any of its stages, and it and its constructor be in peril of sinking into a slough of despond, doubt and disbelief – because the foundation upon which it is to stand will not have been carefully prepared on rock-solid ground to bear its ever-towering weight. Study the vital "Foundation" chapters first!

The term 'initiate' is here used in both a loose and a literal sense. In the former, initiation refers to the age of Bar/Bat-Mitzvah (BM), which will be exactly defined in chapter eight, though it could also apply to the non-Jew who opts to enter the Jewish Faith. Such initiates would naturally be expected to acquire an adequate knowledge of at least the basic tenets of the religion *before* their entry into it; and in that sense 'initiation' is intended to include that preparatory period – the longer it be, the better.

Section 1.   "Apprenticeship"
First, a definition: the *bar* in bar-mitzvah is the Aramaic equivalent of the Hebrew *ben* – a 'son'; and *bat* is the Hebrew for 'daughter'. *A* mitzvah is *one* of the commandments given to Moses on mount Sinai, the plural being *mitzvot*: but Hebrew often idiomatically employs the singular of a noun "for the plural," as here; and therefore a BM is a 'son of daughter of commandments' – a person who has reached the juncture in life when he or she is considered to be sufficiently mature

responsibly to fulfil "all the commandments enumerated in the Torah" – so far as they are applicable.

But towards whom is this responsibility then borne? Not yet towards G–d, for He, in His graciousness, does not hold man accountable for this actions "until the age of twenty." This conclusion is arrived at from the fact that only those misled by the pessimistic report of the ten spies, and who therefore disobeyed His command to "Go up and possess the Land which I have given you" who were aged twenty or over were punished – despite their having second thoughts overnight. Even then they were too late!

There is a very important lesson in this: do not put off until tomorrow, until an hour or even a minute later, what you can do now! The opportunity may pass by; other more urgent matters may intervene in the meantime. Urged Hillel with regard to the study of Torah: "Do not say 'I will study when I have some free time'; perhaps you never will *have any!"*

Towards whom *do* you, as a BM have that obligation to fulfil the commandments? Primarily – towards yourself! For you will surely want to be fully equipped to fulfil your obligations to G–d by the time you reach the age of twenty; and you are therefore, in the intervening years apprenticed, as it were, to Him! Just as a student for any profession must study for some years under a master of that profession before he can qualify, so must you, under the Guidance of the Supreme Master, given in His Torah, if you are to qualify as a true Jew!

But there the analogy ends: for whereas the trainee in any other profession *must not* practise what he learns until he is fully qualified, you *are obliged* to put every one of the commandments that comes your way during your 'apprenticeship' into practice immediately; and furthermore, you are liable from BM onwards for any damage you cause your fellow-men – according to Jewish law. It means, in effect, that you should already *know* what *all* your obligations are by the time you reach BM.

Section 2.   **Changed Times!**

Is this possible? It certainly was in Talmudic times when, by the time he had reached BM, the average pupil "had already learned the *whole* of the (Written) Torah by the age of 10, and was half-way into the study of the whole of the Oral Torah (the Mishnah)"! And this remained the general Jewish curriculum until relatively recently – about the end of the 19th. century, until when schools were mostly under the control of religious bodies, and there was no compulsory secular education. And such wholly religious-studies schools are common now in Israel.

But in the Diaspora, where the vast majority of English-speaking Jews live, most Jewish children attend Government or municipal-controlled schools where the curriculum comprises secular subjects in the main, their Jewish pupils obtaining a modicum of religious education at Sunday or twice/thrice weekly 'Hebrew Classes' – if they attend them.

True, the Jewish Day School Movement is gaining ground, and in its excellent schools a considerable part of the curriculum consists of religious subjects – in addition to the compulsory secular ones, extra hours often being added voluntarily to the school day for that purpose. *Their* pupils *may* have learnt the whole Written Torah by BM age – but *they* are not likely to read this book!

For this work is intended for the majority, the 'Hebrew Class' type of youngster, who will be far, far behind in the above-mentioned syllabus by BM age. But this is no cause for despondency, for being disheartened, nor is there time for such emotions! Spend it rather on making up for the time you've lost – as you can, and must!

You *must*, because though, as we shall see (commandment 17), it is a father's duty to teach his children Torah, or have them taught it, by the time they reach BM; but should he not fulfil it, "they must teach themselves thereafter." And you *can*, because "it is at BM age that the *yetzer hatov* begins to assert itself", rousing within you a desire, a thirst to know Him Who breathed it into you – which you can satisfy only by Torah-study.

Section 3. **Ladies Also!**

When we come to discuss this commandment (17) in detail, it will be shown that ladies are as much obliged to study the Written Torah – at least – as men. But at this early, introductory stage it is necessary to nail the malicious lie, ignorantly inferred from a wrong interpretation of the blessing recited by the male each morning thanking G–d "Who hast not made me a woman" (SPB 7), that Judaism confers inferior status upon the woman.

On the contrary! To cite three short rabbinic sayings in rebuttal of this absurdity – and then a true story which refutes this nonsense. "The Holy One, blessed be He, endowed the woman with greater understanding"; Abraham was told to obey Sarah "because he was *her* inferior in prophetic insight"; and "It was on account of the merit of the righteous *women* that our ancestors were redeemed from Egypt".

And the story: A pious couple, because they could not have

children and therefore considered themselves "no use to G–d", tearfully decided to divorce and attempt to 'be of use to Him' with other partners. The pious woman married a good-for-nothing and made a pious man of him; and the pious man married a shrew who made a ne'er-do-well out of him. "So everything depends on the woman" is the moral drawn from this poignant story.

The *sole* reason for the male reciting the above blessing is that he has the privilege of performing a few more commandments than a woman – primarily those from which she is exempt, but not debarred, "because they have to be performed at a specific time" and might therefore interfere with her much more important domestic duties, upon which the welfare of her family and the community depends.

Section 4.   **Get Ready!**

So prepare yourself for getting to know the commandments! R. Joshua b. Perachyah mentions the two most important requisites: "Provide yourself with a teacher, and get yourself a companion": a teacher to elucidate your difficulties and problems, and a companion with whom to discuss them. Very interestingly, Rashi informs us that there are those who say that 'companion' here means 'books': and Hertz (HPB 618) quotes this, adding the comment: "(Books are) the best of companions, and invaluable for the acquisition of religious knowledge."

How true! As to how to acquire them, see suggestion in commandment 11 – but a teacher is still necessary, and a good companion, with whom to discuss the lessons and the books' contents, highly advisable.

As will be observed more than once in the following pages, the ideal language in which to read or study any book – or recite a prayer – is the language in which it was written; and most Jewish classical literature was originally written in Hebrew (or Aramaic). If you have a working knowledge of it (or them), perfect it! But if not, try to learn Hebrew, and in the meantime make use of the English translations into which almost all the classics have been rendered.

There will undoubtedly be found on your bookshelf the three most popular of these, widely used in Synagogue and home, frequently used for reference in these pages, the first for the plain text, and the other two for their excellent commentaries on it: SPB, HPB and HPH. We can now proceed to fashion the two uprights of our ladder, each of five dovetailed constant commandments.

Section   **Notes**
1 E.g. Deuter. 8.1. & 27.1.; Niddah 52a; Shabbat 89b; Numbers chap. 14; Deuter. 9.23; Ethics 2.5.

2 Ethics 5.24; Kiddushin 29b; ADRN chapter 16.
3 Niddah 45a; Megillah 14a & Rashi on Genesis 21.12; Sotah 11b; MR. Genesis 17.7; Kiddushin 33b–34a.
4 Ethics 1.6 and Rashi thereon.

Seven

THE FIRST FIVE "CONSTANTS"

The vast majority of the commandments call for fulfilment at specific times of the day, week, month or year, and a few only once in a lifetime. But there are some which must be borne constantly in mind, every moment of the day. The Chinuch lists six such 'constants' in his introduction: but the circumstances and environment in which Jews live today have greatly changed since it was compiled in the 13th. century, bringing new challenges in their train. Here, therefore, the number is increased to ten, five in this chapter and five in the next, the first three in each group according with the Chinuch, the others additions considered necessary for the times in which we live.

1.   TO *KNOW* THE ETERNAL IS YOUR G–D

Section 1.   This is generally considered to be the first of the so-called "Ten Commandments" (a more correct definition of which is given in chapter 31), proclaimed by G–d before the whole assembly of Israel at mount Sinai: "I, the Eternal, am thy G–d, Who brought thee out of the land of Egypt, out of the house of bondage." And this is taken to be a commandment to believe in G–d.

But can you be *commanded* to *believe* something? Has it not been laid down as one of the foundations of Judaism that man has absolute freedom of will, to choose to think and act as he pleases? Then how can he be told what to believe? It was no doubt because of this dilemma that the earliest of the classifiers of the 613 (the "BeHaG") did not include this first of the 'Ten' in his list!

RN, however, does include it in his – but as a *gezerah*, an imposed divine decree, not a commandment, "Crescas" agreeing with him on the grounds that a command can only be given by one accepted as a commander, and that here G–d is *asserting* Himself as the Comman-

38

der of Israel *before* issuing His *first* actual command – "Thou shalt have no other gods . . ." – the second of the 'Ten' (SPB 91–3).

The Mechilta, illustrating its view with a parable concerning one who was only accepted by his people as king after his having conferred many benefits on them, turns G–d's words here into a question: "Am I, the Eternal Who brought you out of . . . the land of bondage, your G–d?". To this, all the people voluntarily and enthusiastically replied "Yes! Yes!", the acceptance of the Commander transforming His question into a commandment.

Both before and after the actual exodus from Egypt He had performed many other miraculous deeds on their behalf – but not as many as He has since performed for their descendants in the subsequent three-and-a-quarter millenia to this day, delivering them from bondages much more dire than Egypt's. How much more so, then, should we, you and I and every Jew who has survived them, believe in Him?

Section 2.   **Belief Is Not Enough!**
But just believing is not enough! The children of Israel "believed in the Eternal, and in His servant Moses" after the crossing of the Red Sea – yet but a few days later they were grumbling against him and praying "Would that we had died by the hand of the Eternal in the land of Egypt"! To His question, "Am I your G–d?" they exclaimed "Yes! Yes!" – but less than two months later they were worshipping a golden calf!

Yes – I remember starting this volume with the assertion that you cannot even *begin* a serious study of Judaism without first accepting the existence of G–d and the authenticity of His Torah – but that was as a starting-point, out of faith. In his brief statement of the Thirteen Principles of the Faith (SPB.93) RM begins each with "I believe with a perfect faith . . .", the first being in G–d as the Creator. And he similarly opens his shorter work on the commandments (SM) with our duty to *believe* in G–d.

But in his major work on that subject, the *Mishneh Torah* (or "Yad" for short), he commences thus: "The foundation of foundations, the pillar of all wisdom, is *to know* that there is a Supreme Being (or First Cause) Who brought forth all things . . .". For while you cannot be commanded to *believe*, you *can* be commanded to use your rational mind, which distinguishes you from the rest of the animal world, to engage in diligent research which will transform your faith and belief in G–d into *knowing* Him – so far as is humanly possible.

And you are given an assurance that you can do this, subject only

to one condition. "If, from thence, you will seek the Eternal your
G–d, then you will find Him – if you search for Him with *all your
heart and with all your soul.*" Moses summed all this up succinctly in
one verse which is included in the beautiful *Alenu* (SPB 79) prayer,
when he said: "And you will *know* this day, when you lay it to your
heart, that the Eternal, *He* is G–d, in the heavens above and on the
earth beneath – there is none else."

2.   NO OTHER DEITIES – FOR YOU

Section 3. This is the second of the 'Ten' and the 'constant'
commandments, the best rendering of the part that concerns us here
being: "Thou shalt have no other gods in My presence" – which
means, in effect, never and nowhere, for G–d is Eternal and Omnipresent. The Torah recognises that other peoples and religions have their
own gods; and both Moses and David declare the True G–d to be
"the G–d of gods, and the Lord of lords."

The last of the Hebrew Prophets, castigating his people for their
half-hearted service to G–d, says in His Name: "From the rising of the
sun even to the going down thereof, My Name is great among the
nations . . ."; and this is taken to mean: "Even the heathen nations
that worship the heavenly hosts pay tribute to a Supreme Being, and
in this way honour My Name."

But all other gods, including these heavenly hosts, "the Eternal *thy*
G–d hath allotted unto all the peoples under all the heavens" – but
not unto *you*! You must recognise none but the One and Only G–d,
holding Him constantly in mind; and with modesty and without
ostentation, by exemplary Jewish living, demonstrate what serving
Him means.

3.   G–D IS A UNIQUE UNITY

Section 4. This is the Chinuch's and our third 'constant', derived from
the last clause in the opening verse of the *Shema*: "(Hear, O Israel, the
Eternal our G–d), the Eternal is One". This is not intended to convey
merely that there is only One G–d – we can infer that from a
combination of the previous two commandments.

It means, first, that not only is He the *Supreme* Being, but the *only*
One, the sole Source of all power in the universe, and there is none
remotely like Him. "Thus saith the Eternal, the King of Israel . . . I am
the first, and I am the last, and beside Me there is no god"; and again:
"To whom will you liken Me, and make Me equal, and compare Me,
that we may be like?" – a rhetorical question, to which the answer is a
resounding, "No one!"

Secondly, He is not a duality, as the Zoroastrians, among whom the Babylonian exiles lived, believed, consisting of two ever-contending powers of light and darkness, good and evil. Since the Torah was given, and man was "granted freedom of choice between either life and good or death and evil", said R. Eleazar, "man is himself responsible for any evil that overtakes him." As for G–d, "The Eternal is good to all, and His tender mercies over all His works" – though His curative medicine might at times be very bitter!

Neither does G–d share His powers with any spirit and human being to form a trinity, as Christianity maintains. He *does* contribute of His own spirit, as has been explained, to *every* human being, some letting it lie dormant all their lives, others nourishing it and fanning it into a flame which brings them near to Him. But no one is His associate, though many are His messengers.

You may well say: "But I know all this already, I've been brought up to believe it: the age of sun- and moon-worship, of idolatry and polytheism, is long gone by among civilised people! The number of people who believe even in only *one* G–d seems to be ever-decreasing!" All very true – but there are still dangers of two kinds, one of them very old and the other modern.

You will remember that the Names of the Supreme Being translated 'G–d' into English signify His attribute as Judge, most powerful or most influential Being. There are many urges in life, like the pursuit of wealth, power and honour which, should they not be restrained by the discipline of G–d's commandments, could exert a more potent influence over man than His. Therefore we are here commanded always to remember that the Eternal our *G–d* must be the unique influence in our lives, that all our actions must satisfy Him, the ever-present, all-knowing Supreme Judge.

4.   DO NOT INDULGE THE ENTICER!

Section 5. A growing number of fancifully-named groups within the Christian and Moslem religions today are earnestly and zealously attempting to woo the Jew and entice him away from the religion into which he was born – apart from the apostles of other religions and some weird cults – which is why I have presumed to add this and the following commandment to my list of 'constants'.

The impulse which drives them, with all sincerity, is a logical one: if *their* approach to G–d is the right one, which they intensely believe, then the Jewish approach is wrong; and therefore the 'misguided' adherents to Judaism must be convinced of the error of their ways, and be persuaded to acknowledge the 'true' religion or cult. And to our horror we hear of young Jews and Jewesses succumbing to these enticers, due largely to the victims' abysmal ignorance of their inherited religion.

Should, then, any of them knock at your door, accost you at the school gate or on the university campus – their favourite hunting ground, do not indulge them! Slam the door in their face, or abruptly turn your back to them. Warns the Torah: should anyone, even a renegade member of your own family, "entice thee secretly, saying: 'Let us go and serve other gods' which thou has not known, thou nor thy fathers, of the gods of the peoples that are round about thee . . . or far off from thee . . . thou shalt not consent unto him . . .!'"

Have nothing to do with him – or her, as is often the case! Rather retire to your study, and immerse yourself in furthering and deepening your knowledge of your own religion, and thus erase the nasty effect of the encounter.

5.   DO NOT LISTEN TO HIM!

You might imagine, however, that you are sufficiently committed to your own religion to be able to emerge unscathed from a discussion with the would-be enticer: you may be right, but it is much more likely that you will be wrong, dangerously wrong!

You must realise that these soul-seeking wolves in sheep's clothing are selected for their missionary work on the strength of their glib tongues and their plausibility. How much of the Hebrew Bible do *you* know? *They* have been expertly trained to manipulate its text so that it erroneously is made to support their arguments about words, phrases and passages that you might not have even ever read!

Therefore the above quotation proceeds to say: "do not listen to him, neither shall thine eye pity him, neither shalt thou spare . . . him . . . because he hath sought to draw thee away from the Eternal thy G–d, Who brought thee out of the land of Egypt, out of the house of bondage" – which is one of the most grievous sins.

The whole paragraph refers to the enticer being a fellow-Jew, even the closest of relatives, and the enticement taking place in the Land of Israel, governed by Torah law. The omitted phrases advise that the enticer should not be protected, but reported to the authorities, be tried by a court of no less than twenty-three learned judges, and if found guilty, be stoned to death, the informer having to be the first to cast the death-dealing stones – all very unlikely to happen.

But a general warning against listening to *any* enticer can be read into it. "Thine eye shall not pity him" can mean: don't say 'after all, the poor fellow is harmless, only trying to do his job; I'll be polite and just give him a hearing'. Don't! You do not know the harm such misplaced politeness may do to your precious soul! "Thou shalt not spare him" – send him away with a flea in his ear!

The paragraph begins with the extreme possibility that the enticer may be even your brother, son, daughter, wife or best friend who is attracted, or may have already succumbed, to the blandishments of an enticer, and invites you to join him in apostasy. It is today a possibility, though a remote one, and such individuals are the most dangerous, especially if they are versed in Jewish lore, because they know you intimately, and what arguments may appeal to you.

On the other hand, you know them just as well, and may have influence over *them*, and other Jewish sheep who have strayed from their ancestral fold; and to exert that influence to bring them back to the religion of their birth is a great *mitzvah*; for "anyone who preserves a soul of Israel is as if he had saved a whole world".

Yet even in apostasy, they remain Jews! For "An Israelite, even should he sin, remains an Israelite . . . a myrtle, though it stands among reeds, is still a myrtle, and is so called" – very often even by the surround 'reeds' amongst whom it has tried to merge. There is no contracting out from Jewry!

Section 6.   Two Others Almost Impossible – For You!

There is a third Torah commandment, or rather two of them, in this category which I had thought at first not even to mention, since it is so unthinkable a possibility – that you yourself should entice one or more persons to worship other gods! The prohibition against so grievously misleading one person is deduced from the last verse in the paragraph we have been considering, and against making a habit or vocation of it from "and the name of other gods shall not be heard out of thy mouth."

So heinous, indeed, is such a crime that RM reckons it amongst the only four classes of persons whom "the Holy One, blessed be He, does not give an opportunity of repenting having committed it, so great is his sin."

It is wholly inconceivable, then, that anyone like you, one who has already committed himself to fulfil the four commandments preceding this one, should even momentarily contemplate enticing other Jews *away* from their religion!

But then I decided to include them, though unnumbered, first because of that other meaning given to 'other gods' – impulses which acquire greater influence over us than that of obeying the word of G–d; and secondly because the enticement spoken of here refers to wooing a person away from the *whole* of his religion, yet it remains a sin to entice him away from observing any *part* of it.

Most of the 'other-god' influences will be dealt with in the next volume, which is concerned with Jewish life from marriage onwards, and therefore do not belong in this volume; but there is one which very much *does* – the potent influence of the sexual urge which grows apace as the teenage years progress, and which, if given free rein, can literally and religiously 'take a person out of this world'. Much more about it in later chapters.

Another possible such influence is sport, such as fanatically follow-ing all your favourite team's Shabbat games, at home and away: and to persuade another Jew to join you in such a violation of the holy day and neglect of its proper observance is a good instance of one act of enticement, 'sinning and causing others to sin' – another of those four sins which repentance cannot eradicate.

On the other hand, how great a *mitzvah* you would be doing by bringing an apathetic, non-observant friend back to full observance of Judaism, by winning a *Jewish* soul for G–d, through your example and gentle persuasion! "Whosoever causes the multitude to be righteous, through him no sin shall be brought about" – and that should be your constant aim in life.

Section   **Notes**
1   Exodus 20.2; 9th. cent. Baal Halachot Gedolot; RN's commentary on SM. P.1; 15th. cent. Asher Crescas; Mechilta on Exodus 20.2.
2   Exodus 14.31 and 16.3; from sub-title "Yad Hachazakah"; Deuter. 4.29–39. Exodus 20.3; Deuter. 10.17 and Psalms 136.2–3; Malachi 1.11; Menachot 110a; Deuter. 4.19.
4   Deuter. 6.4; Isaiah 44.6; Ibid 46.5; Deuter. 30.15; MR. Deuter. 4.3; Psalms 145.9.
5   Deuter. 13.7–12; Sanhedrin 37a.
6   Sanhedrin 63b; Exodus 23.13; Yad. Teshuva 4.3; Ethics 5.21.

Eight

THE SECOND FIVE "CONSTANTS"

Like the preceding one, this chapter will also consider five Torah commandments which must be borne constantly in mind, the first three again being among those so listed by the Chinuch, and the other two being added by me as such, having become more urgent since his time.

6.   TO LOVE G–D

Section 1. Were all the commandments, all the 613 of them, classified in order of the possibility of adequately fulfilling them, then this would probably be the last, or at least vie with the next one we will be discussing, as we will soon explain, for position as the top rung of the ladder. This raises the question: how then can its fulfilment be expected from a BM before he or she has even completed the uprights firmly enough to carry its ninety rungs?

An even more fundamental question about it should have occurred to you if you studied what was said about the very first commandment: free will and choice being basic to Judaism, how can we be *commanded* to love? Love is an emotion, springing from the heart, and cannot be commanded. True, people talk of 'falling in love at first sight': but even if it is true love, and not infatuation, it is roused *at sight* – and G–d is an incorporeal Spirit!

These two questions will be answered once the text of the commandment has been cited and carefully studied. But in order to do the latter properly, two introductory notes are essential.

First: our duty to love G–d is frequently mentioned in the Torah (Five Books), but *never* is it expressed there as an imperative command "Love G–d!". Furthermore, in the Nach (the rest of the Hebrew Bible) the imperative is only used once in that context – and there it is addressed to those who are nearest to the top rung of the ladder! "Love the Eternal, all His *saintly* ones"!

Secondly: the Hebrew letter *vav*, which as a *word* means a "hook", when used as a prefix is appropriately a conjunction – *any* conjunction, and not only 'and'.

Section 2.   **The Text**
If follows the first all-important verse of the Shema, commanding us to grasp with our minds that the Eternal our G–d is the One unique Supreme Being, and is generally translated as the command: And thou *shalt* love (*ve-ahavta*) the Lord thy G–d with all thy heart, and with all thy soul, and with all thy might – and that is the end of the verse, the next one beginning "And these words . . .".

But *ve-ahavta* can also mean "And you *will* love"; there being no punctuation in the Torah, the verse may not end at "with all thy might" but continue with what follows it; and the *vav* joining them may mean 'when' and not 'and'. All this gives us the translation: "And thou wilt love the Eternal thy G–d with all thy heart, and with all thy soul, and with all thy might when these words which I command thee this day will be upon thy heart."

In other words: you are here given an *assurance* that you *will* love G–d only when all His commandments and guidance, the whole of His Torah, are on your heart, having arrived there through your mind, and having been put into practice, of course. And since G–d has given you the brains and the breath of His spirit with which to achieve this, He has the right to ask you to give *ve-ahavta* its other meaning as well, which makes it the *commandment* 'And thou *shalt* love' Him – because you are equipped with the means with which to attain that top rung of the ladder!

This interpretation has Talmudic support. When we come to discuss the commandment (16) to recite the Shema itself, it will be seen that, so far as the Torah requirement is concerned, the definitive ruling accords with the view of R. Meir that only its first verse *must* have been said with concentrated intent (*kavanah*) for the commandment to be considered to have been fulfilled. But some of his colleagues maintain there that such concentration must be continued to the end of the third verse, to 'upon thy heart' – because you cannot realise G–d's uniqueness until you have attained the love of Him; and *that* can only be achieved when *all* His words are upon your heart.

How is this to be achieved – the goal of every Jew? With your *whole* being, the middle of the three opening verses stipulates, constantly, and with single-mindeness.

Section 3.   **"With Heart, Soul And Might"**
The way you develop a love for G–d through the first of these three media, 'with all your heart', say the Sages, is to put "both your

impulses", the animal and the divine, to work solely in His service.

This is deduced from the use here of the longer form, *levav*, of the Hebrew word for 'heart'; for had the shorter form, *lev*, been used, it could have meant with one or other, but not necessarily both, of these impulses, as just two examples will show. Said G–d, in the verse which is the source of the Hebrew terms for these two impulses: "For the impulse (*yetzer*) of the heart (*lev*) of man is 'evil' (*ra*) from his emergence (from his mother's womb)" – as Jewish tradition renders it.

If this interpretation is taken in conjunction with the dictum that "the *yetzer tov* does not enter a person until he or she reaches BM age", *lev* here can *only* refer to the *yetzer ra*. But once endowed with the higher impulse, that person can serve G–d with the other *lev* as well, the one referred to in "All the upright in heart (*lev*) shall glory", and thus serve G–d with the whole *levav*. How this is achieved will emerge as we go along.

The next medium through which to attain love for G–d is 'all your soul'. The word used for 'soul' here is *nefesh*, the animating element common to all living creatures, which is often employed as a synonym for 'life', as exemplified in the verse (SPB 122): "In His hand is the soul (nefesh) of every living thing. . . ."

This second, and more difficult, requirement is therefore interpreted to mean that you must at all times be ready, should the dire situation demand it (see commandment 10), to give back to Him the life He gave you, as Isaac was prepared to do, and as R. Akiva (HPB 118 and HPH 770) and many, many thousands of Jews, before and after him actually *did*.

And when they did so, all accepted the situation, as did R. Akiva, not as one in which G–d had forsaken them – on the contrary: they saw in the supreme sacrifice of their lives, however, painful the experience usually was, a unique, and even joyful, opportunity of fulfilling the command to love the Eternal with *all* their souls.

Section 4.   **What Is 'Might'?**

Only here, and "in one other place" in the whole Tenach, is the word *me'od* used as a noun, that other instance being an adaptation of our verse, and translated 'might'. On the numerous other occasions it is used as an adverb meaning 'very' or 'exceedingly'. As a noun, then, it means anything of which you have a great amount, and which the Sages apply particularly to "thy money" or material possessions, *all* of which you should be prepared to sacrifice if serving G–d demands that of you.

The question is asked: "Need this third requirement be stated?" Surely if a man is willing to give his very life in G–d's cause, it goes without saying he will give all his money therefor? And the answer is: there are people who value their money more than their lives – and there *are*, and have always been, those who would rather remain in a perilous political climate and protect their possessions, rather than escape with their lives alone to safety.

It was for such people, so attached to their possessions that they will not part from them even to save their lives, that 'with all thy might' was added *after* with all thy soul' – since for them it is the most difficult thing to do! But what of the vast majority, who are more sensible, and are not so attached to their material possessions – or have none: is 'with all thy might' superfluous?

No! The Sages give this very rare noun an alternative reading, connecting it with *midah*, meaning 'measure', and render the phrase: aspire to the love of G–d "with whatsoever measure He metes out to you" in life – wealth or poverty, strength or weakness, good or ill-health! Do the best you can, whatever your circumstances; and then *your* service will be equal to that of the 'mightiest' – for "The Holy One, blessed be He, wants the heart"!

Section 5. **What Of The Mind?**

Is that all, then, that is required to bring us to love the Eternal our G–d – the maximum use of heart, soul and might? What of the mind, the brains with which we think and which give us understanding – does not the Holy One, blessed be He, require us to use *them* in His service, that gift of His which distinguishes us from the rest of the animal kingdom?

A more intriguing question: what *is* the biblical word for 'mind'? There *is* one in common use – *mo'ach*, but it occurs "only once in the whole Tenach," and there it means 'bone marrow', and not the living, thinking mind! Is there then no such word in Hebrew? There is, and it is – *lev*! Just two proofs: The Eternal said of the generation of the Flood: "every imagination of the *thoughts* of his heart (*lev*) is only evil all the day"; and when G–d invited Solomon to "ask what I shall give thee", his reply was: "Give Thy servant an *understanding* heart (*lev*) . . . that I may discern between good and evil" – the function of the *mind*.

And so *lev* can have three connotations: your animal impulses, your divine, spirit, or your mind, in any given text: and this should always be borne in mind whenever you come across the word 'heart' in English translation.

7.   TO "FEAR" G–D

Section 6. That is how this commandment is translated in the almost identical two verses in which it is stated: "Thou shalt fear the Eternal thy G–d, and Him shalt thou serve, and by His Name shalt thou swear"; and "Thou shalt fear the Eternal thy G–d, Him shalt thou serve, and to Him shalt thou cleave, and by His Name shalt thou swear" – all the *vavs*, you will notice, being translated 'and'.

Have you also spotted the difference between the two? In the second, you are told "to cleave" to Him, but not in the first; and it so happens that just as that verb has two opposite meanings in English, either to 'separate' or to 'unite', so has the Hebrew verb *leyirah*, almost always rendered 'to fear', but also meaning 'to revere'.

A person's instinctive reaction to something or someone he fears, is either to back away from the object, or obey that someone out of fear of the consequences should he not do so. But if he reveres an object or person, he will want to approach nearer to it, or obey that person out of reverence for him. And so as regards our relations with G–d.

The first of the two source-texts, it is suggested, refers to the inferior kind of *yirah*, called by the Sages *yirat ha-onesh*, obeying G–d out of 'fear of punishment' should you not do so. But the second, which includes 'cleaving' to Him, which obviously means approaching as near to Him as you can, refers to revering Him, which the Sages call *yirat haromemut*, 'reverence for His Majesty'.

And, translating one of its *vavs* by another conjunction, that second verse can be shown to refer to the superior kind of *yirah*: "Thou wilt revere the Eternal thy G–d, Him wilt thou serve – *when* to Him thou wilt cleave . . ." such service given out of love of Him, and not fear.

It is to this kind of *yirah*, which can only be reached either together with, or immediately following, the attainment of love of Him, that we refer when, in the blessing before the morning Shema, we ask "unify our heart to love and *revere* Thy Name", as HPB (115) understands it – and *not* 'to love and *fear*' as SPB (41) renders the phrase. And that is why I said when beginning discussion of the previous commandment, that it vies with this one for position as top rung of our ladder.

Almost everyone starts out at the beginning of religious adulthood to refrain from violating G–d's commandments out of fear of punishment, and this is the deterrent which persists as the motive of many throughout life. But the ideal towards which *you* should constantly aspire is to make reverence your motive, always saying to yourself when the temptation to sin tugs at your heart: How can insignificant I, ignore the command of His Majesty!

Section 7.   **How To Achieve Reverence**

That will be your instant reaction to any temptation to sin – once you have achieved that unified love and reverence, "RM avers" – but how to achieve it? he asks; and answers: "When man contemplates His great and wondrous works and creatures, and thus realises how incomparable and infinite His wisdom is, he will at once love Him . . . and be possessed of a great yearning to know the Great Name!" He then quotes king David's reverential exclamation: "When I behold Thy heavens, the work of Thy fingers, the moon and the stars, which Thou hast established – what is frail man that Thou should be mindful of him . . .?"

You have a much greater opportunity for such contemplation than even RM had, with the tremendous progress science has made since his day, and the highly acceptable face of television which brings the result of patient research by great scientists into your very home! But even they have only researched a tiny area of His vast Universe, and a relatively small number of the myriads of His creatures.

Even we, almost 3,000 years onwards, can declare as king David did. "How great are Thy work, O Eternal; Thy thoughts are very deep! A brutish man knoweth it not, nor does a fool understand this." But *you*, who are educated and no fool, should strive to know and understand as much of His wisdom as you can in your aspiration to love and revere Him.

8.   STRAY NOT AFTER YOUR HEART AND EYES

Section 8. The source of this commandment is in the third paragraph of the Shema, where we are told that the purpose of wearing the fringed garment (commandment 28) is to ensure that "you will not follow the desires of your heart and your eyes which lead you astray". You will see that it is the longer form of the word for 'heart' used here, and therefore refers to both your lower and higher natures.

RM says that in the latter context it is a prohibition against endangering your faith in G–d by accepting any scientific or religious concepts which are contrary to those laid down in His Torah. Study science, by all means: on the above RM quotation, the author of the Sh.Ar. advises us so to do "in order perfectly to understand G–d's wondrous works". But if its conclusions appear contrary to the Torah, it means one of two things: either you have not studied the Torah deeply enough, or those conclusions are false – for the Torah is eternally true, whereas Science has been proven to have erred at times!

But this commandment is primarily intended as a restraint on the animal instincts in man. "The heart and the eyes are 'agents' of the body: the eyes see, the heart desires – then the body acts" – if you yield to the temptation; and in this context our commandment provides the appropriate juncture at which to discuss the choice of age at which boy and girl become BM.

Section 9.　　　　**The Bar/Bat-Mitzvah Age**

These ages are nowhere explicitly mentioned in the Torah, though it is deduced that, so far as boys are concerned the age is thirteen from the fact that both pairs of brothers were that age when "the *lads* grew up, and Esau became . . . a *man* of the field, and Jacob a quiet *man*"; and when "Simeon and Levi, Dinah's brethren, took each *man* has sword . . ." – the word 'man' in each case not being essential to the narrative, and therefore introduced to teach this lesson.

That age is mentioned for boys in the "curriculum for life", but its author gives no reason for its choice. Commenting on it, Rashi says: "It is a law given to Moses (only orally) at Sinai that anyone who has the physical signs of puberty has reached the responsible age for the observance of some of the commandments of the Torah. The Sages assume that such evidence appears in the majority (of boys) by the age of thirteen." And the same assumption is made of girls "at the age of twelve."

Religious responsibility, then, arrives with puberty, it being assumed that intellectual advancement keeps pace with physical growth; and a girl becomes responsible a year earlier than a boy because "she is endowed with more understanding than a man", and therefore matures sooner, intellectually as well as physically. And it is with the advent of maturity that the *yetzer hara*, the animal impulses begin really earnestly to demand free rein.

But it is also just then that the *yetzer hatov* comes into its own, with the purpose of checking its older rival in the life-long battle for the soul of man. "If G–d created the *yetzer hara*" – for goodly purpose, in its proper time – "He also created the Torah as its antidote" *before* that proper time arrives. There are many devices the cunning tempter can make use of in our age, not least of them the *unacceptable* face of TV.

And so, to paraphrase our commandment, and incidentally to give its verbs their literal meaning: "You shall not search out with your heart and your eyes those temptations which can adulterate the purity of your mind and body." It is hard, very hard, in the permissive society in which you probably live; but if you have the determination, and use the Torah as an antidote to the temptations, you can do it – and will reap rich rewards later!

Section 10.   **A Constant Battle!**
The war between the two rival forces within, increasing in intensity as the teenage years progress, is a constant one: "*Always* must a man (or woman) stir up his higher impulse against the lower urges" – and the battle must commence *at once*, even before you begin to ascend the ladder. For one of the numerous warnings the Sages give us against the cunning machinations of the *yetzer hara* is: "At first it is like the thread of a spider, but eventually it becomes like a cart-rope", – if you give way to it. It is easy to brush away a spider's thread, with disgust – but a cart-rope can pull you down off the ladder, and do you grievous spiritual, as well as bodily, harm! (more on this subject later).

9.   DO NOT DESECRATE G–D'S NAME

and

10.   SANCTIFY G–D'S NAME

Section 11. These are two 'constants' I have added to the Chinuch's list, since they have become much more urgent now that Jews are scattered so widely and freely amongst the other nations. They express the depths of disservice to which the Jew can sink, and the height of service he can render, towards G–d, and towards His people called by His Name.

Both commandments are in the one verse: "You shall not desecrate My Holy Name, but I will be sanctified among the children of Israel; I am the Eternal Who sanctified you." This is one of the verses from which "the Sages infer" that G–d can only be sanctified by the recital of *Kedusha, Kaddish* (both of which mean 'sanctification'), a few other prayers and the public reading of the Torah among no less than ten adult males, since that is the smallest number to which the term 'congregation' is applied.

But the verse has wider application. Speaking to the Jewish people in G–d's Name, Isaiah says: "Thou art My servant, Israel, through whom I shall be glorified". How can this be done? Micah gives the answer: "And the remnant of Jacob shall be in the midst of many peoples as dew from the Eternal, as showers upon the grass . . .", upon which the SBB comment is: 'Israel's moral and religious influence among the nations will be as refreshing and regenerating as the effect of dew and rain on vegetation." By living as true Jews we glorify G–d, and sanctify His Name.

Section 12.   **The Other Side Of The Coin**

On the other hand, to desecrate G–d's Name among the peoples in whose midst we live, to bring disgrace upon the name of His people by illegal or anti-social behaviour, is a most grievous sin, so grievous, in fact, that the perpetrator of such an act falls into a category of sinners whose wrong-doing can only be expiated by death itself.

There is a text which, when read as it is written, says: "And *he* came unto the nations whither they came, and *they* desecrated My Holy Name, in that men say of them 'these are the people of the Eternal, and have gone forth out of His Land'". A footnote suggests that we should read 'they' for 'he', while the Midrash suggests that the 'he' should be 'He', i.e. G–d, Who accompanies His people into exile.

But might it not be that the Prophet meant what he wrote, to teach us the lesson we have all learnt to our sorrow – that when but *one* Jew commits an act of *Chillul haShem*, as this commandment is called, the people among whom we live blame us all, saying '*they* have desecrated' their good name, and therefore G–d's as well?

If only to be spared such unfair guilt-spreading, if you can possibly prevent anyone from committing such an act, you should do so! But religiously, you *must* do so, for "All Israel are sureties one for the other", and those who have the power to prevent others from sinning and do not exercise it, are held guilty with the perpetrators.

As for your own actions, and even words, your constant endeavour must be to sanctify and glorify G–d's Name among Jews and non-Jews by ever demonstrating, practically and without ostentation, that you are "Israel, My servant, Jacob whom I have chosen – a descendant of Abraham My friend", by living according to the laws and the ethics of His Torah!

And now, having set the foundation on which our ladder is to stand, and fashioned its uprights, we can commence to prepare its ninety rungs, one by one.

Section   **Notes**
1 Psalms 31.24; Exodus chapters 27 & 28 passim.
2 Deuter. 6.5; Berachot 13b.
3 Berachot 54a; Genesis 8.21; ADRN 16; Psalms 64.11.
4 II. Kings 23.25; Berachot 54a; Ibid 61b; Sanhedrin 106b.
5 Job 21.24; Genesis 6.5; I. Kings 3, 5 and 9.
6 Deuter. 6.13 and 10.20.

7   Yad Y. Hatorah 2.2; Psalsm 8.4–5; Ibid 92.6–7.
8   Numbers 15.39; SM. N.47; Kesef Mishneh loc. cit.; MR. Numbers 17.6.
9   MR. Genesis 63.10 and Rashi, Nazir 29b; Genesis 25.27; Ibid 34.25; Ethics
     5.24; Yad Ishut 2.7; MR. Genesis 18.1; B. Batra 16a.
10 Berachot 5a; Sukkah 52a.
11 Levit. 22.32; Sanhedrin 74b; Isaiah 49.3; Micah 5.6.
12 Yoma 86a; Ezekiel 36.20 and Rashi thereon; Shevuot 39a-b; Isaiah 41.8.

Nine

PREPARATIONS

Section 1. **The Basic Requirement**

Everyone who goes to Synagogue on Shabbat morning is given an opportunity, if only brief, to have a glance at the writing in a Sefer Torah as it is raised and shown to the whole congregation at the conclusion of the reading of the weekly Portion. Moreover, every BM-boy has himself read at least a few verses from it, and no BM-girl will be refused a closer look at it, on request.

It is not an ordinary 'book' or scroll by any means. Without going into any great detail: the parchment on which it is written must be "of the hide of an animal fit for Jewish consumption and tanned by a Jew for that sacred purpose"; the ink must be made of special ingredients, and the writing done with a quill pen; and most important of all, the *sofer* (scribe) who writes it must be a very G–d-fearing and learned man, whom it takes months, if not years to write just one Sefer Torah.

You will be surprised to learn, then, that one of the commandments which devolve upon you immediately upon your becoming a Barmitzvah – actually the last in the Torah, is:

11. TO WRITE A SEFER TORAH

You may well ask: How can this possibly be expected of me now – or at all? And why has it been placed as the very first rung of the ladder? Both these questions will soon be answered; but first let us look at the source of the commandment. After telling Moses that "thy days approach that thou must die", the Eternal commands: "Now therefore write this song for yourselves, and teach it to the children of Israel, put it in their mouths . . .".

"This song" is but part of the next chapter in the Torah, but it is deduced that the above words comprise a commandment to every Jew "to write the whole Torah which includes this song", and RM

55

proceeds to explain: "If he writes it himself, it is considered as if he personally received it from Sinai. If he cannot, he must either buy one, or employ someone to write one for him". In other words: In one way or another, every Jew, including you, must own his own Sefer Torah. Why?

That one-word question is an answer, in a way, to both your imagined questions above: always seek the reasons *why* you were given the commandments! A great Jewish philosopher, in a book called *Chovot Halevavot*, "The Duties of the Hearts", compares the Jew who fulfils G–d's commandments just *because* he is so commanded, without attempting to discover the reasons for them, to "an ass loaded with a sack of books"!

The fact that he uses the plural form *levavot* which, as we saw in the last chapter, refers to both heart and mind, emphasises the lesson that you must use the brains with which He has endowed you ever to search, always to ask "Why?", you are required to fulfil any positive commandment and refrain from violating the prohibitions.

So we will now consider the reason for our present commandment, and the conclusion we will reach will give further answers to those two questions.

Section 2.   **The Main Reason**
In former times, a Sefer Torah was the sole medium through which G–d's Word could be studied; and as we shall see later, every Jew has to occupy some part of every morning and every night of his life in such study. Therefore "everyone had to have his own copy to hand, so that he can constantly use it, and not be compelled to borrow one from a friend who might need it himself".

Later, after the introduction of paper manufacture, sanction was given to write the Books of the Torah, Nach and other religious literature page-by-page in book form for the purpose of private study. "Nowadays it is a *mitzvah* to write the Five Books of the Torah, the Mishnah and the Gemara, and their commentaries" for personal study; and "this is a greater *mitzvah* than presenting a Sefer Torah to the Synagogue". Some authorities maintained that with this facility, it would be an insult to the Sefer Torah to use it merely for study! And this view was reinforced with the invention of printing in 15th. century, and more so today when that art has made so much progress, and books roll off the presses in thousands!

And that is the *main* reason for our commandment: that every Jew should acquire a library containing *all* the Books of the Torah, Written and Oral, and *all* the traditional commentaries on them, with translations in the vernacular, if necessary – and any other books which will help him to understand the deep words of G–d. *Do* so!

Section 3. **Ladies Also?**

A few of those authorities go so far as to consider the above the *only* reason for our commandment, and therefore declare the commandment to *write* a Sefer Torah not applicable in our times. But if its purpose in olden times was *only* to study therein, why, it is asked, is it ruled that "Even if his father left him a Sefer Torah, he still has to write one for himself"? Cannot he study in the inherited copy?

The answer this authority gives is interesting, not only in itself, but from the corollary he draws therefrom – that ladies, also, have to *write* a Sefer Torah! I cannot enter all the arguments here, but you might get your teacher to go over them with you. See also HPH 889 on how you can 'write' one even today!

I have devoted much space to this preparation for "the study of Torah which leadeth to them all" (SPB 6) in order to set an example as to how you should search for the *reason* of *every* commandment by constantly consulting books in your own library – and those of others – and not leave them unopened and neglected on the shelf!

12.   DO NOT ADD TO THE TORAH

and

13.   DO NOT DETRACT FROM THE TORAH

Section 4. The source of both these commandments is: "Every thing which I command *you*, that you shall observe and do; *thou* shalt not add thereto, nor shalt *thou* diminish from it." See (HPH 805) Hertz' quotation from RM on this, and his own commentary on the verse. To them must be added RM's further observations that the addition and subtraction is forbidden both to and from the Written Torah and the Oral, i.e. the Mishnah – and the definitive rulings derived from the Gemara's discussion of the latter, and codified in the Shulchan Aruch. (see chapter two).

There is another verse which says the same thing even more clearly, yet it is not from there, but from our source-text, that RM deduces that the recognised religious authorities in every age do have the right, in the interest of communal welfare, to add to, or temporarily suspend one of, the Torah's commandments. This may be because of the abrupt change from plural to singular in the source-text, giving the possible interpretation: "You shall not, each individually, add or

subtract . . .", but your judges have divine sanction to do so; and you
must obey them.

But not even the most exalted of individuals, even be he a king of
Israel and the wisest of them all, could subtract even one commandment – as Solomon learnt to his cost. The Torah commands that an
Israelite king "shall not multiply wives to himself, that his heart turn
not away." Solomon, however, said: "*I* will multiply wives, and *not*
let my heart be turned away!" Yet we are told that "When Solomon
was old, his wives turned away his heart after other gods."

This illustrates his own conclusion, "There is no wisdom, nor
understanding, nor counsel against the Eternal". And it is a warning
to you that when, as you most certainly will, come to a commandment for which, try as you may, you can find no reason, or think
neglect of it cannot possibly affect you – obey it, nevertheless: for it
does have a reason, for your *good*, which G–d knows!

Section 5.   **Choosing A Career**
The second of these two commandments must be taken into consideration when you are choosing a career. The Talmud has an adage to
express the inevitable: "If you cut off his head, will he not die?"; and
there are some professions and trades which almost inevitably involve
regular violation of some commandments, which is equivalent to
detracting them from observance. This applies particularly to Shabbat, the observance of which is said to be "equal in weight to that of
all the other commandments" – a statement which can be misunderstood, and which will be explained when we discuss that holy day.

Another factor which you should take into consideration is
whether you will be able to pursue the chosen occupation in places
where such amenities as kasher food and congregational prayer at
least on Shabbatot and Festivals, the dietary and social ties which
ensure the preservation of your Jewish identity, are, or can be made,
available. If you are already engaged in an occupation which does not
satisfy either, and certainly both, of these requirements, you should
change over to another, however difficult this may be, before it is too
late for "Once a person has committed a sin and repeated it, it
appears to him like a legitimate act" – he gets into a rut from which it
is hard to extract himself.

14.   WALK IN G–D'S WAYS!

Section 6. It was explained in chapter two that the Torah, in the strict
sense of that word, consists of two intertwined threads, the legislative
and the narrative: and, apart from its historical content, the purpose

of the latter is to aid us in the fulfilment of this challenging commandment – to see how G–d acts towards man, and follow His example!

On no less than five occasions we are urged to aspire, so far as is humanly possible, to this summit of ethical living, and it is from the last of them that our commandment is drawn. "The Eternal will establish you as a holy people unto Himself, as He has promised you – if you will keep the commandments of the Eternal your G–d, and *walk in His ways.*"

Forty years before transmitting this commandment, Moses had asked the Eternal: "Show me now Thy ways, that I may know Thee, so that I may find favour in Thine eyes", and He had answered: "The Eternal, – the Eternal, is G–d, merciful and gracious, long-suffering and full of kindness and truth, keeping kindness unto the thousandth generation, forgiving iniquity and transgression and sin, and clearing (the guilty who repent) . . .". Into these words the Sages read the "Thirteen Attributes of G–d's Nature" (enumerated in HPH 364).

But even Moses was divinely told that: "Man shall not see me and live" – i.e. no human can know *all* His ways while on earth. But he *can* learn many of them by following His 'foot-steps' through the pages of the Torah and Nach.

Section 7. **Emulating G–d**

To give a few examples: from His bringing Eve to Adam, we learn that we must aid in arranging marriages; and from His clothing them both after their sin, to clothe the naked and the ragged. He visited Abraham who was recuperating, He comforted Jacob on his mother's death, He fed and quenched the thirst of the hungry and parched children of Israel, and forgave them their sins; and He (not 'he was' as in HPH) buried Moses – all to show us how *we* should act towards others.

And from the stories of the lives of the righteous and how He rewarded them, and of the wicked and how He punished them; we can learn how to act, and take warning how not to act, throughout our lives. Strive, therefore, ever to walk in G–d's ways, and the paths set by His pious ones!

But you cannot reach this lofty ethical goal on your own, even with the help of the most extensive library of Judaica. For many Torah texts are terse and difficult, sometimes not meaning what they superficially appear to mean – for, after all, they are the words of G–d which "can be explained in forty-nine different ways"! Your research into G–d's ways must be accompanied with the *meaning* of the following literally impossible commandment, to which passing reference was made in the last chapter.

15.   TO CLING TO G–D!

Section 8. The duty to cleave to G–d occurs in four different places, the second of them, very appropriately, in one of the verses in which the previous commandment is mentioned, and immediately following it. The first of the four reads: "The Eternal thy G–d shalt thou fear, Him shalt thou serve, *and to Him shalt thou cleave*, and by His Name shalt thou swear".

Obviously, it cannot mean what is literally says! Are we not told that "His Glory is above the heavens", countless miles beyond the point any astronaut has ever reached? And even were man able to approach Him, are we not further told "The Eternal thy G–d is a consuming fire"? Of course, this and like descriptions of G–d are poetic, expressing His infinite eminence – though "the Eternal is *near* unto all them that call upon Him . . .", and His glory fills the whole universe!

In any case, G–d is Spirit without body, and one cannot cleave to a spirit. So what does our commandment mean? answers the *Sifre*; "Associate with wise men and their disciples, and I (says G–d) will consider it as if you have indeed ascended on high." It is even opined that "close attendance on Torah scholars is greater than study of the Torah itself", since you can learn from their practice, as well as wise words, of Torah.

Possibly the most poignant story told in the Midrash is Moses' plea before his death that one of his sons should succeed him as leader of Israel, to which the Almighty replied: "Your sons did not occupy themselves with Torah, whereas Joshua served you from early morning to late at night: *he* is worthy to serve Israel!" Moses, our Teacher *par excellence*, undoubtedly taught his sons Torah, but they did not immerse themselves in studying its practice in their father's home. But Joshua "was minister to Moses", and departed not out of the tent of his master – the only human to whom the Eternal spoke "'face to face', as man speaketh to his friend." *That* was cleaving to G–d!

Section 9.   **Choose Your Company!**

The import of this commandment is best explained by RM: "We are here commanded to associate with the wise, continually to be in their company in all spheres – at Service, in committee, in eating and drinking and in business, so that we can emulate their actions, and acquire true belief (in G–d) from their words."

Whenever you hear that a Jewish scholar is to speak, run to "sit at his feet, and drink in his words with thirst"! join Torah study groups, and, above all, choose your close friends carefully, among young people who have the same religious objective in mind as yourself, and preferably who are more learned than you in Jewish knowledge, so that you can always learn from them and their practice of Judaism and even general conversation.

And the most constructive suggestion of all: Why not do as so many young people are doing today – spend your long vacation, or even a longer period between ending school and entering into university or occupation, at a Yeshiva or Young Ladies Seminary in Israel – where you can learn to read Hebrew fluently, so important, as we shall see in the next chapter, for the study of Torah in its original language!

Whatever you decide, remember that next to your parents and family, the most potent influence on your life are the friends you make. Wisely choose the Jewishly wise, thus fulfilling the commandment to cleave to G–d, walking in His ways and ascending our ladder with them!

Section	**Notes**

1   Y. De'ah 271; Deuter. 31. 14 & 19; Ibid 32. 1–43; SM. P.18; Bachya in chap. *Avodat Elokim.*

2   Chinuch 613; Y. De'ah 270.2 and *Baer Hagolah* thereon.

3   Aruch Hashulchan 270.5ff.; Sanhedrin 21b.

4   Deuter. 13.1; SM. N. 313 & 314; Deuter. 4.2; Ibid 17.11; Sanhedrin 21b; I. Kings 11.4; Proverbs 21.30.

5   Shabbat 103a; MR. Exodus 25.12; Yoma 86b.

6   Deuter. 8.6., 10.12, 19.9., 26.17., and 28.9. Exodus 33.13; Ibid 34. 6–7; R. Hashana 17b; chapter 3.

7   Genesis 2.22; Ibid 3.21; Ibid 18.1 (see HPH); Ibid 35.9 (see Rashi); Exodus 16.12. & 17.6; Numbers 14.20; Deuter. 34.6; MR. Numbers 14.20.

8   Deuter. 10.20., 11.22., 13.5 and 30.20; Psalms 113.4; Deuter. 4.24; Psalms 145.18; Berachot 7b; MR. Numbers 21.14; Exodus 33.11.

9   SM. P.6; Ethics 1.4.

Ten

THE "SHEMA"

Section 1.   **Introduction On Kavanah**

When performing a positive commandment, is it essential for you to have *in mind* at the time the fact that, and the reason why, you are performing it, or is the mere act sufficient to satisfy its fulfilment? To put the question in rabbinic form: is *kavanah* necessary or not? This is discussed in a number of places in the Talmud: and because the first of the arguments concerns our current commandment, the subject will be briefly considered here.

An extremely improbable supposition is made to illustrate the viewpoint of those who maintain that *kavanah* is not required. "A person throws a keenly sharpened and perfectly smooth-edged knife" with the intention of transfixing it into a wall, and by a million-to-one chance, an animal whose flesh is permissible happens to pass by at that very moment, and in the course of its flight the knife slaughters it in exactly the correct way!

Though the knife-thrower had no intention whatsoever of slaughtering the animal, R. Natan declares it *kasher* – fit for Jewish consumption, and "so the law rules". But all it proves is that if a *shochet* performs the act of slaughter in the correct manner, though he did so mechanically, with other thoughts in mind, it is valid.

Shechita is but one commandment, and the Talmud continues the argument concerning others, surprisingly reaching no decision either way. The Sh.Ar. rules in favour of those who maintain *kavanah* is necessary, but later authorities qualify this ruling, restricting its application to Torah commandments, and only then in certain circumstances.

For your general guidance, it will be well if you bear in mind always the conclusion reached there: "All these arguments are about *after* the commandment has been performed (i.e. whether one done without *kavanah* has to be repeated *with* intent); but as regards *before* fulfilling them, *all* authorities are agreed that *every* command-ment (Torah or rabbinic) *must* be performed with *kavanah*" — and particularly the one we are about to study: for should 'anyone recite the Shema and not direct his heart (to what he is saying) in the first verse, 'Hear, O Israel . . .', it is arguable whether the obligation has been fulfilled."

16. TO RECITE THE SHEMA MORNING AND NIGHT

Section 2. The name "Shema" is given to three Torah paragraphs (SPB 41–44), and is derived from their first word. The Shema is not a prayer, in the strict sense of that word, since we do not ask G–d for anything in it; but a solemn declaration of our acceptance of Him as our One-and-Only G–d, and our resolution to attain true love of Him by fulfilling all His commandments.

That the Shema has to be recited daily, morning and night, is deduced from its first paragraph which tells us to speak of them when, *inter alia*, "thou liest down and when thou risest up". *You*, as an individual, may go to bed and get up at *any* time of the day or night – and indeed part of the Shema is usually said by individuals whenever they *do* retire and rise at reasonably normal hours. But apart from those occasions, there are two times, one in the morning and the other in the night, when *all* Jews should be saying the Shema.

The Torah, as has been stated before, was given to the people of Israel, to be implemented in the Land of Israel, with a predominantly agricultural economy. The industrious farmer there made the most of the daylight hours, getting up just before dawn and "going forth unto his work and to his labour until the evening" – ready, more or less, for "the sweet sleep of the labouring man".

But before leaving, and immediately on returning home, he was used, even before having anything to eat, to recite the Shema – as parts of the Morning and Evening Services, as we shall see in the next chapter. And though most Jews are not agricultural workers today, nor do they live in countries where, as in Israel, dawn and nightfall are always at a reasonable hour, those two times have ever remained the *ideal* for the twice-daily recital of the Shema – or as soon as possible thereafter.

Section 3. **The First Of The Day – For Ladies Also?**
As you must know from the first chapter of *Genesis*, a Jewish day begins in the evening – precisely, when three medium-sized stars can, or could be visible (though, as we shall see later, something of the profane weekdays is added to Shabbatot and Festivals). This, there-fore, is also the ideally 'fresh' moment for reciting the night-time

Shema for "the zealous who perform their religious duty as early as possible", amongst whom it is hoped you will always be, and especially on the day you become a BM, for that is the very first Torah commandment you can fulfil!

Yet it does not begin to get 'stale' "until a third of the night-time has passed," but it is so by midnight, though the Sages enacted the Shema may be said until then – one of the stakes in their fence around the Torah "in order to keep man from the sin" of falling asleep before reciting it, and awaking too late to do so. However, in a case of emergency or forgetfulness, the Shema *may* be said at any time of the night, until shortly before dawn.

Though, for the reason given in chapter six, it is ruled that "women are exempt from reciting the Shema", the Sh.Ar. advises: "It is nevertheless fitting that they be taught to acknowledge the yoke of G–d's Kingdom; and that they should therefore recite at least the first verse". However, the MB there, who cites many authorities who maintain ladies are duty-bound to say much more, concludes: "All argument is about the extent of their *obligation* – but of course ladies can voluntarily take upon themselves the duty to say *everything*."

And so, young lady! although you do not *have* to say the Shema at all, according to the Torah, and even the Sages advise that you only recite the first verse; you *may* say it all – and G–d will surely bless you for doing so! I will have more to say on your obligations in the next chapter.

You should by now have acquired at least the three books listed at the end of chapter six, and especially Dr. Hertz's two masterpieces which are almost indispensable to the English-speaking person not at home in the Hebrew language, who seeks a broad knowledge of the Jewish religion, its prayers and their history. You will frequently be asked in the following pages to study these two commentaries.

As regards the Shema as a whole, there is no better exposition of it and the commandments it contains than Hertz's (HPB 116–127 and 263–269, and HPH 769–771). It is assumed that you have studied these, and we will therefore concentrate here on some interesting lessons he omits.

Section 4.   **A Word For Every Limb!**
The first all-important verse of the Shema is sandwiched, as it were, between two rabbinic praises of G–d not contained in the Torah text. A separate reason for the inclusion of the second will be given later: but why does the first precede the Shema? And why is it only said when recited privately, but not in congregation?

If you count the words of the complete Shema, from that word to the end of the third paragraph, you will find that it contains 245 words. Now the human body has "248 parts", and therefore in order that there should be a word for *every* part, in congregation we wait after we have individually recited the Shema to hear the Reader repeat its last two words and the first of the next paragraph. You do not hear these three words when praying privately, and therefore you compensate for this by commencing with the three words for "G–d, faithful King"!

Said R. Ami: "Let not the recital of the Shema be a light thing in your eyes, for it contains 248 words corresponding to the parts in the human body. (It is as if) the Holy One, blessed be He, were saying: 'If you guard *My* commandment to recite the Shema, I will guard all *your* limbs'"! So enunciate every word clearly and with deliberation – and not only of the Shema, "but also of all praises and Prayer, and when reading and studying the Tenach."

Section 5. **In What Language?**

The Talmudic Sages strictly adhered to the Torah command "to follow the majority" – as they interpret the last clause in that verse – when deciding the law. After giving careful consideration to all views on a particular subject, "they took a count and decided" according to the majority and even the most distinguished in the minority loyally abided by that decision.

Thus, when the great Rabbi Judah the Prince argued that the Shema must be recited in "these words", i.e. in the Hebrew original, his colleagues overruled him and decided that it can be said in any language, deducing this from the two words *Shema Yisrael*, which *they* render "Understand, O Israel", extending it to include the language in which you recite it. In other words: better in the English you understand than the Hebrew you do not – but best is in the Hebrew you *do* understand, having taken the trouble to learn it fluently.

And that is the law: "One may recite the Shema in any language" – but must be careful not to make mistakes in that language, and be as clear in enunciating it, as with the 'holy tongue' – which is what they call Hebrew. And, as we shall see, the same applies to almost all prayers and blessings.

Section 6. **The First All-Important Verse**

I introduce a detailed consideration of this verse with two questions, the first rather surprising: where and when did it originate; and whom are you addressing when you recite it in private (for in congregation it may be the other members)? A moving Midrash suggests answers to both these questions – and why the non-Torah verse was inserted immediately after *Shema Yisrael*. . . .

Of course, Moses wrote it into the Torah at G–d's dictation – but the words were "first uttered at the bedside" of him who gave Israel their name, by all his sons in unison. How came this about? Jacob, we are told, had summoned them all "that I may tell you what will befall you in the end of days" – but he did *not* tell them their future, because "at that moment the Divine Presence, and the spirit of prophecy with it, departed from him," G–d not wanting him to reveal the future.

Jacob, however, thought the reason for its departure to be some unfitness in his sons, so he asked them: "Is the G–d of Israel in heaven your Father? Perhaps in your hearts you wish to break away from Him?" And they all answered: "Hear, O Israel! the Eternal is our G–d, the Eternal is One!". When the Patriarch heard this he exclaimed: "Blessed be the name of His glorious Kingdom for ever and ever!" – that second non-Torah verse.

The Midrash continues: "Therefore, when the Jew says it every day, morning and night, it is the Patriarch he is addressing, saying: "Hear O Israel – from the Cave of Machpelah: that which thou didst bid us we still practise, for – the Eternal is our G–d, the Eternal is One!" – and it is him we address whether we recite it in public or privately. The ancestral bond still holds fast!

A more prosaic answer to the second question may be: you are addressing *yourself*, your divine soul, your *yetzer tov*, rousing it morning and night to do battle against the cunning, never-resting *yetzer ra*, the lower, animal impulses within you. Perhaps that is why R. Yose maintains that "your ears must *hear* what you utter with your lips", giving yourself this battle cry!

Section 7.   **Its Meaning**

R. Yose draws this inference that the ear must 'hear' your saying of the *Shema* from that very word, giving the verb its most common meaning. But, as we saw above, that verb has at least one other meaning – to 'understand', the only one it *can* have, for instance, in the verse "But they did not know that Joseph understood (*shome'a*) them, for the interpreter stood between them" whilst his brethren were conversing in Hebrew amongst themselves. The verb is so translated there – and should be here as well: "Understand, O Israel! . . .".

The dictionary defines 'to understand' as 'to grasp with the mind' or 'to be able to follow the working of', and both of these definitions can help us to obtain one possible interpretation of our verse: "Grasp with your mind, O Israel, that the Eternal is our G–d, the Eternal is One" – by being able to follow the working of His ways. That can only be achieved through Torah study (commandment 17), remembering all G–d's commandments therein and doing them conscientiously leading to the summit of the ladder, the love of G–d with heart, soul and might (commandment 6) – and that embraces the whole of the Shema and the Torah.

As previously mentioned, this verse of the Shema, at the very least, must be recited with complete concentration and intent; and for this reason, in order to exclude the possibility of any distractive sights, "it is customary to cover the eyes with the right hand while reciting it; and, as an aid to banishing all extraneous thoughts, to make the affirmation in a loud voice".

Section 8. The Rest Of The Shema And Its "Sandwich"

The other commandments included in the Shema have already been, or will eventually be, discussed in the appropriate sequential place in the BM's life. But one question relevant to the night-time recital of the Shema must be answered here. Its third paragraph concerns the commandment (28) of *tsitsit*, and when we come to deal with it, it will be seen that the wearing of the fringed garment is obligatory only during the daylight hours. Why then do we include this paragraph in the *night*-time Shema?

HPB (309) gives the reason: because that paragraph concludes with the Eternal's reminder that it was for the purpose of being our G–d that He redeemed our ancestors from Egypt, and therefore this remembrance must be with us and be mentioned "all the days *and* nights* of thy life"; and it is because of its mention here in its last verse that the whole paragraph is said nightly as well.

But the Shema alone is not all, for the Sages enacted that "both the night and morning recital must be 'sandwiched' between some blessings" (SPB 116–122 and 38–46), and the last of these must be *immediately* followed by the Prayer (see next chapter); and everyone who does this is assured that "no harm will come to him (or her) throughout that day *and*, if he does so regularly, is ultimately destined for 'the world to come'".

In other words, you have to say the whole of the Evening Service. However, if for some reason you cannot do that at the most fresh moment, you should then recite the Shema only in fulfilment of the Torah commandment, and repeat it again as a reading from the Torah when you recite the full Evening Service.

Section	**Notes**

1 Chullin 12b; Y. De'ah 3.1; E.g. Eruvin 95b and Pesachim 114a; Or. Ch. 60.4–5 with MB. notes 10–11.

2 Psalms 104.23; Eccles. 5.11.

3 Or. Ch. 235.1; Pesachim 4a; Berachot 2a; Ibid 20a-b; Or. Ch. 70.1. and MB. there.

4 Makkot 23b (see *Soncino* edit. p. 169. note 5); Tanchuma Kedoshim 6; Or. Ch. 61.22.

5 Exodus 23.2; Chullin 11a; E.g. Eruvin 13b; Berachot 13a; Or. Ch. 62.2 and MB. note 3.

6 MR. Genesis 98.3; Genesis 49.1; Pesachim 56a; Berachot 15a.

7 Genesis 42.23; Or. Ch. 61.4–5.

8 Berachot 12b; Or. Ch. 66.8; Berachot 9a.

Eleven

TORAH STUDY AND PRAYER

Section 1. These two commandments form the subject matter of this chapter because they are closely linked, the first with the purport, and the second in the liturgy, to the one that precedes them – so important that the whole of the last chapter was devoted to it.

17.   TO STUDY TORAH

There is a verse in the Torah which appears to be the ideal source-text for this commandment, since it so clearly expresses the duty to learn *all* G–d's commandments. "And Moses summoned all Israel and said to them: Hear, O Israel, the statutes (*chukkim*) and the judgments (*mishpatim*) which I speak in your ears this day, that you should *learn* them, and observe to do them."

Could there be a more explicit statement of your duty not only to learn both categories of the commandments, but also that the objective of that learning is to observe and do them, than this? Yet it is not in this verse that the Sages see the source of our commandment; and all the enumerators of the 613 by-pass this verse, not including it in their classification of them. This may be because the Torah's contents are more than just the commandments (see chapter two and commandment 14) – but there is a more profound reason why the Sages chose another verse.

The one they selected, in their wisdom, is: "and thou shalt *teach* them diligently unto thy children . . ."! Why? Because, of course, no one can teach before he or she has learnt! And the fact that the BM is called upon to fulfil this commandment (SPB 275) five years before he is expected to marry and raise a family, is proof of the theory that the years between BM and marriage comprise a period of apprenticeship, it being assumed that by the time that next important juncture in

69

your life arrives, you will be fully qualified to guide your children in the Torah way.

Section 2.   **A Tall Order!**

That is a tall order! The source-text is preceded by the verse "and these words which I command thee this day shall be upon thy heart" – which includes 'in your mind', you will remember; and 'these words' refer to the *whole* of the Torah, in the widest sense of that term. It has been shown how much of that you would have been taught by BM age when Jewish education comprised the complete curriculum in Jewish schools, and how far the average BM in the Diaspora actually is from achieving it by that age.

It is in a situation such as that arising from the modern educational system that the first verse quoted assumes importance. The *source-text* tells us that it is a father's duty, in the first place, to teach his children, or have them taught by a competent teacher, up to that stage by BM age; but if, for whatever reason, he does not or cannot do so, then it is deduced from that other verse that the son, after reaching that age, "must teach himself, for it is written, 'and you shall *learn . . .*'".

The one Hebrew word translated 'and thou shalt teach them diligently' occurs only one other time in the Torah where it means to 'sharpen' (a sword); and from that the Sages infer that its occurrence in our text means: "the words of the Torah shall be *clear-cut* in your mouth, so that if anyone asks you about them, you should not have to hesitate, but be able to answer him immediately". And that 'someone' will eventually be your child(ren) who will probably be very inquisitive, and ask tough questions!

And so, young man, you have much leeway to make up if you are eventually to qualify literally to 'teach your children' when that time arrives – by first learning, and getting into the regular habit of practising 'these words' during your bachelor days. For it must be stressed briefly here – though the subject truly belongs in the next volume, that you will not have to teach them just the *words* of the Torah, a duty which you will probably depute to trained teachers who can do that better than you; but to show them how those words are translated into practical Jewish living.

This is clearly indicated in the first-quoted verse – "so that you should learn them, *and observe to do them*". To 'observe' (or 'guard') is taken by the Sages to mean to guard against violating the negative commandments; and to 'do', to perform the positive ones. And to these must be added all the ethical lessons to be culled from the narrative section of the Torah – again, in its widest sense.

Section 3.   **What Of The Ladies?**

Before answering this question – a snippet of Hebrew. As you probably know, *bain* is 'a son' (*ben* being 'the son of'), and *bat* is 'a daughter', their respective plural forms being *banim* and *banot*, and their construct ('the . . . of') *b'nai* and *b'not*. However, unless the context obviously refers to 'sons' only, the masculine plural forms are always treated as common gender. For instances: when the Almighty said, "You are the *banim* of the Eternal your G–d", He was not referring to men only! And the term *b'nei Yisrael* is invariably *translated* "the *children* of Israel", to include both sexes.

But there are a few places in which the Sages deduce that the masculine plural must be restricted to its literal meaning, 'sons', and that the commandments in which they occur apply to men only – and *talmud-Torah* is one of them! Thus they deduce, from associating them with the verses preceding and following those in which they occur, that *banecha* in our source-text, and *benaichem* in a similar context, refer to sons only, "and therefore daughters do not have to be taught, and mothers do not have to teach their children." The inference is then drawn from the first text quoted that ladies are not obliged to teach themselves either.

Does this mean then that girls, the future mothers of our people, in which capacity they spend more time and have more influence over children than the fathers, should be left in ignorance of all Jewish knowledge and practice in their children's most formative years, when they are most in need of religious and moral guidance?

Just a glance at the staff of any Jewish Day School or set of Hebrew Classes will show you that it is not so, the majority of its members usually being young ladies *trained* in Teachers' Seminaries established by the orthodox community for the specific purpose of becoming knowledgeable and loyal Jewish teachers, wives and mothers. Are then those Seminary pedagogues at best occupying their time in performing an unnecessary task, or at worst breaking the law? Of course not!

The arguments in the Talmud concerning teaching girls Torah are intensely interesting, ranging between the extreme views of Ben Azzai who says "they *must* be taught it," and R. Eliezer who maintains "they *must not* be." RM and the Sh.Ar. rule that these views do not conflict, the first referring to the Written Torah, and the other to the Oral Torah.

Though they finally qualify even this compromise by ruling that it is better, in the first place, that ladies be not taught even the Written Torah, but should they have been, no wrong would have been done; they admit that a lady who teaches *herself* Torah receives reward therefor – but not as much as a man who is so *commanded* to do: because it is harder to obey a command than to act of one's own free will.

The Rama's comment on this is: "Nevertheless, a woman is duty-bound to learn laws having particular relevance to a woman. And a mother is not duty-bound to teach her son Torah – though if she *helps* her son or her husband so that *they* can occupy themselves in Torah, she shares their reward with them."

Section 5.   **Definitive Opinion?**

Just before his death, Moses commanded the priests and elders to, every seventh year: "Assemble the people, the men, *the women* and the children, and the convert that is within thy gates, that they may hear, and that they may learn, and fear the Eternal your G–d, that they may *observe to do all the words of this Torah*" – a copy of which, which he had just completed writing, he handed to them. Discoursing on this, R. Eleazar b. Azariah asked: "If the men came to learn, and the women to hearken, why did the little ones come? In order to grant reward to those who bring them."

Combining these two texts, the *TaZ*, one of the two main commentators on the Sh.Ar., comes to a conclusion which should be accepted as the definitive law regarding ladies and Torah-study. "They should be taught, of set purpose, the text and the plain meaning of the Written Torah, *as is the custom every day*, but not deeper intellectual research into it (i.e. Talmud study), into which the Sages forbade they should be initiated."

According to the TaZ, then, it is the study of the *Oral* Torah that parents and/or teachers should not initially teach ladies – but if they nevertheless do so, no wrong is done: However, it is to be assumed, ladies may study it (amongst) themselves – and be rewarded for doing so! And this should be their ideal, in preparation for marriage and running a truly Jewish home, and training their children in the ways of G–d.

Section 6.   **When And How**

Torah-study is one of those commandments (SPB 6) which have no fixed measure: on the one hand you can turn this forty-nine-faceted more-precious-than-rubies treasure round again and again, contemplating and waxing grey and old over it, without fathoming all its beauty and mysteries; while on the other, "in times of extreme pressure or emergency only", the twice daily recital of the Shema, so

important a commandment in its own right, "can double" for this one
as well.

But in normal times, which I trust yours will always be, the
minimum requirement is "to study at least one chapter each day and
one chapter each night", in fulfilment of the duty "This Book of the
Torah shall not depart out of thy mouth, but thou shalt meditate
therein *day and night*" – as we promise to do (SPB 117) in every
evening Service of the year. And one of those 'chapters' – for it may be
longer or shorter than a chapter in the English Bible – should be the
parashah of each day, for the Sidra (Portion of the week) read in
Synagogue every non-festive Shabbat consists of seven *parashiot*.

R. Joshua b. Levi told his children: "Complete your *parashiot* with
the congregation (in the Synagogue every Shabbat), twice the Hebrew
text and once Targum"; and that has become every Jew's staple daily
diet for mind and soul. 'Targum' means translation into the vernacular: in Babylon it was Aramaic, in Europe mostly Yiddish, and in
Moslem countries either Arabic or Ladino.

For you, it is English: so 'twice in Hebrew and once in English'; and
the best way for you to carry out R. Joshua's instruction is to study
each day's *parashah* verse by verse with its English translation and
commentary, and then to re-read the Hebrew text as a whole,
knowing the second time what it all means.

As for the second daily chapter to satisfy the minimum requirements of our commandment, you might ask your rabbi or teacher to
draw up a programme for you. I would suggest the consecutive study
each day, in the same way as that of Torah, of the Books of Nach
from Joshua to Malachi. If you add just one chapter every Shabbat,
you will be surprised to learn that you will have completed the whole
of the Hebrew Bible in one year!

You can choose your own times day and night for this study, but
the ideal times are immediately following the Morning and Evening
Services. The importance of doing so is conveyed by the Sages'
statement that one of the first two questions asked on the post-
mortal day of judgment is "Did you set aside daily periods for Torah
study?"

Finally on this commandment – though much more could be said
about it: remember its purpose – "so that they may learn *to observe
and to do*"! R. Yochanan severely censured "one who studies Torah
and does not fulfil it – it would have been better for him had he never
been born!", he opined. And rightly so – for "it was for that purpose
you were born"! Remember also: we have been talking about the
minimum time you should daily devote to study of Torah in its widest
sense – and there is *no* maximum! (SPB 6)

18.   TO PRAY TO G–D DAILY

Section 7. We are often told in the Torah to serve G–d, and talmud-Torah and worship in the Temple are illustrated as two forms of such service. But when we are told "to serve Him with all your *heart*", the Sages ask: "What is service with the heart? You must say this means prayer."

It is from here that RM deduces the commandment that all Jews have to pray daily. But he goes on to say that neither the number of daily services, nor the form of, or time for, such prayer are part of the *Torah* commandment.

He therefore observes that women must also pray daily, for the commandment "has no fixed time for its fulfilment" – and that "is the law" – but more about this later. "*Everyone* must pray daily, first declaring the praises of G–d, then beseeching Him for one's needs, and finally thanking Him for His past kindnesses." (Note well these three constituents of prayer and their order.)

But the habit of praying at *three* specific times daily is traced back as far as the Patriarchal Age, it being deduced from Torah texts that "Abraham introduced prayer in the morning, Isaac in the afternoon, and Jacob at night." King David says, "Evening, morning and noon-time will I pray and moan"; and Daniel was accustomed to "kneel three times a day and pray and give thanks before his G–d".

The Midrash has preserved a set of such simple prayers corresponding to the three changes in the day. "In the evening a person should say, 'May it be Thy will, O Eternal my G–d, to bring me forth from darkness to light'; in the morning, 'I thank Thee . . . for bringing me forth from darkness into light'; and in the afternoon, 'May it be Thy will . . . as Thou hast favoured me to see the sun in its brightness, so mayest Thou favour me to see its setting'".

Section 8.   **Before, During, And After The Exile**
In the time of the First Temple, "the priests sacrificed and prayed for the whole people", blessing those Israelites who were there, especially on the Three Harvest Festivals when "all Israel came to appear before the Eternal their G–d in the place which He chose" – and those who were not there, from afar. The latter recited the Shema morning and night, and possibly an extempore prayer when they felt the need, or perhaps at the three day-change times.

And so, more or less, their religious life continued during the Babylonian Exile, though it is possible that, when they met together for companionship on foreign soil, they nostalgically broke into impromptu singing of some of the Psalms of David which the Levites used to chant with musical accompaniment at Temple Services – and it has been suggested that these social gatherings were the origin of the Synagogue.

Some time after the Return from that Exile, the "Men of the Great Synagogue" (HPB 614), "A hundred and twenty elders among whom were many prophets" including, according to tradition Haggai, Zechariah and Malachi (said to be a pseudonym for Ezra), formulated *the* Prayer (*Tefillah*), then called 'the eighteen blessings' (*she-moneh-esreh*) in a fixed order, for all Jews to recite everywhere. Though a nineteenth blessing (HPB 143) was later added, some people still call it 'the 18', but it is popularly known today as the *Amidah* ('standing' – SPB 46–56) because it has to be said in that position.

These great men of the Great Synagogue also composed all the prayers and blessings we now find in the Siddur, though a few were added later to commemorate or celebrate different occasions. All these facts you can find for yourself in the excellent introduction to HPB, and its splendid introduction to, and commentaries on, *the* Prayer and all the other prayers and blessings throughout the year and for all occasions.

Here, therefore, I will only call your attention to some of Hertz's most important comments, expand where he is brief, and add some observations which he omitted.

Section 9. **Services: Their Times**

Unlike Torah-study, Services including the Amidah *do* have 'a fixed measure'. Instituted after the destruction of the Temple, when the priests could no longer sacrifice and pray for the whole people, the Services replaced those sacrifices, which, in turn, had been offered at the times when the Patriarchs had prayed.

To put it another way: the priests' Service in the Temple having ceased, *every* Jew assumed his role as a member of "a kingdom of priests", "rendering for bullocks the offering of our lips". And these equations of prayer to sacrifice and every Jew to a priest play a great part in practical Jewish living, as will emerge in later chapters. To take but one example relevant to our subject:

The Torah says that both the rich man's bullock and the poor man's offering of a handful of fine flour are equally acceptable as "a sweet savour unto the Eternal". From this the Mishnah derived the adage: "It is all one whether a person offers much or little, so long as he directs his heart to Heaven".

This saying is applied to Torah study, and can also apply to the Prayer: for it is ruled that "anyone who is under pressure who feels he cannot concentrate his mind on the whole of the Amidah, may say an abridged form of the thirteen middle blessings (SPB 56, HPB 159): for a little with *kavanah* is better than a lot without, since "the Merciful One wants the heart" – which brings me back to . . ..

Section 10.   **Ladies And Prayer**
Though, according to RM, the Torah commandment only requires one prayer of one's own choosing per day, as stated above, he of course rules that *men* must carry out the rabbinical enactment to pray three times daily in the set form. But as for *women*, according to RM "it may be possible that even the Rabbis require no more of them" than the one prayer of their choice daily.

RN, however, disagrees with RM, maintaining that daily prayer "is *not* a Torah commandment", the phrase 'to serve Him with all your heart' meaning in *whatever* way you serve Him, do so whole-heartedly. He naturally also accepts that men must fulfil the rabbinical enactment to pray thrice daily – but he maintains that women must also say the morning and afternoon Amidah! But why? Do not the Sages thus convert it into a 'fixed-time' commandment, from which category women are exempt?

Were prayer a *commandment*, replies RN, that would indeed be so – but it is not: "it is a measure of divine graciousness in offering to hear and answer whenever we call unto Him . . . It is part of our service to Him to learn to cry to Him *in times of trouble* such as war, drought, sickness, etc.". The (thirteen middle blessings of the week-day) Amidah are "supplications for divine mercy" (and women excel in that over men!).

This view of RN is the dominant one, since most halachic authorities agree with him, concludes the MB, and he continues: and since it is fitting that women should say (at least the first verse of) the Shema, which must be followed by the thanksgiving blessing (SPB 44–46) for our redemption from bondage, which itself must be immediately followed by the Amidah, which contains a prayer for our future redemption – women must, in effect, recite the whole of the Morning Service proper, especially if they wrap the Shema in its sandwich of blessings!

And, according to this view, ladies must also say the short Afternoon Service – but not the Evening one: because that Service, as distinct from the night-time Shema, was originally a voluntary one, since there were only two daily sacrifices (SPB 11) morning and mid-afternoon, only "the fats and remaining pieces of sacrifices being burnt on the altar at night." *Men* later accepted the Evening Service as obligatory, but not women – though there is no harm in their doing so!

Section 11.   **Are Prayers Answered?**

Not always! In the prayer on the Shabbat preceding a new month (except Tishri) we ask the Eternal that during the coming month "all the desires of our heart for *good* shall be fulfilled": you may *think* that what you are asking is good for you; but He knows it is not – so your prayer will go unanswered. Again: what you ask for may be good for you, and will still not be granted if you have not exerted all the faculties He has given you to the full in striving to achieve that aim yourself.

That is inferrable from the Hebrew verb for 'to pray' – *lehitpallel*, which is the reflexive form of a verb meaning "to judge". It tells us, then, that before we can entreat G–d for anything, we must first judge ourselves to make sure that we have tried our utmost to realise the objective we seek.

So it is no use, for instance, praying to G–d for knowledge, the first and most important of the thirteen week-day petitions in the Amidah, 'Please! – let me pass my exams!', if you play when you should be using the brains with which He has endowed you to the utmost in acquiring that knowledge – and so with all other petitions.

Much, much more can be said on this subject – but not here! I suggest you add to your library one of the translated abridged Shulchan Aruch books, and study a few paragraphs each day: for "If not now, when?" May all your prayers be deservedly answered!

From today onwards then, as soon as the stars appear, recite *Arvit* (the Evening Service) with its Shema, and then study the day's *parashah*, thus fulfilling the halves of two Torah commandments, and another complete one which the Sages have reduced to only one-third! Can you see how?

Section	**Notes**

1 Deuter. 5.1; Ibid 6.7; Ethics 5.24.
2 Kiddushin 29b; Deuter. 32.41; Kiddushin 30a; Deuter 5.1.
3 E.g. Genesis 42.5 and Levit. 6.9; Deuter. 14.1; Ibid 11.19; Kiddushin 29b.
4 Sotah 20a; Yad. Talmud-Torah 1.13; Y. De'ah 246.6.
5 Deuter. 31.10–13; Chagigah 3a; Y. De'ah 246 note 4.
6 Ethics 5.25; Y. De'ah 246.1; Menachot 99b; Joshua 1.8; Berachot 8a; Shabbat 31a and Kiddushin 40b; MR. Levit. 35.7; Ethics 2.9.
7 Deuter. 11.13 and *Sifre* thereon; Ta'anit 2a; Yad. Tefillah 1.1–2; Kiddushin 29a; Or. Ch. 106.1; Berachot 26b; Psalms 55.18; Daniel 6.11; MR. Genesis 68.9.

8   Tamid 32b; Deuter. 31.11; Megillah 17b.
9   Exodus 19.6; Hosea 14.3; Levit. 1.9 & 2.2; Menachot 110a; Berachot 5b;
    Or. Ch. 110.1.
10 MB. 106 note 4; on SM. P.6; Berachot 20b; first note this section; Berachot
    27b and MB. 237 note 1; Berachot 2a.
11 I. Samuel 2.25; Ethics 1.14.

Twelve

DUTIES TOWARDS PARENTS

After having performed the first Torah commandment of every Jewish day – the Arvit Service including the Shema, the first persons you will probably meet with will be your parents, and the other members of your family – if any. Your duties towards them – some of those other relations included, as we will later see, will form the next four rungs of our ladder, two of them positive Torah commandments, and the other two prohibitions.

19.   HONOUR YOUR FATHER AND MOTHER

Section 1. Need I tell you the source of this commandment? Of course not! It is one of the "Ten Commandments" (SPB 91–93), first uttered by G–d Himself at mount Sinai, and later repeated by Moses. It is referred to as "the hardest of the commandments to fulfil", which at first glance appears surprising: but there are sound grounds for this opinion, the most potent of them in our days being the one called 'the generation gap'.

So much more swiftly, compared with the leisurely pace in former generations, does the social climate change, with ever-increasing novel media of pleasure, often involving the loosening of moral restraints; that, by the time a child reaches the teenage years, his or her parents are considered to be too conservative, 'square', unable to 'understand the times we live in'!

However, a gap between people can only be created by their apartness, and is widened when they move in different directions towards dissimilar goals. But when parents and children travel the road of life hand-in-hand towards the *same* goal, directing their steps along the Torah route, whose "ways are ways of pleasantness, and all its paths peace", there can be *no* gap between them, no unpleasantness, no quarrelling.

This is the Jewish way, inspiringly exemplified by the first two fathers of our people – though there was a whole century gap in their ages! "And they went both of them together", we are told of Abraham and Isaac, repeated a second time after father had informed son that "should there be no lamb for an offering, you, my son, will be the offering" – and still "they went both of them together", the one to sacrifice and the other to be sacrificed – as they thought – because that was the route that G–d had charted for them!

Thousands upon thousands of Jewish parents and children have, in the distant and not so distant past, marched on that path, voluntarily as well as under compulsion, to demonstrate that their was no gap between them in their love of G–d – with no angel of His saying to the murderers 'Stay your hand'! But hopefully such ordeals are forever gone, and you and your parents should walk through *life* together, "that thy days may be long, and that it may go well with thee"!

Section 2.   **Examples Of Filial Honour**
Most of the general examples given by the Sages of the ways in which children should honour parents apply when the latter are destitute, sick or aged, like "feeding them, clothing them, aiding them when they have to go out and come in". Such will never come your way, I ardently pray – or at least not for many a year; and so I have left this aspect of the commandment to the next volume, when you will be the middle generation between your own children and your parents.

But the Sages also give many inspiring examples of individuals who ideally demonstrated their fulfilment of this commandment. I quote just one of the many, chosen because it shows how right Ben Zoma was when he asked-and-answered: "Who is a wise man? He who learns from *all* men", be they Jewish or not.

R. Eliezer the Great's disciples asked him to give them an example of *kibbud-av-va'em*, as our commandment is called in Hebrew. "You are asking *me*!", he replied; "Go and see how Dama b. Netina, a certain idolater of Ashkelon, acts towards his father!" He told them that Dama had been offered one thousand gold pieces for jewels he possessed, and required for the High Priest's *ephod*. But he refused to sell – because the key to the jewel-box was under his sleeping father's pillow, and he did not want to disturb him! Thinking that it was greed and a seller's market which held Dama back, the would-be buyers repeatedly raised their offer until they reached ten thousand.

At this stage, Dama's father woke up. The son went and brought the required jewels, and handed them to the Sages, who wanted to give him the ten thousand gold pieces. But he would only accept one thousand offered originally, exclaiming: "Heaven forbid that I should profit from honouring my father!" He was a high official: on one occasion his mentally deranged mother slapped him in public, and he merely courteously bowed to her and whispered in her ear "That's enough, mother!". That's *honour*!

You yourself can think of ways of honouring your parents, fulfilling and even anticipating their every wish, rather than, whenever either of them ask you to do anything, sulkily saying 'O alright!', or procrastinating with 'Just wait till I've finished this game!'. It is the spirit in which it is done, more than the act itself, that counts.

Section 3.   ***His* Earthly Representatives!**
You will have noticed that the commandment to honour your parents comes between your duties towards G–d and those towards your fellow-men. "They are His partners in your existence", His representative on earth, the link between Him and your fellow-men. From the fact that the verse "Honour the Eternal with thy substance . . ." begins with the same word as our commandment, the Sages drew the inference: "Holy Writ equates the honour due to parents with that due to the Omnipresent". Therefore: "When a man honours his parents, the Holy One, blessed be He, says, 'I credit it to them as if I had dwelt among them and they had honoured Me'".

When R. Yosef heard his mother's footsteps approaching, we are told, he would say: "I will rise before the approach of the Divine Presence"! Any parents reading this should note from this and the 'they' in the previous quotation, that *they* must be deserving of their children's honour by *acting* as His representatives on earth!

Section 4.   **Extension of Commandment**
When the word *et* precedes a noun in Tenach it indicates that that noun is the object of the sentence. But as it is not placed before *every* object, the Sages maintain that where it *does* occur, it has *meaning* also, "extending that noun to include someone or something else". From the *ets* and *vav* in our commandment, "step-mother, step-father and elder brother" are included among those who should be honoured; and the Sh.Ar. adds grandparents (and parents-in-law) – but none to such a degree as parents. It can be assumed that adoptive parents are also included, since: "He who brings up children is called father, not he who (merely) begets them".

20.   FEAR (REVERE) YOUR MOTHER AND FATHER

Section 5. The source of this commandment is: "You shall every man fear (revere) his mother and his father (and you shall keep My

Shabbatot; I am the Eternal your G–d)." The same is said of our duty towards the Third Partner in our creation: "The Eternal thy G–d shalt thou fear (revere) . . ."; and therefore, as with honour, we must fear (revere) our parents as we do G–d – exceptions, soon to be mentioned, apart.

That daughters are also included in this commandment is deduced from the use of the plural, 'you', and not the singular 'thou' in the verb. However, it is explained, the verse continues in the masculine, because whereas a son must *always* fulfil the commandment, a daughter, once she is married, must follow her husband's wishes, and not her parents', should there ever unfortunately be a clash of instructions between the two.

'Fear' means just that – fear of punishment should you disobey them. And since a child usually fears his father more than his mother, since it is he who normally inflicts the punishment – which is a good thing: for it is still true that "He that spares the rod, hates his son; but he that loves him, disciplines him in good time": for this reason the Torah here mentions the fear of *mother* first, to stress that she is to be feared as much as father. On the other hand, when speaking of the *honour* due to parents, since most children respect their mother more, because she always soothes them, and tries to protect them from father's disciplinary measures, the Torah puts *him* first, to stress that he must be shown the same honour and respect; for if and when he chastises you, it hurts him as much as it hurts you, and loves you no less than mother does.

That the verb used here (*tira'u*) also means to show reverence, and that that is probably its main meaning, is proven by the examples the Sages give as to how the commandment is implemented. "What is *yir'ah*?" they ask: and answer: it means that a child should not stand or sit in a place or seat reserved for a parent; not contradict them when they speak; and not take the side of an opponent arguing with them. Like R. Yosef, children should courteously rise when father or mother enters the room; and should not address them, as is the 'with it' habit in many families today, by their first names.

Although the law is "that a parent may renounce the right to be shown all the signs of honour and respect", it is a very unwise child who avails him- or herself of such licence: first because though such renunciation absolves the child from the divine punishment that would be incurred had it not been conceded, it is *still* a *mitzvah* (good deed) on the child's part to ignore, such renunciation. Secondly, because it can leads to too much familiarity and worse – as we shall see when discussing the next commandment.

Section 6. **What Of Absence From Home?**

Jacob was absent from his parents' home for thirty-six years, the first "fourteen in the School-house of Eber" studying Torah, and the other twenty-two working for his wives and possessions and leisurely travelling home. For his absence during the latter period, he was punished 'measure for measure' by being deprived of the company of his favourite son for exactly that period of time – for Joseph was seventeen when he was 'kidnapped', and thirty-nine at Jacob's reunion with him in Egypt.

Jacob was not punished, however, for the period he spent in the School-house studying Torah, from which it is deduced that such study takes precedence over remaining at home in order to fulfil the commandment to honour parents in person. If, then, your studies take you to an out-of-town University, and especially to a Yeshiva or Seminary to study Torah, you are not only absolved but commended – though nowadays you can frequently, if not daily, enquire about your parents' welfare, and inform them of yours, by phone or letter.

But if you should take a flat on your own in order to be free of your responsibilities towards them – and perhaps to escape their restraint upon you, then you would be neglecting these two important commandments, unless relations become so strained that violation of the following two Torah prohibitions becomes a real and frequent danger.

Section 7. **Who Comes First? Father, Mother, Or . . .**

Though he turned out to be the son of a widow, a young man asked R. Eliezer: "What should I do if both my father and my mother ask me for a drink of water at exactly the same time?" He replied: "Leave your mother's honour (till afterwards), and serve your father first; for both you and your mother are duty-bound to honour your father." Though the question was poignantly hypothetical, the answer was not – for that "is the law".

Male chauvinism? Discourtesy? Ladies first? Not at all! It is merely recognition of the fact that there must be one ultimate arbiter in a family: and the potential 'rod-swayer', rather than the 'soother-with-words' is more likely to succeed in filling that role – though any *gentleman* in those circumstances would instruct his child to serve *mother* first: for "A man must always be heedful of the honour due to his wife, because blessings rest on a man's home only on account of his wife."

But there is someone who takes precedence even over your parents in the matter of honour and reverence – your Torah teacher or rabbi.

For whereas "your parents prepare you for life in this, temporary, world, the teacher who taught (and is still, I trust, teaching) you the greater part of your Torah knowledge prepares you for the future, eternal world" – after 120 years here! In accordance with this reasoning, if your father is a sage equal in wisdom to your teacher, then father *does* take precedence. But where the appointed rabbi of a city or congregation is concerned, "both a man and his father are bound to honour the rabbi."

It was to set an awesome example to all future would-be rebels against the Rabbis that such a terrible punishment was meted out to those "who rebelled against our very first Rabbi", Moses. To preserve unity in a community, there must be one ultimate authority, and that is the rabbi. That is why, after Moses had told Joshua to consult with the elders before taking any decision after assuming the leadership, G–d instructed Joshua to lead them himself: "Show them your authority! (if necessary) take a stick and strike them on their head! There is only *one* leader to a generation, not two!" And so with every Congregation.

I mention this here because it applies to you as well. Many Congregations have "Junior Membership": if yours has one, join it; if not, take the initiative in starting one! But whatever the situation, the rabbi of the Congregation you attend merits your honour, reverence, and obedience – though you may, and should, question him about any sermon, *shiur* or instruction he gives which you do not understand.

Section 8.   **Any Exceptions?**
Are there any exceptional circumstances in which you may refuse to honour, revere, obey your parents? Yes – but only painful ones, alas, with which I earnestly pray that you will never be confronted. The commandment to honour (and obey) them follows immediately upon that to keep the Shabbat holy in the "Ten Commandments"; while, as you will have noticed, keeping Shabbat is actually mentioned in the *same verse* as the commandment to fear and revere your parents. From this the Sages, probably translating the *vav* that joins them as 'but', deduce that a child *must not*, after BM, obey a parent who asks him or her to break any of G–d's commandments.

The tremendous responsibility which this places upon parents is plain to see, and will be dealt with fully in the next volume. *You* should, in the meantime, always bear in mind that you are now an apprentice to parentage, and should train yourself, 'get into the mood', for it. But what can you do if you *are* asked, even commanded, by your parents to violate one of His commandments, when you are totally dependent on them for everything? It is a very, very difficult situation, one in which few parents would involve their children, especially not *yours*!

But if they nevertheless do, probably not realising the seriousness of what they are doing, here are some suggestions. If, on a Shabbat morning, mother proposes, 'Let's go into town and do some shopping'; or father invites you to go to the office with him, have lunch in a non-*kasher* restaurant, and then go to a football match – politely decline the enticing bait, and say you prefer to go to Synagogue. If one or other of them says, 'If that's what you want, I'll drive you there', say you would prefer to walk, however far it is.

As a last resort, however, if their anti-Torah demands persist, if mother does not keep a *kasher* home – Heaven forbid! – then, if you earnestly want to train yourself as a loyal Jew, you must pluck up courage, and leave home! There are now, happily, many ways in which you can do this, especially if you go to Israel on *aliyah* – with your parents' permission, of course, if you are a (civil law) minor.

I have known some determined boys and girls who have followed this advice, and have settled down happily and Jewishly. I have known others who, by only threatening to leave home, have induced their parents to change their whole life pattern and become observant Jews themselves – and what a wonderful *mitzvah* those children performed!

May you never have such problems! May you and your parents walk harmoniously, hand-in-hand along the pleasant and peaceful pathways of Torah-true life, with the Third Partner taking delight in you all.

21.   DO NOT CURSE YOUR FATHER AND/OR MOTHER

Section 9. The source of this commandment is: "For whatsoever person (Hebrew: *ish ish*) there be that curseth his father and/or his mother shall surely be put to death". It is repeated in almost, but not quite, similar words: "And the curser of his father and/or his mother shall surely be put to death". From the doubling of the subject – *ish ish*, in the first verse it is deduced that "both a son and a daughter are included in the prohibition"; and from the second that it is wrong to curse them "even after their death".

Further inferences drawn are (a) that the conjunctive *vav* can mean either 'and' or 'or', i.e. the sin is committed whether one curses only one parent or both together; and that only when the curse includes G–d's Name is one liable, theoretically, (see chapter thirty-one), to suffer the said penalty.

It is forbidden to curse *anybody*, and this is but one of four Torah commandments prohibiting us from doing so, the other three being included under one 'umbrella' commandment (50). Just imagine for one moment what a child who commits this sin is doing: he or she is calling upon the divine Partner in his or her being to inflict harm upon one or both of the other partners! I could not possibly imagine *you* doing so – which is why this paragraph is in the third person!

22.   DO NOT STRIKE YOUR FATHER OR MOTHER

Section 10. Source: "And he that smiteth his father or his mother shall surely be put to death". The kind of smiting for which one is culpable is "only one in which he wounds them", causing a bruise or blood to flow, assumably struck in anger – which is why I said earlier that it is unwise for father and son to become too familiar with each other, when disagreement can lead to fisticuffs.

Some parents can at times be tactless, unreasonable, over-bearing and provocative, rousing resentment, anger and heated verbal rejoinders from their children. You will see later on, when we discuss the commandment (49) forbidding putting "a stumbling-block before the blind", that one of those who is considered as having violated it is "a father who beats his grown-up son"; for in doing so, he strongly tempts the son to retaliate in kind, and thus to violate the much more serious commandment not to strike a parent.

Should you ever unhappily be involved in such a situation, remember it is your parent who is provoking you! Put a firm rein on your tongue, stay your hand – follow the example of Dama! And should such or other impossible conditions persist, you might be compelled to do what R. Assi did when his aged, widowed mother insisted that he find her a young "husband as handsome as you"! He left home – in fact, went on Aliyah to Israel!

RM, quoted by the Sh.Ar., includes under the first of these two commandments a child "who shows contempt for a parent even in speech or insulting gestures", warning that the Omnipotent would repay such a one 'measure for measure', citing in support the verse "Cursed is he who dishonoureth his father or his mother".

May peace and harmony ever reign between you and your parents until you and your wife or husband come to set up your own home – and thereafter, of course! May you ever respectfully walk in unison with them along the pleasant paths of the Torah!

Footnote. Though the Torah undoubtedly refers to a blow struck in anger, the Sages extended the application of the last commandment to even helpful acts which almost inevitably cause a bruise to develop or blood to flow. Thus, when Rav caught a thorn in his flesh, "he would not allow his son to remove it, lest it result in the spurt of a drop or two of blood".

For the same reason, RM, again followed by the Sh.Ar., ruled that a dentist should not extract parents' teeth, nor a surgeon operate on a parent – unless there was no one else available competent enough to do so.

Section   **Notes**

1   Exodus 20.12 and Deuter. 5.16; Tanchuma *Ekev* 2; Proverbs 3.17; Genesis 22.6–8 and Rashi; Deuter. 5.16.
2   Kiddushin 31b; Ethics 4.1; A. Zarah 23b & MR. Deut. 1.15.
3   Kiddushin 30b–31b; Proverbs 3.9.
4   Pesachim 22b; Ketubot 103a and Y. De'ah 240.22 & 24; MR. Exodus 46.5.
5   Levit. 19.3; Deuter. 6.13; Kiddushin 30b; Proverbs 13.24; Kiddushin 31b; Ibid; Y. De'ah 240.19 & *Pitche Teshuva*.
6   Megillah 16b–17a (also Rashi on Genesis 25.17).
7   Kiddushin 31a; Y. De'ah 240.14; B. Metsia 59a; Ibid 33a; Keritot 28a; Numbers chapter 16; Sanhedrin 8a.
9   Levit. 20.9; Exodus 21.17 and Sifra thereon; Exodus 21.17 and the Mechilta thereon.
10 Exodus 21.15; Sanhedrin 85b; Levit. 19.14; M. Katan 17a; Kiddushin 31b; Yad. Mamrim 5.15 and Y. De'ah 241.6; Deuter. 27.16.

Footnote. Sanhedrin 84b; Yad. Mamrim 5.7 & Y. De'ah 241.3.

Thirteen

FOOD AND MATERIAL FRUGALITY

Section 1. You have not sat down to your meal yet, and we have not yet discussed the commandments, laws and customs connected with one, as we will soon do. Nevertheless you should already know that, if a meal is started with a symbolic piece of bread (*lechem*), you do not, generally speaking, have to recite separate blessings over the other individual items consumed during the course of the meal, as you would have had to do had it not included any bread. Do you know why this is?

It is because, in a wider sense, the word *lechem* can mean a whole 'meal' or 'feast', and therefore the blessing over *lechem* can include everything eaten at a meal. Thus when the Torah informs us that the forty years' affliction and suffering and manna-eating that our forefathers had to experience in the wilderness was "that He might make thee know that man does not live by *lechem* alone . . .", it obviously means by eating, by feeding the body alone.

In other words, we do not 'live to eat' but 'eat to live', to sustain our lives so that we can be of service to G–d and man. However, we are not incorporeal angels, and we *do* have to eat something! *What* we may or must not eat is dealt with with in Chapter nineteen: for the present I am assuming that your mother runs a strictly *kasher* home, and that all that she serves you will be unquestionably permissible – and to your liking! What we are concerned with here is *how much* you should eat, and how to eat it in the traditional Jewish way.

23.   DO NOT EAT AND DRINK TO EXCESS!

To be perfectly honest with you, I am stretching a point by including this commandment deriving from the law concerning a "stubborn and rebellious son", among those applicable today. For even when it *was* enforceable, it could only apply for a very short time – "the three

88

months following a boy's Barmitzvah day." The reason why I *do* include it is on account of the 'warning' which accompanies it, and the rules affecting all of us, at all times, deduced from it – as we shall soon see.

Section 2.   The Son That Never Was!

Though it will be a purely academic exercise, it is worth-while spending a little time in considering the case of the "stubborn and rebellious son" as the Sages interpret it. Briefly, his story is this: At an early stage in those three months, he steals money from his father, buys a specific, excessive quantity of meat and drink, and ravenously consumes them in the company of wholly idle and disreputable louts. In the presence of two reliable witnesses, both his parents warn him not to repeat this foul act; he ignores them, does it again, and they jointly bring him before a three-man court, where he is flogged, again warned to desist, refuses, and is eventually put to death – "so that he should die innocent, and not guilty" of much worse crimes to which such unbridled appetite would inevitably lead.

Can you imagine any parents initiating such a course of action? It is not very surprising, then, that when R. Yonatan declared that he had actually "seen such a son, and had sat on his grave", R. Shimon refused to accept his report, maintaining that an actual case of this kind "never *did* happen, and never *will* happen!" Why then does the Torah include it as a commandment? he himself asked; and answered "that you may study it, and receive reward therefrom" – as with all the theoretical decrees of death and the sacrificial laws. In this instance, I would rather translate it: "That you study it, *and benefit from so doing*" – by learning the lessons it teaches.

Section 3.   The "Warning"

It is a principle of Torah law that "no penalty is decreed unless the Torah itself has somewhere issued a warning against the commission of that crime or sin," – a 'do not!' There are some single verses which serve as the warning against many malefactions: there is the one, for instance, which warns us against disobeying the rulings of the recognised rabbinic authority in any age – "thou shalt not turn aside from the decision they shall declare unto thee to the right nor to the left." And there is another, employed as a warning against many wrong acts, as will become apparent as we proceed – including acting as a "stubborn and rebellious son".

It is – translated literally, "You shall not eat upon the blood", which, in our present context, is taken by RM as the Torah forewarning "against eating which can lead to the shedding of blood" – and this is the kind of eating of the stubborn and rebellious son, who was only condemned on account of such repulsive eating, as it is said, 'he is a glutton and a drunkard'".

And *that* warning is given to all of us, for all time. At this earliest stage of your responsible living, the Torah here warns *you* not to develop that son's habits, "Not to be" – to quote Solomon's trenchant version – "among the winebibbers, among the gluttonous eaters of flesh", especially at today's prices of these commodities! The habits you cultivate *now* will most likely become ingrained for life, and you should be very selective in how you choose them.

Young Lady! This commandment does *not* apply to you, since the Torah speaks only of a *son* and not a *daughter*. Why so? Because, it has gallantly been explained, "it is not the way of ladies to eat and drink excessively"! In any case, you are just about at the age when young ladies begin to measure their intake of calories, in order to gain and retain the kind of slim and winsome figures which *most* of the opposite sex today find attractive – though they did not always, and do not, in some countries, even today!

Section 4.   **How Much To Eat**
King Solomon wisely says: "The right-living man eateth to satisfy his hunger; but the stomach of the wicked will always want." I will have more to say on this subject later: but for the present I leave it with the observation that many more die before their time from *over*-eating than from malnutrition; and with another story about Hillel and his strolling disciples, illustrating a verse very similar to the above: "The pious man doeth good to his life (*nefesh*); but he that is cruel troubleth his own flesh".

Once when he had concluded his studies with his disciples, Hillel the Elder walked along with them. They asked him: "Master, whither are you bound?" He replied: "to bestow kindness upon a guest in the house." They asked: "Have you a guest *every* day?" And he answered; "Is not the poor soul (life) a guest in the body? Today it is here, and tomorrow it is here no longer!" Nevertheless, he was going to see to it that that 'tomorrow' was as far off as possible – by eating just enough to sustain his health and strength; and it is truly surprising how little that need be! But you must eat *enough*, young lady! None of these dangerous, newfangled slimming diets!

24.   DO NOT DESTROY ANYTHING USABLE

Section 5. I introduce this commandment here because over-eating and over-drinking, apart from being injurious, are so obviously a violation of this commandment also. Though its contextual application is restricted in time and place, the laws derived from it are many and constant. The source-text is: "When thou shalt besiege a city a long time, in making war against it to take it, *thou shalt not destroy* the trees thereof by wielding an axe against them; for thou mayest eat of them, but thou shalt not cut them down; for is the tree of the field man, that it should be besieged of thee? Only the trees of which thou knowest that they are not trees for food, them thou mayest destroy and cut down . . ."

Of course the assumption is that the besiegers will win the war and then benefit from the fruit of those trees. But the *inference* is that you are at war with men, not with the fruits of G–d's good earth; and even should you lose the war, that fruit must be left for the victors — for *it* is not warring against you. What a far, far cry from the horrible scorched-earth and defoliation strategy perpetrated in recent wars, let alone the devilish devastation of the Hiroshima bomb and the threat of its giant successors!

The commandment applies in normal, peaceful times as well, of course; R. Hanina was convinced that his son had died "because he had cut down a fig tree while it still bore fruit" — and we will soon see how *bal-tashchit*, as the commandment is called in Hebrew, affects other foods. It is also extended to any useful article or being. R. Hisda "used to lift up his long garments when walking through thorns and thistles, explaining that should his feet be injured, nature would heal them, but not his garments should they get torn!"

Section 6.   **Meat And Vegetarianism**

Until the Flood mankind lived on a wholly vegetarian diet, but from Noah onwards "every moving thing that liveth" was permitted for human food until the Torah was given, when this was restricted to certain species of animal, fowl and fish. Even this permission was later restricted to occasions "when thy soul (appetite) longeth to eat flesh," that is only "when an exceptional desire for meat seizes one."

R. Eliezer b. Azariah lays down there a 'scale of diet': a man of only modest means should eat only vegetables; a higher wage-earner, fish; those still better off should have meat once a week; while those with the highest income alone could indulge in meat every day! This accords with Rashi's comment on the cited verse: "The Torah here teaches the proper way to live, that is: not to eat meat except in times of abundance and wealth."

It should be noted that the Torah only *permits*, and does not *command*, the eating of meat. There is a popular mis-statement that 'there can be no rejoicing except with meat and wine': but it is an

amalgam of two separate sayings: "*When the Temple was in existence* there could be no rejoicing save with *meat*; but now that the
Temple is no longer in existence, there is no rejoicing save with
wine." Still, most of us have a liking for meat, especially on Shabbat
and Yomtov.

Vegetarianism, therefore, is not only eminently permissible, but
also highly praiseworthy, at least until the Temple is rebuilt – so long
as the reason given for adopting it is not because the slaughter of
animals for meat is 'cruelty', which is an affront to G–d whose
"tender mercies are over *all* His works" yet permits flesh for human
food, this being one of the purposes for which animal, fowl and fish
formed part of His creation.

Section 7.   **But Not For Sport**
But no Jew can disagree with the contention that killing animals and
fowl purely for sport is not one of those divine purposes. As an
example of "the man who stood not in the way of sinners" Shimon
Ben Pazzi cites "one who does not attend contests with wild beasts"
or "one who does not participate in hunting wild beasts with dogs"
(Rashi) – or, nowadays, with shot-guns. RM rules "that hunting for
pleasure is a violation of *bal-tashchit*"; and, when asked by a rich and
influential leader of his community whether it was permissible to go
hunting with the local royal scion, a great halachic authority replied
"that is not a pastime for a Jew".

Finally on this aspect of unnecessary destruction – a quaint Jewish
reservation. It is a custom to wish someone who puts on a new article
of clothing: "may you wear it out and renew it." However this is *not*
said when the article is made of leather – because renewing it must
involve the killing of an animal! "This is a very weak reason" for not
expressing the wish, the paragraph concludes – presumably because
the leather can come from an animal which has been slaughtered for
food; "but nevertheless many are particular about this." As for killing
animals for furs or busbies, that is another matter: but if it involves
cruelty, Judaism must object to it.

Section 8.   **Other Foodstuffs**
As with meat, so with other foods: you should eat as much of them, in
their most simple and cheapest varieties, as will sustain a healthy life.
R. Hisda maintained that a person who could eat barley bread, the
cheapest kind in his days, yet ate more expensive wheaten bread, was
guilty of *bal-tashchit*; and R. Papa passed the same stricture on "one
who could manage on beer, yet drank wine"! They did not know of
tea and coffee, which were not introduced to Europe, even, until the
17th. century, both of which are reputed to contain a certain element
of poison, and are therefore inferior as drinks to plain water!

Does this mean that you have to live an austere, ascetic life, sustaining yourself on "a morsel of bread with salt, and water by measure" which will ensure that "you will be happy in this world, and it shall be well with you here and in the world to come"? Well, it would certainly do you no harm to live such a life, including the added recipe there of "sleeping on the ground"! But that is the regimen prescribed for one who is determined to devote all his time to "toiling in the Torah", and not waste a moment of it earning more than the bare necessities of life — as Hillel did, and not for the average person.

This text, a Principal of the Gateshead Yeshiva once told me, was quoted to him by a wealthy but niggardly Jew when approached to contribute towards an adequately stocked kitchen for resident students at his Yeshiva. The Principal retorted: "That text includes the phrase 'If you do this' — and I suggest that only if you live such a life can you demand it of my students to do the same"! No doubt if *you* did this, it would ensure you good health, and undoubtedly happiness in the world to come — but not in this one!

No: you will remember that "the avowed abstainer from wine was termed a 'sinner' because he denied himself something which G–d permits;" and the opinion is authoritatively expressed that "everyone will ultimately have to account for every enjoyable item of food which he saw but did not make a point of eating." R. Eleazar was so mindful, of this, we are told, that he especially saved money with which to buy delicacies and eat them at least once in their season!

Almost all the Torah's blessings are expressed in material terms — good things to eat, and plenty of them, as in the second paragraph of the *Shema* and many other passages. Indeed, we are told that what the priests have to have in mind when they pronounce their well-known blessing over us is: "May the Eternal bless you" — with material wealth; "And keep you" — so that no robbers deprive you of it!

Yes, all this is true: but, as the wisest of men said: "To every thing there is a season, and a time for every purpose under the heaven." There *are* times for enjoying all G–d's good things: I will only hint at them now by reminding you that we are now talking about weekdays, on which your diet *should* be restricted to a healthy minimum. Perhaps consideration of the following discussion will help you.

Section 9. **Is It *True?***

An ardent and emphatic social worker once asked me: How can you possibly declare to G–d thrice daily, "the eyes of all wait upon Thee, and *Thou givest them their food in its due season*: Thou openest Thy hand *and satisfieth every living thing with favour*" — when two-thirds of the world's population are starving? A challenging question, is it not? Yet the answer should readily come to you from all that has been said above. One of the main reasons why those two-thirds are starving is that the other third eats three times as much as it need, and are therefore guilty of wilful destruction of the starvelings' sustenance – quite apart from the good food they throw into dust-bins!

We believe that no creature, and certainly no human being, enters this world 'accidentally' – by chance: and G–d *does* provide food for them all. However "He hath given the earth to the children of men", and "Thou hast given him dominion over the works of Thy hands, and put all things under his feet" – *and* given him absolute control to do as he will with it!

It is *man* who, either by guzzling away the portion of others, or by letting fertile land lie permanently idle, or by scorching already productive land in brutal warfare, or by manipulating markets, storing up mountains of food and lakes of drink 'to keep prices steady', and even, at times, dumping thousands of tonnes of grain and fruit into the sea or pits because 'it's not worth selling them' – it is *man* who causes starvation and malnutrition, by his maldistribution of G–d's overall provision of 'their food in its due season'. And if those so many nations, possessing vast areas of unexploited fertile land, would devote but half of the energy and love which little Israel has devoted to its comparatively few acres of erstwhile barren land, turning desert into fruitful fields – instead of constantly warring with each other and others, there would not only be no hunger in the world, but abundance for all, man and beast, as G–d does *potentially* provide.

That is what I told that sincere social worker. There is no necessity for hunger anywhere. It is man's fault, not G–d's, if the Prophet's metaphor for individual independence and plenty, "They shall sit every man under his own vine and under his own fig-tree, and none shall make them afraid," has not yet been realised in up-dated terms; and that it was towards its achievement, as soon as possible, that he, the social worker, and I, and all people of goodwill are aiming. And *you* can make *your* contribution by eating only your own portion of G–d's bounty in measure, and helping others to gain their rightful share of it, in whatever ways you can.

The Talmud and RM give much good advice regarding healthy diet, and you can find much – though by no means all – of it collected in the chapter on "Rules for Physical Well-Being" in the *Laws and Customs of Israel*. I have only laid the groundwork on which to build a healthy useful and honest life – by eating only what you need, by not wasting *anything*, "even to the extent of a grain of mustard"; and using your influence on others to do the same, both at home and elsewhere, such as parties and other social celebrations.

Section 10.   **Thank You, My Provider!**
In those periods of the year when the time of your evening meal is close to that of Arvit, you should not sit down to eat before reciting that Service. This is another of the 'warnings' drawn from "You shall not eat upon the blood", i.e. do not eat before you have prayed for your blood – that is, your life.

Apart from the Benediction which only *kohanim* are commanded to pronounce upon Israel, the only other blessing which the Torah *explicitly* commands *everyone* to recite is that made after eating, which we shall be talking about in the next chapter. But, as you must know by now, there are many more blessings that we say – you have just said no less than 24 in the course of *Maariv*! Where do *they* come from? They are *implicit* in the Torah, and drawn thereout by means of the first of (SPB 14–15) Rabbi Ishmael's "Thirteen Principles Of Interpretation" (in future called "RI–13" for brevity) – a *kal va-chomer.*

Kal means 'light-weight' and *chomer* means (comparatively) 'heavy-weight'. The principle has many usages, but I can only mention the way it is employed here. If we are commanded to do the heavier thing, surely our own common-sense should tell us that we have a duty to do the lighter one in the same context! Let me explain: If you are hungry, and you ask mother for something to eat, and she gives you it, you will certainly thank her for it as she gives you it, *before* you start eating it – that's 'easy' (another meaning of *kal*). But it's not so certain that you will thank her again *after* having eaten it – that's 'harder' (another meaning of *chomer*), though of course *you* would!

So here: G–d commands us, as we shall see, to express our thanks to Him *after* we have enjoyed the produce of the good earth – which is the less likely, once your appetite has been satisfied; surely your own sense should dictate to you to thank Him *beforehand*, when you are still hungry! To put it in the words of the Talmud: "If he says a blessing when he is full, how much more so should he do so when he is hungry!"

The Torah only requires a blessing to be recited after eating "seven particular species with which the Land of Israel is blessed;" but the Talmud logically argues: just as they are things which, after having been enjoyed, require a blessing, so everything that is enjoyed has to have a blessing. This is then extended to our other senses: just as we must think G–d for enjoying the sense of taste, so we must thank Him when enjoying the sight, hearing and smelling; until the final deduction is reached "it is forbidden to man to enjoy *anything* of this world without saying a blessing" – even the sense of touch, in a way, when putting on a new garment.

It is then deduced, from an apparent contradiction in the Psalms that anyone who does *not* recite a blessing is, as it were, robbing G–d: one verse states "The earth *is the Eternal's* and the fulness thereof", while the other states: "The heavens are the heavens of the Eternal, but *the earth hath He given to the children of men*"! It is therefore deduced, in order to harmonise the two, that only with a blessing as 'purchase-price' does anything of His good earth legitimately become ours, so that without reciting it, we rob Him. All these 'pleasure' blessings can be found in SPB 385–390, and you should learn at least some of them by heart: for you cannot go hunting for a *Siddur* when you are caught in a thunder-and-lightning storm, or you see a beautiful gazelle in the zoo!

Section 11.　　　　　　　**Other Blessings**

You will already have realised that there are other kinds of blessings, besides "thank-You" – those recited in *praise* of G–d, like the 'slices' containing the *Shema*; and those said in *prayer* in the *Amidah*. There are also the blessings recited before fulfilling a commandment or performing a *mitzvah*, when about to put on *tallit* and *tefillin*, for instance, or to light the Shabbat and Festival candles.

All the blessings were carefully composed by the Men of the Great Assembly nearly two-and-a-half millenia ago; and are recited at various times of each day "in order to remember the Creator continuously, and to fear and revere Him." The Sh.Ar. commences (in the abridged version, the *Kitzur*, right at the beginning, in large type) with the quotation "I have set the Eternal always before me; surely He is at my right hand; I shall not be moved." For that is the purpose of all the commandments, all the prayers, and all the blessings – to remind us that we are ever in His Presence.

By reading *mai-ah* for *mah* in the verse "And now, O Israel, what (*mah*) doth the Eternal thy G–d require of thee, but to fear (revere) the Eternal thy G–d . . ." R. Meir translates it: "And now, O Israel, 100 (blessings) doth the Eternal thy G–d require of thee . . ." daily. And from this is derived the law: "Every Jew is duty-bound to recite at least 100 blessings each day. As we go along, we'll tot them up, and you will discover, perhaps with some surprise, that on weekdays the total comes to more than that – by leading an ordinary, traditional Jewish life.

Section 12. **Inner Cleanliness**

"Anyone who has a call to nature but does not obey it, yet eats, is like an oven which is heated up on top of its ashes." In other words: you should never sit down to a meal before at least attempting to rid your body of food and drink previously consumed. Inner cleanliness is even more important than outer cleanliness, and to pile new fuel on top of the burnt-out ashes is simply nauseating; is "a violation of 'You shall not make yourselves detestable,'" and is the cause of many serious illnesses.

So, to use the Talmudic term, 'examine yourself' before you sit down to a meal, and, according to Dr. RM, also after each meal – for a reason that should now be patent; before you go to bed, and as soon as you get up. On each and every occasion you respond to the call in a practical way, be it the most meagre, you must wash your hands thereafter – if only in the interests of hygiene, and then recite the blessing (SPB 5) called *Asher yatsar,* in which we thank G–d for the proper functioning of our bodies, such wondrous and complicated creations, without which regular functioning "it would be impossible to stand before Thee" and perform our duties to Him and our fellow-beings.

Section 13. **Intention And Language**

Intention, when reciting any blessing, is more important than exactness, as we shall see in a moment. You should never "hurl a blessing out of your mouth", on which MB quotes the *Sefer Chassidim:* "When reciting a blessing known by rote, one should concentrate his mind on the Name(s) of his Creator Who has been wondrously kind to give him the bread or the fruits to enjoy, and the commandments to perform. He should not recite it as a matter of habit, uttering words without thought. It was because they did this that G–d became angry with His people, and said: "This people draw near, and with their mouths and lips they honour Me – but have removed their hearts from Me . . ."

Almost every blessing opens with "Blessed art thou, O *Eternal our G–d, King* of the universe," and those which do, are not valid without mention of "His Names and Kingship". When uttering the Names, counsels the Sh.Ar. there, we should have in mind when saying the First that "He was, He is, and He ever will be, Master of the universe"; and when saying the second, that "He is all-Powerful, Master of every possibility and of all forces."

You already know, of course, the blessing for bread – though for the sake of completeness, it will be mentioned in the next chapter; and when you say it, you say it in Hebrew. An unlearned shepherd named

Benjamin, however, not knowing either the exact blessing or Hebrew, was heard by Rav to say "Blessed be the All-Merciful, the Master of this bread" in his own language, Aramaic, before eating his sandwich – and Rav ruled that he had fulfilled his obligation by so saying.

From this story we learn two things: that because the shepherd put his heart into what he was saying, and mentioned one of the attributes of G–d, though not His actual Name, his words were acceptable. And secondly, like the *Shema*, the *Amidah* and, as we shall soon see, 'Grace after Meals', any blessing may be said in any language one knows – though again, as with the others, Hebrew is best.

Finally with regard to blessings, even before you start saying the first six most important words, you should have in mind what the ending is going to be: that is, you should know what it is you are reciting the blessing upon, what it is you are thanking G–d for. For to recite the wrong blessing is to take two of His Names in vain, which is a very serious thing.

You are now sufficiently equipped to make the necessary preparations for your meal – unless, that is, you have a pet animal or bird that requires feeding! If you have, you must feed *it* first – a duty which is deduced from the verse in the Shema: "I will give grass in thy field for thy cattle, *then thou* shalt eat and be satisfied"! How's that for kindness to animals? We will have more examples of this inborn trait in the Jewish character.

Footnote

The vast extension of the one Torah commandment – to bless G–d after having eaten seven particular species, to scores of blessings to be recited *before* enjoying *anything* with *any* of our senses, and after all foodstuffs and drinks, is the first of the seven rabbinic enactments which have *almost* the force of Torah commandments. Combined with the 613 they make 620 – the numerical value of *keter*, the Hebrew word for 'crown'; and each one of the seven is indeed a precious jewel, fit for a Torah Crown, as you will agree as each is revealed in its due place. But for the present – can you imagine how much the poorer Judaism would be without this one?

Section	**Notes**
1	Deuter. 8.2–3 (see also Eccles. 10.19 and Daniel 5.1); Ibid. 21.18–21; Yad. Mamrim 7.6–7.
2	Sanhedrin 71a–72a
3	Sanhedrin 54b; Deuter. 17.11; Levit. 19.26; Yad. Mamrim 7.1; Proverbs 23.20; Chinuch 248.
4	Proverbs 13.25; Ibid 11.17; MR. Levit. 34.3.

5   Deuter. 20.19–20; B. Kama 91b; Ibid.

6   Genesis 9.3; Levit. chap. 11; Deuter. 12.20; Chullin 84a; Pesachim 109a; Psalms 145.9.

7   Psalms 1.1; A. Zarah 18b; Yad. Melachim 6.10; Y. De'ah 117, P. Teshuva note 44; Or. Ch. 223 end.

8   Shabbat 140b; Ethics 6.4; Nedarim 10a; Y. Kiddushin, end; Sifre on Numbers 6.24; Eccles 3.1.

9   Psalms 145.15–16; Ibid. 115.16; Micah 4.4; Chinuch 529.

10 Berachot 10b; Levit. 19.36; Berachot 35a; Ibid.; Deuter. 8.8; Psalms 24.1 and 115.16.

11 Yad. Berachot 1.3; Psalms 16.8; Deuter. 10.12; Menachot 43b; Or. Ch. 46.3.

12 Shabbat 82a; K. Sh.Ar. 4.1; Levit. 11.43; Shabbat 33a.

13 Berachot 47a; Or. Ch. 5, MB, note 1; Isaiah 29.13; Berachot 40b; Deuter. 11.15.

Fourteen

THE EVENING MEAL – AND AFTER

Section 1.   **"The Table Before The Eternal"**

All animals must eat, and man is an animal. But if he is civilised, his eating habits are different from the rest of the animal kingdom. Other peoples and religions have their particular table manners, and the Jew has his. RM refers to the knowledgeable and observant Jew as 'the chacham – wise man', and he says of him: "Just as the wise man is distinguishable by his wisdom and opinions, so should he be in his actions, in his eating and drinking" and others which will occasionally be introduced.

Not only does the Jew have to know before Whom he stands in prayer, but also before Whom he is sitting when he eats. Speaking of the centre-piece in the Temple of the future which was shown him in a vision, Ezekiel begins by referring to it as "the *altar*", and concludes with "this is the *table* that is before the Eternal". From this the Sages draw the lesson: "As long as the Temple stood, the altar atoned for Israel; but now, a man's table atones for him".

That is not the only transformation the loss of Temple brought about: it also transformed every Jew into being, as it were, his own priest, an acting and active member of the Eternal's world-wide "kingdom of priests and holy nation". Joining up these two ideas, every Jew is an officiant at the table-altar before the Eternal whenever he sits down to eat, the food being "My bread which is presented to Me" which, if it is fit (*kasher*) and offered in the right spirit and appropriate accompanying words of prayer and praise, is "a sweet savour unto the Eternal".

If you remember, I urged you to study the *whole* of the Torah, including the non-functioning laws; and I now make a special mention of the laws regarding the Temple and its Service, for they are the basis of much of our current practical Jewish life. You have already seen how the daily Services and their timing stem from them;

100

and you will now see how the table–altar equation inspires most of our eating traditions and customs. Let us look at some of them.

Section 2.   **"Lifting Up The Hands"**

Of the priests we are told: "They shall wash their hands with water . . . when they come near to the altar to minister". And so, when we are about to break bread at our tables, we carry out the rite of *netilat yadayim*, which does not mean 'washing' but 'lifting up' the hands, in accord with the verse: "I will wash my hands *in purity*, then encompass Thy altar, O Eternal". For netilat-yadayim is not a matter of hygiene, since the hands must be pure already before performing it: it is a religious rite, "lifting up your hands in holiness, then bless the Eternal".

Netilat-Yadayim is another of the rabbinic 'Torah-crown jewels', for which they found support in the Torah itself, but not from the priestly ritual. At the end of a long chapter detailing laws of diet and physical purity, the Eternal says: "Sanctify yourselves, therefore, and be holy, for I am Holy". The first clause, say the Sages, refers to "washing the hands *before* a meal" and the second to "washing them *at the end* of a meal". (More about the latter later.)

The blessing is recited as the hands are being wiped (SPB 375), and they must be wiped thoroughly; "with the hands lifted up. Whoever eats bread without first wiping his hands is as if he eats unclean food".

Section 3.   **"Bread From The Earth"**

Immediately after the hands have been wiped, with not a word of conversation intervening, the bread is taken in hand, and the blessing "Who bringest forth bread from the earth" is offered. The loaf or roll is then cut or broken – but before putting a piece in your mouth, it is customary to sprinkle a little salt on it. Why?

Because the table is an altar before the Eternal, the bread substituting for the offering: and "with all thine offerings shalt thou offer salt".

It is true, of course, that it is because G–d gives rain and sunshine in their due season, that we have any bread at all – but the ready loaf does not come directly from the earth! After detailing all the labourers and craftsmen, from the ploughman to the baker who are involved in the intermediary processes, Ben Zoma graciously acknowledged all their work – and that of those who spin and weave, exclaiming "All kinds of craftsmen come early to my door, and I find their finished products before me!" The interdependence of men on the labour and skill of one another is much more close-knit today, and we should also always show appreciation of such intermediaries for their labours on our behalf between raw material and end product.

The last of the Prophets, speaking In G–d's Name, castigates the priests of his time for "despising My Name by offering polluted bread upon Mine altar . . . the blind, the lame and the sick, saying 'the table of the Eternal is contemptible' and 'it is no evil'". They should have known from the earliest of times, from the days of Cain and Abel, that only the most choice and fit of offerings, however modest their kind, are acceptable to Him.

It is not only flesh, fowl and fish on our altar-tables that must be of the choicest fitness, unquestionably 'kasher', but every single item we eat, including bread itself, which is nowadays generally *treif*, the opposite of kasher, unless it is *known* to be fit for Jewish consumption; and the same applies to cakes, sweets, and even drinks. You, most probably, eat at your parents' table on which, it is to be hoped, there is no 'polluted bread', in the widest sense of that term – but if there is anything of dubious *kashrut* there, politely urge that it be removed, or at least refrain from consuming it.

Furthermore, bearing in mind that your bread is your 'offering before the Eternal', it must be treated with respect, and not be used "to prop up a dish" – or a book or newspaper; nor treated with contempt by being thrown about – especially in the form of pellets! And remember not to waste any: even the crumbs left over can be fed to the birds.

Section 4.   Other Hand-Washing And Table-Talk

In Talmudic times they used to wash the hands during meals, and especially between milk and meat dishes, because it was then the popular habit to eat with the hands; and also at the end of a meal, when it was considered "a bounden duty" even more important than netilat-yadayim, in the view of some, for a reason that no longer applies today. It was not so long ago, historically speaking, that the finger-bowl used for this purpose disappeared from the table.

But nowadays cutlery is universally used among civilised people, and the 'middle washing' of the hands in the course of a meal has disappeared completely from the Jewish table, as has that at the end of a meal, generally speaking. But MB cites a number of weighty authorities, including the Gaon of Vilna, who maintain that, even today, "everyone should be heedful of 'the last water' at the end of a meal" – and a minority still are.

Naturally, when the family gather round the table for a meal there is a lot of general conversation – though you should not talk with your mouth full, "lest the food goes down your windpipe instead of the gullet, which is dangerous"! But there should be another kind of table-talk as well – words of Torah.

The table is the altar, but it is "words of Torah" which transform the food upon it from 'sacrifices to idols' into offerings on 'the table of the Omnipresent' – and it is the above verse from Ezekiel which is cited as proof-text. And why not make a point of discussing the Torah portion for that week, a halacha or two, or even something from the Prayer-Book – like the *Ethics*, from which this transformation view (SPB 260) is taken?

On weekdays, pre-occupied with our affairs and studies, we usually eat meals in a rush, and some say that, as a last resort, the next commandment we are about to discuss can be considered as covering for this duty as well. But MB disagrees, and suggests that you then say at least the beautiful Psalm "The Lord is my shepherd" (SPB 414 – in a different context) "because it is both 'words of Torah' and a prayer for sustenance".

25.   TO RECITE *BIRKAT HAMAZON*

Section 5. Other religions say a short 'Grace' before commencing a meal, corresponding to our *Hamotsi* – as the blessing over bread is popularly called; but they have nothing corresponding to the Torah commandment stated in the verse: "When thou shalt have eaten and been satisfied, then thou shalt bless the Eternal thy G–d for the good land He hath given thee", quoted in the actual *Birkat Hamazon* (SPB 377–383), commonly called 'Grace after Meals' but meaning 'Blessing for Food'.

A 'thank-You' has to be said to its Giver after *everything* we eat, as we have seen: a short one called *Boray nefashot* (SPB 387) for most individual things, and a longer one, called *al hamichyah* (Ibid 385) after any of the 'seven species', detailed two verses before our source-text. It is only after eating "bread which satiates a man's appetite" that the whole Birkat Hamazon ('B–H' in future, for short) has to be said – or rather chanted, as a reminder of the praise and thanks offered to G–d, vocal and instrumental, in the course of the Temple Service. (See SPB 220, where the word *sheer*, rendered 'Psalms', means 'song'.)

The 'blessing for *food*' is actually only the first of the *four* blessings comprising B–H. "The second is for the land, the third for the re-building of Jerusalem (complete with Temple), and the fourth a praise of Him Who 'is good and bestows good'". There are various opinions as to who composed them in their present form, but the consensus is that it was Ezra and his Beth-Din who formulated the first three, though the essence of each is there traced back to Moses, Joshua and David-and-Solomon respectively. The fourth was later added by the Sages of Yavneh, after Rome gave permission to bury those slain in the last revolt against them at Bethar. It could have gone without saying, so self-evident is it, that ladies also are obliged to thank its Giver for the food they eat by reciting B–H. But lest anyone be misled that this is a 'fixed-time' commandment from Moses' statement "The Eternal will give you flesh to eat *in the evening*, and bread to the full *in the morning*", the Mishnah explicitly rules: "ladies are obliged to recite Birkat Hamazon".

Section 6.   **Emergency And Forgetfulness**
Originally instituted for the use of workmen paid by the hour or the day, so that they should not deprive their employers of more of their work than absolutely necessary, a shortened form of the B–H was permitted, "consisting of the first blessing in full, and the other three merged into one" (SPB 384–385 gives its now popular version). It has now been adopted for times of emergency – but not because of sheer laziness or a desire to rush out to play or not to miss a TV programme!

What if you forget altogether to *bensch* – which is the popular (Yiddish) name for B–H? You should, in the first place, make a point of *not* forgetting, for the law changes with circumstances. But generally speaking: if so much time has passed that you are hungry again, "the commandment is lost"; but if not, and you have already left the table or home, you should preferably return to the table at which you ate, or at least bensch where you happen to be.

Should you not remember whether you recited B–H or not, the ideal thing to do is to wash again, say *Hamotsi*, eat a small piece of bread, and say B–H over that and what you previously had together. But even if there is no bread available where you then are, you must still bensch; "for B–H is a Torah commandment", and all such must be possibly repeated when there is a doubt whether they have been performed or not.

Section 7.   **Meal Times**
When you have your meals depends, of course, on local social custom and your own personal circumstances. But it should be interesting to spend a little time on seeing what those times were in Biblical and Talmudic times, and how, surprisingly, we more-or-less conform to them.

When we come to consider Shabbat laws and customs, it will be seen that a distinctive feature of that holy day is to eat an extra 'third meal' in its honour, from which it naturally follows that on weekdays they had only two meals, in the true sense of that word. For at breakfast time they just had a snack, "bread dipped in salt and a pitcher of water", after Shacharit, which was about 6 a.m. Then, round about noon they had a substantial meal, agricultural "labour-ers" having theirs a little earlier. But the main meal of the day was in the evening after Arvit, at about 6 p.m.

We usually eat three times a day, but with most people the evening meal is still the main one, and either breakfast or the mid-day meal is just a snack. Again, while the times we eat them are perhaps a little different, especially the first meal of the day, the space between them does not vary too much from those in former times. The important thing is to eat more sparingly at least in one of your daily weekday meals, so that you will really enjoy the extra third meal on Shabbat.

RM, who was a renowned and much sought-after physician in his day, opens a long and entrancing chapter on eating habits as follows: "Since preservation of perfect physical health is essential if one is to 'walk in G–d's ways' – for the invalid cannot concentrate his mind on getting to know his Creator, it is everyone's duty to keep far away from everything which is injurious to the maintenance of good health ... Gluttonous eating is like poison, and the root of many illnesses".

So eat wisely, both in measure and wholesomeness, as advised in the last chapter, so that you can enjoy a good night's rest, and awake early and zestfully in order to give a full day's service on the morrow to your Creator and fellow-beings.

Section 8.   The 'Rest' Of The Night

I use the word 'rest' here in both its senses: the remainder of the evening until you retire for the night, and the hours you will spend abed refreshing yourself. Assuming you retire around 10 p.m., you will have some three hours after your evening meal to while away. How should you spend them?

Partly, no doubt, after a hard day's work, mental or physical, in relaxation in the opposite sphere – some energetic sport according to the season in the former case, something more tranquil, like reading a book or listening to music or TV-viewing about which more a little later. You might have some home-work to do, and, if you did not fulfil it immediately after Arvit, you should not forget your night-time duty of talmud-Torah – and even if you did fulfil it then, there would certainly be no harm in adding a little more before you retire.

What you should *not* do immediately before preparing for sleep is to read a book or view a film of a violent nature – or even worse than that! You will remember that G–d only answers the prayers of those who exert themselves to the utmost in achieving that for which they are praying: and in the pre-retirement 'mini-Service' (SPB 391–396) you will ask of Him "Let not my thoughts trouble me, nor evil dreams and evil fancies; but let my rest be perfect before Thee" – and the kind of literature and viewing mentioned are just the things to disturb your rest and engender evil fancies and dreams!

Our Sages widely differ in their opinions on the value of dreams, from the extremes of R. Meir who maintains that "dreams are of no consequence" to the view that "a dream is one-sixtieth part of prophecy"; and the intermediary opinion of R. Shimon b. Yochai that "just as wheat cannot be without straw, so there cannot be a dream without some nonsense" – but some sense as well. But few will disagree with R. Yochanan's view that "a person is only shown in a dream *what is suggested by his own thoughts*".

Pure thoughts, stemming from a healthy mind, ensure restful sleep – as does a cleansed body. Doctor RM advises you for this reason to "examine yourself" for inner cleanliness, evacuating all waste from your innards before bed. A useful hint is to take a difficult biblical problem with you to bed, and you may well wake up with the solution! Said R. Yochanan: "if at the moment of rising a text occurs to one – this is a minor kind of prophecy"!

26.   TO AFFIX A *MEZUZAH*

Section 9. This Torah commandment, "and thou shalt write them on the doorposts (*mezuzot*) of thy house" really belongs in the next volume which will deal with the time when you set up your *own* home: for it was your father's duty to affix mezuzot on the doorposts of the house you now live in; and it is there that the commandment will be dealt with in detail.

But since you are now a BM, and assuming you have your own room, be it only a bedroom, it is now *your* personal duty not only to make sure there is a mezuzah on its right-hand doorpost, but also to check that, if there is one there, the writing on the parchment inside is *kasher*. For it is liable to deteriorate with time, and requires "examination twice in every seven years." And, young lady, "women are subject to the obligation of mezuzah" as well.

On entering the bedroom, you touch the mezuzah with the tips of your fingers and kiss them on the point of contact – as you should do on entering or leaving any other room. On this occasion you thereby remind yourself that G–d is Omnipresent, even in the privacy of your bedroom, an inducement to conduct yourself modestly and with propriety there.

27.   REPENT YOUR SINS!

Section 10. The commandment to repent one's sins will be discussed in detail when we deal with Yom Kippur – though you do not have to wait until the Day of Atonement to repent them. It is contained in the command that when someone has committed a sin against his fellow, and thereby trespassed against the Eternal as well, "then they shall confess their sin which they have done" to G–d, after having made amends to his wronged fellow.

Three times each weekday in the Amidah we beseech our Father and King to forgive us our sins and pardon our transgressions (SPB 48), it being taken for granted that we have beforehand put things right with any fellow we have also sinned against. We make sure that we do this by following the advice of the moralists: "Before going to sleep each night, every person should minutely review all his (or her) actions of the whole day, and if he should find that he has committed a sin, he should confess it, and undertake never to commit it again . . . He should also forgive everyone who has sinned against or annoyed him, and thus merit long life".

The very last thing you have to do just before getting into bed – "or lying on your side in bed", suitable covered, body and head, is to say the prayers for the night mentioned above, called by the Sages "the reading of the Shema beside the bed". It is a mini-Shema-sandwich, beginning with a blessing to Him "Who makest the bands of sleep to fall upon mine eyes, and slumber upon mine eyelids"; and ending with: "Into His hands I commit my spirit, when I shall sleep and awake; and with my spirit, my body – the Eternal is for me, so I will not fear!"

Said R. Meir: "When man sleeps, his soul (*neshamah*) ascends and draws life for him from Above. And R. Eliezer supplements this with: "The Holy One, blessed be He, created the sleep of life, so that man lies down and sleeps whilst He sustains him, heals him, and gives him life and repose".

So retire confident in His Trusteeship! Have a sleep of sweet repose! Then rise, refreshed by Him, to serve Him with every breath (*neshamah*) you draw in! Goodnight – *Leil menuchah!*

Section   **Notes**
1   Yad. De'ot 5.1; Ezekiel 41.22; Berachot 55a; Exodus 19.6; Numbers 28.2 & 8.

2 Exodus 30.19; Psalms 26.6; cf. Psalms 134.2; Levit. 11.44; Berachot 53b; Sotah 4b.
3 Levit. 2.13; Berachot 58a; Malachi 1.6–8; Berachot 50b; Or. Ch. 171.1.
4 Chullin 105a; Ta'anit 5b; Ethics 3.4; Or. Ch. 170 note 1.
5 Deuter. 8.10; Psalms 104.15; Berachot 48b; Exodus 16.8; Berachot 20b.
6 Or. Ch. 191.1; Ibid 184.1ff. with MB.
7 B. Kama 92b; Shabbat 10a; Yad. De'ot chapter 4.
8 Horayot 13b; Berachot 57b; Ibid 55a; Ibid 55b; Yad. De'ot 4.16; Berachot 57b.
9 Deuter. 6.9; Y. De'ah 291.1; Berachot 20b.
10 Numbers 5.6–7; MB. 239 note 9; Ibid. note 6; MR. Genesis 14.9; PRE. chapter 12.

Fifteen

O WHAT A BEAUTIFUL MORNING!

Section 1.   **Day Dawns**

Interpreting the verse "They (the Eternal's mercies) are new every morning; great is Thy faithfulness", R. Alexandri says: "From the fact that Thou renewest us every morning, we know that great is Thy faithfulness to resurrect the dead": for "sleep is one-sixtieth part of death"' that is, by returning our *neshamah* each morning from on High, where it "drew new life from Him above", refreshed and re-charged with energy, it is, as it were, as if (SPB 6) "He restoreth souls to dead bodies".

This was not the lot of all who went to bed last night in apparent good health, confidently looking forward to greeting this new morning: Of the hundreds of millions of His creatures on earth, many thousands so full of hope of getting up 'as usual', probably did not do so. Whatever one's age, he or she has not an 'automatic right' to rise each morning, but does so, *every* morning – only by the 'grace of G–d'.

And therefore, immediately on realising, on the return of consciousness, that you have been so graciously favoured, you should give fervent thanks to your Guardian by declaring: "Thank You! O Living and Enduring King, for having restored my soul to me in mercy – great is Thy faithfulness!" You know it by heart, of course, for it is the very first prayer your Dad or Mum should have taught you when you first began to lisp words – the well-known *Modeh Ani*. And though SPB only includes it (p. 438) for recital by 'young children', I would have thought that the desire, and the need, to render this spontaneous "Thank You!" becomes greater each day we grow *older*!

This prayer may be said even before you wash your hands, because it does not contain any of G–d's Names. But your head should be covered: so, unless you piously wear a nightcap while asleep, you should prepare a kippah at your bedside for this purpose.

Section 2.   **Morning** *Netillat Yadayim*
It used to be the general custom, and still is with some, to prepare a
jug of water and an empty basin at the bedside before retiring, to be
ready at hand on awaking for the duty of rinsing the hands to the
wrists in a specific manner – by pouring water on each of them
alternately, starting with the right hand, three times. If, however, you
have a sink and tumbler in your bedroom, or your bathroom is within
a couple of yards of it – the maximum distance you may walk without
such rinsing, you can dispense with that preparation. This is not a
hygienic exercise, but a religious ritual. Why is it performed, and why
in this specific way?

The prime reason given is – for your own good: for, while your
divine spirit is on High, a spirit of uncleanliness usurps its place; and
though it departs with the return of your *neshamah*, it persists in
clinging to your hands, and can only be dislodged by rinsing them in
this particular way. This is compounded by the fact that "while you
are asleep, your hands can, without your being aware of it, contact
unclean parts of the body" and it is therefore "injurious to touch the
mouth, nostrils, ears or eyes before rinsing the hands."

However MB there gives another reason which harmonises with
our theme of each Jew now being his own priest: just as, before the
priests entered the Temple to perform the daily Service, they had "to
wash their hands as an act of consecration," so we formally dedicate
our hands, and all our selves, to *our* daily service to Him.

Even dressing is part of that service, and there are many little
traditional customs regarding it, based on two considerations mainly:
first, that, as mentioned before, even in the privacy of your bedroom
you are still in His presence, and therefore you do not run about
naked, or with any part of the body usually covered, exposed; and
secondly, because the right side or limb is always given precedence in
the Torah, you always clothe that side of your body first, i.e. put your
right sleeve, sock, shoe, etc. on first. But if your shoes have laces, you
tie the *left* one first – because *tephillin* are *tied* onto the *left* arm –
unless you are left-handed, as we shall see.

All these are customs which distinguish the Jew from others – as is
even the covering of the head: but the latter has become a distinctive
symbol of the orthodox Jew, and its development as such deserves a
short section on its own.

Section 3.   **Head-Covering**
From what has just been said about dressing, it should be quite easy
to find a rational explanation yourself why the head should always be
covered. Although G-d's glory fills the whole earth, we nevertheless

customarily speak of Him as being in heaven; and since our heads are the part of our body nearest to Him in this context, they, like the rest of our limbs, should be decorously and modestly covered in His Presence – which is everywhere. Nevertheless, it used not to be so, except for women, and especially married ones, but not men! "Men sometimes cover their heads, and sometimes not; but women's hair is always covered, and children are always bare-headed."

Among the deeds which they believed would earn them special reward, suggested by a number of Sages, R. Huna mentioned the fact that he never walked four cubits bareheaded. Arising from this, every self-respecting Jew followed that example – the reason he gave being "the *Shechinah* is above my head." But it still remained just a pious custom, followed by many only when praying, studying holy works, and reciting *Birkat Hamazon* and all other blessings. Yet though this view had the support of no lesser an authority than the Vilna Gaon, who maintained that covering the head at other times was only a special sign of piety for those "holy ones, who stand before the Eternal continually", it has so been adopted by all who consider themselves observant orthodox Jews.

The reason for this is probably that given by the *Taz*, "that since it is the Christian custom to show respect by *removing* the head-cover" both in the house of worship and the home, whereas Jewish *covering* of the head originated for that self-same purpose; to ignore the latter at any time would be a breach of the prohibition "And you shall not walk in the customs of the nation" among whom you live, when they diverge from your own customs.

I would prefer the positive reason for the head-covering – the Eternal's command to Moses "And for Aaron's sons shalt thou make . . . head-tires (caps) for splendour and for beauty;" and, once again, each of us today is his own priest, and should dress and act as such.

Section 4. **Preparations For Service**
Having removed the impure and harmful residue of sleep from your hands, you can now proceed with your other preparations for the day. R. Yochanan lists them in their order, and sums up their collective effect, thus: "If one consults nature, washes his hands, puts on the *Tefillin*, recites the *Shema*, and says the *Tephillah* (*Amidah*), Holy Writ accounts it to him as if he had built an altar and offered a sacrifice upon it, as it is written: 'I will wash my hands in purity, and will compass Thine altar, O Eternal, that I may make the voice of thanksgiving to be heard, and tell of all Thy wondrous works.'"

After carefully washing your hands, you should, at this stage, recite the two blessings *al netillat yadayim* and *Asher yatsar*: but since you will then probably be just in pyjamas and/or dressing-gown, their recital is usually deferred to head the other blessings which you will be saying anon. Unless you have a bath or a shower every morning, you should then wash your face, ears and neck thoroughly – and "teeth, throat and mouth, because you are about to give utterance to the Holy Name, which should be done in absolute purity".

You should then proceed to dress in the manner described above. As to the nature of your clothing, it should be "respectable and clean, without any stains or grease, etc.; it should be neither richly ornamented, so that all stare at the wearer, nor ragged, which would put the wearer to shame – but pleasant and in-between".

28.   TO WEAR A 'FRINGED' GARMENT

Section 5. In actual fact, the Torah does not command us to wear such a garment, but only enjoins that if we *have* a four-cornered garment, and wish to wear it, it must then have 'fringes' put in it before we don it. But so enthusiastic should a Jew be to seek out any possibility of fulfilling G–d's wish that, though we are not now accustomed to wear such garments among our clothing, we *go out of our way* to make a special four-cornered garment so that we can fulfil the commandment; and this 'extra' is a *sine qua non* among orthodox Jews.

The commandment, which comprises the third paragraph of the Shema (SPB 43–44), was given to the children of Israel in the wilderness. They were told "to make them a fringe upon the corners of their garments throughout their generations, and that they put upon the fringe of each corner a cord of blue." Now in those days, and for centuries after, the main male top garment was a long and broad one-piece toga-like sheet, worn either over the head to shield it from the sun, or thrown over the shoulder, usually the left.

With fringes conspicuous in each corner wherever he went through-out the day, the Jew would then have been constantly reminded of their purpose – "to remember all the commandments of the Eternal and do them; and that you go not after your own heart and your own eyes, after which you are wont to go astray." Though this type of garment is still fashionable in many Asian and African countries, it is not so in those countries in which the vast majority of Jews live. Nevertheless we do, as stated, deliberately render ourselves liable to fulfil the commandment, so that its purpose may be achieved.

The cord of blue was inserted in each corner "because blue resembles the colour of the sea, the sea reflects the colour of the sky, and the sky resembles "the colour of the Throne of Glory". The constant sight of the blue in the fringe, then, reminded them of Him Who sits on that Throne, and acted as a spur to fulfilling His commandments, and not being led away astray from them. Why then do we not have this important reminder in our *tsitsit* – as the fringes, and therefore the commandment, are called – today?

Because of the difficulty of obtaining the authentic dye for its colouring, and, when it *was* obtainable, on account of the expense. The main ingredient of *techelet*, as the dye is called, is "an extract from a shell-fish or sea-snail called a *chillazon* caught only "from the promontory of Tyre as far as Haifa," and "comes up from the sea only once in seventy years ... and is therefore so expensive". Moreover, because of the possible lucrative profits, many counterfeits cropped up, difficult to distinguish from the genuine article!

For these reasons it was decided to have only white cords in the *tsitsit* – because of the difficulty of obtaining the genuine article and its expense, which would be an imposition on the poor; and the danger of counterfeits. So that when *we* look at our blue-less fringes, we automatically remember that there *should* be a cord of blue there – and why it should have been. Its absence teaches two other useful lessons: that only the genuine article is good enough for G–d's service; and that every commandment should be, or should be made to be by the community, possible for every Jew to perform.

There are two kinds of fringed garments we are accustomed to wear: the one simply called a *tallit* (garment), which is worn at every Morning Service of the year – but one; and occasionally at other times, as an over-garment, in a somewhat similar way they used to wear it of old; and the *tallit kattan* (small garment) or, as it is often called, the *arba-kanfot* (four-corners), which is worn all day, *every* day, as an under-garment – though some have at least the *tsitsit* in view always, since the whole purpose of wearing them is to *see* them, and remember G–d's commandments by so doing!

There are many laws regarding the ideal materials and size of both kinds of *tallit*, the length, knots and method of twining the *tsitsit*, and so on, which you must study for yourself. But, in order to guard you against putting on an inadequate garment, and making a vain blessing on it, I will say briefly: a *tallit kattan* which is two-foot long both back and front and two foot wide, with a seven-inch aperture for the head; which has a five-knot, eight-thread *tsitsit* at each corner, separate from each other – satisfies the minimum requirements. You must look to see whether they *are* satisfied – especially after your *arba-kanfot* has been laundered, before putting it on.

The *tallit kattan* has its own blessing – which is not given in SPB, probably because its compiler assumes that you are going to say the Morning Service immediately after dressing, in which case the blessing you recite over the *tallit* (SPB 1) will cover the *arba-kanfot* as well, the latter then not requiring a separate blessing; and we are advised "so to do at all times". However, you may belong to one of those congregations in which young men do not wear a *tallit* until they are married, in which case you *must* make a blessing over the *tallit kattan* – which is the same as that on the tallit, except that the words *al mitzvat tsitsit* are substituted for *lehitatef batsitsit*.

The Midrash compares one who wears tsitsit to a person who has fallen overboard, to whom the ship's captain throws out a rope saying: "take hold of this rope, and do not let go! For if you do, you will lose your life!" While the Talmud declares: "This commandment is equal to all the other commandments together", because by 'looking upon it, you will remember *all* the commandments and do them'.

Section 6.   **What About The Ladies?**
The discussion on this question is one of the most fascinating in the Talmud, turning largely on the interpretations of the one word *u're'item*," and *you* shall *see* them": if the stress is on 'you', then the unfortunately blind would be freed from wearing *tsitsit*, for they cannot see them; if the stress is, however, on 'see' i.e. by natural daylight, then no one need wear them at night. The argument continued: but finally, though "our Rabbis" – that is the majority of Sages, maintained that *all* must observe the commandment, it was the opinion of one, R. Shimon, which prevailed, who said "women are exempt" – because, by not having to be worn by night, *tsitsit* becomes a set-time positive commandment from which women are exempt.

But later authorities went on arguing about it! RM ruled that they *may* wear them, "and we do not object to their doing so"; Rashi goes to the other extreme, saying they are absolutely exempt, and must not do so; while his grandson, Rabbenu Tam is more permissive than RM, even allowing ladies to recite the blessing over the *tallit* – which RM does not! Next comes the Sh.Ar. which, while agreeing with this last view, frowns upon women donning a *tallit* "because it looks like 'showing off'"! But this cannot apply to the *tallit kattan*!

Interpreting the Israelites' praise of the Almighty, "This is my G–d, and I will adorn Him," the Sages take it to mean: "Adorn thyself before Him in fulfilling the commandments! Make a beautiful *sukkah* in His honour . . . beautiful *tsitsit* . . .!" I agree whole-heartedly with Rabbenu Tam, and do not see why ladies should not adorn Him, on Shabbatot and Festivals, with beautiful *tallitim*, rather than, or at least in addition to, fine gowns and hats! Even the Sh.Ar. agrees that if they insist, they have the right to wear them – but, alas, none dares to start the fashion!

29. DO NOT WEAR GARMENTS OF "MINGLED STUFF"

Section 7. As with the food they serve you, so with the clothes they buy you, I have assumed – but not with as great confidence – that your parents have provided you with *kasher* clothes, i.e. suits, costumes etc. which do not contain *sha'atnez*, "mingled stuff, wool and linen together", which this verse forbids. It is one of the commandments which Rashi cites as an example of "a Royal decree, which has no reason whatsoever, against which the *yetzer hara* scoffs, saying 'What is it for? Why is it forbidden?'" Yet many *have* suggested reasons for the commandment, but I can only give two – those of RN and RM.

RN explains: "G–d created each species of flora and fauna individually, and commanded each to produce seed 'of its own kind'; what G–d has separated, we should not mix together, especially animal matter (wool) with vegetable matter (linen)". RM suggests that "the wearing of such mixed garments would be a violation of 'and you shall not walk in the customs of the nations': for wearing such was a specific religious ritual among heathen priests" – even among the Egyptian Copts of his day.

So serious is violation of this commandment considered that "If one finds mixed stuffs in his garment, he must take it off even in street." RM goes even further: "If one sees even one's teacher in the street wearing a garment patently containing *sha'atnez*, the pupil should immediately rip it off his back: because respect for persons does not set aside a clearly-stated Torah prohibition, (though a rabbinically enacted prohibition always gives way if compliance would involve dishonouring a fellow-being)". Be sure *your* clothing contains no *sha'atnez*; and if you are not sure, don't put the garment on, but submit it for examination to a bureau especially set up for this purpose. It may cause a furore at home – but G–d comes First!

30. DO NOT SIMULATE THE OPPOSITE SEX!

Section 8. I must here introduce another Torah commandment concerning clothing and toilette because the many weird cults which have latterly sprung up in Western society have, alas, attracted some of our Youth, giving it a relevancy which it did not have a few decades ago. It reads: "The apparel of a man shall not be on a woman, neither shall a man put on a woman's garment; for anyone who does these (things) is an abomination to the Eternal thy G–d."

It is explained that this does not refer to one who dons the garb of the other sex in fun or a play – "for there is no abomination here!"; but to dressing up in the clothes of the opposite sex and associating with them, pretending to be one of them. I cannot believe for a moment that *you* would do such a thing – though what with the unisex craze, men's hair growing longer and women's shorter, you have to be careful!

The Sages extend the commandment to include actions which have a flavour of such conduct. Thus a man is forbidden to shave his armpits and more private parts, to use cosmetics, wear jewellery "or pluck out or dye greying hair". Even for one "to look in a mirror" was once considered a contravention of this commandment, unless it was to remove a speck from his eye or some other useful purpose, such as seeing if the *tefillin* are in exactly the right spot. But the ban was later lifted "in places where it is customary for men to use mirrors".

As for ladies, they are – or were – forbidden to bear military arms on the basis of this commandment, an unfortunate necessity which is the prerogative of men. It is on this ruling that certain orthodox elements in modern Israel rely when protesting against women serving in the Armed Forces of the State. However it is quite possible that the Sages who laid down this ruling in the first instance, had they lived today, would have permitted ladies, armed for their own protection, serving in non-combatant roles when there is a shortage of *man*-power in the enemy-surrounded sovereign State of Israel today.

31.   DO NOT SHAVE WITH A RAZOR

Section 9. You may, or may not, have reached the shaving stage, young man – but even if you have not yet, you normally will in the course of the teenage years covered by this volume. The prohibition is contained in the second half of the verse: "(You shall not round the corners of your head), and you shall not shave the corners of your beard."

The first half of the verse is also a commandment, which can barely be considered currently applicable, involving a hair style which RM says is a "heathen priests' custom" – shaving the crown of the head together with the top two 'corners' of the beard, which I'm not counting. Nevertheless, it may be on account of this part of the verse that Jews always leave visible and appreciable side-burns reaching uninterruptedly from crown to below the cheekbones.

The second part of the verse refers to shaving any 'corner' of the beard, of which there are five: one on each cheekbone, one on each jawbone, and one on the chin. (This is a consensus of opinions: others have different ideas as to where exactly the five 'corners' are, so it is safest not to shave *any* part of the face.) The shaving of each 'corner' is a separate violation – five violations in one fell swoop of the razor!

But not to worry! The Hebrew word here translated 'shave' literally means to 'destroy', and the Sages limit the verb to removing the hair "only with a razor". To do so with scissors, clippers, electric rotary shavers is permissible – and there are many very good ones to be had, which is just one of the ways in which modern technology helps you to avoid breaking the commandments. But you should always take care to leave reasonably thick *peyot* (corners) down to the cheekbones.

RM again gives following heathen customs as the reason for this prohibition. Another suggested reason is that the beard is one of the distinctive features of the male, and should be preserved as such. In fact, the lack of a beard is considered a deficiency in manhood. R. Yochanan justifiably – though conceitedly? – claimed: "I am the only one left of Jerusalem's men of outstanding beauty!" But he was not reckoned among the most handsome, because he lacked a beard which is, according to R. Yehoshua, "the glory of the face".

And it appears obvious from the Tenach that this was indeed the purpose of the commandment – for Jews to preserve the distinctive glory of manhood. As just one example, take the story of the grave insult paid by Chanan, king of Ammon, to king David's servants, "by shaving off half of their beards". The victims were so deeply ashamed that they stayed away from their homes in Jericho until their beards had grown again.

A full beard, obviously the best way of preserving all the five corners, wherever they are, is back in fashion – and, almost without exception, enhances its wearer's looks! So why not decide now, young man, that you are going to grow one, always keeping it well trimmed.

As for *you*, young lady, you can shave with a razor wherever you like – but be careful, of course! You can adopt any hair style your fancy takes – as long as it is not deceptively masculine!

Now you can get dressed in the Jewish way – but do not take too much time over it, unless it is well before dawn. You must not let your next duty, reciting your morning Prayers, 'get stale'.

By the way: have you been keeping a tally of the blessings you have recited in the first twelve hours of your day? At our last count, after *Arvit* last night, it was twenty-four. If I am right, it has now reached a minimum of thirty-two, if you have left your ablution blessings the *tsitsit* one with which to commence the Morning Service – at which we will meet again very soon.

Section	**Notes**
1	Lament. 3.23; MR. Genesis 78.1; Berachot 57b.
2	Or. Ch. 4, MB. notes 1 & 11; Exodus 30.19.
3	Nedarim 30b; Kiddushin 31a; Or. Ch. 8, note 6; Ibid, his note 3; Levit. 20.23; Exodus 28.40.
4	Berachot 15a; Psalms 26.6–7; Or. Ch. 4.17 and MB. note 37; Yad. De'ot 5.9.
5	Numbers 15.38–41; Menachot 42b; Exodus 24.10; Menachot 42b & 44a, and Shabbat 26a; MB. 8. note 24; MR. Numbers 17.6; Menachot 43b.
6	Menachot 43a–b; Yad. Tsitsit 3.9; R. Hash. 33a; Eruvin 96a, Tosefot; Or. Ch. 17.2; Exodus 15.2; Shabbat 133b.
7	Deuter. 22.11; Rashi on Exodus 15.26; RN on Levit. 19.19; SM. N. 42; Levit. 20. 23; Yad. Kilayim 10.29.
8	Deuter. 22.5; Nazir 59a; Shabbat 94b; A. Zarah 29a; Y. De'ah 156.2, Rama.
9	Levit. 19.27; Yad. A. Zarah 12.1; Makkot 20a; Ibid 21a; B. Metsia 84a; Shabbat 152a; II. Kings 10.4–5.

Sixteen

FROM PRE-DAWN TO HOME-LEAVING

Section 1. Cleansed inside and out, neatly and decorously dressed, you are now ready to render thanks to your Creator and Guardian for all His goodness towards you by reciting the Morning Service (*Shacharit*). But you cannot do that before first putting on your (*tallit gaddol* and) *tefillin*: for the centre-piece of that Service is the Shema, in which the obligation to wear them is mentioned; and therefore "anyone who recites the (morning) Shema without *tefillin* is as if he were bearing false witness against himself" – stating the obligation without fulfilling it!

Tefillin are put on the body, and so anyone who wilfully neglects putting them on is a 'sinner with his body'. On the other hand, "he who puts on his tefillin regularly will live long; for it is written, 'the Eternal being upon them, they will live'". Let us then consider these so important commandments – for donning both parts of the tefillin constitutes *two* commandments.

32.   TO PUT ON THE *SHEL-YAD*

and

33.   TO PUT ON THE *SHEL-ROSH*

The word 'tefillin' is non-biblical, but the Targum's (Aramaic) translation of the word *totafot*, rendered 'frontlets' in English, and used only three times in the Torah, all of them referring to the 'box' we put on our head. The word is generally regarded as being the Aramaic plural of the Hebrew word *tefillah* ('prayer'), and that is the name "the Mishnah gives to each box by itself."

The Hebrew name given to the 'boxes' is *battim* ('houses'), that put on the arm being known as the *shel-yad* ('of the hand'), and on the head, *shel-rosh* ('of the head'); while the leather thongs with which we fix them in place are called *retsu'ot* ('straps'). You will already have been taught the exact spots on which the *battim* are placed – on the very centre of the brain, and on the biceps of your weaker hand, inclined towards the heart.

Why they are placed on these specific spots is explained in the beautiful meditation (SPB 1) before donning them, and in Hertz's comment (HPB 46–49) on it and the commandment as a whole. There are many detailed laws applying to the proper fulfilment of this commandment, climaxing with the binding of the Hebrew Name "Almighty" on your hand – and you should make a study of them in your abridged Code of Jewish Law (CJL).

Various reasons are given why the two component parts of what appears to be one complete commandment should be considered as two separate ones. For instance: you may have a temporary injured arm or head, or somehow discovered that one of the *battim* is invalid or its *retsua* broken; in which case you put on the *bayit* you can – and you are then credited with having completed a full commandment.

Since such eventualities seldom occur, I would like to think that the doubling of the merit ascribed to donning the tefillin puts the act into the category whereby, as we say at the end of reading every chapter of the *Ethics of the Fathers*, "It pleased the Holy One, blessed be He, to make Israel worthy, wherefore He gave them a copious Torah and many commandments" – an explanation the Sages sometimes give for an apparently superfluous statement in the Torah. (See important note HPB 627 on this.)

Section 2.   **Right Placement: Perfect Condition**
If merit is to be earned, however, the tefillin – meaning the *battim*, the *retsu'ot* and their knots, must all be in their exact places. To have the *shel-yad*, for instance, at the elbow bend, or the *shel-rosh* on the top of your head or in the centre of your forehead, is like binding a bandage above or below the wound it is meant to protect! Worse, perhaps: because to recite the blessings with the tefillin in such positions is to utter G–d's Names to no purpose – in vain. That is why a BM-to-be practises putting tefillin on at least a month before he is duty-bound to observe the commandment.

And, of course, the tefillin themselves must be *kasher* – perfectly fit in every way for use. It is worthwhile quoting here at some length what MB has to say on this subject: "great is the error of those who buy tefillin and *retsu'ot* from someone because he sells them cheaply; for they are probably second-rate or even faulty in script. Every Heaven-fearing man should seriously consider that if he is particular about his clothing and other secular possessions being in perfect condition, surely he should not be miserly when buying 'heavenly requisites', but should ensure that they are the most *kasher* he can obtain, even if the price is high".

The price is high today – but surely the conscientious scribe is worthy of his hire! Nor do you buy new tefillin every year or so, as you do suits, which can cost even more! Tefillin can last a lifetime, "if used regularly, without requiring periodic inspection", though it is advised that the conscientious should have them examined, like the *mezuzah*, twice in seven years, since they may deteriorate owing to perspiration.

So do not be fobbed off with a cheap dubious pair, nor with your deceased grand-dad's! Do not let yourself be persuaded to use your father's or your older brother's tefillin, either before or after he dons them – or because he does not! Insist on your own new pair, with an authoritative seal of *kashrut*: for such a pair is worth more than their weight in gold to you – if worn regularly!

Section 3.   **When Worn, And How Long**

One of the four paragraphs inserted in each *bayit* of the tefillin tells us that we should wear them "as a *sign* unto thee upon thy hand . . . that with a strong hand did the Eternal bring thee out of Egypt". The Exodus and the observance of Pesach are the main theme of that paragraph, which concludes with the verse "Thou shalt therefore keep this statute *mi-yamim yamimah*".

The word *yamim* is occasionally used idiomatically in Hebrew to refer to "a full year", and this phrase is here translated "from year to year", as R. Akiva understands it, alluding to the main theme of the paragraph – the annual observance of Pesach.

But *yamim* literally means 'days', and because this last verse follows immediately the command to wear tefillin, R. Yose the Galilean concludes that *this* is the statute to which it refers; and, translating the phrase "from *day* to *day*", he deduces from it that the tefillin are only to be worn during the daylight hours. Furthermore, the prefix *mi-* can mean 'some of, but not all': and from this is derived the rule that they are *not* put on on *some* days – those whose observance itself is "a sign" of our loyalty to G–d, as well as of the Exodus, Shabbatot and Festivals.

But for how much, or how many, of the daylight hours should we wear the tefillin? Ideally, *all* of them, until sunset, like the *arba-kanfot* (commandment 28) – and such was the way of the Talmudic Sages. Thus when R. Zera was asked by his disciples by what merit he had been blessed to live to a ripe old age, one of the acts to which he ascribed it was: "I have never walked four cubits without (thoughts of) torah and (wearing) tefillin".

However, so holy are the tefillin that no profane thoughts must occupy one's mind while wearing them – quite apart from the impracticability of keeping them on all day in the places we live and the occupations most of us follow. Therefore though "the commandment is to wear them all day, because they require a pure body and constant intent it is customary *not* to wear them all day – but everyone should be heedful of having them on while saying the (morning) Shema and Amidah".

Section 4.   **What About The Ladies?**
"Women are exempt from donning tefillin because it is a commandment dependent for its performance on fixed times" – since they are not worn on Shabbatot and Festivals (or during the night hours). Yet while they are permitted, and at times even encouraged, voluntarily to fulfil 'fixed-time' commandments, such as reciting the Shema and Amidah (see commandments 16 and 18), concerning the tefillin the Rama says: "Even if they wish to oblige themselves to don them, we must protest"! Why? MB comments: "because tefillin require a pure body, and women are negligent in taking care"! What I feel sure he intended was a reason which you yourself, young lady, can infer from the law there that even a man who is suffering from diarrhoea or other incontinence, or who is in great pain, is exempt from putting on tefillin, because either he cannot keep his body clean or his mind concentrated while wearing them – and 'a hint is enough for the wise'! Yet it is interesting to note that Michal, daughter of Saul and wife of David, "did wear tefillin, and the Sages did not attempt to prevent her"!

One final note on this subject for you, young man. Should you for any reason not have donned your tefillin for the Morning Service, you must, if you are then fit and able, put them on for that day's Afternoon Service: for they *may* be put on at *any* hour of the daytime, since they *should* by rights be worn *all* day.

Section 5.   **The Tallit**
There is a general rule common to the performance of all commandments and recital of all prayers and blessings that "if you have two or more of them to perform or recite, the one most frequently performed or recited must come first", the other(s) following in the order of *their* frequency if more than one. The tallit is put on *every* day of the week, the tefillin on only six in a normal week, and even less in a Festival one; and therefore the tallit must always be put on before the tefillin.

The wearing of both kinds of *tallitim*, the *tallit kattan* or *arba-kanfot*, and the *tallit gaddol* – or simply tallit, as it will henceforth be called here, has already been discussed at length (commandment 28), and that is one of the two reasons why I put its donning in parenthesis as one of the two items to be worn when saying the morning Shema. The other is: you might just possibly be a member of a section of our people who do not put on a tallit – though always wear the *arba-kanfot*, of course – until they are married. So if, as is most likely, you do not fall into that category, put on your tallit first.

Section 6.   **The Morning Service**
Like the Evening Service (popularly called *Ma'ariv*, but officially named *Arvit*), the Morning Service, *Shacharit*, consists of the Shema, sandwiched between blessings, followed immediately by the Amidah (SPB 38–56). But unlike Arvit, this essential core of Shacharit has large preliminaries and shorter additions at its conclusion (listed and detailed HPB 4) which have become integral parts of the Service. You should *study* it, outside prayer-time, in HPB (4–238!) with its copious commentary, but *pray* from SPB, so that you should not be distracted by that commentary, however relevant and interesting, from your actual prayers.

The morning and afternoon Amidah, you will remember, were instituted in place of the Temple sacrifices which used then to be offered, and timed to coincide with the times of those offerings. The morning sacrifice began when an observer, especially stationed on the Temple mount for the purpose, announced "there are flashes", or "the whole of the eastern sky is lit up", just as the sun began rising above the horizon.

And that moment was established, therefore, by the pious men of Jerusalem as the ideal time for saying the morning Amidah, in conformity with the words, "They will revere Thee with the sun", i.e. at sunrise; for the Amidah opens with three blessings in praise of G–d.

But just as the priests commenced their many preparations for the sacrifice "a little before or after cockcrow", which is an hour or so before sunrise, so those pious men donned their tallitim and tefillin, recited the preliminary blessings and 'songs of praise', and said the Shema with its blessings, in that hour before sunrise, so that they could commence the Amidah 'with the sun'.

To do this all the year round in Jerusalem, and Middle Eastern countries generally is *relatively* easier than for us living in the Western hemisphere: for there the difference between sunrise in midsummer and midwinter is little more than two hours, while in the West it can be well over five hours. But not to worry! R. Yehoshua says we may recite the morning Shema "until a quarter of the daylight period hast passed", and R. Judah says we can pray the Amidah until a third of the period has elapsed, be it long or short – and the law is so laid down.

Nevertheless, in accordance with the principle which should motivate all our service both to G–d and man, "When a commandment (or good deed) comes to your hand, do it *at once*" – the very first moment it can be performed. This applies to our commandment, especially in the late autumn, throughout the winter, and early spring, when no great effort is called for in order to "revere Him with the sun".

It is somewhat surprising that though the Jewish day begins at nightfall and with Arvit, both the Prayer-Book and the Sh.Ar. commence with morning duties and Shacharit. The latter opens with the stirring call: "(Every Jew) should strengthen himself like a lion to get up in the morning, so that *he* should rouse the dawn", and not the dawn him; "At the very least, he should not let the time when congregational prayers are recited pass him by".

Section 7.   **Congregational Prayer**

Both Hillel and R. Tsadok counsel the Jew "Do not separate yourself from the *tsibbur*". That noun is derived from a verb meaning "to gather *en masse*"; and the noun, of rabbinic origin, refers to people, either in the wider sense of a whole community, as in "we do not lay a hardship on the community (*tsibbur*) unless the majority can endure it"; or in the narrower, and more common, sense, 'a congregation at prayer', which can consist of as few as ten post-BM males. Ladies are not included in that number (*minyan*) because the times of Services usually conflict with their equally, if not more, important domestic responsibilities – though they are made very welcome if they *do* join the congregation.

Any such gathering of ten or more men for prayer *anywhere* constitutes a congregation, be it a private house or a business office – as long as it is clean and decorous (i.e. without unseemly decorations on wall or calendar!). "In every place where I cause My Name to be mentioned, I will come unto thee and bless thee".

Nevertheless, it is better to pray in a 'Synagogue' – the Greek term for what we call 'the *beit-ha-knesset*', 'the house of assembly', which is, after all, the community's centre dedicated for that purpose. But best of all is to pray in a *beit-hamidrash*, a prayer-house which is also a 'house of study' (see HPB 17), timely attendance at which, morning and night, is (SPB 6) one of those especially meritorious deeds "of which a man enjoys the fruits in this world, while the stock remains for him for the world to come".

There are certain most important parts of a Service, like *Kedushah*, the reading of the Torah, and the highest praise of the Almighty, the Kaddish – and particularly that recited by mourners for the repose of the souls of their parents, which can only be said in a *minyan*, not to mention the repetition of the Amidah, morning and afternoon, which is recited by the *sheli'ach-tsibbur*, the 'agent of the congregation' or Reader, on behalf of those who are not able to do so for themselves – though, like the Shema, "the Amidah and other prayers may be said in English" by the individual worshipper, silently.

Copious praise and rich reward is heaped by the Sages, supporting all their statements on biblical sources, on those who pray with the congregation, and especially on one "who has the merit of being counted among the first ten, each of whom is given a reward equal to that of all who follow them, even be they a hundred"!

Section 8. **Weekdays Also**

In most Synagogues it is only on Shabbatot and Festivals that the hundred, or even scores, follow the first ten arrivals, while on weekdays it is a struggle to get even that minimal number – if the attempt is made at all. If it *is*, help as often as you can; if it is *not*, you might try to initiate a weekday *minyan* yourself; for, though it is stated in another context, it applies to all worthy communal causes: "He who causes others to do good is greater than the doer" – and, of course, you will be a doer as well!

Unlike Balaam, I cannot claim to "know the mind of the Most High", but there is a Talmudic saying that "the positive can be implied from the negative". When, then, the Sages give biblical text-support for their conclusion that "Whenever the Holy One, blessed be He, comes into a Synagogue and does not find ten persons there, He immediately becomes angry", it may be inferred that He is delighted when He *does* find ten there, and rewards those present as richly as if they were followed by hundreds of others! And if *you* have caused it to happen . . .!

If, however clash of times or pressure of studies or work make it impossible for you to attend Morning Service from Monday to Friday, you have no excuse for not doing so on Sunday, while on those other days you can do one of the next two best things: either pray at home *at the same time* as the congregational Service, so that your prayers can be joined to theirs; or pray *by yourself in the Synagogue* before or after that time.

Section 9.   **The Synagogue Itself**

Ezekiel said in G—d's Name: "Although I have removed them far off among the nations, and though I have scattered them among the countries, yet have I been to them a *little sanctuary*"; and this is taken to refer to "the Houses of Prayer and the Houses of Study in the exile," miniature and temporary substitutes for *the* Sanctuary in Jerusalem until it is rebuilt – speedily, in our days!

In his first note on a chapter dealing with "the laws concerning the holiness" of these exilic substitutes, MB equates their sanctity with that of the Temple itself, citing the commandment concerning it "My Sanctuary shall you reverence, I am the Eternal", and deducing therefrom that the Divine Presence which resides in them must be revered just as it was in the Temple.

For this reason, no levity, secular talk of business affairs and the like – or of sport, and no eating or drinking, is permitted in the Synagogue; neither may it be used for convenience, such as a short-cut from place to place, a shelter from the rain, or shade from the sun. The Synagogue is a House of Assembly for all the community, a House of Prayer only, where "I shall be sanctified among the children of Israel".

If you want more information about the history of the Synagogue, the vital role it has played in Jewish life throughout the ages, and its adoption by Judaism's two daughter-religions, see introduction to HPB. Here I will conclude this subject with an impetus to your Synagogue-going – a divine assurance, given, through Solomon, called "the beloved of the Eternal", the builder of the Temple, the 'Synagogue' par excellence:

"Happy is the man that hearkeneth unto Me, watching daily at My gates, waiting at the posts of My doors" – waiting for the Synagogue doors to open! – "For whoso findeth Me findeth life, and obtaineth favour of the Eternal".

Section 10.   **Breakfast – And The Tally!**

Shacharit over, see you doff your tefillin in the proper order – exactly opposite to that in which you donned them, bind them up neatly, and put them away in their bag in such a way as your hand will automatically reach for the *shel-yad* first tomorrow morning, since it has to be put on first. Then take off your tallit, fold it carefully in its creases, and put *it* away – so that it will be the very first article to be taken out the next day.

Now you can have your breakfast – and while you are doing so, you might take paper and pen and tot up how far you have got to reaching your goal of at least one hundred blessings per day since

Arvit last evening. When you retired for the night, the tally had reached thirty-two; and now, if you said the whole of Shacharit, I am sure you will be surprised to discover that it has already jumped to eighty!

Whatever you have for breakfast, whether it is a meal starting with bread, or just a cereal with milk and an apple, at least another four blessings will be required – and you still have the Afternoon Service (*Minchah*) to pray, with the nineteen blessings of its Amidah, which will bring the total to over one hundred! And you will undoubtedly have a mid-day lunch or snack – apart from the natural functioning of your body, for which you also have to give thanks. No more counting, then!

So, sustain your body with just sufficient nutritious food to be able healthily to serve your G–d and your fellow-beings devotedly; thank your divine Provider first for His bounty, and then your mother for preparing it and serving you; help with the washing up if you have time – and she will let you!

And now, if you 'strengthened yourself like a lion to get up to serve your Creator' in good time, you should have half-an-hour or so in hand before having to leave home to complete one day's talmud-Torah minimum requirement – if you did not do so immediately after Shacharit. Then you will be ready for "when thou goest by the way – to school, we are going to assume. See you then!

Section   **Notes**

1 Berachot 14b; R. Hashanah 17a; Menachot 44b; Isaiah 38.16; Menachot 38a; e.g. Chullin 66b.
2 Or. Ch. 37 note 4; Ibid 39.10.
3 Exodus 13.1–10; e.g. Genesis 24.55 and Levit. 25.29–30. Menachot 36a–b; Exodus 31.17 and Deuter. 5.15; Megillah 28a; Or. Ch. 37.2.
4 Or. Ch. 38.1–3; Eruvin 96a.
5 Zevachim 89a.
6 Tamid 30a; Berachot 9b; Psalms 72.5; Tamid 26a.ff; Berachot 9b; Ibid 26a; Mechilta Bo 63.
7 Ethics 2.5 and 4.7; see Genesis 41.49 and Exodus 8.10; B. Batra 60b; Exodus 20.21; MB. 90 note 27; Or. Ch. 101.4; Berachot 47b.
8 B. Batra 9a; Numbers 24.16; Nedarim 11a; Berachot 6b; Or. Ch. 90.9.
9 Ezekiel 11.16; Megillah 29a; Or. Ch. 151.1ff; Levit. 19.30; Ibid 22.32; II. Samuel 12.25; Proverbs 8.34–35.

Seventeen

OUT AND ABOUT

Section 1. Nearly half this book has by now been presented, yet it would appear that its sixteen chapters have ranged over only some fourteen hours of but *one day* – and you have not yet set foot out-of-doors! But that is really an illusion: for these fourteen hours have to serve as a pattern for their counterpart in each of the approximately *three hundred* weekdays in the (solar) year; and you will, on average, spend at least fourteen hours of each day in your home, asleep and awake, praying and playing, eating and drinking, studying and conversing, during your teenage years.

So the preceding chapters have, in effect, afforded guidance for more than half your life: and that, in the setting where your whole character has been developing, and will continue to develop, through the learnt and practised word of G–d, and with the aid of His representatives and partners in you – your parents, by the example in Jewish life they set you, and the encouragement – and, if necessary, judicious correction – they give you.

There have no doubt already been, and there will surely be in the future, other human agencies which will influence the moulding of your character. But it is primarily as a 'home-built' personality that you are about to step into the wider society on the other side of your front-door; and the impression of the Jew you will imprint on their minds will depend on how much of G–d's and your parents' good example you have absorbed and made part of your personality.

In this section of the book we are going to consider your attitude and relationship towards all sections of that very wide and variegated society – the practical application of the last phrase in the Shema which remains to be examined, *uvelechtecha vaderech*, "when thou walkest by the way". Just as the modern paraphrase of "when thou sittest in thine house" would be "when you are at home" with which the previous chapters have been concerned; so "when thou walkest by the way" can be taken to mean "when you are anywhere out-of-doors".

Section 2. **Just One Word**

But before we step out, I want to address to you a plea which the Sages say Moses intended to convey by the inclusion of one seemingly puzzling word in the Shema – the word *hayom* in the verse "When these words which I command you *hayom* (today) shall be on your heart". The puzzlement arises from the fact that Moses uttered these words in the last days of his life, after having taught the people for forty years; and they had been adding "precept to precept, line to line, here a little, there a little" all those forty years! So why did he say "which I command you *today*" forty years later?

To convey the plea, says the *Sifre*, not to let G–d's words appear in their eyes as an antiquated royal command, to be observed – if at all – apathetically and with reluctance; but as a fresh and precious command, given anew each day, every day – *today*! And, indeed, it is! For, in almost his last words on earth, Moses said: "To love the Eternal thy G–d, to obey Him, and to cleave to Him; – for *that* is thy life, and the length of thy days" – for which purpose He restores your *neshamah* refreshed every morning!

So, as the days and weeks, months and years, go by, and you pray again, and *bensh* again – do not recite them listlessly, "as command-ment(s) of men learned by rote"; but on each and every occasion as if you are doing so for the first time, with joy and thankfulness in your heart!

Section 3. **Another Way Of Showing Love**

You will remember that it took quite some explaining to harmonise the *command* to love G–d with the fundamental principle of freedom of will which Judaism postulates; and that such love can only be truly attained on arrival at the very top of the ladder, after all the other possible commandments have been fulfilled – a rarefied height attained by very few, yet attainable by all!

It was perhaps for this reason that Abaye gave a simpler interpreta-tion of "And thou shalt love the Eternal thy G–d" which is achievable even on the way to the summit. It means that "the Name of Heaven be beloved because of you. If someone studies Torah and Mishnah, and attends on the disciples of the wise, is honest in his dealings and speaks pleasantly to people, what will everyone say of him? . . . 'Look how fine his ways are, how righteous his deeds!' Of him does Scripture say: 'And He said unto me, thou art My servant, Israel, in whom I will be glorified.'"

But you cannot demonstrate anything, whether it be a scientific theory or a way of life, unless you are yourself well-versed in the relevant details. So you must persist daily in revising what you have already learnt, and then add a little new knowledge to it: for, as that great teacher and exemplar of Jewish living, Hillel, said: "He who does not *in*crease his knowledge, *de*creases it" – i.e. if you do not continually add to your store of learning, what you have already acquired will slip away and in half the time it took you to acquire it!

An interesting parable is given to illustrate this: Two people (you and knowledge personified) meet and then part, walking in opposite directions. By the time each had walked only *one* mile, they were *two* miles apart! Thus, if you desert your learning for one day, it won't stay put and wait for you; it also goes away, or is submerged or dissolved in the fruitless thoughts and words which overflow it, and will be twice as far away the next day!

You are about to go out and come into association with 'the world and his wife', all sorts of people – as you should, except for the bad ones. For Jews do not believe in living the life of a hermit, shunning the company of one's fellows: Hillel said, "Do not separate yourself from the community"; and the Sages in general advised, "A person's disposition should always be pleasant (or intermingled) with people". There *is* a need for, and great value in, daily setting aside a period or two for private, silent meditation, before approaching G–d in prayer, for instance, as did the pious men of old; or in reviewing your day's deeds before retiring at night. But essentially we are social creatures, and can only implement Abaye's interpretation of 'Love of G–d' in association with our fellows.

Section 4.   **Who Are Your "Fellows"?**

The Hebrew language is poor in some respects – like verbal tenses, and rich in others: and it is particularly rich in terms used for human – and other – beings, both as separate individuals, and in their relationship one with the other; and before discussing the Torah laws which will come into force when meeting your 'fellows', it is very important to consider them all and the significance of each. To take the first group first:

There are no less than four words, all translated 'man' in English, yet each has a slightly different nuance in Hebrew. They are:

(a) *Adam*, referring, as you can guess, to every single member of the human family – all the descendants of the very first *adam*, Adam. It has no plural, the term *bnei-Adam*, the children, or descendants, of Adam, being used in its stead;

(b)   *Enosh*, "derived from Adam's grandson of that name", used mainly in *Psalms* and *Job*, meaning almost the same as *adam*, but having special regard to man's mortality and frailty. It occurs only "once in the Torah"; but its plural form, *anashim*, is very common;

(c)   *Ish*, usually referring to a "religiously adult person" – like you; or to one in the prime of life, or a husband. Like *adam* it has no plural of its own, *anashim* being used instead; and

(d)   *Gever*, "always used for the male", as distinct from the female, in the Torah; but often used as common gender in *Nach*.

But there is a fifth term, even more comprehensive than *adam*, which the Sages coined and used very widely in the plural. With only one exception, it occurs, in verbal or substantive form, in the two Books of *Samuel*, meaning "meat" or "to eat (bread or meat)". In its popular plural form, *beriyyot*, it has been assimilated to another very similar but different noun derived from the verb to "create", i.e. *bree-ot*, and is commonly translated "creatures". Let that be so: but we should remember that it means *all* living, food-eating creatures.

Thus, among the many occasional blessings you have to make (SPB bottom 387–389), is one to be recited when, for instance, you go to the zoo and "see an elephant, an ape, a long-tailed ape" etc. – "Blessed is He Who makes different kinds of creatures (*beriyyot*)". It is very important to remember this, as will become evident later; and that is why, everywhere in this book that noun is translated "fellow-beings", and not narrowly "fellow-*men*" – unless the context demands the latter.

Section 5.   **Your Fellow-*Men***

The language is even richer in terms referring to relationships between men – apart from that between parents and children of which we have already spoken. There are no less than six such terms, and here they are:

(i)   *Ach* and *achot* respectively mean (full or half) "brother" and "sister": but they are also used to include near male and female relatives, such as nieces and nephews, and uncles and aunts. That's why Abraham was not really asking Sarah to tell a lie by saying she was his *achot*, because she *was* his niece – though he did mean to deceive Avimelech; and why it was not strange for Abraham to say to Lot, "for we are *achim*", and Laban to say to say to Jacob "Are you not my brother . . .?", because they were uncle and nephew. The terms were then extended to include (SPB 72) "our brethren, the whole house of Israel" – ladies as well!

(ii)   *Raiya*, which derives from a Hebrew verb "to join", and means an associate, a fellow-Israelite, usually a "friend", as it is often translated – but not always so. When Moses saw "two Hebrew men striving together, and said to the wicked one 'why wouldst thou smite thy *raiya*?'" it obviously does not mean 'friend'! Neither can it mean that when we are warned in the "Ten Commandments" not to "bear false witness against thy *raiya*". It certainly does not mean "neighbour", in the commonly accepted connotation of that word, though it is almost everywhere translated so.

(iii) *Amit*, which, with only one exception, occurs exclusively in the Book of *Leviticus*, always with a pronominal suffix. It derives from the noun *am* – a 'nation', and means a "fellow-national". On "In righteousness shalt thou judge *amit'cha*" – the full significance of which we will be considering in chapter eighteen, the Sages, taking the word as a synthesis of two others, *am* and *itcha* (with you), say it means a fellow national who is with you, your equal, in learning and good deeds. But this word, also, is almost invariably translated "neighbour".

(iv) *Ben-am*, also always with a pronominal suffix, and in the plural, as in "to the land of the children of his people (*bnai-ammo*)." It means almost the same as the previous term – "a son of his nation" – a fellow-national; but, as we shall see when we study the one commandment in which it occurs, in context, there *is* a difference between the two.

(v) *Chaver*, from the Hebrew verb meaning "closely knit together", occurs only but sparsely in *Nach*, not at all in the Torah, and refers to close associates either for good purposes or evil. But it is used extensively in the Talmud in the same way almost as a synonym for *raiya*. Thus, on the one hand you are advised "get thee a companion (*chaver*)" with whom to revise your studies; while every morning you pray (SPB 8) "deliver me this day from . . . a bad companion (*chaver*).

(vi) Last, there is *shachen* – also mentioned in that prayer, which really *does* mean "neighbour", that is somebody living next-door or close-by, derived from the verb *lishkon*, to "reside".

Section 6.   **No Apologies!**
I make no apologies for this rather lengthy and detailed introduction to the chapters on "You and your Fellows", for without these definitions, you would find it very difficult to appreciate the full significance of many of the Torah commandments in which they occur. There is another important lesson here: these variations in meaning, either ignored or blurred in translation, and at times even mis-translated, should alone, apart from the many untranslatable idiomatic usages in the Hebrew language, impress upon you how vital

it is to acquire a thorough knowledge of that language, and study the *Tenach* in the original.

Now you can put your *kippah* away, your cap in its place, and open the front door. I'll meet you outside!

Section	**Notes**

1 Deut. 6.7.

2 Isaiah 28.13; Rashi on Deuter. 6.6; Deuter. 30.20; Isaiah 29.13.

3 See commandment 6; Yoma 86a; Isaiah 49.3; Ethics 1.13; Y. Berachot, end; Ethics 2.5; Ketubot 17a; Berachot 30b.

4 Genesis 4.26; Deuter. 32.26; Rashi on Genesis 25.27; Exodus 10.11 and Deuter. 22.5; e.g. II. Samuel 13.5–10; Berachot 58b.

5 Levit. 18.9; Genesis 12.13, 13.8 and 29.15; Jastrow dictionary; Malbim on Exodus 11.2; Exodus 2.13; Ibid 20.13; Zechariah 13.7; Levit. 19.15; Shevuot 30a; Numbers 22.5; Psalms 119.63; Isaiah 1.23; Ethics 1.7; Exodus 3.22 and 12.4.

Eighteen

"WHEN YOU GO BY THE WAY"

Section 1.   **Walking Out**

Says RM: "Just as a scholar should be distinctive through his wisdom and disposition . . . so should he be in the manner in which he walks. He should not do so arrogantly, with his head in the air and roaming eyes, or mincingly, like the ladies, heel-to-toe; neither should he run like a madman, nor cringe like a hump back! Rather should he look downwards, as when praying. Said Solomon in his wisdom: 'When a fool walketh by the way . . . he telleth (showeth) everyone that he *is* a fool'" – and *vice versa*.

This does not mean, however, that you should ignore passers-by. On the contrary: "One should always strive to be on the best of terms with his brethren and relatives – with all men, even with the stranger in the street, so that he may be beloved above and well-liked below, and be acceptable to his fellow-creatures (*beriyyot* – including cats and dogs!). It was related of R. Yochanan b. Zakkai that he greeted everyone, even a stranger, before they had a chance of greeting him".

Whom will *you* meet with first as you emerge from home in the morning? The milkman, perhaps, or the postman, the paper-boy (or girl) or the refuse-collector? Whoever it may be, you be the first to wish him or her, and everyone you meet thereafter, a pleasant "Good morning"; and, in an age when good manners are often scoffed at, do not neglect the courtesy of raising your cap to a lady – or anyone deserving your respect. Except for the cap, all this applies to you also, young lady!

You will have undoubtedly heard the famous story concerning the heathen who came to Shammai and promised to convert to Judaism if that Sage could teach him "the whole of the Torah while standing on one foot "! Shammai was a builder – and a very fiery-tempered man – then; and, in angry response to the would-be convert, the Sage got hold of his measuring-rod and drove the other away. Yet that same

Shammai counsels us: "Receive *all* your fellow-men (*adam*) with a cheerful countenance"!

That is not the end of the story – the denouement will come when we discuss our next all-important Torah commandment. Why I stop here is to impress upon you the lesson which this change-of-character in Shammai teaches us. He *must* have changed from the ill-tempered person he was, to an exemplar of the 'cheerful countenance' he advised others to show at all times: for otherwise he would have been among those "who preach well, but do not act well" – a discrepancy which would have disqualified him to be numbered among the Talmudic Sages! And there is a most important lesson here.

Section 2.   **Developing *Your* Character**

The character with which you are born is a complex mixture of many genes inherited from your parents and theirs before them through the generations. If you are – as we should each consider ourselves to be – an average person, it is composed of numerous traits, relatively good and bad. Says Maimonides:

"Every human being has many moral characteristics, very different and divergent one from the other. There is the quick-to-hot-anger and the absolutely placid, the conceited and the very humble, one of gross physical appetites and the pure of heart . . . The proper path to pursue is somewhere between the two extremes . . . and this is the path referred to in the commandment (no. 12 in this book) 'And thou shalt walk in His ways.'"

Notice my use of the phrase "*relatively* good and bad traits" above, and compare it with the explanation of the terms *yetzer tov* and *yetzer ra* given earlier. For even the 'bad' traits have to be exercised at times: there are occasions in life when you may, indeed should, get angry, show pride, indulge your appetites, and so on – as we will see as we go along. Your research should be into trying to discover when, and to what extent, each characteristic, 'good' and 'bad', should be displayed, so that you can mould your personality to fit exactly into the pattern set for the ideal human being by G–d.

You might have been bequeathed the genetic fate to be born wild, self-centred and passionate, like Ishmael or Esau, when you will find the road to the 'medium path' hard-going; or it might have been your good fortune to be quiet and serene like Isaac and Jacob – whose descendants, after all, we all are, and you'll find the way easier. Whether it be one or the other, or, most likely, somewhere between the two, "According to the effort is the reward". And that reward? "He who finds the exact medium between each pair of opposing traits is called a pious man (*chasid*)".

Your parents and teachers have no doubt been helping you throughout your religious minority to discover, and habituate you in following, these precise media, and they will assuredly go on doing so – if you will let them! But now it depends primarily on *you*; yours is now the religious responsibility. And, to quote another of Hillel's famous sayings: "If I am not for myself, who will be for me? . . . and if not now, when?" No one can have a greater effect on perfecting your character than yourself: and there's no better time to start than *now* – before you get bogged in the rut of uninspiring routine of the self-satisfied, self-seeking masses. For there is a middle clause to this saying of Hillel: "And being for my own self, what am I?"

Section 3.   **Get Yourself A True Friend!**

Your parents, so long as you are under their roof and dependent upon them, are the greatest influence, apart from yourself, in building your character. Your teachers, and particularly your religious instructors, which you should *always* have, also play an important part so doing. But, say both our 'holy teacher' – Rabbi Yehudah the Prince, and R. Chanina, there is one whose influence is even greater than a teacher's! "Much have I learned from my teachers," they both say, "even *more* from my colleagues (*chaverai*), and *most* from my pupils".

That is why R. Yehoshua b. Perachya, after advising everyone to provide himself with a teacher, continues "and get yourself a chaver" – a true and trustworthy friend. Interestingly, Rashi first gives the opinion of some that the 'friend' here meant are "books" – and the right sort can indeed be the truest and most enduring of friends. But then he gives the more literal meaning, 'a *real* friend', because "Two are better than one, as they have a good reward for their labour." How can you learn more from a friend than from a teacher?

Hillel again: "An impatient man cannot be a good teacher" – because he dislikes being interrupted with pupils' questions; on the other hand, "a shy pupil will not become a bright scholar" – because he is afraid to ask questions, especially of an impatient teacher, which so many are! But with a real friend, one as clever as or cleverer than yourself – if that's possible! – you can discuss problems and lessons without any restraint, and you will both benefit from the cut-and-thrust of debate. So get yourself a real friend!

Section 4.   **Who Is A "Good Friend"?**

What are the ideal qualities to look for in a good and true friend? They are mainly two: someone who is morally good, with whom you can tread the right path in life; and who will tell you the truth about yourself, even if it hurts!

Said R. Me'ir: "Love one who reproves you, and hate him who flatters you: for the rebuker brings you to life everlasting, while the flatterer takes you out of this world." A *real* friend pulls you up when you are about to do wrong, and 'tells you off' when you have already done so; but the fawning flatterer, by overlooking and even encouraging such behaviour, eggs you on down the path of wrong-doing. R. Yochanan b. Nuri once said: "I call heaven and earth to witness that the more R. Akiva was rebuked through me, the more love he showered on me!"

On the way to school, in the play-ground and class-rooms when you arrive there, you will meet and have many companions and acquaintances: in fact, you should strive to be friendly towards all of them. But from amongst all of them, carefully choose one or two who will really be loyal and helpful permanent friends, who will be to you, and you to them, an *ach-raiya-amit-and-chaver* all rolled into one! They, together with your parents and teacher(s), and your own constant studies and practical effort, will help you to fulfil your duties towards your fellows, the most important and comprehensive group of which we are now going to consider.

34. DO NOT TAKE REVENGE ON YOUR FELLOW-CITIZEN –

35. DO NOT BEAR A GRUDGE AGAINST YOUR FELLOW-CITIZEN –

36. BUT LOVE FOR YOUR RAIYA AS FOR YOURSELF!

These three commandments comprise one verse, and are closely connected. Says the Torah: "Thou shalt not take vengeance, nor bear a grudge against thy fellow-nationals (*bnai-amecha*), but thou shalt love *for* thy fellow-Israelite as for thyself."

That last clause, however, has popularly been taken out of its context, extended in scope to include *all* men, and mis-translated to mean "Thou shalt love thy neighbour (i.e. all men) as thyself." Do not misunderstand me! That goal of universal love between *all* men *is* the ultimate Jewish ideal, the vision of the Prophets, when, "under the Fatherhood of the One G–d," "all the peoples will call upon the Name of the Eternal, to serve Him with one consent".

This is further proven from a discussion between "R. Akiva and Ben Azzai". The former had maintained that the commandment "Love (for) thy fellow-(Israelite) as for thyself" was a great fundamental principle of the Torah; upon which Ben Azzai commented: the verse at the very beginning of mankind's existence, "This Book is of the generations of *adam*: in the day that G–d created *adam*, in the likeness of G–d did He make him; male and female He created them . . ." – *this* statement, he argued, is much more fundamental than that chosen by R. Akiva; for it distinctly indicates the brotherhood of *all* men.

Nevertheless, that is *not* what our commandment means, for two reasons: first, because *raiya* and *adam* do not mean the same thing; and secondly the translation "Love thy 'neighbour'" completely ignores the prefix *lammed* on the second word – *le-raiacha* – meaning 'for'. Let me explain.

Section 5.   **Love Cannot Be Commanded!**

We have seen how the *commandment* to love G–d could only be given because He has provided us with the means of getting to know Him and His ways – the Torah, and the assurance that when we eventually *do* get to know Him, we *will* love Him. But as for man, we have also seen, the precious life which He gives each one of us has priority over all others – unless *He* demands that we return it to Him; so we cannot be *commanded* to love another person as ourselves! It may happen: you *may* 'fall in love' with someone 'at first sight', or love may gradually develop between two people – as I hope it will between you and your 'intended'. But even that cannot be *commanded* – as perhaps your parents will have to learn!

In any case, love between people is expressed in Hebrew either by the verb being followed by the word *et*, as in "but if the servant shall say: I love (*et*) my master, (*et*) my wife, and (*et*) my children . . ."; or by *kenafsho*, 'as his own life', as in "And Jonathan loved him (David) as his own soul" – and never by either the prefix *lammed* or the word *kamocha*, as in our commandment. What that *does* mean is that you should earnestly desire, and strive to obtain, for your fellow-Israelite all that you desire and have for yourself – *to start with*!

These last three words are important, and anticipate any false accusation that Jews are a selfish people, thinking only of their own! Their many benefactions among the nations, the many ways in which the young State of Israel, with all its own growing problems, has aided newly-independent nations in Africa and Asia, resoundingly give the lie to such base allegations. Our *ideal*, Judaism's ultimate goal, is Ben Azzai's – the universal, loving brotherhood of *adam*: but the individual cannot leap from his sheltered home to the United Nations' forum at one bound!

What our commandment says, in effect, is that we have to shoulder our social obligations in gradually widening circles — without over-leaping any. It assumes, as we have, that you already know and fulfil your duties to the smallest social unit — your family; that you will support and defend your *chaver(im)*; and that you will show team-spirit at school — so long as the particular objective is just. But when it comes to your fellow-Jew and another requiring help from you which you can only give to one — your fellow-Jew comes first.

That's what our commandment says: it is not selfishness, it is not parochialism, but human nature, which inherently feels a closer affinity to members of one's own religion or nation before others. *Every* such entity, be it Christian, Moslem, Buddhist, British, French, American — or whatever, would acknowledge such a priority — to its credit and not to its shame, in identical circumstances.

We will soon see what "loving for thy fellow-Jew", initially, encompasses. But let us take the limited sphere of giving financial aid as an example. Analysing each word, and expanding upon the verse "If thou lend money to any of My people that is poor with thee . . .", R. Yosef interprets: "If you must choose between 'My people' and others, *My* people have preference; between rich and poor, the poor come first; between *thy* poor (i.e. your own family circle) and other poor of your town, your relatives come first; between the poor of your city and those of another town, your own citizens come first" — and so on, in ever-widening circles, step by step.

But there is much more to 'loving for others' than just giving money — though that is very important — if you have it! — since it can be transformed into so much good. There is service, acts of kindness, which can help to bring others to your own more fortunate status — "as thyself". Have you enough to eat, decent clothes, a comfortable home, good health, a good education? Then you are commanded to make every effort you can to help those who have not, to obtain them. And if you look round, you will be surprised to find how much scope there exists to do so — even at *your* age, and even without much money, or none!

We must now consider the two other commandments to which "Thou shalt love for thy *raiya* as for thyself" is the climax.

Section 6.   **Revenge And Grudge-Bearing**

What is revenge? Up-dating the example given in the Talmud: You arrive in class having forgotten your pen, your desk-mate has a spare one and you ask him to lend you it — and he refuses. Soon after, he comes without a pencil, *you've* got a spare one which he asks you to lend him, and you reply, "No! because you didn't lend me your pen!"

That's revenge – unbecoming of you, since you are showing yourself to be just as ungracious as he was!

Even "If thine *enemy* be hungry, give him bread to eat; and if he be thirsty, give him water to drink . . . and the Eternal will reward thee"! And this class-mate of yours is no enemy – just unhelpful! While *you* must always repay evil with good. That's G–d's way with us – every day!

Bearing a grudge is not as vindictive as taking revenge, for the grudge-bearer actively responds; but it is still unworthy, and therefore ethically forbidden. An example: You ask someone to lend you something, and he refuses. Some time later he asks to borrow something from you, and you agree, but say: "I'm not like *you*, who refused my request the other day". By saying that, you show that, ever since his refusal, you have clouded your mind and heart with resentment of his action – instead of forgetting it immediately.

These two commandments have wider application than the first, for it is against *bnai-amecha*, which means your fellow-nationals, and can include Gentile as well as Israelite. Any positive acts of loving-kindness you can manage to do, you should do first for your fellow-Israelite, and then, if you still have the means, time and can make the effort, for others. But harmful deeds or words you must do or say to *no one*, and especially not to the non-Jew – for it would be a double violation: of the one or both of these two commandments concerned; *and* of disgracing the name of the Jew.

Two interesting views, one concerning the futility of taking revenge and bearing a grudge, and the other concerning the reward for refraining from doing so, are worth recording. "Nothing happens unless G–d wills it": therefore if someone hurts you, he is acting as His agent in chastising you for some wrong *you* have done! So why blame the agent? Secondly, "Everyone who forgets and forgives wrongs done to him by his fellows, has all his own transgressions passed over"!

Both these views must have prompted David's order to Avishai, when Shimei cursed the king: "Leave him alone, and let him curse – for the Eternal hath bidden him. It may be that . . . the Eternal will repay me good for his cursing me this day".

We can now re-assemble the three commandments in their original single verse, and see how they connect up. "Do not take vengeance or bear a grudge against your fellow-citizen, for you should love for your *raiya* as you do for yourself" – and would you like him to take vengeance on, or bear a grudge against *you*? Do you not want him to seek *your* good as he seeks his own? In other words: Do unto others as you would have others do unto you.

That, but in a negative sort of way, is how the gentle Hillel accepted the challenge of that would-be convert, whom his colleague Shammai had chased away, as related at the beginning of this chapter, when he asked to be taught the whole Torah while standing on one foot. "What is hateful to you," Hillel told him while in that stance, "do not do to your associate (*chaver*). That is the (essence of the) whole Torah, the rest is commentary (on it) – *go and learn!*" One comment should be added: It is said that among those 'associates', Hillel intended everyman's closest and ever-present Associate, G–d, to be included.

Finally, a striking analogy from the Jerusalem Talmud on all three of our commandments, with an eye to Ben Azzai's ideal of the brotherhood and unity of all the descendants of Adam: "If, in bringing down the axe with your right hand to chop a side of meat, you hit your left hand, would you then revenge yourself on your right hand by maiming it as well?" All mankind is one body, and if even *one* of its members is hurt, all should feel the pain. Conversely, the whole body of mankind should strive for the welfare, and towards earning the love, of every one of its members.

We have not yet exhausted the Torah's commandments regarding love for, or towards, our fellow-beings. There are still two groups of people not yet mentioned here, *for* one of which we are commanded to love as for ourselves, and to show *instant* love towards the other – yes, *commanded* to love on sight! Who these are, and why they are singled out for special mention, will be revealed in a chapter devoted mainly to our duties towards these two groups.

37.   DO NOT HATE YOUR BROTHER IN YOUR HEART

Section 7. This is the first of another three closely-knit commandments occurring in a single verse – the one, in fact, immediately before that containing the last three commandments considered. It reads, in the English translation: "(a) Thou shalt not hate thy brother in thy heart; (b) thou shalt 'surely rebuke' thy 'neighbour' (*amitecha*); and (c) thou shalt not bear sin because of him." We shall consider each one separately, and then put them together again where – and how – they belong. But first a necessary introduction about the difference between 'hatred' and 'enmity'.

When discussing earlier in this chapter the make-up of an individual's character, it was mentioned that the terms 'good' and 'bad' in regard to the traits it contains are relative: that is, the 'good' ones are those by which our conduct should generally be governed; and the 'bad' ones are those which we should generally shun. But the latter also have their purposes, to be used rarely or often – but always under strict control.

Hatred is one of these 'bad' emotions, for it can be the cause of many sins and grave crimes – even murder. Thus we read: "If a man hate his neighbour . . . and smite him mortally that he die . . .". Yet hatred *was* implanted into our nature by the Creator, which must mean that it has its use *some* time – and it has, as we shall soon see. It follows from this that our present commandment cannot mean 'never hate anybody, or any thing, at any time'.

Another necessary elucidation before tackling the intent of our commandment. There are two Hebrew words to describe anyone who dislikes another: *oyev* and *soneh*, the first an open 'enemy' who leaves you in no doubt that he doesn't like you; and the other, literally 'a hater', who hides his dislike of you in his heart. Pharaoh was an example of the first type: "The enemy (*oyev*) said, 'I will pursue . . . I will draw my sword, my hand will destroy them!'"; and an example of the secret hater is given by Solomon when he says: "Trustworthy are the wounds of one who loves (you); but the kisses of an enemy (*soneh*) are deceptive", pretending to be your friend.

Now we can analyse our commandment: You must not secretly hate (*tisneh*) your brother *in your heart*! You should not either, of course, display open hatred towards him without cause – but if you do *that*, you will not be violating "*this* commandment, but the one which commands you to love your fellows". If you think you have reason to hate, then, 'get it off your chest', bring it out into the open, and don't let it rankle and fester inside you as fertile soil for the growth of wormwood and gall!

However, "There is a time to hate" as well as to love. It is *achicha* 'your brother' you are here commanded not to hate, which, in its widest sense, means one who, like you, recognises the Fatherhood of G–d, or at least respects *your* belief in Him – but not one who defies and blasphemes Him. "Do I not hate them, O Eternal, that hate Thee?" asked David; "And do I not strive with those that rise up against Thee? I hate them with the utmost hatred; I count them mine enemies (*oyevim*)".

But he was speaking as the king of the only people who then believed in G–d, about the idolatrous enemy-nations round about who sought to destroy His only people – as others later also tried. Yet even for the individual G–d-fearing person today there can be a duty to hate: for "The fear of the Eternal is to hate evil" – and evil-doers, as we shall find out when we come to our next commandment. However, I have already quoted Solomon's recipe for the treatment of an enemy; and he assures us: "When a man's ways please the Eternal,

He makes even his enemies (*oyevav*) to be at peace with him" – but he still has to be on the eternal look-out for the *soneh*, the hidden enemy! But that is another commandment soon to come!

38.   "THOU SHALT 'SURELY' REBUKE THY 'NEIGHBOUR'"

Section 8. The phrase "and they shall stumble one upon the other" is taken by the Sages to mean "one will stumble for the sin of another"; and from this they draw the awesome conclusion that "all Israel are sureties one for the other – when it was in their power to prevent the sin, and they did not prevent it". Our commandment ordains that if you have the power, any influence, to prevent someone from doing wrong by rebuking him – 'telling him off', you must do so.

The word translated 'surely' is really the infinitive of the verb to 'rebuke', the Hebrew reading *hochaiach tochi-ach*, the Torah way of emphasising the verb somehow. Here, our Sages say, it is employed to stress that, if he takes no notice of you the first time, you must rebuke him again and again, even to a hundred times – or until such time as he strikes you, or threatens to! Should that happen, you are allowed to hate him till he makes amends.

Before you start rebuking anybody, however, before you say to him "remove the mote from between your eyes", make sure he cannot retort "You remove the beam from between *your* eyes!" i.e. that you are not guilty of the same, or even a more serious, sin than the one you are rebuking him about! Again, you are only required to rebuke your *amit* – "your equal in Torah and good deeds", i.e. one who has a moral conscience. As for the conscienceless, "Do *not* reprove a scorner, lest he hate thee; reprove a wise man, and he will love thee."

From this verse is derived the important general rule that "just as one is commanded – in our commandment – to say that which will be obeyed, so one is commanded *not* to say that which will *not* be obeyed." This is especially so when the sinner acts out of ignorance of the law, and you are absolutely sure that, whatever you may tell him about the law, he will continue so to act; for you will be turning him from an ignorant, into a wilful, sinner – which is much worse. Say the Sages of such people: "Let Israel go their way! It is better that they should err in ignorance than sin knowingly"; but the consensus is that this applies only where commandments not explicitly mentioned in the Torah are concerned.

The final law is that where the public generally flout a Torah commandment, "the rabbi must inform them just once of their violation, even if he knows his words will be unavailing", so that no one, at a later date, can say "Why didn't you tell us?". But as for the individual and his friend or acquaintance – that's you and your friend – he or she must reprove the sinner time and time again, as above, in private concerning a wrong committed in private, and there-and-then if it is committed in public "so that the Name of Heaven be not desecrated" – but remember the conditions!

39.   SHAME NO ONE IN PUBLIC

Section 9. This last of the three commandments cannot be understood except as a clause qualifying the previous one, and it is rather surprising that it should have been considered as a separate commandment at all. Many explanations are given of the puzzling words 'and bear not sin because of him', some of them untenable. The simplest seems to be: 'do not bear a share in the responsibility for his sin which you might have prevented him committing', "just as Aaron was held responsible with Moses" because he did not prevent his brother striking the rock.

The Sages, however, take it to mean that reproof of an *amit* even in private must be gentle and tactful, "and must not put him to shame". To put him to shame in public, moreover, "is as though he shed his blood; and anyone who does this to another, "though he has knowledge and good deeds to his credit, has no share in the world to come" – whatsoever the reason for so doing may be. Our commandment, therefore, became the source of the general commandment *never* to put another to shame in public. (See also on "Murder".)

40.   JUDGE YOUR 'NEIGHBOUR' FAVOURABLY

Lest you should infer from all this talk about rebuking and shaming your fellow that it is your duty to 'act as G–d's policeman', seeking out the weaknesses of others, I conclude this chapter with this gracious commandment. It, also, is one of a group of three in one sentence, addressed to judges, and advising them how to treat litigants who appear before them. The whole verse reads: "Ye shall do no unrighteousness in judgment; thou shalt not respect the person of the poor, nor favour the person of the mighty; in righteousness shalt thou judge thy neighbour (*amitecha*)".

In a way, however, we are all 'judges', called upon to pass snap judgments on the words and actions of the many persons with whom we daily come into contact. 'What did he *really* mean by that remark?' we ask ourselves; 'Why did he do that?' – and we pass judgment. When so doing, this commandment instructs us, always think the best of your *amit*: if there is doubt in your mind, give him the benefit of it, and "Judge all men (*adam*) in the scale of merit".

Rashi's comment on this last quote is: "Whatever you hear (or see) about him, decide that he intended well – until you can verify that he did not! For if *you* judge *him* favourably, Heaven will judge *you* favourably". Hertz cites from a Chassidic Rabbi's beautiful personal prayer as a preface to *Shacharit*, in the course of which he used to plead: "Endow us with the vision to see the good qualities in everyone, and to close our eyes to his defects"!

Just one delightful example of a 'favourable judgment': Hillel's wife was putting the finishing touches to a meal for her husband and some guests, when a distressed man appeared at the door and informed her that he had no food with which to entertain the customary minimum *minyan* who were invited to his son's *Brit-milah* shortly to take place. The kindly lady gave him all she had prepared, and hastily set about replacing it. Hillel and his guests had a long time to wait – but he said nothing when it was eventually served. After the guests had gone, he asked his wife what had caused the delay – quickly adding: "Don't think for a moment that I blame you! For I always 'judge you in the scale of merit'"!

It is 'these words' – words and thoughts of Torah, of Jewish learning, which 'shall be upon thy heart ... when thou walkest by the way'. Well, this chapter has provided you with many such words to ponder over on your way to school, and perhaps to discuss with your *chaver tov*. I will be returning with a few more towards-your-fellow commandments during your mid-morning break – but before that we'll meet in the class-room.

Section	Notes

1   Yad. De'ot 7.1 & 8, cf. Isaiah 3.16; Eccles. 10.3; Berachot 17a; Or. Ch. 89.2; Shabbat 31a; Ethics 1.15; Chagigah 14b.
2   Yad. De'ot 1.1ff; see chapter 4; Ethics 5.26; Ibid 1.14.
3   Makkot 10a and Ta'anit 7a; Ethics 1.6; Eccles. 4.9; Ethics 2.6.
4   ADRN 29.1; Arakin 16b; Levit. 19.18; Malachi 2.10; Zephaniah 2.9; Y. Nedarim 9.4; Genesis 5.1–2. (see HPH. 563 and Malbim on Exodus 11.2.)
5   Exodus 21.5; I. Samuel 18.1–3; Exodus 22.24.
6   Yoma 23a; Proverbs 25.22; Chinuch 241; as first note here; II. Samuel 16.11–12; as first note; Y. Nedarim 9.5.
7   Levit. 19.17; Deuter. 19.11; Exodus 15.9; Proverbs 27.6; Sifra (Chinuch 238); Eccles. 3.8; Psalms 139. 21–22; Proverbs 8.13; Ibid 16.7.
8   Levit. 26.37; Shevuot 39a–b; B. Metsia 31a; Arakin 16b; Proverbs 9.8; Yevamot 65b; Betsa 30a; Or. Ch. 608.2.
9   Numbers 20.12; B. Metsia 58b; Ethics 3.15; Levit. 19.15; Ethics 1.6; HPB. 2; Derech Eretz Rabba 6.

Nineteen

DOUBLE
CONSECRATION

Section 1.   **Chinuch**

This Hebrew noun used for 'education' occurs nowhere in the Tenach, and the verb from which it is derived only five times. Two of them refer to the formal initiation of a "private house" for residence, and another two, "the House of G–d" for service – all four rendered 'to dedicate'. This immediately reminds us of another noun derived from the same verb, one which *does* appear in the Torah describing "the dedication of the altar" in the wilderness, and which has given its name to the popular *Chanukah* festival.

However on the fifth occasion the verb occurs, the one which concerns us here, it is translated otherwise – 'to train up', the whole verse being rendered: "Train up (*chanoch*) a child in the way he should go, and even when he is old, he will not depart from it". What *is* 'training', and who should do it? The dictionary defines to 'train' as "to cause to grow up in the desired manner"; and the above translation makes it apparent that it is the father or teacher who decides what the 'desired manner' should be.

But what kind of training is here intended? The SBB commentator opines that "the intention is not 'the way of uprightness and good living', but 'for the way in which he is to spend his life.'" But the Sages are not so exclusive. They view the *chinuch* as both spiritual training for the upright life *and* how to spend it, "to teach him Torah *and* a craft;" and it is well worth while quoting at some length Malbim's comment on this verse, primarily to show how the decision as to what that 'craft' shall be is arrived at.

Section 2.   **Chinuch Is Also Dedication**

Malbim renders the Hebrew of the verse literally: 'Dedicate the child according to *his* way; then, even when he is old, he will not depart from it,' and he explains: "He commands two things: (a) the child

146

should be led by persuasion from a very early age towards perfection in thought, action and character, since such early habits will become engraved in his nature till old age; and (b) to train the child for an occupation *according to his own aptitude and nature*, which he will indicate by his eagerness to follow a certain career. Thus occupied, in the way *he* wants to go, he will be content – i.e. dedicate himself to it – until old age, which will *not* be the case if he is forced into an occupation against his will."

Your religious and spiritual Chinuch is now your own responsibility, and that of your 'craft' Chinuch still your father's, as we shall soon see. You are now probably pursuing both, the latter being for a career of your choice, arrived at in consultation with your parents and teachers who, next to you yourself, best know what your true aptitudes really are, the one important proviso having been kept in mind – that the practice of the selected career must not inevitably involve violation of the lessons derived from the other Chinuch, which must always take precedence.

Dedicate yourself to achieve the best results in both spheres of Chinuch. Respect your teachers, religious and secular, and they will respect you, to your intellectual and moral enrichment. "Sit amid the dust of their feet, and drink in their words with thirst"! And "let your eyes *see* your teachers", as well as hear them; for a lesson can be learnt even from a physical nuance of theirs. Rav, who used to sit in a position in the academy from which he only had a back view of R. Meir, once quoted these words to his colleagues, remarking: "Had I had a front view of him, I would have been even more keen!"

"The beginning of wisdom is *get* wisdom; with all your getting get understanding"! And now is the time to do so, while your brain is relatively fresh and absorptive, receiving knowledge "like ink written on clean paper," and "like a sieve, which lets out the bran and retains the fine flour." *Dedicate* yourself to acquire all there is to know in your chosen sphere, and then you will qualify in it *maxima cum laude*!

Do not waste your time *now*; do not be distracted from your studies by too much fun and sports. In his prayer to G–d, Moses asked: "Teach us so to number our days, that we may get us a heart (mind) of wisdom." He learned "and revised his learning" to the utmost of his great intellectual capacity, though his Teacher had been the Omniscient Himself!

Section 3. **When Do You Qualify Religiously?**
Chapter 6 tells you why you should have been – and how, in former ages you might well have been, qualified to fulfil your religious

responsibilities by BM age; and chapter 11 stresses how important it is that "You (yourself) must learn and observe to do" those command-ments which either you were not taught, or that you *were* taught but did not learn or have forgotten, by the time you reached that age.

That your father had a duty to teach you Torah, and must still teach you a craft or profession is deduced from the verse "See to a livelihood with the wife whom thou lovest": for since, as we shall see in a moment, he has a duty to find life-partners for his children, he must obviously train his son(s) to earn a livelihood in order to be able to support wife and children in dignity.

This obligation to find partners for his children — more often than not with mother's active help! — is drawn from Jeremiah's famous message to his brethren taken into exile in Babylon, instructing them to stay where they were, to settle down and marry, "and take wives for your sons, and give your daughters to husbands."

I shall have a little more to say about marriage in chapter thirty-four of this volume, and a lot more in the opening chapters of the next. I only mention it here because marriage should come when you complete your vocational training, at which stage you 'qualify' for your 'master's degree', becoming, to a great extent, master over your own fate and, for the first time, over that of others — the smallest but most important social unit, a family.

Says Raba: "While your hand is still on your son's neck — i.e. while he is still dependent upon you — teach him a craft and get him married." How long that period lasts is argued by two Sages, both of them basing their respective opinions on the '*chinuch* verse', which, for this purpose, they translate 'Train the *youth* in the way he should go'; but disagree on the extent of the 'youth' years, one maintaining that they are from sixteen to twenty-two, and the other from eighteen to twenty-four.

By the time *you* marry, then, whenever it is, you should have qualified, young man, for both your bachelor's and master's degrees — and *you*, young lady a year or two earlier in age, with domestic science as one, at least, of your vocations!

Section 4.   **'Eating Out'**
You now know how best to apply yourself to your studies — and don't forget not to be shy, but to ask, and ask again, if you do not quite understand what the teacher means! Questing and curiosity are the richest sources of sound knowledge — and remember that you will thereby be doing your teacher a favour! For, as quoted in the last chapter from the mouth of none less than *the* Mishnah Teacher, "I learnt more from my *pupils* than from my teachers and colleagues

combined". I know from experience that many-a-time a teacher has to make deep research before he can adequately answer a really good pupil's questions!

But it is not only study that you will indulge in at your school, college or university. Those establishments are 'little worlds' in themselves, and very useful grounds for your training in the social virtues as seen with Jewish eyes. For you, or you and your one or two special friends, should not keep yourselves to yourselves – or even isolated among your fellow-Jewish colleagues in an inter-denominational school. By all means, club together to discuss Jewish topics, and specific problems which might affect you as a minority group within a major one. But ideally you should integrate into the whole 'little world', as training for harmonious and respectful life in wider society ahead.

How to do that we will consider anon; but first we must talk a little about more basic things, such as food, since this is the first time – in this book – that you will be 'eating out', unless you are fortunate enough to go home for your mid-day meal, where, I am continuing to assume, all the dietary laws are scrupulously observed. Neither will you have any problem if, again, you are lucky enough to go to a Jewish school, etc. which serves mid-day meals or has a *kasher* canteen, or if your mother gave you lunch to take with you, But if not . . .

There are many Jews, alas, who have two standards: they keep their homes *kasher* – but they are not so particular about what they eat away from it, either in restaurants or even other people's homes. I do not want *you* to get into that careless habit: the same laws as regards diet apply 'when thou walkest by the way' as when 'thou sittest in thy house' – at home, and away from it; and it is in your school years that bad habits can take root and become part of your regular way of life. Don't let them!

Section 5.   Do Not Eat . . .! Why Not?

In chapter 13 we talked about how – and how not – to eat Jewishly, and how much. Here we are going to see *what* Jews may eat, and what not. But first the question should be asked: why should our diet be restricted at all; why for instance – as you must surely already know – may we not have bacon-and-eggs for breakfast? Hygiene, as many maintain, may have been a contributory reason in very hot countries before refrigeration was invented, but facts are there for millions to see that it is not so now!

Many Jews enter international sporting events, like the Olympics, tennis and football, even as complete teams from Israel: but it is seldom that they get much further than the first round of the competitions – though they do well competing against each other in the Maccabiad. It is the bacon-and-ham, black-pudding, oyster and caviarre eaters that win all the medals and cups internationally – with one or two exceptions (not particularly known for their observance of *kashrut*)!

Is there then a reason? According to Rashi there is not: whenever he cites examples of *chukkim*, which he defines as "commandments with no apparent reason, but are the King's decree", he always commences with the prohibition against eating pig-meat, which is symbolic of all the forbidden foods. But every commandment *must* have a reason – even if only G–d knows it: Solomon is said to have "known the reasons for 612 of the 613 commandments" – and the one he did not know was *not* this one!

The reason, the one which applies to *all* the commandments, and especially the *chukkim*, is given in an interpretation of the verse: "As for G–d, His way is perfect; the word of the Eternal is refining; He is a shield unto all that take refuge in Him." It is: "The commandments were only given in order to refine man. And why? So that He can be a shield to all that trust in Him."

Whether we understand the reason why they were given or not, the commandments are for *our* good, not G–d's: "If thou hast sinned, what doest thou against Him? . . . and if thou be righteous, what givest thou Him?" They are His means of refining, of disciplining us – and especially the more-than-half animal part of us, so that we can attain that standard of holiness which will fit us to fulfil our high responsibility to Him, ourselves and mankind.

The Hebrew word translated 'refine' is normally used for the process of purifying gold and silver from the dross which clings to it: and that is exactly what the observance of the dietary laws and other disciplinary laws does for us – purify and sharpen our mental and spiritual faculties, earning us G–d's protective shield. He, the Divine Physician, knows all our ailments and weaknesses, and prescribes preventive and curative medicines for them. The Doctor knows the purpose of each of them – though we may not!

So let us now see what may, according to the Torah, be eaten. Because, in effect, there is only one source for obtaining permissible meat and poultry – an establishment authorised to sell them by the ecclesiastical authorities, be it a butcher or delicatesssen shop or *kasher* restaurant; and because, by the time you buy them, all the preliminaries to cooking have already been done for the purchaser, even, in most cases, the extraction of the blood; I am only numbering the main commandment in each class, and briefly mentioning their particulars under Roman numerals.

41. ONLY EAT PERMITTED MEAT

Section 6. (i) "Whatsoever parteth the hoof, and is wholly cloven-footed, and cheweth the cud, among the beasts – that may you eat." Thus, for example, the pig may *not* be eaten, only because, though it is cloven-hooved, it does not chew the cud; nor the camel or hare which, though they chew the cud, are not cloven-hooved.

(ii) Even the permitted animals "thou shalt kill . . . as I have commanded thee," says Moses. Since the details of this method, which are very many, are nowhere stated in the Torah, all the regulations regarding *shechita*, as it is called, are, like those concerning the nature of the *tephillin*, classified as *halachah leMoshe miSinai* – laws given to Moses while on mount Sinai, and transmitted by him only by word of mouth to Israel.

(iii) It follows from this that "You shall not eat anything that dieth of itself", i.e. of natural causes. This is taken to include any animal killed by any method other than *shechita*, or when faults occurred in the *shechita* process itself. An animal which dies in either of these ways is termed *nevelah*; and it is incidentally interesting to note that the Midrash states: "In the Hereafter, the Holy One, blessed be He, will make a banquet for His righteous servants, and whoever has not eaten *nevelah* in this world, will have the privilege of enjoying it in the Hereafter" – a reward for self-discipline here!

(iv) Again it follows from (ii) that "You shall not eat any flesh that is torn of beasts in the field". Such meat is called *teraifah*, and the term was first extended to include the flesh of any beast with symptoms of any illness or abnormality from which it would have died naturally within a year, discovered during a compulsory inspection of its innards by the *shochet* after satisfactory *shechita*; and then to any foodstuff whatsoever which is not *kasher*.

(Of passing interest are the Torah's suggestions as to what should be done with *nevailah* and *teraifah* respectively. The former which, in either instance, may be perfectly healthy flesh, "thou mayest give unto the stranger . . . or unto the foreigner"; but a *teraifah* in its original connotation, i.e. an animal torn by wild beasts, "you shall cast it to the dogs". Why the dogs in particular? "To teach us that G–d does not withhold reward from any creature: for it is said: 'And against any of the children of Israel shall not a dog whet his tongue' (when they leave Egypt). Says the Holy One, blessed be He, 'Give him his reward'"!)

(v) From the phrase "thou shalt not eat the life (*nefesh*) with the flesh" it is deduced that "it is forbidden to eat a limb or piece of flesh severed from a live animal" – i.e. while it still shows signs of life, which is downright cruel. Neither may we eat (vi) "the sinew of the

thigh" (see context for interesting reason therefor), nor certain fats, nor lots and lots of "detestable things that swarm upon the earth" — from the mouse and rat to the worm in fruit or vegetable, comprising many more Torah commandments.

A special section is merited for the prohibition (vii) "You shall eat no manner of blood, whether it be of fowl or of beast, in any of your dwellings," because of G–d's utter abhorrence of such consumption. For He issues the stern warning, "I will set My face against that soul that eateth blood, and will cut him off from among his people." 'Setting My face against', says Rashi, means: "I will lay aside all My other pre-occupations, and attend to him". And understandably so: for the animal's soul is in its blood; and anyone who consumes it animalises his own soul, feeds the animal instincts within himself!

For this reason, very careful steps are taken to remove all traces of blood from *kasher* meat by what is called '*kashering*' it: that is, soaking it is water to remove and soften the surface blood, and then liberally sprinkling it with special salt to extract the inner blood. The liver contains so much blood that it be at least "half-grilled" before being eaten. All this is now increasingly done — except for the liver treatment — by the authorised butcher; but if he does not, it has to be done at home. And, as stated above, many ready-cooked meat foods are available.

42.   EAT ONLY PERMITTED FOWL

Section 8. A list of all forbidden fowl and birds is preceded by: "Of all clean birds you may eat," without giving any features to look for before killing them for food — for the laws of *shechita* apply to fowl just as to animals. However, the Sages do provide us with signs of permissible fowl and bird: "an extra large middle toe, a crop, and a gizzard, the inner lining of which can be easily peeled off." To refrain from eating any forbidden species is another Torah commandment.

The favourite — or, rather, most popular — *kasher* fowl is, of course, the chicken: but also common are duck, geese and turkey; while the pigeon — if you can get it, is a rare delicacy. They are 'clean', say some commentators, because they are not birds of prey, which most of the 'unclean' varieties are. But the ideal reason for not eating the latter is because "it is a decree of the King".

43.   EAT ONLY PERMITTED SEA-LIFE

Section 9. Only "These may you eat from all that are in the waters: whatsoever has fins and scales in the waters, in the seas, and in the rivers." The next verse, forbidding us from eating any sea creatures not having fins and scales, is a further commandment, thus excluding crustacea like crabs, lobsters, shrimps, etc. Yet another commandment is read into the words "You shall not make yourselves detestable with *any* swarming things", covering any other form of sea-life.

Since it is only the blood of fowl and beast which is forbidden, that of fish is permitted – though "it must not be collected in a container for drinking," because others may think it is animal or fowl blood. This principle of not doing things allowed because they might *appear* wrong to others – called *marit-ayin*, 'what the eye sees', or 'for appearance sake' – plays an important part in Jewish ethics, since we are counselled to "be clear before the Eternal *and* before Israel", and to "find grace and good favour in the sight of G–d *and* man" – whenever possible.

Because the verb to "gather" is used with regard to fish, in contradistinction to 'slaughter' with reference to animals, it is deduced that "*shechita* is not necessary where sea-life is concerned". So you may make angling a hobby with a clear conscience!

Generally speaking, everything within, or that issues from, a *kasher* animal or fowl, like milk and eggs, is permitted to be eaten. But as regards the latter, if a drop of blood is found in an egg, it is very possible that it is the sign of fertilisation – that the creation of a new chick has begun, which would make the egg forbidden for food. Though in Talmudic times they were able to distinguish between such a blood-spot and a harmless one – which they just plucked off and threw away, then using the egg; nowadays it is customary "not to use any egg with any blood-spot".

44.   DO NOT EAT MILK WITH (OR AFTER) MEAT

Section 10. Three times the Torah states "Thou shalt not boil a kid in its mother's milk", and since nothing in the Torah is superfluous, the Sages say each refers to a different prohibition: (i) to cooking animal and milk, or their products, together; (ii) to eating such a cooked mixture; and (iii) to having any benefit from such a mixture. Originally "fowl was excluded (from this ban) since it has no mother's milk"; but the Sages added it, "but only insofar as the *eating* of them is concerned."

The prohibition was then extended from eating meat and milk *together*, to eating milk or its products *after* meat, the interval between them varying from one hour to six hours according to custom – the latter, longest wait being supported by RM: "He who has eaten animal or fowl meat should not eat milk dishes afterwards until a 'meal-time' has passed, which is about six hours"; and that is the minimum time which "everyone with a breath of Torah in him" should wait.

Nevertheless, I must tell you – though I do not know whence it comes, that British Jews generally appear to have a long-standing tradition of waiting just half that time, three hours, between meat and milk (and the Sephardim among them only one hour!). What *you* will do depends on how strong the 'breath of Torah' inspires you.

Section 11.   **Summing Up**

Though unnumbered, I have here included many Torah commandments, most of them about things you may *not* eat – but not all of these, by any means! I have not mentioned, for instance, the prohibitions against eating flies, wasps, earth-worms and snakes! I do mention them now because I want you to appreciate the full force of an illuminating and encouraging Talmudic passage which reads, more or less:

For refraining from eating blood and loathsome creatures the Torah holds out the fulsome promise: "It will go well with thee, and with thy children after thee, if thou doest what is right in the eyes of the Eternal". On this R. Shimon comments: "If this is the reward for refraining from eating things for which a person has an instinctive loathing, how much greater must be the reward, for oneself, and for generation after generation to the end of all generations, for one who refrains from eating and doing things for which his body and soul yearns – but does not, because he wants to do only that which is right in the eyes of the Eternal!"

These dietary laws were introduced here, as stated above, because this is the first time you are eating 'on your own', away from home. But they are meant, of course, to guide you throughout your life, wherever you are – even as a guest in someone else's house. Their observance is one of the ways in which you achieve holiness, nearness to your Creator. One chapter which contains most of them ends with the verse: "For I am the Eternal your G–d: sanctify yourselves, therefore, and be holy – for I am holy; and do not defile yourselves . . ." with the eating of forbidden food.

And remember this: most inter-meal 'snacks' bought in tuck-shops – toffees, filled chocolate-bars, cakes, ice-cream etc. have some admixture of forbidden ingredients. *Everything* should be considered by you as of suspect *kashrut,* unless you have ascertained that there are no grounds for such suspicion. Be careful! Discipline yourself! Be holy!

A good appetite! I'll meet you again soon, probably while you are eating. And by the way: do not forget your blessings, before and after you eat the produce of G–d's good earth, thus making it your own!

Section   **Notes**

1   Deuter. 20.5 (twice); I. Kings 8.63 and II. Chron. 7.5; Numbers 7.11 & 84; Proverbs 22.6; Kiddushin 29a.

2   On Proverbs 22.6; Ethics 1.4; Isaiah 30.20; Y. De'ah 246.9; Eruvin 13b; Proverbs 4.7; Ethics 4.25 and 5.18; Psalms 90.12; Rashi on Levit. 1.1.

3   Deuter. 5.1; Kiddushin 30b; Eccles. 9.9; Jeremiah 29.1–14; Kiddushin 30a.

4   Makkot 10a.

5   E.g. Genesis 26.5 & Levit. 18.4; MR. Numbers 19.3; Psalms 18.31; Job 35.6–7.

6   Levit. 11.3; Deuter. 12.21; Ibid 14.21; MR. Levit. 13.3; Exodus 22.30; Chullin 42a; as third note here; as fifth note here; Ibid, Rashi; Deuter. 12.23; Chullin 102b; Genesis 32.33; Levit. 7.23; Ibid chapter 11.

7   Levit. 7.26; Ibid 17.10; Y. De'ah 73.1.

8   Deuter. 14.11; Chullin 59a.

9   Levit. 11.9; Ibid v. 43; Keritot 21b; Numbers 32.22; Proverbs 3.4; Numbers 11.22; Chullin 27b; Y. De'ah 66.3.

10 Exodus 23.19 & 34.26 and Deuter. 14.21; Chullin 113a; Y. De'ah 87.3; Yed. M. Asurot 9.28; Y. De'ah 89 Shach note 8.

11 Makkot 23b; Deuter. 12.28; Levit. 11.44.

Twenty

WORDS, WORDS, WORDS!

Section 1.   **The Gift Of Speech**

After the Creator had breathed into the father of all men "the breath (*neshamah*) of life", Adam became a *nefesh chaya*, 'a living soul' – which is exactly the same description given to all the rest of the animate creatures of land, air and sea! How then did this divine breath elevate the human above those other denizens of the earth? By the fact that *their* life-forces were of earthy origin, already inherent in them as, by the command of G–d, they swarmed forth from land or waters; whereas man was – and still is – a *golem*, a lifeless form, until the breath of G–d stirs him to life.

There are three partners in man: father and mother make their respective contributions towards the formation of his body; and then G–d endows it with "the spirit (*ru'ach*), the divine breath (*neshamah*); brightness of facial features; sight and hearing; the ability to speak and walk; and knowledge, understanding and discernment."

Many other living creatures possess some of these faculties, often excelling in one or other of them over man – but they do not have a *neshamah*, that direct infusion of the divine spirit (*ru'ach hakodesh*, the holy spirit), breathed exclusively into man. Thus, comments Rashi, while man did, indeed, like all other living creatures, become a *nefesh chaya*, "he was the most developed of them, having been (additionally) endowed with a rational mind (*de'ah*) and speech."

And the *Targum Onkelos*, the Aramaic translation of the Torah endorsed by the Sages of the Talmud, while rendering nefesh chaya literally as "a living soul" where it refers to other creatures, translates the identical words as 'a speaking spirit' when used of man's creation.

To summarise, then: the *neshamah* which G–d breathes into every human being gives him not only life itself, with divinely-refined animal senses; but also endows him with the ability to think,

156

consider, and decide between right and wrong; and the gift of speech and others means of communication which follow from it.

Scientists, with the aid of superb modern technological means, have, with patient research proven beyond doubt, and demonstrated to the millions through the wonder of colour television, that animals, fowl and fish also communicate with their own kind through a manner of 'speech', and have even learnt to understand some of that chatter. Indeed, with his supreme human wisdom, Solomon is said to have been able to understand them: "If an ass brayed, or a bird chirped, he knew what it meant" – and the complete history and nature of all "flora and fauna".

But their neighing and braying, chirping and croaking, is primitive and changeless, not cultivated and developing, nor uttered with afore-thought, like man's speech. Speech was given to man as an aid to fulfilling the purpose for which man himself was created: to establish the kingdom of G–d on earth, by promoting the brother-hood of all men under His Fatherhood. To employ it for the opposite purpose, to entice men away from G–d, or to cause disruption among them, is to be worse than the animal.

Section 2. **When And What To Speak**

The tongue – and, by extension, the pen – is the most powerful human organ, for good or evil. "Death and life are in the power of the tongue, and they that indulge it shall eat the fruit thereof," i.e. will be held responsible for the effects of the words they utter. Yet despite this, and the two sets of precautionary guards with which the Creator has enclosed it – the teeth and the lips, the tongue is the most exercised organ of the body for most people.

When *should* we speak? If we take the advice of R. Shimon b. Gamaliel, never – or very seldom! For he says: "All my days I have grown up among the wise, and I have found nothing of better service than silence." Of course, he was talking about general, social conversation – not such speech as prayer, study, teaching and intellectual discussion. And his advice is certainly recommended for foolish people: for "Even a fool, when he is silent, is considered wise."

But *you* are no fool! You move among people, you mix in society; you have class-mates and friends, and if you always sit like a dummy among them, you may well be doing the wise thing, but you'll probably be considered a fool! You will probably not eat your mid-day meal or snack isolated away in a corner by yourself, but either in the dining-hall or the playground, among your friends and colleagues; and you or one of them will no doubt initiate a conversation.

What to talk about? How to use that gift of speech to best advantage? Logically and sensibly, in discussion of the lessons just learnt. But the most frequent topic of leisure-time chit-chat is other people; and regarding such conversation, you would do well ever to bear in mind the latter part of R. Shimon's warning that "he who talks too much usually comes to sinning", as we shall soon see.

The weather's a constant and harmless enough topic of conversation, but how long can you talk about that? Sport is another, permitting of longer discussion, though it can become dangerously over-heated – and many a rash word is said in excitement! Having exhausted these two subjects, what's left? Politics, maybe, or the acceptable face of television – but not the other, which you should not have viewed in any case!

Section 3.   **"Who Wants Life?"**
Have you ever heard of a Rabbi Israel Meir Poupko? Most probably not. Perhaps it might help if I add the clue that he lived in a town called Radun. No? Then I'll give you another clue: he was the author of a commentary on the Or.Ch. called the *Mishna Berura*, from which so many laws have been cited in this book. So popular did it become that the author became known as "The Mishna Berura" – but he had an even more popular name, "The Chafetz Chayim", the title of another book he wrote.

He took that title from the verse we recite every Shabbat and Festival morning: "Who is the man that desireth life (*chafetz chayim*), and loveth days that he may see good therein?" This book, and a complementary one called *Shemirat Halashon* (Guarding the Tongue), explain in great detail the answer given in the next verse: "Keep thy tongue from evil, and thy lips from speaking guile." They are inspiring books, listing and elaborating upon the very many Torah and rabbinic commandments which can so easily be violated by the wagging tongue, leading to the conclusion that we should follow the example of David when he said "I will take heed to my ways that I sin not with my tongue, I will keep a curb on my lips . . .".

It would well be worth your time, money and effort to get these two books, study them under a good teacher – if you cannot by yourself, and revise them constantly, if you "desire life, and love days to see good therein." We will now consider those Torah commandments particularly relevant to you in your relationship with others.

Section 4. **A Sin To Tell A Lie?**

Peculiarly enough, though the Torah contains the statements "Keep thee far from a false matter (or 'word')," and "You shall not lie one to another", neither of these is numbered among the 613 commandments, both being seen as specifically referring to the general context in which they respectively occur.

The first is a general warning to judges to display the highest integrity, and avoid the slightest show of partiality, many examples of the dangers that may befall the unwary being cited in the Talmud. The second verse, deduce the Sages, is a warning against *swearing* falsely in connection with loans received, or property held for safe-keeping.

So *is* it a sin to tell a lie in the course of ordinary conversation? Of course it is! Comments Hertz on the first of these two verses: while it refers to "the administration of justice, this warning has the wider application as a rule of life of the highest importance." R. Chanina states "The seal of the Holy One, blessed be He, is truth"; and R. Shimon b. Gamaliel asserts that "truth is one of the three foundations upon which the preservation of society rests."

Nevertheless, there *are* occasions when not only may you tell a lie, but it is positively praiseworthy to do so – in the pursuit of love and peace! And proof of this, the precedent, was established by G–d Himself, in Whose ways we are commanded to walk. Sarah based her disbelief in the promise that she would have a child on the grounds that both she *and Abraham* were old: but the Eternal asked Abraham, "Why did Sarah laugh, saying . . . 'I am old'?" – without mentioning her reference to Abraham's age.

On this Bar Kappara commented: "Great is peace! For even (the Author of) the Torah made a mis-statement in order to preserve peace between Abraham and Sarah!" Following this divine example, Aaron, we are told, was wont to approach each party to a quarrel and plead: "Do you realise how much heart-ache your friend is suffering because of your quarrel?" – although neither of them had said a word to him! This resulted in their renewing their friendship the next time they met.

And the great Hillel advises us: "Be of the disciples of Aaron, loving peace and pursuing peace, loving your fellow-creatures (*be-riyyot*), and attracting them to the Torah". Speech is a divine gift, and here you have two examples how, apart from "speaking about them" in prayer, audible study, which helps the memory, and intellectual discussion; you can employ it, through restraint and the 'white', peace-promoting lie, to the benefit of your fellow-men. Perhaps this is why the Torah does not say categorically "Do not *ever* lie" – but that it *is*, generally speaking, a grievous sin to do so, is inherent in the commandment we are now to consider.

45.   "DO NOT UTTER (OR ACCEPT) A VAIN REPORT"

I am really stretching a point in including this commandment among those applicable to you (and me) Torah-wise, for in its context it refers only to court cases; and is a warning to a litigant not to talk about, and a judge not to listen to, any details of the dispute in the absence of the other litigant. This is because in such circumstances the litigant present may be tempted to lie, and the judge(s) may thus be influenced in his favour.

It is the Sages who extend this commandment to include *any* indulging in what is commonly known as *lashon hara* – an 'evil tongue', one which utters anything to the discredit of another *even if what he says is true*! For the Hebrew phrase in this verb is not – as the English translations would have – a 'false' (*sheker*) report, but a 'vain' (*shav*) one, useless gossip, which can do no good, but only harm.

The above source-text follows immediately upon the words "You shall throw it to the dogs" – i.e. *treifah* meat; and from this juxtaposition R. Eleazar b. Azariah moralises: "Everyone who relates *lashon hara*, and everyone who *accepts* (willingly receives) it . . . deserves to be cast to the dogs"! The listener is as guilty as the gossiper, since he encourages him. "Why are the fingers like pegs? So that he who hears an unworthy thing can plug them into this ears! And why is the whole ear hard and the lobe soft? So that he who hears an unworthy thing can bend it into his ear!"

R. Dimi gave two examples of how even praising another can be classified as the 'evil tongue', a person who, having been lavishly entertained by a generous and caring host, "goes out into the street and publicly sings his praises" for the hospitality received from so-and-so. Those who hear it will then come and 'plunder' the good man, either by robbery or importuning him for free board-and-lodgings!

His other example is put in the form of a warning: "A man should never speak in praise of his friend, because through praising him he brings about criticism of him". RM observes that such praise is ill-advised only in the presence of the friend's enemies, who will be enticed to cite his faults; and considers such praise as merely a shade, or tinge (Hebrew: *avak* = dust) of *lashon hara*. Under this heading RM also includes damning with faint praise, and such statements as "I'm not going to tell you what I know about so-and-so!"

46.   DO NOT TELL TALES!

Section 6. This prohibition *is* a Torah commandment, and is so close in nature to *lashon hara* that the two are sometimes interchanged or confused. But there is a difference between them, as will soon emerge.

Its source is: "Thou shalt not go about as a tale-bearer (*rachil*) among thy people . . .". In this form the noun occurs only here, twice in *Proverbs*, where it is also translated 'tale-bearer', and thrice in the *Prophets*. A more common form of the noun is *rochel*, which is always translated 'merchant': and because in one instance reference is made to one "perfumed with . . . all the *spices* of the *rochel*", the term is taken especially to refer to a spices-selling pedlar — but not the unusual kind told about in the following story!

He attracted great crowds when he cried out: "Who wants to buy the medicine of life?". When R. Yannai heard him through his study window, he called out, "Come here, and sell me it!" Said the *rochel*: "Neither you nor people like you need it!" But when the Rabbi insisted, the *rochel* brought out the Book of *Psalms* and showed him the verses: "Who is the man that desireth life . . .? Keep thy tongue from evil, and thy lips from speaking guile". This unusual *rochel* was selling copies of the *Psalms*!

The *rachil* is someone with a perpetually wagging tongue, what is now commonly known as 'a good conversationalist'. Generally speaking, he can tell a good story about anything or anyone 'at the drop of a hat'; but specifically he "carries the talk of this one to that one, and that one to this one." He speaks the truth: they *did* say what he says they said: he possibly means no harm — but what an awful lot he can cause!

"He that goeth about as a tale-bearer revealeth secrets; therefore meddle not with him that openeth wide his lips," cautions Solomon. For, as with *lashon hara*, the listener to the *rachil*'s tittle-tattle becomes his accomplice through lending him a willing ear. And *rechilut*, as this sin is called, if not *lashon hara*, is the main conversational content of most social get-togethers.

Of particular interest is the example of tale-bearing the Mishna gives: of one of a bench of judges who, after a guilty verdict had been agreed upon by a majority vote, says: "*I* was for acquittal . . . but what could I do, since *they* were in the majority?" The Torah ordains "after the majority must one incline" — except to do evil; and the minority must silently fall in with the majority.

Section 7.   **The Foul Mouth**

The phrase *lashon hara* literally means "the bad tongue", and the prohibition against it certainly includes the use of filthy, obscene language – so certainly, in fact, that the Torah does not demean itself even to mention *nibbul-peh*, as foulness of mouth is called. Yet it does, just once, use more words and letters than necessary, in order to teach us to use only pure language.

When Noah was commanded to take of all the species of animals into the ark, G–d said: "Of every clean (*tehorah*) beast thou shalt take seven and seven . . . and of the beasts that are not clean (*lo tehorah*) two (and two) . . ." – instead of just 'unclean' (*teme'ah*). From this R. Yehoshua b. Levi concludes: "A person should never utter a gross expression with his mouth"; and others give examples of even greater circumlocution in order to avoid and word 'unclean'.

Need I say more? If it is less graceful to say 'impure' than 'not pure', how much more unacceptable are the many obscenities and shameless expressions and rude expletives which have almost become the general currency of conversation today! The divine gift of speech should never be sullied by their utterance.

To quote one telling Talmudic example of nibbul-peh, a whit paraphrased: "All know the purpose of marriage; yet against anyone who speaks obscenely about it, even if a decree of seventy years' happiness has been sealed for him, it is reversed for evil."

Though not nibbul-peh – yet very often disgracefully accompanying it, there is a kind of "taking G–d's Name in vain" – to which general reference will be made at a later stage. To exclaim "By G–d!" or "O my G–d!" and the like, other than in the course of praying, is unnecessary mention of the Holy Name, which has, alas, become very common practice. Even worse, though less prevalent among Jews, is to use the names of the gods of others, or their "Messiah", in such expletives, which is a violation of the Torah commandment "Make no mention of the name of other gods; neither let it be heard out of thy mouth."

Always bearing in mind all these moral and religious evils, putting a tight curb of teeth and lips on your tongue whenever one of them strains for release, ponder on this advice: "He that restraineth his words displays good sense . . . and he that shutteth his lips is esteemed." Above all, ever heed the two following commandments.

47.   ALWAYS KEEP YOUR WORD!
and
48.   NEVER BREAK YOUR WORD!

Section 8. These are derived from two sources: "That which has gone out of thy lips thou shalt observe and do; according as thou hast vowed freely to the Eternal thy G–d, which thou hast spoken with thy mouth": and "When a man voweth a vow unto the Eternal . . . he shall not break his word; he shall do according to all that proceedeth out of his mouth."

Both texts, it will be seen, speak of oaths or promises made to G–d. But RM, from the apparently superfluous ending of the first – the 'repetition' of "which thou hast spoken with thy mouth" after "which has gone out of thy lips"; and its almost literal reiteration in the second source; concludes that both commandments apply to *any* verbal undertaking we give, to man as well as to G–d, and even if not uttered in the actual form of a vow.

And so it should be: for every promise made to another is made in G–d's Presence, to one of His children – your brother or sister. Playing on the word *hin*, which is a liquid measure, and its resemblance to *hen*, which means 'yes' (in Aramaic), in the phrase "a just *hin* shall you have" – which appears to be superfluous: R. Yose b. R. Yehuda says "It teaches us that your 'yes' should be just, and your 'no' should be just." Abaye says it teaches another important lesson relevant to our theme: "One must not speak one thing with the mouth, and think another with the mind."

One of the characteristics of "G–d's Gentleman" who is typified in, and therefore gives this popular name to, Psalm 15, is: "He promises (even) to his own hurt, yet changeth not." On this the *Soncino* commentary observes: "The sanctity of the plighted word, even if it proves disadvantageous, is stressed in Jewish ethics." A Jew's word, even without written corroboration, must be his bond! Incidentally, the eleven characteristics enumerated in this Psalm are said to "epitomise all the 613 commandments", and qualify those who display them to "dwell upon Thy holy mountain", though they are all purely moral and ethical!

It would appear that the second of our commandments is just the other side of the same coin – but it is not so! It contains implicitly the warning that, once you have given a promise, you should make all haste to keep it in good time, lest circumstances which you could have, but can no longer, control (led) intervene between the word and the deed.

You will remember that, in the text, these commandments refer explicitly to promises to G–d, concerning which the Torah says: "When thou shalt vow a vow unto the Eternal thy G–d, thou shalt not be slack to pay it: for the Eternal thy G–d will surely require it of thee, and it will be sin in thee" – if you do not honour it while you can. And the same applies to promises made to your fellows – and to donations promised to your Synagogue, other communal institutions, and charities.

49. DO NOT MISLEAD ANYONE

Section 9. The actual wording of the commandment from which this prohibition is derived is: "(Do not curse the deaf), and do not place a stumbling-block before the blind; for thou shalt fear thy G–d – I am the Eternal." (We will deal with the bracketed part later.)

The plain text, of course, means exactly what it says: If you see a blind person coming along the road, do not put a stone, banana-skin, or any such obstacle in his path, so that he should stumble and fall! But only a wicked sadist would do such a thing: and, to use a rabbinic adage descriptive of such a person, "Are we then dealing with wicked people?" Certainly not!

And so the Sages extend the term 'blind' to those who are blind not of eyesight but in other ways – like Adam and Eve, who were 'blind' to evil until they had eaten of the Tree of Knowledge, after doing which "the eyes of both of them were opened" – which does not mean that they could not previously see with their actual eyes! In the same way, Isaiah complains about the spiritual leaders of his times: "His watchmen are blind, without knowledge . . .", i.e. they could not 'see' the difference between right and wrong.

Based, says the *Malbim*, on the fact that in the source-verse the verb translated 'place' literally means 'give', the Sages read into it the inner meaning that it is prohibited to *give* potentially harmful advice to anyone blind to a sphere of knowledge in which you have 'sight'; to encourage him, in his ignorance, to do something which will be to your advantage; or to infuriate him to such an extent that he will do something wrong which he will regret and pay for when his anger cools down. I'm sure you can yourself think of other examples of the sighted leading the 'blind' into sin, bad habits, or just pure mischief!

It would be wrong of you to persuade a friend to exchange, say, his good camera for your watch which you know – but he does not – to be faulty! It would be wrong of your father to rouse your temper to such a degree that you feel like hitting him – which is technically a capital offence!

All these are examples adapted from some given in the Talmud. Another they give is offering a drink to someone who is under pledge to give up drinking – similar, nowadays, to offering a cigarette to someone trying to give up smoking.

50. DO NOT CURSE *ANYBODY*!

Section 10. In chapter twelve the biblical capital offence of cursing your parents is listed. From the bracketed part of the source-text of the previous commandment, "thou shalt not curse the deaf", together with the italicised words in the half-verse "and a ruler *within thy people thou shalt not curse*", the Sages deduce that it is prohibited to curse any living person, even be he deaf, and cannot therefore hear you (though the mention of the living deaf excludes the dead from the prohibition!).

Although, according to the Torah, this sin is only committed when one calls upon G–d, by any of His Names in any language, to curse another, the Sages extended it to include any formula, even if a Name is not mentioned. And I introduce it here because it is one of those evils from which you should guard your mouth, since its incidence is not as rare as it used to be.

Cursing can do harm! "Though we have not the ability to understand how a curse affects its victim, or how mere speech can do harm, yet we do know that it does. I would humbly suggest that since the gift of speech is a portion of the Divine, He gave it the power to have effects outside its own sphere, for good or evil." Thus, because Jacob, unaware that his beloved Rachel had stolen them, indignantly declared to Laban, "With whomsoever thou findest thy gods, he shall not live!", Rachel died prematurely. Moreover, a curse can have a boomerang effect! Because king David pronounced five curses on Joab, "all of them were fulfilled in *David's own* descendants – as the Talmud there shows in detail.

Section 11. **Who Knows?**

You might ask: Who will know if I secretly give someone bad advice or curse someone in strict privacy? *You* know the answer, as well as I do! But, just in case you might forget that G–d is present everywhere and always, the verse containing these two prohibitions concludes with "but thou shalt fear thy G–d – I am the Eternal", as if as to say: true, no human can hear you, but *I* can! This warning and reminder is given "of everything known only to the heart" of the performer.

There is a soul-searching prayer called *Zakkah* (purification) said just before *Kol Nidrei* in which the repentant itemises the limbs of the body, and humbly confesses how they have been used for purposes other than those for which they were divinely intended. Here is what it says about the vocal organs:

"You created within me mouth, tongue, teeth, palate and throat, together making possible speech by which You have distinguished man from animal. But I have been worse than an animal, for I have made my mouth impure with obscene talk, *lashon hara*, lies, *rechilut*, quarrelling and shaming my fellows in public." And of the ears: "I have defiled them by listening to *nibbul-peh, lashon hara* and all forbidden things." You should see what is said of the other limbs!

So, young lady and gentleman! Follow the Torah which is a "tree of life to them that lay hold of it". And always bear in mind that "Whoso guardeth his mouth and tongue, guardeth his life from troubles" – and the lives of others!

Section	**Notes**
1	See chapter 4; Niddah 31a; on Genesis 2.7; Ibid 1.20 & 24; Mr. Cant. 1.1.9; I. Kings 5.13.
2	Proverbs 18.21; Ethics 1.17; Proverbs 17.28.
3	Psalms 4.13–14; Ibid 39.2.
4	Exodus 23.7; Levit. 19.11; Shevuot 30b–31a; B. Kama 105b; Shabbat 55a; Ethics 1.18; Genesis 18.12–13; MR. Genesis 48.18; ADRN 12.2; Ethics 1.12.
5	Exodus 23.1–3; Sanhedrin 7b; Makot 23a; Ketubot 5b. Arakin 16a; B. Batra 164b; Yad. De'ot 7.4.
6	Levit. 19.16; Cant. 3.61; MR. Levit. 16.2; Psalms 34.13–14; Y. Pe'ah 3b (1.1); Proverbs 20.19; Sanhedrin 29a; Exodus 23.2.
7	Genesis 7.2; Pesachim 3a; Shabbat 33a; Exodus 23.13; Proverbs 17.27–28.
8	Deuter. 23.24; Numbers 30.3; SM. P.94 & 157; B. Metsia 49a; Levit. 19.16; Makkot 24a; Deuter. 23.22.
9	Levit. 19.14; Yoma 6a; Genesis 3.7; Isaiah 58.10; Pesachim 22b.
10	Exodus 22.27; Chinuch 231; Genesis 31.32; MR. Genesis 74.9; II. Samuel 3.29; Sanhedrin 48b.
11	B. Metsia 58b; Proverbs 3.18; Ibid 21.23.

Twenty-One

FOR SPECIAL CONSIDERATION

Section 1. Until now we have been speaking generally, of your attitude towards your 'equals', in school and elsewhere. Ideally, of course, as has been mentioned before, *all* men should be equal; and that is the end towards which Judaism is ever aspiring.

But the facts of real life are different. Apart from those in skin colour, which should not affect our attitudes one iota, there are other divisions among men – of nationality and religion, of culture and education, and of degrees of material wealth and social security; and there are few countries in the world, if any, where most of these divisions, if not all, are not prevalent.

The Torah, given in the desert at Sinai, recognised that all these divisions would pertain in the settled Land of Israel, and regulates as to our duties towards each of them. Thus provision is made for the Levite – one giving full-time service to G–d or the community, and therefore unable to earn a livelihood by "the labour of thine hands"; the 'stranger' – to be defined soon in detail, but it includes one of another nationality or religion; and the orphan and widow, who lack normal security.

Particular attention is drawn to maintaining in dignity "thy poor and needy brother in thy land – for the poor shall never cease out of the land"; though the Torah does foresee a time when "there will be no needy among you, when the Eternal will surely bless thee in the land . . . which He giveth thee for an inheritance to possess it – if only thou diligently hearken unto the voice of the Eternal thy G–d, to observe to do all this commandment . . ." i.e. the whole Torah.

In this chapter we shall be considering what the Torah requires of you, in your post-BM, pre-marriage years, in your attitude towards all these categories – and others, on account of either the special respect due to them, or the danger of getting involved with them! But first we must consider the two main categories existing among most nations, represented in the Torah by the *ezrach* and the *ger*.

There are two words in the *Tenach*, the first always, and the second almost always, translated 'stranger' – *ger* and *nochri*: though the latter is sometimes translated 'foreigner', which is what it really means: one of a foreign nation, either passing through, or temporarily residing, in accordance with his own beliefs and customs, in your land. Thus the Torah envisages the awesome scene of "the foreigner (*nochri*) that shall come from a far land" to see the devastation with which G–d had afflicted His Land, because its citizens had "forsaken the covenant of the Eternal, the G–d of their fathers." This, also, is the reason why "the *nochri* alone may be lent money on interest" – because he is "here today, and gone tomorrow", and therefore the chances of repayment are more risky. But *ger* is the more common term.

Moses referred to himself as a *ger* in the land of Midian, not a *nochri*. There is a legend, quoted from a work called "The Chronicles of Moses", which maintains that, after fleeing from Egypt, Moses fought in the Ethiopian army, and was eventually appointed king over that country, over which he reigned for forty years, departing thence at the age of sixty-seven! Even so, he would have still spent thirteen years in Midian – so he was no transient *nochri*, but a *ger*. Let us now see what this word, over which there is much confusion, really means.

Section 2.   **Ger And Ger**

Some over-simplify its meaning: Rashi says: "Every occurrence of the word *ger* refers to one not born in a particular country, but has come from another country to reside there." It does, of course, mean that, as Moses description of his stay in Midian shows – but not always. On the other hand, when R. Eliezer the Great asked: "Why does the Torah, in thirty-six different places – and some say forty-six – warn us against mistreatment of the *ger*?", the *Soncino* edition translates the word 'proselyte", i.e. convert to Judaism, which meaning it bears more often than not – but again not always.

The Malbim painstakingly details and examines all forty-six of them, and shows that well over half of them indeed refer to the convert to Judaism – in Hebrew *ger tsedek* – whenever the word is qualified in one of the following ways: (a) by the *ger* being equated with the *ezrach* – the Jewish-born Israelite or Levite, as in "as the *ezrach* among you shall be the *ger* . . .", and "I have given them to the Levite and to the *ger* . . ."; when the *ger* is described as either (b) "one who sojourneth with you (*itecha*)" or one (c) "who sojourneth in your midst (*betoch'chem*)", the difference between these two being that (b) refers to the newly-received convert, and (c) to the convert of long-standing.

Uncertainty arises in two cases: when the description "the *ger* who is within the gates" is used. It obviously cannot mean a *ger tsedek* in the advice we have already come across once, that "that which dieth of itself thou mayest give unto the *ger* that is within thy gates, that he may eat it"; whereas the identical phrase in the "Fourth Commandment" *does* refer to the convert, as we shall see when considering the observance of Shabbat.

The other kind of uncertainty arises where the term *ger* is used without any qualification or description. Its meaning has then to be deduced either from the context or by reference to other texts. However, it can be assumed that in all legal texts, where *ger* does not refer to the *ger tsedek*, the convert who has accepted fulfilment of all the commandments, it refers to the *ger toshav*, the permanent or long-term resident alien, a status available to anyone in biblical times who renounced idolatry while enjoying that status in Israel – and, it is to be assumed, to any Israelite in any other country who did not show disrespect to *its* god(s).

Section 3.   **Love For The *Ger* As For Yourself**
I now quote in full one of the verses from which one of the above excerpts was taken, to show that it refers to the convert. It reads as follows: "As the *ezrach* among you shall be unto you the *ger* who resides with you (*itecha*), and thou shalt love for him as for thyself, (for you were *gerim* in the land of Egypt)": that is, you have to fulfil all your duties towards him as you have to towards your fellow Jewish-born brother.

Which is as it should be: for elsewhere the Torah legislates: "As for the congregation, there shall be one statute both for you and for the *ger* who resides among you (*betoch'chem*), a statute for ever throughout your generations; as you are, so shall the *ger* be before the Eternal. One law and one ordinance shall be both for you, *and* for the *ger* that resideth *with you* (*itecha*)."

A question arises: if equating *ger* with *ezrach* by itself, and the qualification "who resides among you" always refer to the convert; and if, as we are taught to believe, nothing, not even one letter, is superfluous in the Torah; why, in both of these quotations, is the phrase "who resides *with* you" added? (Another even more difficult, though much more obvious question is posed by another phrase in the first of these quotations. See if you can find it! I shall be posing it later in this chapter.)

The answer is that this additional phrase refers in particular, you will remember, to one who has just been, or even is only in the course of being, converted to Judaism. It is at this sensitive stage of his (or her) induction to our religion that he looks for that encouragement, warmth and love from members of the *ezrach* community which the Torah commands. And he deserves it — therefore this warning in these two verses and elsewhere.

Said Resh Lakish: "Beloved is the convert to the Holy One, blessed be He, more than all the masses that stood at mount Sinai! Why? Because had the latter not heard the thunder and seen the lightning, the mountain roaring and the ram's-horn sounding, they would not have accepted the yoke of the Kingdom of Heaven. But *this* one (the convert) saw and heard none of these — yet he came of his own accord to submit himself to that yoke! Can anyone be more beloved than he?"

Section 4.   **Attitudes To Converts**

And there are many other sayings in praise of the convert. Both R. Eleazar and R. Yochanan agree that "The Holy One, blessed be He, exiled Israel among the nations only in order that converts might attach themselves to them." R. Eliezer said: "The Omnipresent swore by His throne of glory that if anyone should come to be converted from any nation in the world, he should be accepted — except from the Amalekites" (who are now extinct — but see end of this chapter).

Deducing it from the words "and the *souls* that they had *made* in Haran", the Midrash draws the lesson that "If one brings a convert near to G–d, it is as though he had created him": and it proceeds to prove that not only Abraham and Sarah, but also Isaac and Rebecca, and Jacob and Leah, made it part of their lives' work to convert heathens to believe in G–d.

True, there are other views opposing the acceptance of converts. R. Chelbo inelegantly said: "Converts are as hurtful to Israel as a sore on the skin" — though this has been interpreted to convey that, so sincerely do converts fulfil all the obligations Judaism imposes upon them that they cause the skin of the less observant born Jews to itch! While the answer given to his own question by R. Eliezer the Great, cited above: Why does the Torah in so many places warn against inconsiderate treatment of the convert? is, "because his 'turn' is evil" — i.e. should such inconsiderateness cause him, through disillusionment, to turn away from Judaism, he can do much evil.

But consider the story, which I relate only very briefly here, of R. Shimon b. Yochai. Because of a little bit of 'innocent' *rechillut* to his parents (see Rashi) by a son of a converted couple, R. Shimon and his son had to hide in a cave for *twelve years*! For "a bird of the air shall carry the voice, and that which hath wings shall tell the matter"; and this 'innocent' report, that R. Shimon had criticised the Romans, somehow reached them, and they sentenced him to execution, from which he escaped to the cave.

Sometime after emerging into freedom, he happened to see the informer in the street, and exclaimed: "Is that man still alive?" So he pierced him with his eyes, and the man became a heap of bones! Yet it was that same R. Shimon b. Yochai who said: "Who is the greater person – he who loves the king, or he whom the king loves? Surely the latter! And G–d 'loves the *ger*, in giving him food and raiment'. Beloved are the converts!" And this leads me directly to our first, and very important, Torah commandment of this chapter.

51.   LOVE THE *GER!*

Section 5. From all that has preceded, it would appear that there is no need for a separate commandment to love the *ger*, and especially the convert, since he is to be treated as 'the *ezrach* among you' and 'thou shalt love for him as for yourself'. Yet the classifiers *do* include such a commandment, not deducing it, surprisingly enough, from any of the above-quoted texts, but from another – the verse following that cited by R. Shimon b. Yochai telling us that G–d loves the *ger*: "Therefore *you* shall love the *ger*; for you were *gerim* in the land of Egypt."

But can this refer to the *ger-tsedek*, the convert? Were our ancestors *converts* in the land of Egypt? Surely they were involuntary resident aliens there! A possible answer to this question is proffered at the end of this chapter.

I would therefore venture to suggest that we indeed do not require a separate commandment to instruct us to love for the convert as for ourselves, though the Torah states it just to leave us in no doubt whatsoever about this duty; and the commandment we have here concerns the *ger-toshav*, the resident alien, the kind of *gerim* we were in Egypt. This view seems to be supported by the question-and-answer: "What is the meaning of the verse 'Thou shalt neither wrong a *ger*, nor oppress him; for you were *gerim* in the land of Egypt?' It has been taught: R. Nattan said: 'Do not taunt your fellow with having a blemish which you yourself have (or had)'".

But how can we be *commanded* to love the resident alien – or, to give him his modern description, the immigrant or refugee, on sight? The Torah itself gives the emphatic answer: "because you – *you know* the life (*nefesh*) of the *ger*, seeing that you were *gerim* in the land of Egypt." The Israelites were then themselves refugees, slaves just released from bondage, wandering in the wilderness. They *knew* what that felt like – especially when Amalek came to attack them!

And this commandment was addressed not to them alone. As we say in the *Haggadah* every Pesach: "In *every* generation one is duty-bound to see himself as if *he* had gone forth from Egypt, as it is written: 'And thou shalt relate to thy son in that day saying, It is because of this that the Eternal wrought for *me* when *I* came forth from Egypt'. Not our forefathers alone did the Holy One, blessed be He, redeem, but us also did He redeem with them, as it is said: "And us did He bring out from there, that He may bring us to give us the land which He sware unto our forefathers." And He *kept* that promise, for the third time, in 1948!

In the more than two thousands years before that date, ever since Jews really had independent rule over their own Land, they have known on hundreds of sad occasions what it means to be alien residents in the lands of others, wandering in the wilderness of nations. If not your parents, your grandparents, and if not they, theirs, were most likely fleeing refugees from persecution and hunger, received sometimes not too gracefully, but with deep gratitude in their hearts, by one of the more liberal-governed countries.

You are no doubt an *ezrach* of the country you live in, speaking its language, and acclimatised to its culture and social life – without, of course, sacrificing one iota of your democratic right to free observance of your religion. It is probably one of those countries which annually receives many immigrants or refugees from persecution as *gerim-toshavim*, resident aliens, who strive eventually to become naturalised *ezrachim* themselves.

You, remembering that your forebears were such *gerim* not only in Egypt but, much more recently, in Russia, Poland, Germany and other countries, must show them instant love and warm co-operation, helping them in school, for instance, with their language and studies, and generally to integrate into the life of their new country. That is how this commandment applies to *you*, now – and always.

52.   DO NOT OFFEND THE *GER* VERBALLY

This is deduced, in the first place, from "And a *ger* thou shalt not offend, (neither shalt thou oppress him); for you were *gerim* in the land of Egypt." The phrase in brackets refers, say the Sages, to actual physical and commercial wrong, which will be included under business ethics in the next volume. The rest means offending the *ger-toshav*, the resident alien; the convert being added later, in verses already cited.

You might think: As long as I do him no actual injury, what harm is there in taunting him with mere words, like saying "Remember the deeds of your ancestors", or "How can a mouth which has eaten unclean and forbidden food study the Torah which was uttered by the mouth of the Omnipotent?" – or the like. He can answer: "*Your* forebears were also once resident aliens, and yearned for the flesh-pots of Egypt!" Both kinds of *ger* can be very sensitive, and we are therefore warned not to offend them even with words.

53.   DO NOT OFFEND YOUR *AMIT* VERBALLY

Section 6. I include this commandment here, not because your *amit* merits special consideration – because he is your fellow-born Jew or citizen. It derives from: "And no man of you shall offend his *amit* – and thou shalt fear thy G–d . . ." It does *not* refer to business wrongs like 'overreaching', as Hertz says – that being another command-ment, according to the Sages, already mentioned there in verse 14; but to insulting *speech*, with which we have been dealing.

You may say: "All right! The *ger* can be sensitive, so I will be very careful as to what I say to him, in order not to offend him in the least way. But what harm is there in taunting my equal in birth and religion?" Therefore the Torah warns against using your divine gift of speech for taunting *anybody*, even your equal; for that was not the purpose for which it was given to you.

Examples of such offences given in the Talmud are: if someone who had not been religious decides to turn over a new leaf and come back to Orthodox observance, do not ever say to him "Remember what you used to do before!" Do not go into a shop and pretend you want to buy something, thus raising the store-keeper's hopes, when you know very well you have not the means to buy it. And just in case you think, "Who knows I'm only pretending?", the Torah adds "thou shalt fear thy G–d" – Who *does* know, even your most private and secret thoughts.

54.   DO NOT HARM THE WIDOW OR ORPHAN

Section 7. These are another pair of individuals for whom the Torah demands special consideration on account of their vulnerability and relative insecurity. It commands: "You shall not offend any widow or 'fatherless child'". The Hebrew word for the latter, *yatom*, means a child deprived of father, or mother, or both. But it is usually translated 'fatherless' because, though in some families it is the mother who 'wears the trousers', or even earns a livelihood for the family, this is normally the province of the father; and therefore when he dies, both his widow and his child(ren) lose their protector and bread-winner.

However, so far as the children are concerned, this commandment applies with even greater weight when they lose both their parents – as so many did in the Russian pogroms and Hitler's Europe, if the children were indeed fortunate enough to survive. Concerning such the Sages say: "Anyone who brings up (or adopts) an orphan boy or girl in his home is regarded by Holy Writ as having given birth to him or her."

This source-verse is one of the shortest in the Torah, consisting of only five (Hebrew) words, and provides an excellent opportunity for illustrating how – as everywhere – each word and each letter, each idiom and grammatical 'irregularity', has a lesson to teach, a moral to excavate – if you only dig deep enough! In order to show you how this is done, I am going to translate the Hebrew of this and the next verse very literally. "Any (kol = all) widow or orphan you (plural) shall not harm. If harm thou (singular) dost harm *him*, if cry *he* shall cry unto Me, hear I will hear *his* cry."

Few Words – Many Lessons!

If the Torah meant *only* these two may not be harmed because they cannot protect themselves, then it could have said, You shall not harm a widow or an orphan, the addition of the word *kol*, therefore, extends the application of the commandment to *all* vulnerable and insecure people, of whom these two are usually the most commonly occurring examples, thus including the cripple, the mentally retarded, and the like.

The use of the plural verb in the first verse only, conveys two lessons: (a) that the Bet-Din, as the legal representatives of the community, must take up the case of these unfortunates, and defend them, if necessary; and (b) that if they and the community close their eyes to the wrongs done them, the dire punishment threatened in the following verse – which I don't even want to cite – will be visited upon all of them.

The emphatic 'harm if thou dost harm' teaches that the slightest humiliation of them, even by one word, let alone a harmful act, will be punished; the double 'cry if he should cry' implies even if one of them should breathe the slightest sigh because someone hurt them, let alone a loud cry, G–d will hear it; and the emphatic 'hear I will hear' means that G–d will more speedily punish the wrong done to them than to anyone else.

All these observations are taken from the *Malbim's* explanation of the *Mechilta* on these verses. He does not say why the second verse refers to the victim only in the masculine; but Ibn Ezra suggests that it will probably be the poor little orphan who will do the most crying – when, for instance, his school-mates make fun of his, knowing he has no father to protect him. I would suggest that it may be because, since customarily it is the (eldest) *male* orphan who takes over protection of the family, it is *he* who seeks redress from G–d, should he not get it from man, when wronged.

RM summarises this commandment thus: "Always speak gently to them, and treat them with every respect. Do not burden them with hard work or harsh words; and care for their money and property more than you do for your own."

Incidentally, this is one of the 'pairs', widow and/or orphan which RN numbers as two separate commandments, while RM, here followed, treats them as one, and examples of all such unfortunates. However it is obvious that if anyone offends or harms both a widow *and* an orphan, he violates two commandments.

55.   HONOUR THE LEARNED AND THE AGED

Section 8. Among the individuals with whom you come into frequent contact, those who have first claim to your honour and respect are your parents and rabbi – or "teacher", which is what the title means. Next in rank come other scholars and the aged, conveyed in the verse: "Thou shalt rise up before the hoary head (*saivah*), and honour the person of the old man (*zaken*)." Where is the learned man mentioned here?

The Sages generally take both *saivah* and *zaken* to refer to "one mature in wisdom" – which is usually acquired only in old age, as it is said, "with the ancients is wisdom". However, reading *zaken* as an abbreviation for *zeh kanah chochmah* – "this one has acquired wisdom", they reach the conclusion that even one who has acquired the wisdom of age while still young demands our honour and respect.

However R. Issi b. Yehudah maintains that while *zaken* does indeed refer to a sage, *saivah* connotes *any* old person, learned or unlettered, and R. Yochanan not only ruled that "the law accords with Issi," but put it into practice. For "R. Yochanan used to rise up before even the non-Jewish, heathen peasants, saying, 'How many of life's ordeals have these experienced!'" Others compromised: while they did not actually stand up on the approach of a non-learned old person, they showed their respect in other ways. Raba, for instance, was very courteous to them in conversation, and sent his servants to give them any help they required; while Abaye respectfully shook them by the hand.

And that is the law. "It is a positive commandment to rise before every wise person, even if he is not old, but a wise youngster; and even if he is not one's teacher – as long as he is superior in wisdom and one can learn from him. It is also a commandment to rise before the hoar-headed, i.e. one aged seventy (and over), even if he is an ignoramus – unless he is a wicked person." But scholarship is Judaism's most cherished treasure, even be it that of non-Jewish savants, as RM acknowledges:

Commenting on the method of calculating the time of the appearance of the new moon, he declares: "We know all this from the books of the wise men of Greece . . . and whenever conclusions are all clear, proven, and cannot be doubted, it matters not whether they are arrived at by the Prophets or the wise men of other nations." For this reason the Talmudic Sages formulated a blessing to be recited "on seeing the sages of other nations" (SPB 389).

There are others who, though retaining but a soupcon of their eminence in Temple times, still merit being honoured by their fellow-Jews. I refer to *kohanim* and Levites, whose status and obligations will be considered in chapter thirty three – because *you* might be one or the other, and will want to know that your duties as such towards G–d and your fellow-Jews of the other 'tribes' are.

As far as those 'ordinary' Israelites are concerned, the only duty left them is the commandment: "And thou shalt sanctify him (a *kohen*), for he offereth the bread of thy G–d" – a duty that still holds sway, though he no longer serves in the Temple. We observe it by always "calling a *kohen* to the reading of the Torah first (and a Levite after him);" and, "if he is a learned man, to give him the honour of leading in the recital of *Birkat Hamazon*".

56.   "REMEMBER WHAT AMALEK DID TO YOU . . ."

Section 9. A very different kind of consideration has constantly to be given to this type of person, the Amalek type. "Ever remember what Amalek did unto thee by the way as you came out of Egypt," the Eternal warns and commands; "How he met thee by the way and smote the hindmost of thee, all that were enfeebled in thy rear, when thou wast faint and weary, and 'he' feared not G–d." These desert-tribe 'warriors' lay in wait, ready to pick off the weak and weary among the freed slaves – and they were blood-cousins of the Israelites, descendants of Amalek, "the grandson of Esau"!

But the biter was bitten when, at the command of Moses, Joshua assembled *his* warriors and "discomfited Amalek and his people with the edge of the sword." Why did G–d, Who had protected them in Egypt, fought for them at the Red Sea, allow this to happen? The above phrase rendered 'and *he* did not fear G–d' can also mean 'and *you* . . .': it is there-suggested "that this is indeed what it means – it was the *Israelites* who did not fear G–d", for they had just questioned "Is the Eternal among us, or not?"; and so He showed them that He *was*, in answer to Moses' prayer.

Another suggestion there is that it was not an armed attack that Amalek made, but a spiritual one: they secretely crept into the Israelite camp "under cover of the protective pillar of cloud and stole souls from among Israel" – and that can happen anywhere, at any time, more so today than there in the wilderness, when the Jew is religiously weak and unwary. And so the positive commandment is reinforced by the negative one:

57. "DO NOT FORGET!"

These are the last words in the source-text, stressing that we must take steps not to forget this danger; and we fulfil both commandments formally by reading this text as a special Maftir on the Shabbat before Purim, because Haman, the villain of that story, was an "Agagite", a descendant of Agag, king of the Amalekites in the days of king Saul.

But we must *ever* remember, and *never* forget, that unless we are strong in our faith, knowledgeable about it, and remain within the camp of Israel, Amalek in many guises stalks about to entrap – which is why I placed commandments 4 and 5 among the 'constants' which form the uprights of our ladder, always to be grasped firmly.

Finally, a possible answer to the question left unanswered in the earlier part of this chapter.

Section 10.   **The Remaining Question**

Could and Israelites have 'converted' to Egyptian idolatry during their long sojourn there? The brief answer is – probably yes, since for almost a century, "from their going down to Egypt until the death of Levi", they were favourably treated by their host; and they were residentially so intermingled with the majority population that the Eternal had to "pass over the houses of the Israelites" when He plagued the Egyptians. If subsequent history is any guide, there must have been many who defected from the faith of their forefathers in such circumstances.

Indeed, it is suggested that "only one in five of the Israelites left Egypt, those who refused to do so having 'died' during the plague of darkness" — a spiritual death, perhaps? But the one-fifth *did* leave, and we are their descendants "My servant, Israel, in whom I will be glorified"! May He so be for ever, by *you*!

Section	**Notes**
1	Deuter. 14.29; Psalms 128.2; Deuter. 15.7–11; Ibid v. 4; Ibid 29.21ff.; Ibid 23.21; Y. Shimoni 168.
2	On Exodus 22.20; B. Metsia 59b; on Levit. 19.33 & 16.29; Levit. 19.34; Deuter. 26.13; e.g. Exodus 12.48; e.g. Levit. 16.29; Deuter. 31.12; Ibid 14.21; Exodus 20.10.
3	Levit. 19.34; Numbers 15.15–16; Tanchuma Lech-lecha 6.
4	Pesachim 87b; Mechilta on Exodus 17.16; Genesis 12.5; MR. Genesis 84.4; Yevamot 109b; B. Metsia 59b; Shabbat 33b; Eccles. 10.20; Mechilta on Exodus 22.20; Deuter. 10.18.
5	Deuter. 10.19; B. Metsia 59b; Exodus 22.20; Ibid 23.9; Ibid 13.8; Deuter. 6.23; as note 3 here; B. Metsia 58b; Exodus 16.3.
6	Levit. 26.17; B. Metsia 58b.
7	Exodus 22.21; Megillah 13a; Yad. De'ot 6.10.
8	Levit. 19.32; Kiddushin 32b; Job 12.12; Y. De'ah 244.1; Yad. Kiddush Hachodesh 17.24; Berachot 58a; Levit. 21.8; Or. Ch. 135.3; Ibid 201.2.
9	Deuter. 25.17–19; Genesis 36.12; Exodus 17.8–12; Mechilta on last note; Esther 3.1 and I. Samuel chap. 15.
10	Rashi on Exodus 6.16 and Sifse Chanchamim note thereon; Exodus 12.27; Mechilta on Exodus 13.18.

Twenty-Two

THE END OF THE DAY

Section 1. School over, you will most probably, after bidding a courteous farewell to your teacher(s), wend your way home, towards the Jewish end of the day at nightfall. How much of that day remains, depends on the season of the year: in mid-summer, it can be six hours or more; while in the depths of winter, it can be less than one hour. And these variations will affect the timing of your fulfilment of the last third of the only Torah commandment to be considered in this chapter – reciting the Afternoon Service.

This we shall presently do, at length and in depth: not only because the brevity of that Service provides a relevant opportunity to discuss its origin and main part, the *Amidah*, at greater leisure; but also because, in a way, it is the most important yet most liable to be neglected, Service of the day. To adapt a rabbinic saying regarding all the blessings we make, "it is the final prayer that is decisive": and this is the last Prayer of every day of the year (except Yom Kippur).

And not only will we, with this one-third-of-a-commandment complete a Jewish day, but you will have learnt how Jewishly to live five-sixths, more or less, of your teenage years – all the six working days of most weeks, only excepting those with Festive days; for the one day we have been spending together is a pattern for them all – except the last hour or two of Fridays, as we shall see.

True it is that Sunday is the official day of rest in the nominally Christian countries in which most of us live, and you therefore do not attend school etc. on that day – though the law of the country permits Jews who observe *their* Shabbat, to work on Sunday. How *you* occupy yourself on Sundays depends on how preciously you value every passing hour: but your religious duties are then no different to those on the other working days.

179

Section 2.   **The Afternoon Service: Minchah**
As explained in chapter eleven, the Morning and Afternoon Services
were instituted to be said at the time when the two daily sacrifices
were offered in the Temple. Concerning these the Torah ordains:
"The one lamb thou shalt offer in the morning, and the other lamb
thou shalt offer at 'dusk' (Hebrew: *bain ha-arbayim*); and a tenth part
of an *ephah* of fine flour for a meal-offering (Hebrew: *minchah*),
mingled with the fourth part of a *hin* of beaten oil." The *minchah*,
then, was not the sacrifice itself, but a meal-offering which accompanied it – both in the morning and 'at dusk'. How, then, came the
name Minchah to be applied to the Afternoon Service in particular?

From the dramatic challenge issued by Elijah to the 450 prophets of
Baal on mount Carmel to see whether their god or his true G–d would
accept a sacrifice by consuming it with fire from heaven. "They called
on the name of Baal from morning to noon, saying: 'O Baal, answer
us!' But there was no voice, nor any that answered." So they
continued dancing and gashing themselves with swords and spears
till the blood gushed out 'until the time of the offering of the
minchah'" – without any success, naturally.

Then, at that precise time, "at the time of the *minchah* offering,"
Elijah prayed to the G–d of Abraham, Isaac and Israel to hear him:
"And the fire of the Eternal fell, and consumed the burnt offering . . .
and all the people fell on their faces and said: 'The Eternal, *He* is G–d,
the Eternal, *He* is G–d!'"

Elijah must have been praying all day, if only to counter the
frenzied outpourings of the false prophets – but he was not answered
until "the time of the *minchah* offering", thus giving that name to the
Afternoon Service. On the strength of this R. Huna said: "One should
always take special care about reciting Minchah; for the Prophet
Elijah's prayer was answered at that time." Another reason for being
very careful about Minchah will be given later.

Section 3.   **The Time For Minchah**
But when *was* "the time of the *minchah* offering"? According to the
Torah it is *bain ha-arbayim*, which is variously translated "at dusk"
"at eventide" and even just "evening". But what do these terms mean,
precisely? For you will surely want to pray at the precise time! Let us
revert to the original Hebrew – as you *always* should – and try to find
out what *it* means: it should not be very hard for you.

You know that *erev* means 'evening'; *arbayim* means 'two evenings', since *-ayim* is a dual suffix; and *bain* means 'between'. The
whole phrase, therefore, means "between the two evenings". What
are they? Explains Rashi: "Between the beginning of the seventh hour

(noon), 'when the shadows of the evening begin to stretch out', and the end of sunset at night-time" – between noon and starlight.

However the Sages base their calculation on the belief that "during the second half of the sixth hour and the first half of the seventh hour the sun stands over the head of all people": i.e. between 11.30 a.m. and 12.30 p.m. the sun is more-or-less stationary – or rather the 'shadows of evening' do not begin to show until the latter time. We will see the significance of this later.

But for the purpose of deciding the exact time for the afternoon sacrifice, the two 'evenings' were considered to be noon and 6 p.m. – in an ideal-length day-time of twelve hours. All the preparations of the sacrifice took one hour, and these were undertaken from 2.30 p.m. to 3.30 p.m., exactly *between two evenings*, each of two-and-a-half hours. The later evening was divided into two halves, each being called a *plag-haminchah*, a 'half-minchah', though the term is now usually employed for the time-division between them, that is, 4.45 p.m.

In the Talmud there is a discussion between the Sages generally and R. Yehudah as to how long the sacrifice took to be offered and consumed: the former maintain it lasted the whole evening until darkness fell, and therefore we can recite Minchah until then; while R. Yehudah said that the offering was completed by the *plaghaminchah*, by which time Minchah must have been recited. The argument was not resolved, and it was therefore ruled "if one follows the one he is right, and if one follows the other he is right".

Section 4.   **Special Circumstances**

So, as with Shacharit, we have three possible times for reciting Minchah: the ideal time, the moment it is possible, so that it cannot get 'sour' – exactly at two-and-a-half hours before nightfall; any time from then onwards until the *plag-haminchah*; even after that division, until nightfall – i.e. "about twelve minutes before the stars appear."

However, there was one day in the year when the afternoon sacrifice preparations commenced an hour earlier, at 1.30 p.m. and, when that day fell on a Friday, as early as 12.30 p.m. That day was "the eve of Passover," when every head of a family had to "slaughter the paschal lamb" also *bain ha-arbayim*. You will remember the general rule that "whatever is performed more frequently takes precedence over what is done less frequently: and therefore the daily sacrifice had to be offered before the once-a-year paschal lamb".

The reason for these earlier times is explained as follows: the proper time for offering the afternoon sacrifice should have been as soon as *bain ha-arbayim* beings, at 12.30 p.m. *every* day of the year, in accordance with the principle "when a *mitzvah* comes your way, do not let it get *chametz*" – do it immediately. However the Torah itself legislates that the fat of the private individuals' offerings, or which there could be many any day, had to be placed on the altar between the morning and afternoon sacrifices. Therefore the latter's preparation was delayed for two hours.

On Passover eve, however, when *all* the people had to prepare their paschal lamb offerings – and all the other requirements of the Festival – after the daily afternoon sacrifice, this was brought forward one hour, to give them more time. But when that eve was a Friday, which meant that they would have to *roast* the paschal lamb as well before the Shabbat commenced, since cooking is forbidden on Shabbat, the afternoon sacrifice was offered at its earliest possible time, namely 12.30 p.m., to allow for this.

Because this reversal to 'proper' time occurred only on an average of once every three years, the Sages allowed the Minchah Service to be said from 12.30 p.m. onwards on *any* day of the year – but only in special circumstances. Two examples of such circumstances are given: "when you have an opportunity to recite Minchah with a congregation at the earlier hour, which you will not have later; or when you will be setting out on a journey about that time, and will not reach your destination before nightfall."

Though there are some authorities who permit the recital of Minchah from this earliest time onwards in *any* circumstances, the consensus of opinion is that it should be recited at the time when the afternoon sacrifice was offered all the year round, according to R. Yehudah – between 3.30 and 4.45 p.m., in a twelve-hour day.

Section 5.   **The Halachic Hour**

That last qualification, "in a twelve-hour day" is very important. In Western countries, unlike the Middle East, such days are very few – just a week or two in early Spring and late Autumn or Fall, in which times an 'hour' is a twelfth part of daytime, and contains sixty minutes. But for halachic purposes, an 'hour' is *always* a twelfth part of any day, be it long or short. Thus in midwinter, when there are only about nine hours of daylight, a halachic hour can be forty-five minutes; and in midsummer an 'hour' can be as long as one hundred minutes.

As twice stressed, the time for Minchah given above refer only to days consisting of exactly twelve hours – and to Greenwich Mean Time. Throughout most of the year, therefore, the halachic hour has to be calculated; and, during the six months of artificial daylight saving adjustment, allowance has to be made for that as well. To give but one example, taking both these factors into consideration: in midsummer, the time for "Minchah Gedolah" – the earliest, 'proper' time, called the 'big Minchah' – is almost 2.00 p.m. (and not 12.30 p.m.); and that for "Minchah Ketanah" – the actual time, called "little Minchah" – 6.15 p.m. (rather than 4.45 p.m.).

To obviate the necessity of making all these calculations and adjustments by the individual, most large Jewish communities publish calendars, prepared by the local religious authorities – for the halachic times vary in different parts of the country, dependent on local latitude. These calendars give the weekly variations in the times for all Services, the beginning and ending of Shabbatot and Festival – and much more useful information. You should obtain one, and consult it regularly.

There is a Yiddish saying "Minchah is a *ganev* (thief)" – because the time for its recital, especially in winter, can steal in and out without your realising it – which is the second reason I promised to give you for having to be very careful with this Service. "Everyone knows when to say Shacharit – as soon as he gets up in the morning, and before becoming involved in his daily affairs. Everyone knows when to say Arvit – when he arrives home after his daily occupations (or before going to bed). But Minchah has to be said in the middle of the day, while still pre-occupied with other matters. Therefore he should make a point of detaching himself from whatever he is doing, and recite Minchah at its proper time: and the reward of one who does so is great indeed."

Take, for instance, an average day in the few weeks in midwinter when Minchah Gedolah is around 12.30 p.m. Minchah Ketanah 2.15 p.m. Plag-Haminchah 3.00 p.m. and the latest possible time 4.30 p.m. What should you do then? It all depends on when your afternoon session at school ends, and how soon you can get home. The ideal time for Minchah is between 2.30 p.m. and 3.00 p.m. when you will probably be at your lessons! So what to do?

If, of course, you are fortunate enough to attend a Jewish school or college, there is no problem: suitable arrangements will be made. If not, you *may* pluck up sufficient courage to ask your teacher for a ten-minute break – or you may *have* such a break between lessons – and it is very probable even a non-Jewish master will be sympathetic, having had the reason for your request explained to him.

If not, then if you can rush home to arrive in comfortable time before 4.30 p.m. you can leave Minchah until then – but make sure you recite it the moment you arrive. Or, and I think preferably, you can find a quiet corner and recite Minchah during your lunch hour, at 12.30 p.m. or after. Whatever you do, organise *something*! Don't let the 'thief' steal away, having robbed you of this most important final third of the Torah commandment to pray!

Section 6.   **The Shortest Service**
You will have gathered from the size of the break I have suggested you should ask for, that Minchah is the shortest Service of the day – primarily because there is no afternoon *Shema*, and therefore no 'sandwich' of blessings. It consists of Psalm 145, introduced by two verses, and concluded with a third, each from different Psalms; the *Amidah*; Confession – on most days; and *Aleinu.*

The introductory and concluding verses added to *Tehillah le-David*, as Psalm 145 is called in the Talmud, are interesting. The first two both begin with the word *Ashrei*, the second containing it a third time, "to remind us – after having said it twice during the Morning Service" – that "whoever recites *Tehillah le-David* three times daily, is sure to inherit the world to come." The first of the two, beginning "Happy are they that dwell (= sit) in Thy house . . ." was the basis upon which the pious men of old established their custom to sit for some time in silent contemplation before praying "in order to concentrate their minds upon their Father in heaven."

The concluding verse was "really added for the Shacharit recital in the *Pesukai d'zimra*" – in order to connect Psalm 145 with the other five Psalms which follow it, all of which begin and end with the word *Hallelujah*, with which this verse also ends; and it remained there on the second and third occasions in the day Psalm 145 is recited.

The rest of Minchah, like *Ashrei* – as this Psalm with its additional verses is popularly called, is a 'repeat' of parts of the Morning Service – but none of it should be treated as such! *Every* Service, throughout your life, should be recited with such devotion and enthusiasm as if it were the very first! There is much, much more for you to learn about *all* the Services, and particularly their centre-piece and climax, the *Amidah, the* Prayer. But you must study this for yourself, in the Shulchan Aruch and annotated Siddur, excellent English translations of which are available.

Section 7.   **What If You Miss A Service?**
What if, either through forgetfulness or in an emergency, you miss reciting one of the daily Services? This is the proper place to discuss this because, as mentioned above, Minchah is the one most likely to be missed. Let's say, for instance, that one winter day you intended getting home in ample time to recite Minchah, but detention was imposed upon your form – not, of course, because of anything *you* might have done!

The answer is you can make amends by "reciting the *Amidah* twice at the very next Service," at Arvit if you missed Minchah, at Shacharit if you missed Arvit, and at Minchah if you missed Shacharit. When this happens, it is the *second Amidah* with which amends are made, not the first – "though it has to be the same *Amidah* as the first," If, for example, you missed Minchah on Friday afternoon, you say the *Shabbat Amidah* twice at Arvit.

If, however, you deliberately miss a Service, the debt cannot be paid. To one who does this is referred the half-verse, "that which is crooked cannot be made straight". Nevertheless, the *Amidah* can be repeated at the next Service – but it is considered not as fulfilment of your duty (*chovah*), but as a gift (*nedavah*). We have here, once again, an analogy with the sacrifices.

There are many variations on this theme, and complications: so my advice to you is: never be forgetful; try to avoid, or overcome, emergencies; and never, never miss any Service deliberately – through sheer laziness or cussedness.

Section 8.   **Words Replace Sacrifices**

We have now seen how, in accordance with the Prophet's advice: "Take with you *words*, and return to the Eternal; say unto Him: 'Forgive all iniquity, and accept that which is good, *so we will render for bullocks the offering of our lips*'" – we daily recite the *Amidah* three times, in place of the two daily Temple sacrifices and the burning of the fats and surplus limbs at night.

As for "forgive all iniquity": most of the sacrifices were offered in atonement for sin, and they were not acceptable unless "they shall confess their sin which they have done . . .". Therefore in every (weekday) *Amidah* is included a plea for forgiveness of sin (SPB 103); and after the morning and afternoon *Amidah*, which correspond to the actual two daily sacrifices, we confess our sins (SPB 111), thus "rendering for bullocks the offering of our lips".

Whether, when the Temple is rebuilt, as it surely will be sometime – and may it be speedily in our days! – sacrifices will again be offered there, is a moot point. Speaking of the Messianic Era, Isaiah says: "Them will I bring to My holy mountain, and make them joyful in My House of Prayer; their burnt-offerings and their sacrifices shall be acceptable upon Mine altar; for My House shall be called a House of Prayer for all peoples, saith the Eternal G–d Who gathereth the dispersed of Israel."

However, referring to the same Era, the very last of the Prophets foretells: "Then shall the offering (*minchah*) of Judah and Jerusalem be pleasant unto the Eternal, as in the days of old, and as in the ancient years" – and though *Minchah* can refer to the sacrifice itself, as we have seen, its real meaning is a *meal*-offering, i.e. a cake of fine flour and oil.

Section 9.   **Will Sacrifices Return?**

The following statement was reported, and presumably endorsed, by three outstanding Sages, in the name of R. Menachem of Gallia: "In the Time to Come all the offerings will be abolished, but the thanks (*todah*) offering will never be abolished": and he supports this with king David's promise that, in fulfilment of the vows he makes when in distress, "I will render thanks-offerings (*todot*), O G–d, unto Thee," the assumption being, *only* such, and no other (sin) offerings.

It was certainly not on the strength of the beautiful, joy-inspiring Messianic chapter thirty-three in his book that the Prophet Jeremiah – quite unfairly, in my opinion – gave the word 'jeremiad', meaning 'a tale of grief', to the English language! Therein he says (v. 11), "When I cause the captivity of the land to return as at the first, saith the Eternal . . . (there will be heard) the voice of them that say:

'Give thanks to the Lord of hosts, for the Eternal is good, for His loving kindness endureth for ever' – even of them that bring offerings of thanksgiving (*todah*) to the House of the Eternal": and again, presumably such and no other kinds of sacrifices.

In an earlier, similarly optimistic chapter, the 'gloomy' Prophet transmits: "Behold the days come, saith the Eternal, when I will make a new covenant with the house of Israel . . . I will put My Torah in their inwards parts . . . and they will all know Me . . . for I will forgive their iniquity, and their sin will I remember no more" – which means that there will be no call for sin-offerings in that blissful Era, but just those of thanksgiving!

The thanksgiving offering (*todah*) was also called "a peace-offering (*shelamim*)." Why? asks the Midrash, and it answers: "Because it made *shalom* between all! The blood, fat, etc. were offered on the altar to G–d, a select portion went to the priest for his services, and the flesh and hide were taken home by the offerer." This is really not much different from what happens today when we have *kasher* meat: the blood is drawn out completely, the butcher removes the forbidden fats, etc., and we have the flesh. As for the priest's share, we invite the poor to partake of it with us, or supply their needs, either directly or through charitable institutions.

Section 10.   **But For The Present . . .**

All this conjecture, however, is about the future, when the Temple is rebuilt, when the Messiah comes and instructs us as to the will of

G–d regarding the sacrifices. For the present, we have only prayer to link us in communion with G–d, directly, and not through any intermediary.

As the priests ascend the Ark steps on Festivals to bless us – the present ceremony being but a pale reflection of that most impressive event in the Temple, the congregation say (SPB 324) a prayer which begins with: "And may our entreaty before Thee be as sweet as burnt offering and as sacrifice." And your observance of the commandment to pray daily – and that of all the others that come your way, or you can make come your way, should be so conscientious that it and they are acceptable "as a sweet savour to the Eternal".

And so I leave you, temporarily, on a Friday afternoon, back at home, with an hour or two in hand before the commencement of Shabbat, so that you can prepare to receive the holy day in the way it should be, as will be described in the next chapters. And you should have such a period of preparation *every* Friday, even in winter: for the law of the country allows you, at your parents' request, to be released earlier, in order to make such preparations.

It is with Shabbat and the Festivals, the holy days of G–d and the Jew, that the next few chapters will be dealing. Not that we have exhausted all the commandments between man and his neighbour. Indeed, most of those on the second tablet of "The Ten Commandments" still remain to be considered. But these are less likely to come your way, surprisingly enough, than those already included; while one of them, in that particular context, would only be violated by a real villain – as we shall see!

We have now ascended more than half way up the ninety rungs of the ladder which you, an average, non-working, unmarried teenage student, can possibly climb towards the summit of the mountain of G–d – and, of course, the *first* ninety rungs for any more adult Jew or Jewess.

Perhaps before Shabbat begins, you will find time to ascend the next three rungs, the three Torah commandments governing the observance of Shabbat, and then, as befits that day, rest on the sixtieth rung, and leisurely study their development in the next two chapters. In the meantime, Shabbat Shalom to you!

(Note. Do not let the numbering of the commandments confuse you! They include the ten 'constants' making up the uprights of our ladder!)

Section	**Notes**
1	Berachot 12a.
2	Numbers 28.4–5; I. Kings 18.16–29; Berachot 6b.

3   Exodus 29.39; Jeremiah 6.4; Pesachim 94a; Ibid 58a; Berachot 26b.

4   MB. 233 note 8; Pesachim 58a; Exodus 29.39; Levit. 6.5; MB. 233 note 1.

5   Aruch Hashulchan Or. Ch. 232.2.

6   Siddur Avodat Yisrael; Berachot 4b; Psalms 84.5; Berachot 32b; Ibid 30b; Psalms 115.18; as note 1.

7   Berachot 26a–b; Or. Ch. 108.9; Eccles. 1.15.

8   Hosea 14.3; Numbers 5.7–8; Isaiah 56.7–8; Malachi 3.4.

9   MR. Levit. 27.12; Psalms 56.13; Jeremiah 31.31–33; Levit. 7.11–12; Sifra on Levit. 3.1.

Twenty-Three

THE SHABBAT: GUARD IT!

Section 1. From its very first occurrence at the creation of the universe, the seventh day of the week was blessed and sanctified by G–d because – so reads the accepted English translation, "in it He 'rested' (Hebrew: *shavat*) from all His work (*melachah*) which G–d 'in creating had made' (literally: 'had created to do')". The significance of the italicised and quoted words, and the changes they necessitate in the accepted translation, will appear in the course of this and the following chapter.

The blessed and sanctified seventh day – not yet given a name, remained so observed by G–d alone for almost 2,000 years, "until the forty-eight year of Abraham," the first person to convince himself through his own powers of reasoning that there was a G–d in heaven. He thereafter, employing those G–d–given faculties to the full, "kept My charge, My commandments, My statutes and My laws", presumably including the sanctity of Shabbat, known since Adam's days.

The sanctification of the seventh day was thenceforth undoubtedly transmitted from generation to generation. The Midrash relates that when Moses first emerged from the royal palace in which he had been reared, "and went out unto his brethren, and looked upon their burdens" – that they were forced to labour a seven-day week; he returned to Pharaoh and said: "If one has a slave and does not give him rest one day in the week, he will die – as will your slaves, if you do not give them one day's rest in the week." And Pharaoh replied: "Go, and do with them as thou sayest."

Thus did the then favoured royal prince Moses gain the concession to re-institute the seventh day as one of rest (*menuchah*) for his toiling brethren: and this is one of the reasons for our saying in the morning *Amidah* of that day (SPB 188), "Moses rejoiced in the gift of his portion" – this concession from Pharaoh. But when, some sixty years later, he returned from Sinai as G–d's emissary demanding "Let My people go!", not only did the obstinate Pharaoh refuse that demand, but he withdrew that concession.

Section 2.   **First Mention Of "Shabbat"**

The word "Shabbat" as the name of the seventh day of the week first occurs in the story of the gift of manna at a place called Marah. The children of Israel were told to gather one *omer* – 3.89 litres – for each person in the family. Some gathered what they thought to be a lot more than this – the greedy ones; and the weaker ones what they imagined to be less. But when they came to measure what they had gathered, they discovered that there was exactly an omer, no more and no less, for everybody!

When, however, they returned from collecting it on the *sixth* day, they found that there were *two omers* for each, and they asked Moses the reason for this. He replied: "This is that which the Eternal hath spoken: tomorrow is *shabbaton*, a holy *Shabbat* unto the Eternal. Bake that which you will bake, and seethe that which you will seethe; and all that remaineth over, lay up for you to be kept until the morning." And on the morrow, the Shabbat, he said to them: "Eat that today, for today is a Shabbat unto the Eternal; today you will not find it in the field." (The greedy tried – but they found none!)

But the commandment regarding the general commandment for the full observance of Shabbat came directly from G–d in the "Fourth" of "The Ten Commandments". These occur twice in the Torah: first in Exodus, at the time when they were actually divinely uttered; and then, some forty years later, when Moses repeated them in his farewell oration to his flock.

There are variations in the two texts, some slight, some major: indeed RM maintains that the second text contains a commandment *extra* to those given in the first – as we shall see in chapter thirty-two. Each of these variations, however slight, has a reason which will be explained in due course: but, essentially, the second text is a re-statement of the first. One of them I must mention and explain before we study the Shabbat commandments, for it will help to make clear why consideration of the Shabbat is being divided into three chapters.

Section 3.   ***Zachor*** **And** ***Shamor***

The very first word in each text of the "Fourth Commandment" is different: in the first, it is *zachor*, 'remember' (to do what you must); and in the second 'observe' or rather 'guard' (against doing what you must not). In other words: the latter word instructs us to refrain from violating the negative commandments concerning Shabbat, while the former enjoins us to remember and do all the positive actions which pertain to its proper observance.

They are, in fact, two sides of the same coin – to such an extent that the Sages say the two words were divinely "pronounced in a single utterance – an utterance which the (human) mouth cannot utter, nor the ear hear" – a uniqueness incorporated in the beautiful poem chanted (SPB 146) in the Shabbat Inauguration Service. The holiness of the seventh day cannot possibly be experienced and really enjoyed without the full observance of both *zachor* and *shamor*. It is with the latter that this chapter will deal, and the former in the next – though, for completeness sake, all the Torah commandments governing the observance of Shabbat will be stated here. Chapter twenty-five deals with the duty to sanctify the Shabbat.

You will be surprised, no doubt, to learn that there are only three of them definitely applicable today. RM enters a fourth in his list of the 613 commandments, but RN, followed by most of the later authorities, consider it to be only a rabbinical prohibition. Nevertheless, I am going to cite it, unnumbered, because rabbinic law is, you will remember, also law, and this one may conceivably apply to you sometime.

The six sources of these four commandments will now be quoted, followed by mention of three other passages which will help us the better to understand the full significance of the Torah commandments – all nine numbered with Roman numerals. Then, after giving a few essential definitions, all will be brought together to give a complete picture as to what is – and is not – forbidden on Shabbat.

58.   SANCTIFY THE SHABBAT DAY

Section 4. This commandment occurs in both texts of the "Fourth Commandment", and apart from the already-mentioned difference in the first word of each, the reasons given for observing the sanctity of Shabbat also differ. They read:

(i)   "Remember the Shabbat day to sanctify it. Six days shalt thou labour and do all thy 'work'; but the seventh day is a Shabbat unto the Eternal thy G–d . . . For in six days did G–d make the heavens and the earth, the sea, and all that is in them, and 'rested' on the seventh day: wherefore the Eternal blessed the Shabbat day and made it holy".

(ii)   "Guard the Shabbat day to sanctify it, as the Eternal thy G–d commanded thee. Six days shalt thou labour, and do all thy 'work'; but the seventh day is a Shabbat unto the Eternal thy G–d . . . in order that thy man-servant and maid-servant may rest as well as thou – that

thou shouldst remember that thou wast a servant in the land of Egypt,
and the Eternal thy G–d brought thee out thence with a mighty hand
and with an outstretched arm; therefore the Eternal thy G–d hath
commanded thee to observe the Shabbat day."

59.   DO NO 'WORK' ON SHABBAT

This commandment is derived from the sections omitted from the
above positive commandment. Again, note the variations:

(iii)   On Shabbat "thou shalt do no manner of 'work', thou, nor
thy son, nor thy daughter, nor thy man-servant, nor thy maid-servant,
nor thy cattle, nor thy *ger* within thy gates."

(iv)   On Shabbat "thou shall do no manner of 'work', thou, nor
thy son, nor thy daughter, nor thy man-servant, nor thy maid-servant,
nor thine ox, nor thine ass, nor any of thy animals, nor thy *ger* that is
within thy gates."

60.   CEASE FROM 'WORK' ON SHABBAT

(v)   "Six days shalt thou do thy 'work', but on the seventh day
thou shalt cease; that thine ox and thine ass may have rest, and the
son of thy handmaid and the *ger* may be refreshed." This is by no
means a repetition of the previous commandment, but adds much
new information, as will be shown.

Do Not Overstep The Shabbat Boundary

(vi)   "See that the Eternal hath given you the Shabbat; therefore
He giveth you on the sixth day bread of two days. Stay you every man
in his place: let no man go out of his place on the seventh day." This
was stated after some of the greedy ones had gone out to gather
manna on the Shabbat, despite being told that there would be none
on that day.

Rashi on this verse sums up the general consensus that this was a
one-time commandment to the manna gatherers, but that the Sages
"extended it for all-time," restricting movement outside the place we
live in, be it village, town or city, further than the "Shabbat limit"
(*techum Shabbat*), variously calculated between 1.14 and 1.68
kilometres – about 1¼ miles. (Further reference to this enactment will
be made later in this chapter.)

Section 5.   **The Sanctuary In The Wilderness**
After detailing the donations that would be requested from the
children of Israel, the nature of the Sanctuary and its furnishing, and

the vestments of the priests towards which their contributions would be dedicated – but before the work was about to commence, Moses warned them that, even in their enthusiasm to see the divine Dwelling-Place in their midst as soon as possible:

(vii) "Six days shall 'work' be done, but on the seventh day there shall be to you a holy day, a 'Shabbat of solemn rest' (Hebrew: *Shabbat shabbaton*) to the Eternal: whosoever doeth any 'work' therein shall be put to death" – even in the course of building the Sanctuary!

With such liberality, promptness and enthusiasm did the people present their gifts that, after but a few days, the wise men who were to do the work came to Moses and said: "The people bring much more than enough for the 'service' of the 'work' which the Eternal commanded to do" – and he had to stop them bringing any more gifts!

When the Sanctuary and all its furniture and utensils were completed, we are told: "And Moses saw all the 'work', and behold they had done it; as the Eternal had commanded, even so had they done it: and Moses blessed them."

(viii) It was on G–d's instruction that Moses fore-warned the people not to occupy themselves with the building of His Sanctuary on the Shabbat, saying to him: "And speak thou unto the children of Israel, saying: 'But My Shabbatot you shall guard, for it is a sign between Me and you throughout your generations 'that ye may know' that I am the Eternal Who sanctify you. . . . Six days shall 'work' be done; but on the seventh day is 'a Shabbat of solemn rest', holy to the Eternal . . .'".

Then follow the two well-known verses which are part of the central blessing in the Shabbat morning *Amidah*: "And the children of Israel shall guard the Shabbat, to observe the Shabbat throughout their generations, a perpetual covenant. It is a sign between Me and the children of Israel: for in six days the Eternal made heaven and earth, and on the seventh day He ceased from work and 'rested'."

(ix) Finally, when giving a complete calendar of all "the appointed seasons of the Eternal which you shall proclaim as holy 'convocations'", Moses heads the list with: "Six days shall 'work' be done, but on the seventh day is a *Shabbat shabbaton*, a holy 'convocation'; you shall do no manner of 'work': it is a Shabbat unto the Eternal in all your dwellings."

Section 6.　　　Weaving Them All Together

Much in these nine quotations might have seemed monotonous and repetitive reading to you – but let me assure you that they really are not. Each contains a different phrase, word, grammatical form or nuance which adds something new to our full appreciation of what the Shabbat means, why it holds such a central place, in Jewish life. And now, to define, elucidate, and put all the pieces together. This process, will involve, both in this chapter and the next, reference to one or more of these nine passages – so use a bookmark!

You will have noticed that wherever the word 'work' has occurred I have put it in inverted commas. This is because there are three Hebrew words, each with a different significance, which are translated 'work': and we must know which of them is or are forbidden on Shabbat. Of course, it may be all three, in which case it would make no practical difference to our guarding the Shabbat – but *is* it all three? And even if it is, it is good to know what the different kinds of 'work' are – so here goes!

(a) *Avodah*: This derives from the verb *la-avod*, and we can gather what kind of work it connotes from the very first three times it is used in the Torah. Before Adam was created "there was not a man to till (*la-avod*) the ground; after he was created, G–d "put him in the garden of Eden to till it and to guard it"; and after he sinned, in order to serve his punishment "by the sweat of thy face shalt thou eat bread", he was "sent forth from the garden of Eden to till (*la-avod*) the ground from whence he was taken."

Many other such instances can be cited to prove that the derived noun *avodah* almost invariably means 'labour' – and hard labour at that. The fact that another noun derived from the same verb, *eved*, means a 'slave' or a 'bondsman' provides, I think, decisive proof. In all the passages above, *avodah* occurs only in (vii), where it is translated 'service' – and then not in connection with Shabbat; while the verb occurs in the phrase in (i) and (ii), "six days shalt thou labour (*ta-avod*) and do all thy 'work'".

That last quoted verse continues: "but the seventh day is a Shabbat . . . on it thou shalt do no manner of 'work'" – and that last word in the Hebrew is not *avodah*, as we shall soon see. Therefore, believe it or not, physical exertion is nowhere explicitly forbidden in the Torah on Shabbat. If you enjoy weight-lifting, for instance, or an arduous game of tennis or football in a private, enclosed garden or yard, you may indulge in them – but see qualifications in the next chapter.

(b) *Ma'aseh*: this refers to any kind of work, or occupation pursued as a means of earning a livelihood, usually a less laborious one than *avodah*. The name Noach – note this well for future reference – means 'rest': and he was so called because "this one shall give us rest in our work (*ma'asenu*) and in the toil of our hands" – by

his reputed invention of the plough, thus lightening the *avodah* of tilling with even more primitive tools.

When Joseph introduced his brethren to Pharaoh, the latter asked them "What is your occupation (*ma'asaichem*)?". And on a number of occasions, Moses promises that obedience to G–d's will result in His "blessing all the work (*ma'aseh*) of your hands" – whatever your occupation may be.

This is the word used in (v) which tells us of one kind of work, our customary weekday occupation, from which we must cease on Shabbat. "Six days you may strive to earn a livelihood," it could be paraphrased, "but on the seventh, cease" – even to think about it! However, on *all* the other many occasions when the Torah speaks of not doing "any manner of work", neither *avodah* nor *ma'aseh* is used but

(c) *Melachah*. What is *melachah*? It is the kind of 'work' from which G–d 'rested' after the Six Days of Creation – i.e. *creative* work: not, of course, making something out of nothing, as He did; but transmuting one thing into another, or uniting two things by means of a firm knot, or writing just two characters – be the 'work' as easy as saying "Let there be light"! For it was merely "with ten utterances that the world was created".

To take but two examples: what can be easier than switching on the electric light or the TV? Yet by doing so, you would be changing current into incandescence or picture – a *melachah*. It is not much more difficult to switch on the car ignition, and press just a little on the accelerator – and thereby performing two *melachot*: kindling fire, and transforming petrol into energy.

These examples show how foolish are those people who argue that, in those far-off biblical days, one had to labour to create fire by rubbing two stones together, and therefore it was then forbidden on Shabbat: but today, you just have to flick a switch, so it should be permitted! Nonsense! It has nothing to do with it!

Section 7. The Thirty-Nine (Main) *Melachot*

The Sages state that there are "thirty-nine principal (*avot* = 'fathers') melachot" which are forbidden on Shabbat, and the mishnah details them. They, in turn, have many *toladot* (generations, or children): and, in order to be fully aware of everything you must not do on the holy day, you should study them in a good English translation of the (abridged) *Shulchan Aruch* – which this book, I remind you once again, is not.

But here are just some of them which can very well tempt you, especially if you are a keen gardener! Digging, planting, picking flowers or fruit, and watering the lawn. Ladies may not bake or cook, sew or knit – nor, of course, may men! You may not kindle or extinguish any fire or light, write or erase any writing, cut your hair or nails, or carry anything from a private into a public place.

As regards the last mentioned, it is to this – carrying from private to public domain and vice versa – that RN, following one opinion in the Talmud, says (vi) above refers, and not to walking beyond the Shabbat boundary, as RM maintains. And even carrying on Shabbat is permitted when, as is the case in most residential areas in Israel, what is called an *Eruv* exists – a method whereby the last dwelling-places at every extreme of the town or area are 'joined together' by wiring etc., thus transforming the whole area into one big 'private domain'. There are few *eruvin* outside Israel, however.

Section 8.   **Who May Not Work?**
From now onwards, we can use the word work without quotation marks, keeping in mind all the time that by it we mean either any of the main *melachot* or their derivatives; or our usual weekday occupation – even school homework – unless it happens to be religious studies!

Who, then, may not work on Shabbat – who, first, is the "thou" in "thou shalt do no manner of work"? It refers, of course to every post-*Bar*mitzvah – but how about the post-*Bat*mitzvah? *Do* ladies have to guard against violating Shabbat? A silly question? You may momentarily think so – but think again, and you will realise that it is *not*! Why not?

Because Shabbat comes but once a week, and "Remember the Shabbat day to sanctify it" is therefore "a positive commandment limited by time, from observing which ladies are exempt". The question is not mine: it is argued about in the Talmud; and, on the strength of this general rule, Abaye actually opined that the Torah indeed exempts ladies, and that they are only obliged to sanctify Shabbat by rabbinical law! However, his regular debating partner, Raba, pointed out that there is also the negative commandment – from none of which are ladies exempt – 'Guard the Shabbat day to sanctify it'; and that "whoever has to 'guard' has also to 'remember' – and that is the law! So you are also included, young lady!

'Thy son and thy daughter' mentioned in the commandment must therefore refer to minor children, below Bar-Bat-Mitzvah age: that is, parents must train them from early age to observe Shabbat – a subject for my next volume, P.G.

'Thy man-servant and thy maid-servant' in the commandment apply to a class of servants which does not exist today, "*bnei-berit*," 'children of the covenant' — non-Jews who had undertaken to observe all the commandments ladies have to observe, including Shabbat. The *ger* in the commandment is the convert to Judaism, because of the qualification "that is in thy gates".

However, the *ger* referred to in (v) is a non-Jewish resident alien, and "the son of thy handmaid" is also non-Jewish. *You* have to cease pursuing your regular occupation (*ma'asecha*) on Shabbat, in order that *they* may be refreshed. What a wonderful religion Judaism is! How social-conscious and humanitarian!

All this is expected of us because of the reason given for the observance of Shabbat itself in (ii): "Remember! *you* were servants in the land of Egypt", and should therefore appreciate what it must have been like to work a seven-day week without respite, as did your fore-fathers before Moses obtained his concession from Pharaoh, and after it was withdrawn.

In (iii) we are told that "thy animals" must not work on Shabbat; in (v) "thine ox and thine ass" are singled out to be given rest; and in (iv) all of them are mentioned — "thine ox and thine ass and all thy animals". From these variations it is deduced that "just as ox and ass — unclean as well as clean animals — are alike in the matter of Shabbat rest, so are all beasts and birds in your care". *All* are entitled to their rest on the seventh day.

And so if you have a cat or a dog — or both, they must also have their Shabbat rest and enjoyment. Referring to (v) the *Mechilta* comments: And should you say, "Very well, I'll tie them up in the stable or the house — that is not rest for them, but pain! Therefore you must let them roam around freely in the field" — and take your dog for a walk!

Section 9. **"Solemn" Indeed!**

The verb in this last-mentioned verse, 'and on the seventh day *tishbot*', everywhere translated "thou shalt **rest**", does not mean that at all, but, as I have rendered it, 'thou shalt *cease*'. This is proven decisively from its occurrence in the verse "And the manna ceased (*vayishbot*) on the morrow, after they had eaten of the produce of the Land; neither had the children of Israel manna any more; but they did eat of the fruit of the land of Canaan that year."

Therefore, as will be shown in the next chapter in greater detail, *yom ha-Shabbat* — the latter noun being derived from the verb 'to cease', does not mean a "day of rest" but a "day of cessation from work". This mis-translation is aggravated when, as in (vii), (viii) and (ix), the double-barrelled expression *shabbat shabbaton* is translated "a sabbath of solemn rest"!

If 'solemn', as my dictionary defines it, means 'grave, serious', or even "characterized by a serious and formal series of acts performed at a slow pace", then this translation completely misrepresents the very essence of Shabbat, which is 'A day of light and rejoicing for Israel', as we joyfully sing (SPB 172) at table on that day; a day on which "it is a *mitzvah* to *run* to – but not away from! – the Synagogue." Solemn, indeed! Slow pace, indeed!

The expression *shabbat shabbaton*, as such nominal and verbal repetitiveness always does idiomatically in Hebrew, is intended to emphasise the noun or verb, and therefore means 'a *complete* cessation' from any manner of work. It is applied *only* to Shabbat and Yom Kippur, the *only* days when such *complete* cessation from work is commanded – as distinct from all the other Festivals, on which *some* kinds of work are permitted, as we shall later see.

Section 10.   **A Bridge**
I have now given you sufficient – but not exhaustive – data, I think, to appreciate what the Prophet meant when he declared: "Happy is the man that doeth this . . . that guardeth the Shabbat from profaning it, and guardeth his hand from doing any evil."

For the purpose of *shamor*, this complete cessation from work, is to give full time and scope for *zachor*, the fulfilment of all the positive aspects of Shabbat, to which the Prophet refers when he later says, "And you shall call the Shabbat a delight, and the holy of the Eternal honourable."

In the next chapter we will see how honoured it is, and how delightful Shabbat can be. And I will conclude this one by relating a delightful story which will serve as a bridge between the two.

The Roman Emperor asked R. Yehoshua b. Chananyah: "Why does your Shabbat food have such a fragrant odour?". "Because," replied the Sage, "we have a certain seasoning called 'shabbat' which we put into it, and which gives it its flavour." To the Emperor's request, "Then please give us some of it", R. Yehoshua replied: "It only has its effect on those who observe the Shabbat; but to him who does not, it is of no use."

To savour Shabbat delight to the full, you must observe it to the full – both *shamor* and *zachor*!

Section   **Notes**
 1   Genesis 2.2; MR. Genesis 30.8; Genesis 26.5; Exodus 2.11; MR. Exodus 1.28; Ibid 5.18.
 2   Exodus 16.14–36.
 3   Shevuot 20b; see Chinuch 24.

4 Exodus 20.8–11; Deuter. 5.11–15; Exodus 23.12; Ibid 16.29; Eruvin 51a
   and 17b.
5 Exodus 35.2; Ibid 36.4–5; Ibid 39.43; Ibid 31.13ff; Levit. chapter 23.
6 Genesis 2.5; Ibid 2.15; Ibid 3.23; Ibid 5.29; Tanchuma Bereshit 11; Genesis
   47.3; e.g. Deuter. 28.12; Ethics 5.1.
7 Shabbat 73a.
8 Kiddushin 29a; Berachot 20b; as note 1; Mechilta on Exodus 20.10; B.
   Kama 54b.
9 Joshua 5.12; Or. Ch. 90.12; Levit. 23.32.
10 Isaiah 56.2; Ibid 58.13; Shabbat 119a.

Twenty-Four

THE SHABBAT: REMEMBER IT!

Section 1. In the last chapter we spoke about *shamor* – guarding against the violation of Shabbat; and in this one, as promised, we are going to see what *zachor* – positively remembering the weekly holy day, means. And here, for the first time, I have given these two divine words their true rendering – remember*ing* and guard*ing*: for this form of the verbs in Hebrew is not the imperative, but the gerund, a verbal noun, conveying the idea of continuous action.

Rashi compares them with "slaying oxen and killing sheep, eating flesh and drinking wine" – in which the same form of the verbs is used – descriptive of the citizens of Jerusalem's revelry while danger threatened from Assyria. And he says *zachor* means: "Set your heart on continuously remembering that Shabbat is approaching;" and as an example of how to do so, he cites R. Eleazar b. Chananya who said: "Remember it from Sunday onwards, so that should a choice item come your way at any time of the week – put it aside for Shabbat."

Shammai actually "ate on every day of his life in honour of Shabbat!" How so? If he found a choice item on Sunday, say, he put it away for Shabbat. But if he found a still better one on Monday, he put *that* aside for Shabbat, and ate the first – and so on. Thus he had Shabbat at heart every day of the week! His disciples therefore advised: From the first day of the week prepare for Shabbat.

We do this verbally as well. I have just mentioned "Sunday" and "Monday", day-names which derive, as do all the others, from idolatry. The Sages only speak of "the first day", the "second day", and so on; and at the end of each Morning Service we introduce the Psalm of the day "which the Levites used to say in the Temple (SPB 84ff) with: "today is the first, second, third . . . day towards Shabbat."

You can at least follow R. Eleazar's example: if, for instance, you

200

see a luscious (kasher) cake through the shop window, or some choice fruit or anything else which may not be available later in the week – buy it, and don't worry about the expense! For "the more you spend in honouring Shabbat (and the Festivals), the more He will give you back" – somehow!

Section 2.   **Preparations**

When the sixth day (Friday) dawns, greater urgency is required. The children of Israel were told that when they gathered the bread that God would rain down from heaven for them, "it shall come to pass on the sixth day that they shall prepare that which they shall bring in." The manna fell early in the morning, "and as the sun warmed, it melted." From this event R. Chisda drew the lesson for all time that "One should always rise early (on Friday morning) in order to make preparations for Shabbat."

You, also, can do so: one of the ways in which we honour Shabbat is to put on clean linen and our best clothes before it commences – *not* leaving it to the morning. Before you go to school on Friday, you should make sure these will be ready for you when you arrive home. If you still have time to spare after *Shacharit*, breakfast and *Birkat Hamazon* – as you should have, it you had the coming Shabbat at heart on Thursday evening, and went to bed earlier so that you could get up earlier: you should ask Mother if there are any small jobs you can do, or any errands you can go in order to help. "No task is too menial for anyone to do in honour of Shabbat."

It is a *mitzvah* to have a thorough wash on the eve of Shabbat. In Talmudic days, when there was no such thing as indoor plumbing, R. Yehudah b. Ilai had a basin of hot water brought to him, had a complete wash, dressed in his best clothes, and looked like "an angel of the Lord of hosts"!

You can do better than that: you can have a proper, comfortable bath – and if you do not look exactly like an angel after you have dressed in your best clothes, you *will* look more radiant than on weekdays! For one of the things with which G–d blessed the seventh day was "the light of a person's face, which is not the same on Shabbat, when it is more radiant, than as it is on weekdays."

Included with bathing is "washing the head, cutting your nails, and, if necessary, having a hair-cut" – in other words, everything that makes you look clean and neat. And as mentioned above, you should put on your best clothes before Shabbat commences, even if, for some reason, you are not even going to leave the house. For it is not for other people to see them that you don them, but in honour of Shabbat and Him Who gave it – Who is in your home as well!

Section 3.   **Switch In Meanings**

As you must undoubtedly know, when G–d at the very beginning of the Creation, formed light out of darkness, He "called the light (*or*) day, and the darkness He called night: and there was evening (*erev*) and there was morning, one day." It is from here, indeed, that we learn that a Jewish day commences in the evening, at nightfall, whatever time of the day that may be.

Need one have any more conclusive proof that '*or*' means 'day-light'? Yet, the Sages, from both the phrase "Praise Him all the *stars* of light (*or*), and the fact that beacons used to be lit on the '*or*' of the relevant day to inform the people country-wide of the beinning of a new month, prove that '*or*' can *sometimes* mean the night-time commencement of a full Jewish day. This they do to explain the law with which the tractate *Pesachim* begins: "On the *or* of the fourteenth (of Nisan) a search is made for leaven by the light of a candle".

On the other hand, whenever the Sages speak of *erev*-Shabbat or Festivals, they are usually referring to the *day-time* of Friday or the day before the particular Festival. Thus, when they describe as "industrious and one who sees profit" the man who works the whole week, but not on erev-Shabbat, they do not intend the Thursday evening to be included. And that is what is popularly understood to be erev-Shabbat – from dawn on Friday, until Shabbat begins.

There *are* people who can either afford, are not able, or have not the opportunity, alas, or who are plumb-lazy, not to work on Friday – or any other weekday (about which more later). Yet even the latter is described as "an indolent man who profits" – because he does not work on erev-Shabbat! But one who is voluntarily idle from Sunday to Thursday, and then works the whole of Friday until the very moment Shabbat begins, is termed "an indolent man who suffers loss".

The majority of people who *do* work, however, work on Fridays as well, but they should nevertheless curtail such work: for "He who does work on erev-Shabbat from *Minchah* onwards . . . will see no sign of a blessing therefrom." As you should know by now, there are, practically, four *Minchah* times; and the one to which this refers will soon be discussed. Before that, I want to talk about a kindred subject . . .

Section 4.   **Tosefet Shabbat**

With reference to Yom Kippur, which is on the tenth of Tishri, the Torah says: "It shall be a day of complete cessation from work for you, and you shall afflict your souls. In the *ninth* of the month in the evening, from evening to evening, you shall cease work on your

Shabbat". There are many questions which arise from this verse, apparent inconsistencies and superfluous words — all of which have something to teach us.

First: the evening of *every* day is the beginning of the next; so "the ninth of the month in the evening" should mean the night *before* Yom Kippur! "But does one fast on the ninth? Do we not fast on the tenth?" One lesson R. Chiyya deduces from this is: "It is thus stated to indicate that if one eats and drinks (plentifully) on the ninth, the Torah accounts it to him as if he had fasted on the ninth *and* the tenth" — for the more you eat on the ninth, the greater will be your affliction on the tenth! And that is exactly what we are urged to do: "It is a *mitzvah* to eat on erev-Yom Kippur and to increase one's meals."

But that is not the main lesson deduced from this verse: there is a much more important one. "If the Torah had said only "in the evening", one might have inferred that he had to fast only after it gets dark: therefore it says 'in the ninth', to convey that he should commence to afflict himself whilst it is yet day. From this we learn that we must add from the weekday to the sacred day. "This tells me only about the beginning: how do I know (that we must add part of the following weekday) at the end? From the words 'from evening to evening'".

For this purpose the verse could have ended at "you shall cease work". Why was the word for "(on) your Shabbat" added? To teach us that this addition (*tosefet*) applies to any day on which 'ceasing from work' is commanded, i.e. Shabbatot and Festivals. But before we consider how much this *addition* at both beginning and end has to be, we must know when Shabbat itself begins and ends.

Section 5.   The Extent Of Shabbat

You already know, from the commandment concerning the recital of the evening *Shema*, that it is definitely night when three medium-sized stars are visible. But there is a period before that, called 'twilight', that is, 'double-light', in English, less picturesque but similar to its Hebrew name, *bain hashamashot*, 'between the two servants' of G–d – the sun and the moon; a period during which both give a little light.

The twilight "is a period when it is doubtful whether it is partly day and partly night, or all of it day, or all of it night." It is therefore inseparably a part of Shabbat at both ends: at the beginning, in case it is part of the night; and at the end, lest it is still day. There are a number of views as to when it begins, but the consensus of opinions is that it is at the moment when the whole sun has just disappeared below the horizon; and it lasts about fifteen minutes – that is, a quarter of a *halachic* hour.

So that is the *minimum* extent of Shabbat itself, and to this the *tosephet* has to be added. How much time should you add? I quote MB: "He who enjoins strictness upon himself, and ceases work half-an-hour, or at least twenty minutes before the sun has completely set, happy is he, for he satisfies thereby even the most strict of the authorities. As for the termination of Shabbat, because of the great seasonal variations in the length of the halachic hour, it is best policy to wait until three stars are visible – small ones."

Nevertheless it is permissible to inaugurate the Shabbat even earlier, from the *plag-haminchah* (one-and-a-quarter halachic hours before the sun has completely set) onwards. But to do so before that time has no validity.

Section 6.   **Self-Employed Or Employee**

We can now return to a consideration of which Minchah it is that, if one carries on one's regular occupation thereafter, "he sees no blessing from that work," i.e. "whatever profit he may then make, he will lose at another time." It depends on what your occupation is, and how you are occupied, in the first place. If you are an employee, working for someone else, it does not apply to you at all. All you can rightfully demand from your employer is to be allowed to leave in sufficient time before sunset to be able to prepare a minimal meal and light the Shabbat candles – unless local custom or law requires otherwise!

But if you are self-employed in manufacture or handicraft, it *does* apply to you – but not if you are occupied in trade, which *may* continue until shortly before Shabbat begins. Which Minchah? "Some say it refers to Minchah Gedolah (12.30 p.m.) and others to Minchah Ketanah (3.30 p.m.) – both halachic hours – and he that adopts the later time does not lose thereby" comments the MB.

All this refers to continuing your regular occupation, but not to doing odd jobs about the house, or writing letters – and certainly not to preparing yourself and your garments, etc. in order to receive the Shabbat in the most honourable and respectful way you can, which is the very purpose for which you are required to take this time off! But why, if you have done all these things, and still have an hour or two in hand before the *plag-haminchah*, may you not receive Shabbat earlier than that time? I can suggest two possible answers.

Section 7.   **"Shalt" Or "Mayest"?**

The main purpose of the "Fourth Commandment" is to tell us to sanctify the seventh day because, as stated in the first text, on that day of Creation, G–d ceased from doing all the *melachah* He had been doing on the first six days. We, therefore, are commanded to follow His example on the seventh day of every week, throughout our generations, as a sign of the everlasting covenant which exists between G–d and Israel.

But, as an introduction to this, as it were, we are told, each one of us individually, 'six days *ta-avod*, and do all thy work'. Now that verb is in the only future tense the Hebrew language possesses, and it means many things, among them 'you will work,' 'you shall work', 'you may work', 'you shall have worked' – and others. Which one – or more – is intended here?

All the translations, and most people, without realising the implication, take it as a command – as part of the commandment: "Six days *shalt* thou labour;" which implies that just as you *must not* do any manner of work on the seventh day, so you *must* work on the other six. And that, for one of the reasons, may indeed be the intention meant to be conveyed by the word: either because the joy and refreshment of Shabbat cannot be fully appreciated except after six days' labour; or it may be because of our partnership with G–d.

I opened the last chapter with the reason first given for Shabbat observance, "because on it He ceased from all His work which G–d 'in creating had made'", and I noted that the literal meaning of the Hebrew of the quoted last words is "which G–d had created to do". G–d did not create a perfect world: "Whatever was created in the first six days,' said R. Hoshaya, "requires further action (*asiyah*): for example, mustard and lupines need sweetening, wheat needs grinding – and man, too, needs perfecting." The world, Nature, is much more developed, and mankind by-and-large much more civilised, than they were in Noah's or Abraham's age – or even just a century ago – but we are very far still from the time when (SPB 79–80) "the world will be perfected under the Kingdom of the Almighty, and all the children of flesh will call upon Thy Name." We have much to do in the course of our respective occupations among our fellow-men, quietly demonstrating through our dealings and relationship with them, how the true Jew strives to achieve that ideal.

For both these reasons, then, we must not reduce the six working days by too much. We have to add the *tosefet* to Shabbat, and may extend it to *plag-haminchah*, but no further – according to the translation 'six days *shalt* thou labour' in perfecting G–d's world. In this way, everyone who observes Shabbat and the weekdays leading up to it in their proper way becomes 'a partner with the Almighty in (perfecting) the works of the Creation'.

Section 8.   **Only If You Have To**

However, it is much more likely, and strongly supported by biblical texts, including sources (vii) and (viii) cited in the last chapter, that "six days *ta-avod*" means "Six days *mayest* thou labour": for in the latter, that introduction to the Shabbat commandment is replaced with "six days shall work be done". On this the question is asked: "Yet another verse states 'six days shalt *thou* labour, and do all thy work' – how can the two be reconciled?" And it answers:

"When Israel fulfils the will of the Omnipresent, their work will 'be done' for them by others; but when Israel do not fulfil the will of the Omnipresent, '*six* days wilt *thou* labour, and do all thy work!'". That this interpretation refers to the *people* of Israel, living in their own land in the Messianic Era, is proven by the supportive verses cited: "And strangers will rise and feed your flocks, and those of other nations will be your ploughmen and your vine-dressers; and *you* will be called priests of the Eternal, ministers of our G–d shall be said of you".

In other words: in that Era, all nations will recognise the G–d of Israel as the One and Only G–d, and that the people of Israel, having been true to the responsibility placed upon them, "Ye are My witnesses, saith the Eternal, and My servant whom I have chosen," will be called upon by all other nations to act as their full-time ministers and priests: for "The lips of the priest will guard knowledge, and they will seek Torah from his mouth; for he is the messenger of the Lord of Hosts." And those nations in turn, as did the non-priests of old, will sustain Israel so far as their material needs are concerned, so that they will be able spiritually to minister to them continuously, without distraction.

But until then, the Jew, like everyone else, has to work to support himself and his dependants, to labour arduously for six whole days every week, if his lot so demands. For, for the vast majority of people like you and me, one's daily sustenance is one of the three things Raba maintains "depend on *mazzal*" (the other two being length of life and children): and if you are unlucky, you may have to toil six days a week in order to earn an honest livelihood – especially in times of national economic depression.

I say 'unlucky' – but if you succeed, you will be happy, and enjoy your Shabbat rest all the more. "When thou eatest the labour of thine hands, happy shalt thou be, and it shall be well with thee." And *no* honest labour is undignified, as the humble occupations of so many of the Talmudic Sages prove. "Flay carcases in the market place and earn a living," Rab advised R. Kahana, who presumably was a *kohen*, "and do not say 'I am a priest and a great man, and it is beneath my dignity!'".

Earning an honest, independent living, if necessary by the sweat of your brow, by toiling six days a week, is an honourable thing. As we shall see in the next chapter, one of the ways in which we sanctify the Shabbat is to have an extra meal on the holy day. It was in this context of the number of meals one then eats – and this context alone! – that R. Akiba said: "Treat your Shabbat like a weekday, rather than be dependent on others". Nevertheless, shame on any community that makes it necessary for anyone so to do! But should anyone ever be in such an unfortunate position, he is urged "to eat just a little less on weekdays", so he can eat that little more on Shabbat.

Excepting Israelis, for most of whom erev-Shabbat is aptly half-day closing, to the majority of Jews, even if they do not work six days a week, Friday is a normal working day and, especially in the winter months, they want to work as long as is permissible. The more fortunate, who can have leisure on that day, can and should occupy that time in Shabbat preparations, both practical and intellectual. But they must fall in with the majority, and not inaugurate Shabbat at an earlier hour than the majority can, i.e. not before *plag-haminchah*.

Section 9.   **All Play (Or Study) – And No Work!**

But however much leisure you may have, even if you've inherited untold wealth from your grandparents, say, you still have to do *some* useful work to earn your existence on G–d's earth – because it is for that purpose that He put you here! It can be voluntary, charitable work, so much required in every community, general as well as Jewish. Of course this is in addition to your duties towards G–d, your leisure providing you with the opportunity to fulfil them with extra care and devotion. "Complete idleness," opined R. Eliezer, "leads to immorality or dullness of mind."

Nevertheless, though study of Torah is the most important occupation in which a Jew can indulge, because (SPB 6) "it leadeth to them all" – i.e. the observance of all the other commandments; Rabban Gamaliel the son of R. Yehudah the Prince said: "All study of the Torah without work must in the end be futile and become the cause of sin". And the Sages, generally, confirmed this.

Reconciling the command that "This Book of the Torah shall not depart out of thy mouth, and thou shalt meditate therein day and night" with the practical necessity of the farmer to "gather in the corn, thy wine, and thine oil", R. Yishmael said that the implication is that Torah-study has to be combined with a worldly occupation – farming or anything else. And logically so: for after long discussion, all the Sages agreed that Torah study "is only the greatest duty *because it leads to action.*"

Section 10.   **Work Up An Appetite!**

The paschal lamb could not have been very enjoyable, because "it has to be eaten after the appetite is satisfied" at the end of the Seder. But your Shabbat Eve meal is part of the day's joy, so you must make sure you will have a good appetite to eat it, by not having any meal during the last quarter of the daylight hours, especially in the winter. I know that there are weeks in high summer when to do this would mean missing the time of your usual evening meal – but I'm telling you what Jewish custom is, while *you* know how long it takes *you* to work up an appetite!

Well, I've told you much about how we keep on remembering that the holy Shabbat is coming, from the very first day of the week onwards; and how we prepare for it, working hard throughout the six days, if necessary, until a few hours before Shabbat begins. If you are a full-time student still, young lady or gentleman, you might have found all the discussion about work rather academic. But it is not really so, for two reasons:

Your studies are *also* work, and as you grow older, jolly hard work, perhaps more exhausting than handicrafts or trading, or practising the profession in which one is already qualified. You, in particular, *should* slog away at your studies six days a week – with breaks for relaxation and sport, in order to ensure that you will qualify with the greatest proficiency in your career.

Secondly, this volume will take you right up to the marriage age, at which the next, P.G., will begin. And you probably *will* be working by that time – and should be! For, by the order in which it sets out the verses "that hath built . . ., that hath planted . . . and that hath betrothed . . .", the "Torah has taught us a rule of conduct: that a man should first build a house (find a home), then plant a vineyard (find a means of livelihood), and only then take a wife."

And now, having spent one chapter on the ways of *guarding* against violating Shabbat, and another on means of *remembering* it – *shamor* and *zachor*; we can proceed to the most important part of the whole commandment *lekadsho* – how to *sanctify* it.

Section   **Notes**

1   On Exodus 20.8; Isaiah 23.13; Mechilta Yitro 8; Betsa 16a; Ibid.
2   Exodus 16.5 & 21; Shabbat 117b; see Ibid 119a; Ibid 25b; MR. Genesis 11.2; Or. Ch. 260.1.
3   Pesachim 2b; Psalms 148.3; Pesachim 50b; Ibid.
4   Levit. 23. 32; Yoma 81a; Or. Ch. 604.1.
5   Shabbat 34b; MB. 261. note 23.
6   Pesachim 50b; MB. 261 note 25; Or. Ch. 251 with MB.

7   Genesis 2.3; MR. Genesis 11.6.
8   Mechilta on Exodus 31.15; Isaiah 61.5–6; Ibid 43.10; Malachi 2.7; Moed
    Katan 28a; Psalms 128.2; Pesachim 113a; Shabbat 118a; Or. Ch. 242.1.
9   Ketubot 59b; Ethics 2.2; Berachot 35b; Joshua 1.8; Kiddushin 40b.
10 Pesachim 70a; Or. Ch. 249.2; Deuter. 20.5–7; Sotah 44a.

Twenty-Five

THE SHABBAT: SANCTIFY IT!

Section 1. 'The world to come' is synonymous with a state of utter bliss and joy which man, in human form, cannot even visualise, let alone experience: it is a state reserved for him in reward for the good he does while on earth, and his share of it commensurate with the extent of his contribution towards establishing G–d's Kingdom here.

Nevertheless, it is possible to savour a sample of that bliss while yet on earth – the joy which the sanctification of Shabbat brings in its train. "Shabbat is a sixtieth (taste) of the world to come;" while the Sages bring proof from each of the three sections of the Tenach that "the observance of Shabbat is equivalent to all the other commandments"!

This does not mean, of course, that a person can murder, rob, swindle and commit other heinous wrongs six days of the week, and have them condoned by keeping Shabbat on the seventh! Neither does the superficially remarkable saying of R. Yochanan, that "He who observes Shabbat according to its laws, even if he practises idolatry like the generation of Enosh, he is forgiven"!

Of course not! What they both mean is: that the person who sanctifies the holy day in the spirit that it should be, will thereby come to observe all the other commandments, and to the realisation that there is a G–d Who created the universe, including man. And from the moment that truth dawns on him, he will forsake his stupid idolatry – and all will be forgiven him. What, then, is that spirit?

Section 2. **The Spirit Of Shabbat**

The Prophet expresses it succinctly: "If, because of Shabbat, you turn your foot away from pursuing your business on My holy day; and designate the Shabbat a delight, the holy (day) of the Eternal honoured, honouring it by not pursuing your secular affair, by not seeking business, nor even talking about it: *then* you will delight yourself in the Eternal" – and get a soupçon of the world to come!

But, according to the *Mechilta* (quoted by Rashi), the Torah says the same thing, even more tersely, in the "Fourth Commandment". Deliberately 'misunderstanding' the scope of the word "all" in "Six days shalt thou labour and do all thy work" it asks: "Is it then possible for a man to do *all* his work in *six* days? Rather does it mean: cease – *as if* all your work is done: don't even think about work!" And then it cites the above verse from Isaiah in support of its interpretation.

With the cessation of all prohibited work, with even all thought of our weekly occupations banished from our minds – even school work! – how do we materialise this spirit, that it should infuse light and joy into body and soul? The answer is really very simple: rest your body, and refresh your soul!

Section 3.   **Rare Noun And Rare Verb**

As mentioned briefly in passing in the last chapter, the noun Shabbat does not mean 'rest' but 'cessation from work'. There are two nouns meaning 'rest' in the Torah – apart from the proper noun, Noach, already mentioned – occurring only five times in all the Five Books, and not once in connection with Shabbat! One of them occurs twice: "But the dove found no rest (*mano'ach*) for the sole of her foot . . .": I do not want to quote the other occasion – and if you look it up, you will realise why. The other is a longer form, occurring three times, as in "And he saw that rest (*menuchah*) was good . . .".

But the verb from which they both derive occurs three times in our source-texts, each one giving a different reason why we should actively *rest* on Shabbat: (1) because after the work of Creation G–d "rested (*vayanach*) on the seventh day"; (2) "in order that thine ox and thine ass may have rest (*yanuach*) . . ."; and (3) "in order that thy man-servant and maid-servant may rest as well as thou."

As is evident from the second and third of these quotations, this physical rest is primarily intended for those who work hard physically during the six weekdays – "as well as thou", if you happen to fall into this category. Even if you do not, "if you are accustomed to have an afternoon nap, you should not deprive yourself of it, because it gives you *oneg* (pleasure)." But, MB warns, it must be *intended* as part of your Shabbat enjoyment, and not as gathering strength for Sunday's work or play!

But most of us do not work that hard six days a week or even five – and that is where the rare verb takes control. Its noun is *very* common – *nefesh*, which we have come across quite often, meaning 'soul', 'life', and something else which we will soon have again. But the verb occurs only thrice in the whole of the Tenach, once in *Samuel,* and twice in the Torah, both in connection with Shabbat: The first tells us that Shabbat is a sign between G–d and Israel because "in six days the Eternal made heaven and earth, and on the seventh *shavat vayinnafash.*" This is the only place in connection with Shabbat that the English translations correctly renders the verb *shavat* as "He ceased from work" – but only because it reserves its usual translation of the word, "and He rested", for the second verb – which it does *not* mean: for the Hebrew for that is *vayanach*, and is so correctly translated there.

The other Torah occurrence of the verb is in the verse which has already been partially quoted; giving the reasons for the institution of Shabbat (a) "so that your ox and your ass may rest (*yanuach*)," and (b) "that the son of the handmaid and the resident alien *yinafesh*" – here more correctly translated "may be refreshed". On this Hertz says (HPH 316): "Even the lowliest in Israel is to be reminded by the Shabbat day *that he has a soul,* that there is a higher life than mere drudgery; he is to receive *spiritual refreshment* on the Shabbat day."

Section 4.   **Refreshing The Soul**

Rashi's comment "How could He, of Whom it is written 'He fainteth not, neither is He weary', and all of Whose 'work' was by word of mouth, write of Himself that He required rest? He did so in order to make the (human) ear understand what it heard". In other words: G–d anthropomorphised Himself so that *we* should understand what was expected of us in the matter of Shabbat observance.

All living creatures require some form(s) of rest. The ox and the ass, symbolic of the forced hard labourer, including the human kind, need *menuchah*, physical rest. That is what Moses, you will remember, demanded of Pharaoh for his enslaved brethren; for without one day's *menuchah* weekly they would die, he warned. Speaking of man's final bodily rest in death, Job says: "There the weary will rest (*yanuchu*)".

Every human being, be he or she the lowliest in social status, "the son of thy handmaid and the resident alien" being representative of them, has a *nefesh*, a soul, human feeling and emotions, and therefore must have *nofesh*, a weekly respite in which to refresh themselves and 'catch their breath'. Both the toiling animal and the humans in our service are, like us, part of G–d's Creation: and the farmer or employer acknowledges the Creator and His work by giving them their *menuchah* and *nofesh*, following His 'example', on Shabbat.

But the *ben-chorin*, the 'free' man, the man of intellect – "and no man is free but he who occupies himself with Torah", needs to refresh not only his physical life-preserving *nefesh*, but also his spiritual *neshamah*, his divinely-inspirited soul. This applies to *everyman* (*adam*): for R. Meir was wont to say: "How do we know that even a heathen who studies (and observes the seven Noachite laws of) the Torah is as a High Priest? From the verse, 'You shall therefore keep My statutes . . . which, if man (*adam*) do, he shall live by them'".

But for the Jew, Torah — knowledge in its widest sense, ethically applied to practical living — is supplemented by the discipline of the ritual commandments, *chukkim* as well as *mishpatim*; and this transforms his *nefesh* into a *neshamah* — a breath of the divine, ever reaching out to its Source.

Section 5.   Shabbat's Extra Neshamah

From the word *vayinafash*, moreover, Resh Lakish deduces the lesson that on erev-Shabbat, as the holy day is about to begin, the Jew "is given an *extra neshamah* until the Shabbat's termination." Connecting this word with the previous one, *shavat*, he interprets: When the Shabbat ceases (shavat) the Jew exclaims "*vai nefesh!*" — "Woe! the (extra) soul is gone!", splitting the word into two!

For what purpose is this extra Shabbat soul given? There are two apparently opposing opinions about this. There is that of R. Shemuel bar Nachman who maintains that "the Shabbat was given solely for the purpose of studying Torah" — that is, to be used to feed the Jew's higher nature, his soul, which has been starving for nourishment throughout the working week.

The other opinion then, is that of R. Chiyya b. Abba: "The Shabbat was given solely for enjoyment". And the source goes on to say: there is no difference of opinion between them. This latter view has reference to those who study Torah all the week, and are therefore entitled to some relaxation of Shabbat; whereas the other refers to working people, who may perforce have to neglect such study all the week, and must make full amends on Shabbat.

I can suggest another way of harmonising the two views. Study is a source of enjoyment to the intelligent person with an active and curious mind — and especially the study of Torah: for "The precepts of the Eternal are right, rejoicing the heart"! After being tied down for most of the week at his regular, possibly exhausting, work of earning a livelihood, such a one will not want to waste the holy day in eating and drinking, lolling and strolling about, all the time. He will want to refresh his soul, enlarge his knowledge.

Very aptly, it is the Torah itself which has the last say in this matter. If you read in full all the source-texts cited — some of them only partially – in chapter twenty-three, you will see that in some of them the holy day is described as "a Shabbat to the Eternal", and in others "a Shabbat unto you". Whose then is Shabbat – G–d's or ours? We will see later, when dealing with the Festivals, that this question is asked primarily regarding them. But the Shabbat is "equated with them for this purpose."

The answer is – a compromise: it is half for the Eternal, and half for you; yet you *should* have enjoyment from both halves, making the whole of the holy day one of *oneg* – delight. How? We will soon come back to that: but since enjoying Shabbat is the Prophet's explanation of one aspect of the Torah commandment to *sanctify* the day, we will first consider what that overall commandment signifies.

Section 6.   **With 'Manna', Light and Wine**

Let us go back to half-an-hour or so before Shabbat commences. You have brought the sanctified radiance of the day to your face by washing, and honoured it by donning your best clothes. Your mother will now be setting the table with two specially-baked loaves (*challot*), reminiscent of the two measures of manna which fell on erev-Shabbat, putting them on a white table-cloth, and covering them with an adorned white cloth, those two representing the layers of dew within which the manna was enveloped.

She does this because it was with this *lechem mishneh*, double measure of heavenly 'bread' that fell on erev-Shabbat that G–d *blessed* the holy day, and by not causing the manna to fall on Shabbat itself that He *sanctified* the day. It is from this source that the two Shabbat loaves thereafter were given the name *lechem mishneh*.

Though the sun, moon and stars were not created until the fourth day of Creation, the light originally created on the first day continued to function, during the night-time as well as the day, until the end of the first Shabbat. G–d was going to withdraw it as soon as Adam sinned in the tenth hour, i.e. two hours before nightfall on the sixth day, for he only abided in the Garden of Eden for twelve hours altogether! But He graciously allowed the light to shine throughout that night, in order not to mar Adam's first Shabbat!

For this reason we kindle lights in our homes on Shabbat Eve – before, of course, the holy day commences; for once it has, it is forbidden to kindle *any* light, even these: and the privilege and responsibility for kindling them is, in the first place, given to the lady of the house. A number of reasons are given for bestowing the mitzvah on her, but this is not the place to give them. For the present we will assume that it is because Mother is thus rewarded for all her work in making the Shabbat the day of joy and light it is going to be, and is usually always at home at the right time. But if, for any reason, she is *not*, someone else *must* light them.

The usual number of candles is two – one for *zachor*, the other for *shamor*, though it is permissible to add to that number. In some families it is the custom to light one for each member – the girls kindling their own: while some light seven, corresponding to the days of the week, or even ten, corresponding to "The Ten Command-ments" – but they do not *all* have to be on the table.

Though when lighting the candles the blessing (SPB 141) "Blessed art Thou. . . . Who has commanded us to kindle the Shabbat light" is made, this prominent and vital – (see Ibid 162. par. 6) – feature of Shabbat is not, in itself, actually one of G–d's commandments, but one of the seven most important rabbinic commandments which supplement the 613 of the Torah – one of the jewels in the "crown (keter = 620) of Torah", all of which have near-Torah status.

However, we can now appreciate that this *mitzvah* is not really an *addition* to the Torah's commands, but the elaboration of one of them – "Remember the Shabbat day to keep it holy"; and this is one of the ways in which we do so, giving it light and joy.

Beside the *challot* and candles, Mother will put a bottle or carafe of wine and a goblet, because "'Remember the Shabbat day to sanctify it' means to hallow it by reciting a blessing over wine as the holy day enters." Why wine in particular? Because "wine cheereth G–d and man" – or most men! But that sanctification (*Kiddush* in Hebrew) comes a little later, and we will talk about it in its proper place.

Section 7.   **To Divine Service!**

You will remember the compromise: half of Shabbat is for G–d, and half for you. We will come to your half soon: but it is appropriate that part of His half should be beginning the Eve and the morning of the day in His House, and ending it there. There are far, far too many who attend Morning Service only, arriving late even then – though this is better than not going at all! But *you* should make a habit of worshipping publicly on all three occasions, and persist in it through-out your life, young man. As for *you*, young lady, not many girls are accustomed to attend the Evening Services – but I am certain you will be made very welcome if you do!

I have always considered the Inaugural Shabbat Service – called *Kabbalat Shabbat* in Hebrew – to be the most enjoyable of all Synagogue Services, the lesser reason for my choice being its ideal length, about forty-five minutes! But my main reason is that it is full of delightful, inspiring song and poetry, communally chanted to a variety of stirring tunes. The most soul-stirring of them all is the popular *Lecha Dodi* (SPB 146–147), "Come, beloved, to meet the bride!", the first letter of each stanza, apart from the opening and recurring refrain, forming an acrostic of the famous composer's name, Shlomoh HaLevi (Alkabetz).

The origin of the refrain itself is interesting. "R. Chanina robed himself and stood at twilight of Shabbat Eve and exclaimed: 'Come and let us go forth to welcome the Queen Shabbat!' R. Yannai . . . exclaimed: 'Come, O bride, Come O bride!'" The Shabbat is weekly welcomed afresh as the royal bride of the Jewish people.

This accords with the story told by R. Shimon b. Yochai, that at the end of the Creation the Shabbat complained to the Holy One, blessed be He, "All the other days have partners: the first day has the second, the third has the fourth, and the fifth has the sixth – but I have no partner!' 'The Community of Israel will be your partner,' G–d replied. And therefore when Israel stood at Sinai, G–d said to them, 'Remember to sanctify your partner, the Shabbat'!" The Hebrew term for 'marriage' is *Kiddushin* – 'sanctifications'.

I am not going to tell you any more about this lovely Service, but will cite you the answer once given to Raba by Abaye: "Go and see what the usage of the people is!" I would only ask you to note that we "sanctify the day", each quietly for himself in the central blessing of the *Amidah*; and we thereafter repeat, aloud and in unison, *its* centre-piece, the Torah verses *Vayechulu*.

R. Yose son of R. Yehudah said: "Two ministering angels accompany a man from the Synagogue to his home on Shabbat Eve, one good and one evil. When he arrives home and finds the candles burning, the table laid, and the couch – (on which they used to recline, in place of our chairs) – covered with a spread, the good angel exclaims: 'May it be even so next Shabbat also!' and the evil angel unwillingly responds 'Amen'. But if not . . ." – I'm not going to tell you what, because it is not going to happen to you!

Section 8.   "Welcome To Our Home!"

As you enter the house – having first touched the *mezuzah* and kissed the point of contact – you welcome these angels, bidding them enter in peace, bless you with peace, and go in peace (SPB 167–168). After Father praises Mother as "The woman of worth" he *has* found – a weekly tribute to all her domestic chores for him and you, we are back to the "sanctification over wine" – Kiddush.

You might have wondered why I did not mention the Kiddush which the Reader probably recited in your Synagogue. It is because it perpetuates a social institution which no longer prevails, and "it is better to direct that Kiddush should not be recited in the Synagogue, which is the custom — not to recite it — in the land of Israel". It was originally instituted for the benefit of the transient poor who had no home to go to, and no host to invite them to their homes, so that each Synagogue provided a 'lodging-house' and board nearby.

Though these conditions happily do not apply today, the custom still persists in the Western world — but no one over Bar-Bat-mitzvah age is allowed to drink of the wine, for they have to make Kiddush for themselves at home. This ban includes even the Reader who recites the blessing over the wine-except when there is not even one under — BM child present, for whom this Kiddush is *now* said to be made, since such are not duty-bound to make it at home.

Why I *do* mention it now is in order to point out the difference between this inessential Kiddush in the Synagogue and the essential one made at home. In the Synagogue it is customary to stand while it is being recited — and doing so "is good for weak knees"! But at home, where the Kiddush is introductory to the meal, "the custom is to sit while Kiddush is made" — except for the first four Hebrew words said aloud, meaning "The sixth day. And the heavens were finished . . ." since their first letters form an acronym of G–d's most holy Name.

R. Hamnuna declares the person who recites Kiddush to be "a partner with the Holy One, blessed be He, in the Creation" by reading *vayechulu*, and they, (the heaven and earth) were finished' as *vayechalu* — 'and they (G–d and the Kiddush-maker) finished' the heaven and the earth! While Mar Ukba is reported as saying that the two ministering angels, who have waited for Kiddush, place their hands on the reciter's head and say: "Thine iniquity is taken away, and thy sin purged." What a beneficial *mitzvah* indeed!

Section 9.   The Joys Of Shabbat

The Shabbat candles are usually lit in the dining-room, and the meal eaten in their glow. But what if it is a very warm night, and on arriving home from Synagogue you decide you would like to eat on the verandah? You may make Kiddush there, and have your meal there, even out of sight of the candles; for "the candles were ordained to give *joy* and not to enforce discomfort — and this is logical"! MB however permits this departure only when great discomfort is involved, and advises, even then, to make Kiddush and eat just a little by the candles, and then to continue outside.

And I suppose the same applies to anyone who does not like wine, or has taken the pledge! He or she need not drink wine from Kiddush — for its institution was intended for pleasure and not for distaste or vow-breaking! As a last resort, Kiddush may be recited

over the *challot*. You don't *have* to eat anything you don't like! But
eating and drinking what you *do* like constitutes the main Shabbat
enjoyment.

Rashi states that the extra soul which pervades the Jew on Shabbat
"engenders a sharper appetite for eating and drinking", giving the
word soul the same meaning as it has in the verse: "All the labour of
man is for his mouth, and yet his appetite (*nefesh*) is never filled." But
the Jew's should be, with just enough on weekdays, and plenty on
Shabbat – by divine command! Said G–d to Israel: "*You* sanctify the
Shabbat with food and drink and clean clothes, deriving physical
pleasure therefrom, and *I* will reward you" for so doing!

In our discussion of commandment 24, opinions were quoted that
anyone who ate food of greater quantity and richer quality than was
essential to keep body and soul healthily together was guilty of
unnecessary destruction of the produce of G–d's good earth – but not
on Shabbat (and Festivals)! On those holy days it is commendable
pleasurably to pay heed to Rav's warning: "Everyone will ultimately
have to account for every delicacy which his eyes saw and his
appetite desired, yet did not eat" – if he could afford it!

When R. Eleazer heard of this saying of Rav, he started saving so
that he could have a reserve with which to buy any delicacy he might
come across, and undoubtedly put it aside for the following Shabbat,
if it would keep, in the Shammai tradition. And that is what *you*
should do, especially with the advantage of refrigeration which he did
not have!

Section 10.   **An Extra Meal Too!**
You will remember that in biblical and Talmudic days they used to
eat two meals on weekdays (chapter fourteen). But on Shabbat they
had three, a hint of this being given in the occurrence of the word
'today' in the verse concerning the manna: "And Moses said: 'eat it
today, for *today* is Shabbat unto the Eternal; *today* you will not find it
in the field." R. Chidka argued that these referred to *day*-time meals,
"apart from the evening one", making four altogether: but the
majority of the Sages ruled that the Shabbat Eve meal was included in
the three.

And so we have *shalosh seudot* every Shabbat, and this is one of the
names popularly given to the third meal, another being *oneg Shabbat*,
derived from the phrase "And thou shalt call the Shabbat a delight
(*oneg*)".

Apart from the sit-down meals you have, you should also eat and
drink during the course of Shabbat many of those fruits, sweets and

liquid refreshments you like, not only for your own enjoyment, but also – since, of course, you will recite a *bracha* before and after each – for the purpose of making up for the loss of many of the minimum one hundred blessings you should make every day. For each *Amidah* on Shabbat contains only seven blessings, compared with the week-day's nineteen; and though, as we shall soon see, there is an extra *Amidah* on Shabbat (and Festivals and New Moon), the shortfall is still twenty-nine blessings. Other ways of making it up will be suggested later.

This encouragement to extra consumption, and the reason there-fore, give a useful reminder that even when the fulfilment of any commandment gives us great pleasure, its performance is basically to be considered as a service to our G–d: for "the commandments were not given to provide enjoyment" primarily, "but as a yoke round Israel's neck", is Rashi's comment – even when you are eating that delicious (*kasher*) ice-cream on Shabbat, in order to make two extra blessings! It is because we are so liable to forget this that the Chafetz Chaim avers in one of his commentaries that *oneg* Shabbat is one of the most difficult commandments properly to perform.

Shabbat Morning Service begins in most Synagogues an hour and more later than on weekdays, so that you can have an extra lie-in: for "Sleep (*SHainah*) on Shabbat (*B'shabbat*) is a pleasure (*Ta'anug*)" (an acronym); customarily supplemented with an afternoon nap. During the other hours of the half of the holy day that is "for you", there are many ways in which you can enjoy yourself: playing chess, for instance, or table-tennis, and even scrabble – if you have markers with which to tot up the scores, so that you will not be tempted to get a pen and jot them down!

I have referred, in chapter twenty-three, to the permissibility, under certain conditions, for playing even strenuous ball-games on Shabbat. There is what appears to be a remarkable conclusion that "the destruction of Tur Shimon (or Tur Malka) – a mountain region containing many townlets and villages, was decreed because they played ball-games" – on the Shabbat, add both commentaries. But one of them gives an alternative reason: "they used to while away *all* their days playing ball, and consequently did not study Torah." *Nota bene*!

And there are many other ways in which you can enjoy yourself – going for a stroll, visiting friends, attending an orthodox Youth organisation's Oneg Shabbat, if there is one in your area, reading a wholesome novel or thriller, and so on. But remember always that only *half* of the holy day is yours, and that the rest of your enjoyment of it should be 'for the Eternal'.

Section 11.   **The Other Half**

Singing traditional table-songs – *zemirot*, is a mixture of both halves
SPB pp. 170–173 and 227–232 contains the six most popular ones,
each having a variety of soul-stirring or jolly tunes; and there are
many more which you can find in special compilations of *zemirot*. But
it is "speaking words of Torah" round the table which transforms it
into an altar, and the meal into a service unto the Eternal.

Nor must you forget, on Shabbat Eve or before going to Synagogue
in the morning, to "complete your *parashot* with the congregation":
i.e. to finish revising the Sidra which is to be read that Shabbat in the
Synagogue, before it is publicly read, so that you know what the
Reader is talking about; for by so doing your "days and years will be
prolonged". There may be a need to revise the *whole* Sidra – if you
have not been doing so parshah by parshah each weekday!

Some people complain that the "Shabbat Morning Service is too
long". In actual fact what they are participating in – *if* they arrive at
the beginning, which most of the complainants, in particular, do
not! – is *two* Services, each of which should take no more than the
forty-five minutes the previous Evening Service lasted, *and* the
Reading of the Torah, which takes more-or-less the same time,
depending on its length – and the number of 'extras' more than the
required seven the Warden(s) decide to honour.

These two-and-a-half hours are service to the Eternal, but they are
spiritually enjoyable as well. They should end by mid-day, because
you must not have a meal until at least after *Shacharit*, the Morning
Service proper, corresponding to the daily sacrifice. But most Congregations follow this immediately with the Reading of the Torah and
the *Musaf* Service, corresponding to the additional Shabbat offering
in Temple times – and "it is forbidden to fast on Shabbat until noon"!
However, most people have a 'snack' before going to Synagogue.

"Assemble The Congregation!"

There may be a sermon between the two Services, and/or a *drashah*
(ethical lecture) or a *shiur* (study meeting) towards the end of
Shabbat. This custom, it is deduced, goes right back to Moses' time,
he having "assembled all the congregation of the children of Israel,"
not for prayer, but to instruct them regarding the laws of Shabbat.
From this it is inferred that G–d meant to convey to Moses:
"Assemble large congregations on Shabbat, so that future generations
may learn from you so to do, to teach them and guide them in Torah
knowledge, that My Name may be praised among My children."

You should utilise the remainder of your "half for the Eternal" in
attending such *derashot* and *shiurim* – and by staying in the

Synagogue for the sermon, and not sneaking out for a chat as the rabbi goes to the pulpit, which is insulting to G–d as well as to him!

Section 12.   The Second *Seudah*

The name "Shabbat" signifies the seventh day – all the 25+ hours of it: and it is with the Kiddush at its *beginning* that we sanctify it. From the fact that the Torah says "Remember the Shabbat *day* to sanctify it," however, it is gathered that Kiddush should also be recited before the *day*-time meal (*seudah*). It need only consist of the blessing over wine – and because it is so little, it is called "the great Kiddush"! Later on, two of our source-texts were introduced (SPB 226–227) to precede the blessing over wine, so that this Kiddush would 'live up to its name'; but the Eve's sanctification blessing (SPB 163), which is the main portion of Kiddush, is not recited in the morning.

And The Third

"Be very heedful of fulfilling the third meal (seudah shlishit)," because he who does so "will be delivered from three evils;" for which reason R. Yose always prayed, "May my portion be of those who eat three meals on Shabbat." It is usually eaten after the Minchah Service, very often communally in the Synagogue – in which you should join, if your Congregation arranges one; and like the other two meals, should preferably be a full meal, with the Hamotsi recited over two loaves – but there is no Kiddush then. Incidentally, "ladies are also duty-bound to eat the third meal."

Some say that just a piece of cake, fish or meat, or even fruit, can constitute this 'meal'; but unless you are absolutely replete from the second *seudah* just finished on a winter Shabbat afternoon, say; you should eat the minimum amount of bread mentioned above, which constitutes a 'meal' – the blessings before and after eating it helping towards your quota of 100!

Section 13.   A Reluctant "Farewell"!

I would remind you of two details already mentioned: that there is a *tosefet*, an addition, of part of the following week-night to the end of Shabbat, as well as an addition of part of the week-day at its beginning; and that the holy day has to be sanctified, preferably over wine, at its termination as well as at its inauguration.

To symbolise our regret at the departure of "the Queen", we delay ending Shabbat as long as possible – at the very least until the sky is starry. Then, after each individual has uttered the "distinction between the holy and profane" (SPB 124) – *Havdalah*, as it is called, in the Ma'ariv Amidah, one of their number publicly recites the

Havdalah 'Service' (SPB 292–293) commencing with the blessing over wine. He then makes a blessing over spices and inhales their fragrance – to sustain his weekday soul after the departure of Shabbat's "extra soul": and finally, by the light of a many-wicked candle, he observes the shadow his nails cast on the palm of his hands – because light was created on the day just beginning.

This recital of the Havdalah in the Synagogue does not absolve those present from making it at home, especially for the ladies, "who have to hear Havdalah just as they have to hear Kiddush". And it has to be recited immediately on arriving home, or at least before having anything to eat.   .

R. Chanina said: "One should always set his table at the termination of the Shabbat, even if he is only going to eat as much as an egg-quantity (of bread)" – "in order to escort the Shabbat on her departure, as we welcome her on her arrival". Some people make quite a meal of it, often in company, and it is called a "Melava Malkah" – "escorting the Queen" on her departure.

Section 14.   **Only The Surface**

Rashi, commenting on the fact that the story of Eliezer's mission to find a wife for Isaac is not only told in detail, but repeated, quotes from the Midrash: "The ordinary conversation of the servants of the Patriarchs is more pleasing to G–d than the Torah of their children. For wheras the story of Eliezer is told and then repeated, many important and basic principles of the Torah are only hinted at". And Shabbat observance is certainly one of these basics.

This is my third, and longest chapter on that subject, culling from a text here and a word there, only the main framework of Shabbat observance, leaving much of the picture for you to fill in yourself. To change the metaphor: I have only scratched the surface – *you* must dig deep below it.

And there is much fertile ground on which to do so! The tractate *Shabbat* has 175 double pages – apart from many references to the holy day in other tractates, especially *Eruvin*: while the Shulchan Aruch has a similar number of chapters on Shabbat. Go and learn!

Apart from the reason already given – that the proper observance of Shabbat can lead to the fulfilment of all the other commandments; there is another reason why I have devoted the space I have, to an outline, at least, of its laws and customs. Though there is one distinctive and far-reaching difference between the observance of Shabbat and that of the Festivals, the manner and the mood in which we celebrate them is very much the same.

Thus you will see, as we now proceed to consider the Festivals, collectively and separately, there will be many aspects of them which will be familiar to you from what you now know about Shabbat.

There is only one word in the source-texts to which I drew special attention but have not yet explained – the word *lada'at* in the divine instruction to Moses to tell the Israelites that the Shabbat "is a sign between Me and you . . . 'to know' that I am the Eternal Who sanctify you." *Who* should know? I have left what I think is the true explanation until now because it is a link between the Shabbat and the Festivals, applying to both.

The English versions render it "that *you* may know" i.e. the Jewish people: but Rashi says it means "that *they* may know" – the nations of the world. By *our* sanctifying Shabbat and the Festivals, *they* realise that the Eternal is our G–d throughout our generations.

Section	**Notes**
1	Berachot 57b; MR. Exodus 25.12; Shabbat 118b.
2	Isaiah 58.13–14; on Exodus 20.9.
3	Genesis 8.9; Deuter. 28.65; Genesis 49.15, Numbers 10.33 & Deuter. 12.9; Exodus 20.11; Ibid 23.12; Deuter. 5.14; Or. Ch. 290.1; II Samuel 16.14; Exodus 31.17; Isaiah 40.28.
4	On Exodus 31.17; Job 3.17; Ethics 6.2; Sanhedrin 59a; Levit. 18.5; see chapter 5.
5	Ta'anit 27b; Pesikta R. 23; Psalms 19.9; Y. Shabbat 45a (15.3).
6	Shabbat 113a; MR. Genesis 11.2; Exodus 16.22; Sanhedrin 38b; Or. Ch. 263.3; Ibid MB. note 6; Mechilta. Exodus 20.8; Judges 9.13.
7	Shabbat 119a; MR. Genesis 11.8; Eruvin 14b; Shabbat 119b.
8	Or. Ch. 269; Ibid & MB. note 6; Ibid 271.10; Shabbat 119b; Isaiah 6.7.
9	Or. Ch. 273.7; Ta'anit 27b; Eccles. 6.7; MR. Deuter. 3.1; Y. Kiddushin, end; Eruvin 54a.
10	Exodus 16.25; Shabbat 117b; Isaiah 58.13; Menachot 43b; R. Hash. 28a; Yalkut Reuveni on Deuter. 5.14; Y. Ta'anit 21b (4.5).
11	Ethics 3.4; Berachot 8b; Or. Ch. 288.1; Yalk. Shim. *Vayakhel* 1; Exodus 35.1–3.
12	Pesachim 106a; Or. Ch. 291.1ff and Shabbat 118a.
13	Or. Ch. 296.8; Shabbat 119b; Or. Ch. 300.
14	On Genesis 24.42; Exodus 31.13.

Twenty-Six

THE FESTIVALS: A GENERAL SURVEY

Section 1. Because it was "divinely blessed and hallowed" from its very inception as the climax of the Creation; because of the frequency of its incidence; and because, as we saw in the last chapter, its proper observance can lead to the fulfilment of all the other commandments; the Shabbat is the first of the six "appointed seasons of the Eternal" listed in *Leviticus* chapter twenty-three; and we refer to it as such in the evening Kiddush (SPB 170) for that day.

Indeed, Shabbat is the *only* one of those appointed seasons the time for whose observance was immovably fixed – every seventh day, adherence to which distinguishes us from Judaism's two daughter-religions. The five Festivals differ in this respect, in that the Torah "gives the Sages authority to alter the times of their occurrence," sometimes by as much as a whole month, for various reasons, examples of which will be given in the next two chapters.

Although that *Leviticus* chapter (to which all verse references following will allude) lists the five Festivals in the order in which they fall in the biblical year, which commences with Nisan, the month of the Exodus, they are usually divided into two groups: the *Shalosh Regalim* – Three Harvest or Pilgrim Festivals, given us (SPB 311) "for gladness and joy"; and the *Yamin Nora'im*, "Days of Awe", popularly called the "High Festivals", with which the ten opening penitential days of the calendar year (beginning with Tishri) begin and end.

The Festivals will be discussed individually and in detail in the next two chapters. Here we are going to see what all of them have in common with each other, and with their 'parent' – Shabbat. It is interesting and useful to note at this stage that RM includes the first of the "Days of Awe" with the Joyous Festivals, giving it, like each of them "the popular name *Yom-tov* ('good day')," thus leaving Yom Kippur in awesome isolation.

61–67.   TO SANCTIFY THE FESTIVALS

Section 2. Glance through the source-chapter and you will see that the first and seventh days of Pesach, the one day of Shavuot, Rosh Hashanah and Yom Kippur, and the first and eighth days of Sukkot is each, like Shabbat, called a *mikra-kodesh*, and each classified as a Torah Commandment, which RM equates with our commandment 58, giving the term the meaning "sanctify it" as you sanctify the Shabbat.

How? Commenting on the last occurrence of *mikra-kodesh* in our chapter (verse 35), Rashi tells us: "On Yom Kippur, sanctify it with clean clothes and prayer; and on the other Festivals, with food and drink as well". Prayer – or rather praise and thanksgiving, for we do not *pray* for our daily needs on Shabbat – is an important element in all of them, and especially together with a congregation, as explained in chapter sixteen. But it is patent here that the term *mikra-kodesh* has a much wider connotation than "holy convocation", as it is translated.

68–74.   DO NOT WORK ON THE FESTIVALS

Again, you will see that we are commanded not to work on any of these seven days, comprising another seven Torah prohibitions. However, to only one of them, Yom Kippur, is the term *shabbat shabbaton* (verse 32) applied, meaning a *complete* cessation from all manner of work, as it is used with reference to Shabbat. The kind of work forbidden on the other Festivals is *melechet-avodah* (see chapter twenty-three for definition of these Hebrew terms) – with one exception which, in effect, is . . .

Section 3.   **A Very Big Concession**
To discover what this concession is, we have to go back to the original institution of the Festival of Pesach while the children of Israel were still in Egypt where we are told of its first and seventh days, "no manner of work shall be done in them, except that which every soul must eat, that alone may be done by you". Although this is explicitly stated of the first of the Festivals, the concession is taken to include them all (except Yom Kippur, for the reason given above).

From this text the Mishnah rules: "There is no difference between the Festivals and Shabbat except in the matter of food". So, unless it coincides with Shabbat, in which case the laws governing that day's observance take precedence, baking and cooking are permitted on any Yomtov. But such preparations call for the use of fire, which is also forbidden on Shabbat – so such use is also permitted: not, however, *creating* a new fire by, for instance, striking a match, but lighting one from an already burning source. Similarly, a gas or electric burner may be adjusted higher or lower, but it must not be extinguished.

Again, the cook may find that she (or he) lacks a necessary ingredient which can be borrowed from a neighbour across or down the street – and carrying in a public thoroughfare is forbidden on Shabbat; and so carrying was also permitted. These two concessions were then further extended: since the lighting of fire and carrying out-of-doors were permitted in the preparation of food, they were also permitted for other purposes such as lighting a cigar or cigarette, carrying your tallit and Siddur to Synagogue – or a toddler who gets tired walking.

Section 4.   **Beware Abusing Them!**

There is always a danger in granting some people a degree of latitude – they have a habit of extending it themselves still further without warrant. To discourage abuse of these concessions, therefore, it is necessary to understand the *reason* why they were granted. As mentioned earlier and will soon be proven, the Festivals are times for especial *enjoyment*, and so Torah and Sages went to the furthest possible extent of making them enjoyable *without compromising the sanctity of the day*, relying on our loyalty and discipline not to abuse them.

How? Let us take one or two examples. The reason why the Torah permits Yomtov cooking and baking is that "warm bread baked today, and a dish cooked today is tastier than that baked or cooked yesterday". (You might ask: but is not Shabbat food, which *must* be prepared the day before, not only tasty but positively delicious? For the answer to that, see end chapter twenty-three.) Therefore the Sages "forbade the cooking on Yomtov of such dishes which would *not* lose their tastiness overnight, lest a person should deliberately leave such work to be done on Yomtov itself, *and thus diminish her (or his) enjoyment* of that Festival".

Another example: if puffing at the pernicious weed adds to your Yomtov enjoyment, you may light-up cigarette or pipe from a burning candle or gas-ring, as mentioned. But this concession leads to so much even unintentional abuse by forgetfully flicking on a lighter, that some authorities wanted to forbid smoking on Yomtov altogether. They were then a minority, and so the permit continued – but had they lived today, when we know how much harm such addiction can do, their view would probably have prevailed and been extended all the year round, on health grounds!

If, however, you are careful not to do any *melachah* which is forbidden on these days, and you sanctify them in the manner prescribed, then during the year you will have climbed another fourteen rungs up our ladder, to within one rung of three-quarters of its reach — and there is another Torah commandment to come associated with most of the Festivals. But first we must give attention to some of the rabbinical enactments concerning them, and particularly one which affects their observance in the Diaspora.

Section 5.   **Diaspora "Second-Day Festival"**

Up to now we have been speaking of the seven *Torah* ordained Festival days: but rabbinic enactment — which is also 'Torah' in the wider sense of that term — adds another six to them for Jews living outside Israel, called *Yomtov-sheni shel galuyyot*, 'second-day Festival of the Diaspora'. They are: the second days of Pesach and Sukkot; and extra day added at the end of these two Festivals; and the extension of Shavuot and Rosh Hashanah to two-day Festivals. (The last-mentioned gradually became, and is now observed by everyone there as, a two-day Festival in Israel as well, the probable reason for which will be suggested when we discuss that Festival in detail.)

It all has to do with "the moon He made for seasons" (SPB 243) — the three-word Hebrew phrase for this, incidentally, being the sole reason why this long Psalm was selected for special recital on New Moon days. The Jewish month is lunar, and as you will have seen in the source-chapter, the Festivals have to be observed on specific dates in the months, and it is therefore essential to know when a month begins. When *does* it?

Nowadays, of course, that is no problem — we just consult a Jewish calendar, or *lu'ach*. But it was not so in biblical and Mishnaic days. When the Eternal said to Moses and Aaron in Egypt: "This month shall be unto you the beginning of months; it shall be the first month of the year unto you", He was not only telling them that Nisan, the month in which Israel became a free people, was to be thenceforth the first in the nation's year, but much else.

He actually *showed* them the moon in its renewal phase, and *commanded* them, and the spiritual leaders who succeeded them in future generations, to sanctify and publicly proclaim a new month when the moon was at that exact phase. (This, and all the following data on this subject, is taken from RM's classification and codification of this currently non-functioning commandment.)

Section 6.   **Determining The New Month**

On the day after the twenty-ninth of each month, a court of no less than three Sages, each an expert in astronomy, who had already calculated that the new moon might appear on that day, sat and awaited the possible arrival of witnesses who claimed to have seen it. They were warmly received, and strictly questioned in detail; and if their evidence, under examination, accorded with specifications and calculations of the experts, that very day was sanctified and proclaimed as the first of the new month: otherwise, it remained the thirtieth of the old, and the following day, automatically and without any proclamation, was the first of the new month – since no Jewish month has more than thirty days.

The proclamation, in the first instance, took the form of a country-wide-and-long chain of hill-top beacons. But when mischievous sects misled the people with false beacons, the practice was discontinued, and in its stead messengers were sent post-haste in all directions; and, with expedition, they could reach all population centres in the country in time – but hardly outside of it, and certainly not the far-flung communities in the Diaspora!

In earlier times, therefore, these communities, not knowing whether the day after the twenty-ninth of a month had been proclaimed the first day of the next, apparently always treated it as such, just in case it had been – and observed two days Yomtov. If they were right, then they had observed the Festival on the correct day, i.e. the first day Yomtov: but even if they were wrong, they *still* observed it on the correct day – the second day Yomtov!

All this, however, became academic from the middle of the fourth century onwards, when the then President of the Sanhedrin, Hillel II, because of restrictions placed upon that supreme religious body by the Romans, and the dearth of expert astronomers in Judea, published the perpetual calendar which is still our guide to the beginning of months (and years, which will be referred to in the next chapter). Presumably then, Jews everywhere now know the exact dates of the Torah Festivals – yet the second-day Yomtov is still observed in the Diaspora. Why?

Section 7.   **Even With Perpetual Calendar!**

That question was asked and answered by Abaye: because the authorities in the Holy Land sent a message to the Jews in the Diaspora which said: "Give heed to the customs of your ancestors . . . for it may happen that some future Government will issue a decree (to destroy all Jewish literature, including calendars), and confusion will arise again" – and, indeed, such attempts have often been made.

A novel reason why Diaspora Jewry still have to keep two days Yomtov, one which is particularly relevant today, has been suggested: the observance of the second day is a punishment imposed on them for not living in Eretz Yisrael. Not surprisingly, its source is the *Jerusalem* Talmud. But can there be a more prosaic, more factual reason? It is here suggested that there is.

For practical purposes, a month must consist of so many complete days, but the exact period between one new moon and the next is approximately twenty-nine days and twelve hours (add forty-four minutes and three-and-a-half seconds for exactitude). When the calendar was compiled, therefore, ten of the twelve months in an ordinary year alternately had twenty-nine and thirty days, half a day being taken off the first in each pair, and added to the second, and the last day of the latter, the thirtieth, was *also* observed as new moon (Rosh Chodesh) since it included half of it!

And the same would apply to every day in every month – it would be either half-a-day long or short; and therefore a two-day Festival would include both halves! But if this is so, why not two days in Israel as well, since there is no longer any witnessing of the new moon there? The answer may be: if the two-day Festival is a 'punishment' on Diaspora Jews for living there, the one-day Yomtov is a 'blessing' on Israeli Jews for living *there*!

Whatever the reason, the Diaspora Jew must observe the two-day Yomtov. Some maintain that when R. Eleazar included (SPB 262) "one who despises the Festivals (*mo'adot*)" among those who, even if they have Torah knowledge and good deeds to their credit, have no share in the world to come, he meant neglect of the whole of the Festival; while others say he intended only the intermediate or 'weekdays' (*chol hamo'ed*) of Pesach and Sukkot.

But it may well be that the truth lies in a compromise between these two views, and he was referring to the Diaspora Jew who abandons observance of *Yomtov-sheni shel galuyyot*. If you want to enjoy the 'blessing' of only one day Yomtov, then, – go and live in Eretz Yisrael!

Section 8. **Additional Service**

New Moon days were in the past, and will in future times be, observed as semi-Festival days, and today they still have in common with Shabbat and all the days of all the Festivals the recital of a fourth Service called *Musaf* ('additional'). You will remember that the three weekday Services were instituted to replace, and correspond with the times of, the sacrificial Service in the Temple; and on each of the above days there were additional festive sacrifices there.

We are reminded of this by the reading of the Torah verses referring to the particular day's special offerings either as that day's Maftir or, on the intermediate days of Sukkot and Rosh Chodesh, as the day's Portion itself. On the latter occasion, the Reading commences with the sacrifices offered on weekdays and Shabbat. On all those days a further mention of the particular day's sacrifices is made in its Musaf Amidah.

75.   TO REJOICE ON YOMTOV

Section 9. The Torah employs exactly the same variations in the purpose it gives for the observation of the Festivals as it does for that of Shabbat (see chapter twenty-five); and from them the Sages deduce that all the Festivals except Yom Kippur should be spent in the same way as Shabbat – half the day in service to the Eternal, such as prayer and study, and the other half for your own enjoyment.

However it would certainly not be to your discredit if, apart from partaking of its three meals, you spent most, or even all the rest of the Shabbat in study! On the contrary: such sanctification of the holy day, especially if you can only manage to devote the minimum of time to prayer and study on weekdays, would undoubtedly be to your eternal credit!

But as far as the Festivals are concerned, you are positively commanded to *enjoy* yourself, and give enjoyment to others. "And thou shalt rejoice on thy feast – thou, thy son and thy daughter, thy man- and thy maid-servant, the Levite and the stranger, and the fatherless and the widow that are within thy gates." How? A man should make himself merry and of good heart with wine, etc; his children by giving them pop-corn and nuts, etc.; his womenfolk by buying them new clothes and ornaments, according to his means; and the poor and other unfortunates by feeding them. Though this is stated primarily of the three Joyous Festivals, it also applies to Rosh Hashanah, though with certain reservations, as we shall see later.

This commandment is given in the context of the celebration of the Three Joyous Festivals, as stated above, on which all the families of the Land of Israel, and even from beyond its borders, were wont joyfully to wend their way to Jerusalem, where the menfolk in particular presented themselves before the Eternal at His Temple, and there made festive and thanksgiving offerings, taking back to their lodging-places the major portions of them for the festive meals.

Section 10.   **To The Paterfamilias**

The commandment is primarily addressed to the paterfamilias, enjoining him, in the first instance, to enjoy the Feast with "whatsoever thy soul desireth, with oxen and sheep, with wine and strong drink, and/or with whatsoever thine appetite asketh of thee" – as long as it is *kasher*, of course! But just as important, he is commanded not to be greedy and selfish, but to share his divinely-given bounty with his wife and famly, and retainers they may have, by giving them gifts *they* enjoy, and with the poor and hungry of the house of Israel generally.

At the end of every three years, the farmer in Temple times had to make sure he had separated all the tithes and other gifts due from him, and had transferred them to those to whom they rightly belonged. After this he had to aver before the heavenly Provider: "I have done according to all that Thou hast commanded me" – which implies, says the Mishnah, "I have myself rejoiced, and caused others to rejoice (with Your bounty)". And after the Temple was destroyed celebration of the Feast-days was adapted to approximate as closely as possible to that of those days.

As you will see, the commandment calls for giving expression to the virtues of charity, kindness and hospitality in the particular sphere of home and family over which mother and father, rather than you, have sway. Moreover the practice of these virtues involves expenditure which only the gainfully-employed can afford – far more than what is left over after the average teenager has drawn from his/her 'pocket-money' the cost of personal needs!

In fact, so important is the practice of these virtues *all the year round* that there are separate Torah commandments relating to them, which are being held over for the next volume of this work dealing with true Jewish living from marriage and livelihood-earning on-wards – though you should, in the meantime, do as much as you can, with the little you have, in practising them.

There is, however, one aspect of Festival rejoicing which you *can* fulfil *now*: for it is not only the hungry for *food* that have to be entertained especially on the Festivals, but also those who yearn for congenial *company* in which to celebrate them. The Torah mentions the fatherless, the widow, and the 'stranger' – who could be a colleague studying or working far away from his home, or a convert to Judaism (see chapter twenty-one).

All of them may have the means to regale themselves with every delicacy – but they are lonely, and would eagerly accept an invitation to celebrate the Festival within the warmth of an observant family circle! *You* might have one or more such among your acquaintances, and ask your parents to invite him (or them) to join your festive table, "so that the Eternal thy G—d may bless thee in all the work of thy hand which thou doest".

Section 11.   **The *Eruv Tavshillin***

This law is not numbered, because it is not a Torah commandment but a rabbinic enactment – perhaps half of one of the 'seven crown jewels' with which they adorned the Torah (see last chapter), the other half being the *eruv techumim* (see chapter twenty-three). Though it is normally father who performs the rite, so that mother can avail herself of the concession it grants; it may be that *you*, young lady or even gentleman, may have a penchant for baking or cooking, which may be one of the ways in which you get *your* Yomtov joy – which is one reason why I enter it here.

When the manna was first about to fall, Moses was divinely instructed to inform the people that with the double portion which would fall on the sixth day of the week they should "bake that which you will bake, and cook that which you will cook" for that day, and to prepare their meals for the following holy Shabbat with the remainder. In these instructions the Sages found support for their regulations:

Only when the sixth day is an ordinary weekday, as it was then in the wilderness, may food be prepared on it for the Shabbat, but not when it is a Festival – unless an *eruv tavshilin* is prepared before that Festival begins. This is read into the double use of the verbs, i.e. you may bake and cook on Yomtov for Shabbat only if you have already begun doing so before the Festival started. And, from the mention of baking *and* cooking, it is gathered that the *eruv* should consist of both something baked, like a roll, a matza-cake or a slice of bread, and some-cooked, fish, meat or an egg – a complete mini-meal.

The phrase *eruv tavshilin* means "a mingling of dishes" – of those cooked on Yomtov-Friday with that already prepared before Yom-tov, whether on Wednesday or Thursday, dependent on whether Yomtov is Thursday and Friday or Friday and Shabbat. Before Yomtov beings, the *eruv* (SPB 308) is raised and the blessing and declaration made over it.

It is then carefully put away, and *may* be eaten at any of the Shabbat meals. Ideally, however, the roll or matza-cake should be used, *but not eaten*, as one of the two 'chalot' at the Shabbat's evening and morning *seudot*, used to make the *Hamotsi* over at the *seudah shlishit*, and then eaten together with its cooked dish. Incidentally, a 'third meal' is not customary on Yomtov.

Two reasons are given for the *eruv* enactment: so that *Yomtov* should not be belittled, the *eruv* demonstrating that, were it not for its institution, it would have been forbidden to cook on the Festival even for Shabbat, let alone for the following weekday; and so that *Shabbat* should not be belittled, the *eruv* demonstrating that Yomtov should not begin until Shabbat preparations have at least been begun – and it is for this reason that it is urged that the *eruv* should be made with the choicest chalah and cooked dish.

Every householder should make his own *eruv* on behalf of all his family, and anyone who deliberately does not do so is considered a sinner. But even in that case, and certainly on occasions of forgetfulness or mishap, he is 'covered' by the *eruvin* of those who *have* made them: for in the declaration it states the *eruv* is "for us and for *all who reside in this city*"; and every rabbi makes his for all the members of his community – just in case!

You are not a family-man yet: but should your father have forgotten to make his, or was somehow prevented from doing so, *you* can act on his behalf, since every family should have its own *eruv*. There are many other interesting laws concerning this rite – but you will have to study them for yourself.

Section 12. **Reciting *Hallel***

This is another of the 'seven crown jewels' with which the Sages adorned the Torah – to recite *Hallel*, some of David's Psalms of "Praise" on the three Joyous Festivals, basing their enactment on the Prophet's saying: "You shall have a song as in the night when a Feast is sanctified; and gladness of heart as when one goeth with the pipe, to come into the mountain of the Eternal, to the Rock of Israel".

This is taken to mean: There shall be special songs of praise to the Eternal on those Festivals sanctified on their Eve with Kiddush, with gladness (*simchah*) of heart; and when pilgrimages are made to the Temple to appear before the Eternal Rock of Israel – the *Shalosh Regalim*. Though it is very probable that many of those who were going to Jerusalem and the Temple for Sukkot arranged to leave a fortnight earlier so that they could be present there on Rosh Hashanah and Yom Kippur as well, Hallel is not said on these two Festivals. Why not? The ministering angels are said to have asked the Almighty that very question, and He answered: "Is it possible that the King should be sitting on the throne of justice, with the books of life and death open before Him, and Israel should chant Hallel?"

Though Rosh Hashanah is included with the Three as a Yomtov, a day for feasting and enjoyment, we are advised to celebrate it as such with a measure of restraint – for after all, it *is* the opening Day of Judgment. Why treat it as a Yomtov at all then? That will be answered when we discuss that Festival in detail; and the same applies to Yom Kippur, only more so – though, as we will then see, it used to be one of the two most enjoyable days in the Jewish year!

Hallel (SPB 295–300) is also said on Rosh Chodesh (New Moon

days); but since it is only a very minor festive day, only 'half Hallel' is then said, two excerpts being omitted. Why it is that this abbreviated form of Hallel is also said on six of the eight days of Pesach will be explained in the next chapter.

We can now proceed to discuss the five Torah Festivals in their traditional two groupings, and the specific Torah commandments governing each of them, as distinct from those they all have, more or less, in common. Do not, however, forget the latter: add them to, and observe them with, each Festival's own commandments.

Section	**Notes**
1	Genesis 2.3; Rosh Hash. 25a; Yad. Yomtov 1.1.
2	SM. P. 159–160, 162–163, 165–167; N. 323–329.
3	Exodus 12.16; Megillah 7b.
4	Yad. Yomtov 1.5–8.
5	Exodus 12.2; Yad. Kiddush Hachodesh; SM. P. 153.
7	Betsa 4b; Y. Eruvin 3.9.
8	Numbers 10.10; I. Samuel 20.18; Amos 8.5; Isaiah 66.23; Numbers chapters 28–29.
9	Pesachim 68b; Deuter. 16.14; Or. Ch. 597.1 & 529.2; Pesachim 109a.
10	Deuter. 14.22–29; Ibid 26.14; Maaser Sheni 5.12.
11	Exodus 16.6–23; Betsah 2b & 15b; MB. 527 note 48; Or. Ch. 529.1; Ibid 527.7.
12	Isaiah 30.29; Arakin 10b; R. Hash. 32b; Or. Ch. 597.1.

Twenty-Seven

PASSOVER – AND SIX WEEKS

Section 1. The three Festivals commonly called Pesach (Passover), Shavuot (Pentacost) and Sukkot (Tabernacles) are collectively described in the Prayer-Book (SPB 311) as *mo'adim le-simchah*, "appointed times for joy", and *chaggim le-sasson*, "festivals for gladness', descriptions which, incidentally, provide the form in which we greet each other on these occasions. The first well-wisher greets friend with *"chag same'ach!"*, to which the other responds in like manner or preferably with *"mo'adim le-simchah!"*

As we saw in the last chapter, Shabbat and all the Festivals are called "the appointed times of the Eternal"; but only these three are specifically described as 'for joy', hence their name "The Joyous Festivals", and only they are called *chaggim* in the Torah, where the collective name for the three is the *Shalosh Regalim*.

These two words literally mean "three feet", referring to the commandment "Three times (*pe'amim*) in the year shall all thy males appear before the Lord, the Eternal" on the Temple Mount – which could only be approached *on foot*, hence the names "The Three Foot Festivals" or "Pilgrim Festivals". (Even the Hebrew word here translated 'times' occasionally means 'feet' or 'foot-steps'.)

When making these appearances, G–d commands that "none shall appear before Me empty; every man shall give as he is able, according to the blessing of the Eternal thy G–d which He hath given thee". Therefore everyone brought with him a festive offering called a *chagigah* – hence the name *chaggim* for these three Festivals.

Agriculturally, the first two of these Festivals must coincide with the opening and closing of the grain harvest, and the third with the fruit harvest, upon which the national economy in ancient Israel depended so vitally – as it does, indeed, in modern Israel, though perhaps to a lesser extent. They are therefore sometimes called "The

Three Harvest Festivals". We can now proceed to consider them in the order they occur in the biblical year.

Section 2.   **Pesach: The Springtime Festival**
When dating the Festivals, the Torah does not give the months names but numbers: and it ordains that the Feast *we* call Pesach should begin "in the first month . . . on the fifteenth day of this month . . ." – the month *we* call Nisan. Now, as can be adduced from the last chapter, an average Jewish year of twelve lunar months has 354 days, whereas a solar year, by which the seasons come round, has 365.

Were *all* our years to consist of twelve lunar months, it would mean that if Pesach began one year in mid-March, it would fall in mid-February three years later – and mid-December six years after that (which is, incidentally, what happens with the Moslem fast-month of Ramadan, they having such a year).

But the Torah directs: "Be ever watchful for the month of the *aviv*, *then* keep Pesach unto the Eternal thy G–d; for in the month of *Aviv* the Eternal thy G–d brought thee forth out of Egypt by night". This tells us two things: that *aviv* is the season when "barley is in the ear (*aviv*)" – the Spring; and that the month in which barley, "the first-fruits of your harvest" is reaped – which is the agricultural reason why the month in which Pesach falls used to be called "Aviv". (*The names of the Jewish months now in use are not Hebrew, but adaptations from the Babylonian month-names, "brought up by the returning exiles" to Jerusalem.*)

In Temple times, then, the Sages watched not only for the new moon, but also for the arrival of Spring; and when they calculated it would be late, they declared a 'pregnant' year, adding a whole month after the last of the old year, Adar, and calling it Adar Sheni (Second Adar). And when Hillel II. fixed the calendar he inserted seven such years at varying stages of every cycle of nineteen.

Thus Pesach is always in the Spring, when all Nature bursts forth into new life, when Israel emerged from the winter of bondage to the spring of national freedom – which is why the Festival is called "the season of our Freedom" in its Amidah and Kiddush (SPB 311 & 313).

But if you examine all the texts hitherto quoted and others, you will see that the name "Pesach" is applied only to the *first evening* of the Festival, the Seder night, when the *korban Pesach*, the paschal lamb, was eaten. For example: "In the first month, on the *fourteenth day of the month at dusk is the Eternal's Pesach*".

Section 3.   **The Feast Of Unleavened Bread**
The verse following the one just quoted reads: "And on the fifteenth day of the same month is the feast of unleavened bread unto the

Eternal; seven days ye shall eat unleavened bread" – and that is the name given to the whole of the Festival, in Bible and Prayer-Book, *chag hamatzot*. I will not insult you by telling you why it is called that, but only cite the source-verse: "And they baked the dough which they had brought out of Egypt into unleavened cakes, for it was not leavened; for they had been driven from Egypt and could not tarry. . . ."

We shall soon see that "seven days shall you eat matzot" is not the commandment it appears to be. The Torah is much more concerned that you should *not* eat its opposite – *chametz*, leaven, not a crumb of it, not a drop: so concerned, in fact that it devotes no less than six commandments to ensure that we can have no contact with it – and the Sages add their own. All this is not really surprising, when you bear in mind that for 357 of the (solar) year's 365 days we eat *chametz* without even thinking about it. The six commandments are:

76.   REMOVE ALL LEAVEN FROM YOUR HOME

That 'duty' to eat matzot for seven days (eight in the Diaspora) is first mentioned in the paragraph of instructions for the observance of the first Pesach – yes, we'll still call the Festival that for convenience' sake! – and is followed by "but (*ach*) on the first (*rishon*) day you shall cause all leaven to cease from your homes". Obviously this cannot mean on the first day of Yomtov! What then does it mean?

The Sages first show that *rishon* can mean the *preceding* day, and then that the word *ach* limits it to half a day, giving the meaning: by mid-day on the day before Pesach all leaven shall have been removed from your home. They then build their own fence round this Torah commandment by enacting: a thorough search for *chametz* throughout the home on the previous evening – or the one before that if Yomtov begins on Sunday, carefully leaving in one place sufficient food for meals until two hours *before* mid-day on Erev-Pesach, after which time *chametz* may not be eaten; and disposing of any remainder by one hour after that.

77.   YOUR LEAVEN NOT TO BE SEEN *ANYWHERE*

Section 4. This is an extension of the previous commandment: not only in your home, but in any place you possess or occupy, must leaven not be seen during Pesach – places like your office, business premises, personal locker, etc., and therefore must be removed from there also before Pesach. This is deduced from "neither shall leaven of yours be seen *in all thy borders*".

78.   NOR OTHERS' LEAVEN IN *YOUR* POSSESSION

The source of this commandment is the clause, "seven days leaven *shall not be found* in your homes" – even if it belongs to someone else, and you have responsibility for its safe-keeping. Should a non-Jewish friend, however, enter your home eating a bread sandwich, you do not have to tell him to leave – but must not let him use your table or plate! And see that any crumbs are removed!

79.   DO NOT EAT *CHAMETZ* FROM MID-DAY EREV-PESACH

As mentioned above, refraining from eating leaven in the two hours *before* mid-day is a rabbinic 'fencing' enactment; but not to eat it *after* mid-day on Erev-Pesach is a Torah commandment, derived from an interesting source. We are told that when the paschal lamb was being slaughtered, "thou shalt eat no leavened bread with it". From this it is deduced that *chametz* must not be eaten once that slaughtering had commenced; and as explained when considering the earliest time for the daily Minchah Service, (chapter twenty-two), on occasion that was as early as noon.

It is also forbidden to eat matza during the whole day of Erev-Pesach from dawn – or at least from two hours before mid-day, in order to work up an appetite for the Seder. Another reason is to have an interval between eating matza at other times, just because you like it, and eating it in fulfilment of the commandment to do so at the Seder, soon to be entered. For this latter reason many people refrain from eating matza two weeks earlier – from Rosh Chodesh Nisan onwards.

80.   DO NOT EAT *CHAMETZ DURING* PESACH

You may consider this commandment wholly superfluous after the previous four. If we must dispose of our own *chametz*, and remove that of others, seven hours before Pesach begins; and if we must not eat it six hours before; how can it possibly be imagined that it may be eaten on Pesach itself, when all these precautions are to ensure that only "unleavened bread shall be eaten throughout the seven days"?

It is precisely *because* those four are only precautionary, and therefore do not incur the dire penalty that eating *chametz* on Pesach itself does, that *this* commandment is stated time and again: "for whosoever eateth leavened bread from the first day to the seventh day, that soul shall be cut off from Israel" – by the hand of Heaven.

Section 5.   **What Is *Chametz?***

At this stage it should be explained, briefly and not exhaustively, what *chametz*, rendered 'unleavened *bread*' into English, is. It *is* such edibles as bread, cakes, etc. baked from those grains from which matza can be baked, the dough having been allowed to ferment, i.e. become leaven, by either standing idle without being kneaded for more than eighteen minutes, or made to ferment by the addition of some leavening ingredient such as yeast – which is why the dough from which matzot are baked must *not* contain such an ingredient, and may *not* stand idle as long as that.

The five such grains are: "wheat, barley, spelt, rye and oats;" and to these, Askenazi Jews only add "rice, millet and pulse." However the term *chametz* also includes liquors made from these grains, such as beer and whisky.

81.   OR ANYTHING WITH *CHAMETZ* ADMIXTURE

This commandment extends the previous one to include eating anything containing even a minute admixture of *chametz*, be it only one ear of corn found in a large pot of chicken and soup after it had been warmed up on Pesach; or the taste of a *chametz* dish absorbed by a metal pot during the year, which clings to it even after normal washing. For this reason such pots may not be used on Pesach unless they are subjected to a particularly scrupulous course of scouring through the application of heat great enough to extract that remnant taste.

Why such stringency, and why so many commandments? The first either to distance us as far away as possible from *chametz* which we are used to all the year round, or because anything mistakenly admixed with a small amount of it may be eaten after Pesach. And the second either for the first of those two reasons, or because "the Holy One, blessed be He, was pleased to make Israel worthy, therefore He gave them a copious Torah and many commandments" (see HPB 627).

82.   *DO* EAT MATZA – THE FIRST EVENING

Section 6. As mentioned earlier, "seven days shall you eat matzot" is not a commandment ordering you to eat matza *every* day of Pesach – in fact, you do not *have* to eat it on *any* of its *days*! This is deduced, by means of the eighth of R. Ishmael's thirteen principles (SPB 14), from the inconsistency between this verse and another which says, "*six* days shalt thou eat matzot . . .". This makes the eating of matza on the seventh day voluntary and, in accordance with that principle, on all the other days as well.

However, speaking of the first Pesach in Egypt, the Torah says that the paschal lamb *must* be eaten "in that *night, with matzot* and bitter herbs", as was the case later, as long as there was a Temple, and the lamb could be offered. But even when that offering could not be made, it is deduced from "in *all* your dwelling-places shall you eat matzot", matzot (and bitter herbs) must be eaten *that evening* – wherever you live, Temple or no Temple.

"Seven days shalt thou eat matzot" therefore means: if you eat any bread during Pesach – and most people do since it is the staple diet of most, then it *must* be *unleavened* bread. *It should be noted that just as wherever the biblical 'seven days' have been mentioned here, the eighth day must be added in the Diaspora; so does the obligation to eat matza on the first night include the same obligation on the second night there.*

83.   RELATE THE EXODUS STORY!

Section 7. "And thou shalt tell thy son in that day, saying: 'It is because of this did the Eternal do for me when I came out of Egypt". 'Thou' means every father, in every generation, who is commanded to say, "when *I* came out of Egypt", i.e., had it not been for the Exodus, which brought our people into being, he would not have been there to tell the story (*Haggadah* – the name of the book in which it is related).

'Thy son', though masculine singular, refers to all the children of the family, the youngest able to do so asking the four set questions, and he and the others adding any others which occur to them – and there should be quite a number, the Service at the time (called the *Seder,* meaning 'order') having fourteen different parts, most of them of an unusual nature, which have to be performed in their proper order.

'That day' refers to the first day of Pesach, and specifically to the Seder on its Eve, when 'this' – the first matza on which the commandment is to be performed, and the bitter herbs are lying for all to see on the table.

The rest of the Haggadah comprises the set answers to the four set questions – in a roundabout way; but it can, and should be, supplemented by answers to the children's other questions, and father's own additional comments: for "the more one tells of the Exodus, the more is he to be praised" – like the five Sages at Benai-Verak, who were so engrossed in telling of its miracles all through that night that they had to be reminded that the time for reciting the morning Shema had arrived!

If all the children have left home, having their own families to whom to tell the story, husband should relate it to his wife – though both of them will probably be with (one of) the children, glowing with pride at seeing how the tradition is being handed down to the next generation. But even if one is on one's own, he (or she) should still recite the Haggadah for him- or herself, "that thou mayest remember the day thou camest out of Egypt all the days of thy life". However, no family or community should allow *anyone* to celebrate a Seder alone – which may well be the reason why the Seder nights are the only two Feast Eves when no Kiddush is made in the Synagogue Service, as it is every Shabbat Eve in the Diaspora (see chapter twenty-five).

Section 8.   **Dew Continue, Rain Cease!**

Throughout the autumn and winter we praise G–d in every Amidah we recite as He "Who causes the wind to blow and the rain to fall"; and, during the latter season only, we pray in every weekday Amidah that He may "give dew and rain for a blessing upon the face of the earth" (SPB 46 and 50).

But when Pesach, the Festival of the spring in which the grain harvest commences, arrives, Ashkenazi Jews in the Diaspora intone a very moving prayer called *Tefillat Tal* ("Prayer for Dew") in the repetition of the Musaf Amidah, beginning with "Grant dew to favour Thy land", and ending with "For Thou art the Eternal our G–d, Who causest the wind to blow and the dew to descend – may it be for a blessing, and not for a curse, for life and not for death, for plenty and not for scarcity!" – with the implication that the rains may thenceforth cease.

From then onwards those Jews omit the praise, and pray just for "a blessing on the face of the earth" until the autumn arrives again, "because dew and winds are never withheld". Sephardi Jews, however, continue to praise Him as He "Who causeth the dew to descend", i.e. that He should not *withdraw* the blessing – which He could do if He so willed; and their custom has been adopted by almost all congregations, Ashkenazi as well as Sephardi, in the Land of Israel, which so greatly depends on precious dew.

Unfortunately, though they include other once-a-year-only prayers, and even some said but once or twice in a lifetime, and not normally recited out of Daily Prayer-Book, neither SPB nor HPB include the Prayer for Dew or that for rain to be mentioned in the next chapter.

But you can find them in the appropriate *Machzor* (Festival Prayer-Book), a set of which you no doubt have on your bookshelf.

84.   THE OMER: COUNTING DAYS AND WEEKS

Section 9. "From the time the sickle is first put to the standing corn shalt thou begin to number seven weeks". The first grain to ripen in Israel was barley; but the sickle was not generally put to it before "an *omer* of the first-fruits of your harvest" was brought to the priest on the morrow of the first day of Pesach, and he had waved it before the Eternal as a thanksgiving for the harvest.

An *omer* is a measure of approximately 2.1 kilogrammes. How it was ceremoniously reaped as the first day of Pesach ended, and the preparations for and the form the offering took are described in detail in the Mishnah – and you should study it. Once it had been offered, the farmers betook themselves each to his own barley ingathering.

The seven weeks had to be counted from that night onwards – and not only the weeks, but the days as well: for the last quotation above continues: "unto the morrow after the seventh week shall you number fifty *days*". The Temple is no more, neither is the *omer* offered: but the commandment to number individually those days and weeks, called *Sefirat ha-Omer*, the Counting of the Omer (SPB 367–370) remains – the longest 'non-constant' single commandment the individual has to fulfil.

Before giving some consideration to the other six of these weeks, however, we must conclude our study of the first of them, the days of the Festival after the first Yomtov – going in a backward movement, for a reason that will soon emerge.

Section 10.   **Qualified Rejoicing**
The first Pesach and the Exodus reached their climax on the seventh day when (SPB 35–37) "the Eternal saved Israel out of the hand of the Egyptians, and Israel saw the Egyptians dead upon the sea shore . . . Then sang Moses and the children of Israel . . ." And they had good cause, indeed, for singing that majestic tribute to their Warrior Deliverer: had it not been for His salvation, the people of Israel would not have come into being – at least not then; nor any of the consequences that flowed therefrom. That is why that Exodus and that song were chosen for the portion of the Torah to be read on the Seventh Day of Pesach.

Yet when the ministering angels wanted to celebrate that event with song, we are told, "the Holy One, blessed be He, remonstrated with them, saying: "The work of My hands are being drowned in the sea –

and *you* want to *sing?*" What a profound moral we have here! The Sovereign Lord of all peace (SPB 109) must perforce at times become a 'Man of War': but even when this involves bringing death to His and His people's enemies, He is sad – for *all* men are the work of His hands, and He loathes having to destroy any!

And we are commanded to walk in His ways (commandment 14): We are advised: "Rejoice not when thine enemy falleth . . .", especially when, as Egypt did, he once befriended you and gave you hospitality in troublous times. Moses and the children of Israel did not sing *for joy*, but "unto the Eternal, because *He* had been exalted" by the triumph of their righteous cause.

And therefore, on every anniversary of that historic event (and its second day in the Diaspora), we temper our rejoicing by saying only *half* Hallel, as on the minor Rosh Chodesh day. But that Seventh Day is Yomtov, after all, and has greater sanctity than the intermediate days of the Festival which precede it: and so we say only half Hallel on those days as well, so that it should not appear that they are more important than the Yomtov following them.

Section 11.   **The Intermediate Days**

Those days between the first and last Yamim-Tovim – five in Israel and four in the Diaspora – are called in Hebrew *Chol Hamo'ed*, the 'weekdays of the Festival', because there are some things which you may do on them, if essential, as if they were ordinary weekdays, and some which are forbidden just as they are on Yomtov. Even when one of them is Shabbat, as it is more often than not, it is still called *Shabbat Chol Hamo'ed*; but it must of course be observed in the same way as any other, by complete cessation of work.

Since the Torah is not explicit as to what additional work is permitted on Chol Hamo'ed that is forbidden on Yomtov, it is deduced that "it was left to the Sages to make the decision." The five categories of these permitted works have been summarised thus: (a) anything which, if not done on Chol Hamo'ed, would cause financial loss; (b) anything which contributes to the enjoyment of the Festival; (c) anything which a poor man need do to provide himself with Yomtov necessities; (d) essential public works; and (e) any amateur job outside one's regular occupation.

Section 12.   **Linking Past To Future**

Not mentioned in the last chapter as one of the things which the Three Joyous Festivals have in common, is the custom to recite on each of them – in our case the last day of Pesach, *Hazkarat Neshamot*, a Memorial Prayer for the Souls of the departed, commonly called *Yizkor*, which they, in turn, have in common with Yom Kippur. The reasons for the omission are three:

First, because the custom has no Torah or Talmudic origin; secondly, because even the Shulchan Aruch only mentions it in connection with Yom Kippur, the Torah name for which, Yom Kippur*im* (Day of Atonement*s*), it is suggested, implying that the Day atones for both the living *and* the dead – thus giving the custom tenuous Torah support; and thirdly, because some authorities oppose the custom being followed at *any* time, maintaining that only a person's actions in *this* life decide his status in the Hereafter.

The custom has been traced back to the times of Judas Maccabeus historicised in two books of the non-biblical Apocrypha. When that hero went to give burial to some of his slain warriors, it is related, he found that they appropriated local idols, which sin he assumed to be the cause of their death. He therefore made a collection of money, and sent the proceeds to Jerusalem therewith to buy a sacrifice to be offered as atonement for them. Perhaps this is the source for the additional custom of promising charitable donations when Yizkor is said, as "atonement for the soul of the departed".

Another possible source cited for the custom is the non-inclusion of Amon among those kings "who have no share in the world to come", though his equally wicked father, Menasseh, *was* included in it – because of the righteousness of Amon's son, Josiah. From this is derived the saying that "a son can confer privileges on his (dead) father". Josiah, however, *consistently* "did that which was right in the eyes of the Eternal": charity alone, though a very important aspect of 'righteousness', is not enough in itself to achieve so great an objective!

Nevertheless, Yizkor, often even unaccompanied with charitable donations, has become a very popular influence in Jewish life, attracting many to the Synagogue on those days of the Three Festivals when it is recited, who would otherwise not attend then. It also gives us an opportunity to pay tribute to the generations gone by, whose loyalty to Judaism was transmitted to us, as we undertake to hand it down to future generations (SPB 44).

And, in a way, Yizkor also helps us to understand why the weeks of the Omer after Pesach, the harvest season which is usually a joyous time among other peoples, have become a sad interlude in the Jewish year.

Section 13.   **Mournful Omer Days**

The traditional reason for observing semi-mourning from after Pesach until the thirty-third day of the Omer is the death during that period of 24,000 disciples of R. Akiva from a mysterious and cruel bout of choking. This has been put in an historical setting: R. Akiva was a committed supporter of Bar-Kochba who raised a rebellion against the Roman occupation forces of Judea. He is reputed to have thrown all those thousands of his disciples into the hopeless battle against overwhelmingly superior forces, with disastrous results.

Others (HPB 939) attribute the commemorative mourning to the massacres of Jews by the Crusaders, who left on their 'holy' mission to clear the Holy Land of 'infidels' just after being urged on in church sermons on Easter — which corresponds in time approximately to Pesach, killing the 'infidel' Jews in the communities en route.

Whatever the source, no weddings or hair-cutting are allowed for a period of thirty-three days, some counting them from the second day of Pesach to the thirty-third (*LaG* — *lamed* being numerically equal to 30, and *gimmel* to 3) of the Omer, others from the beginning of the month Iyar to three days before Shavuot. But *all* observe LaG b'Omer as a semi-Festival, when all joyful celebrations may be held, because the plague ended on that day — or Bar-Kochba had some unrecorded and temporary victory on it.

Modern Israel has added two more joyful and bright days to relieve the gloom of the Omer, as we will see in chapter thirty. "Weeping may tarry for the night — but joy cometh in the morning"! Our people's night has been a long, long one; but the bright dawn of Medinat Yisrael has already broken forth!

Another reason given for counting the forty-nine days from that on which the Exodus began is that, in Egypt, the Israelites had been associated with the forty-nine degrees of idolatrous and moral impurities — to the very nadir of all immorality. Each day of their trek in the desert air cleansed them of one of these impurities, so that on the fiftieth day they had been purified completely, enabling them to receive G–d's pure Torah at Sinai — an event which happened to coincide with the Festival we are now to consider. Chag Same'ach!

Section   **Notes**
1   Exodus 23.14–17; Deuter. 16.16–17; e.g. Isaiah 26.6 and Cant. 7.2; as note 2.
2   Levit. 23.6; Deuter. 16.1; Exodus 9.31; Levit. 23.10; Y. Rosh Hashanah 1.2; Levit. 23.5.
3   Levit. 23.6; Exodus 12.39; Ibid 12.15; Pesachim 5a; Or. Ch. chapters 441 & 445.
4   Exodus 13.7; Ibid 12.19; Deuter. 16.2–3; Or. Ch. 471.1–2; as note 1; see MB. 443 note 1; Exodus 12.15.
5   Pesachim 35a & 46a; Or. Ch. 442.5; Pesachim 30a; Or. Ch. 447 & 451; MB. 447 notes 1 & 103.

6   Exodus 12.15 and Deuter. 16.8; Pesachim 120a; Exodus 12.8 & 20.
7   Exodus 13.8; see Haggadah; Deuter. 16.3; Or. Ch. 487.2.
8   Ta'anit 3a.
9   Deuter. 16.9; Levit. 23.10–11 & 16; Menachot chapter 6 (but chapter 10 in Mishnayot); SM. P. 161.
10 Exodus 14.30 & 15.1; Megillah 10b; Proverbs 24.17; Or. Ch. 490.4 and MB there, note 7.
11 Chagigah 18a; MB 530 note 1; Levit. 23.4.
12 Or. Ch. 621.6 and MB. note 19; Encyc. Judaica vol 7. 632. II. Kings 21.19 to 22.2; Sanhedrin 104a.
13 Yevamot 62b; MB 493 note 4; Psalms 60.6.

Twenty-Eight

SHAVUOT AND SUKKOT

Section 1. Though Pesach is, as we have seen, the first of the 'Joyous' Festivals, "you do not find the Torah refer the term 'rejoicing' to it even once. Why? because on Pesach the grain crop is judged", its quality and quantity, according to the nation's merit. But had not the harvesting of the barley crop begun on the second day of that Festival? Yes! But even imminent prospects of a bumper crop can be dashed in a day by "fire and hail, snow and smoke, and the stormy wind which fulfil His word"!

Anything could happen in the course of those six weeks; and the *omer* offering was as much an entreaty for fair weather until the whole harvest was completed, as a thanksgiving offering for its commencement. Besides, although barley is one of the two grains with which the Promised Land was said to be blessed, it was considered as animal fodder – a very important commodity, but not for man's bread, unless he is very poor!

But once the seven weeks had clemently passed, and the granaries were filled with *all* the varieties of corn, including the last to ripen and the choicest, wheat – *then* "thou shalt observe the Feast of Weeks (*Chag Shavuot*) unto the Eternal thy G–d . . . and thou shalt *rejoice*" before Him. The year's staple food for man and animal is safely gathered in, and there is cause for *simchah* – but not joy unbounded, for there was still another harvest to come.

Just as an offering of unleavened barley was waved before the Eternal on Pesach, so "two wave-loaves . . . of fine flour, baked with leaven for first-fruits" of the wheat harvest on Shavuot: and just as the omer was offered so that the grain harvest may be blessed, so "the Holy One, blessed be He, said: Bring before Me two loaves on *Atseret* that the fruit of your trees may be blessed."

247

Section 2.   **The Sages Own** *Atseret*

That name 'Atseret' which the Sages give to Shavuot is very remarkable, in a way – for Shavuot is the only one of the Three Festivals to which the Torah does *not* apply that name! It is used once to describe the last day of Pesach, and twice in referring to the day after the seven days of Sukkot the latter actually being called *Shemini Atseret* – but never in connection with Shavuot. Why then did they call it the Atseret? We will consider the word itself in greater detail when we come to the Festival with it in its name, but for the present we will look at just one aspect of it.

The noun is derived from a verb with which you should be acquainted, for it appears in the second paragraph of the Shema where the Almighty warns that should Israel not obey Him then "He will close up (*atsar*) the heavens, and there will be no rain, and the land will not yield its fruit . . .". The noun therefore means 'closure', and in our context, a 'closing Festival'; and that is how the Sages regarded Shavuot – the closing Festival of Pesach. The latter celebrates the *opening* of the grain harvest, and Shavuot its *closure*.

Perhaps they were led to this conclusion by the fact that, apart from the two it has in common with all the other Festivals, Shavuot has no commandment of its own. Again, each of the others has a tractate of the Talmud named after it, while Shavuot has none; and whereas the laws of Pesach, for example, occupy sixty-four chapters in the Shulchan Aruch, Shavuot has only one short one at their tail-end, containing three paragraphs, two of them dealing with the portions of Torah and Prophets to be read, and the third with the Festival's customs, mostly concerned with the second, deduced, reason for its celebration as:

Section 3.   **"The Season Of The Giving Of Our Torah"**

And this is how we describe Shavuot in our prayers, the description having nothing to do with the harvest. This Festival is unique in that the Torah does not give the actual date on which it is to be observed, only telling us that it is the fiftieth day after the First Day of Pesach, which is why it is called in English "Pentecost", from the Greek word for 'fifty'.

But our Sages, examining the chronology of the verses introductory to the giving of the Torah at Sinai, which is the Portion read on (the first day of) Shavuot, reach the majority opinion that it took place on the sixth of Sivan, though R. Yose contended that it was on the seventh – which gives an additional reason why Diaspora Jewry observe two days Shavuot, but Israelis only on the sixth, which coincides with 'Pentecost'.

Were it not for this happy coincidence, Shavuot might have been a mere 'harvest memorial' *chag*, especially in those countries of exile where they were not allowed to own any land, working which might have kept the remembrance of all the Harvest Festivals in mind, as they are celebrated in different ways in Israel today. But as the Torah-Giving Festival Shavuot was kept vibrantly alive until now.

Section 4. **Some Festival Customs**

The customs observed on Shavuot reflect both its aspects. Since, before ascending mount Sinai to receive the second tablets, Moses was instructed to arrange that "neither the flocks nor the herds shall pasture before that mount", it is the custom among some to bestrew Synagogue and home on Shavuot with sweet-smelling herbage, plants and flowers. Because the Torah enjoins that "the seven weeks shall be *complete*", and no Jewish day definitely ends until the stars appear, it is customary not to hold the Arvit Service in the Synagogue on Shavuot Eve until that time.

It is assumed from the words "And Moses brought forth the people out of the camp *to meet G–d*" that His Presence had arrived before them and had to await their coming, they being afraid to meet Him until Moses succeeded in persuading them. To demonstrate, on each anniversary of this epoch-making event that we not only do not fear Him and the Torah He then gave, it is the custom to stay in the Synagogue the whole first night of Shavuot studying the Torah, anticipating His coming, until the Morning Service held as dawn breaks!

Just one more custom, one that merges the two aspects of the Festival. It is to have two special loaves on the table – which, you will remember, is likened to the altar, when we arrive home from Service on Shavuot morning, to remind us of the two which were then offered in the Temple. One of them, however, should be baked with 'milk and honey', because the clause "Honey and milk are under thy tongue" is taken to be a poetic reference to the Torah; and it also recalls the repeated description of the Holy Land as one "flowing with milk and honey". A cheese and honey cake can take their place – but care must be taken not to eat even a crumb of the dairy produce with the meat dish that should follow, after changing the table-cloth and rinsing your mouth thoroughly. Milk and meat *must not* mix!

None of the *mikra'ay-kodesh* is meant to be observed and enjoyed for one or two, seven or eight days, and then forgotten: each of them brilliantly but transiently highlights a vital element in the totality of Judaism, its glow intended to brighten and inspire all our days.

We saw in the last chapter that it is our duty to remember the

Pesach Exodus, and its purpose stated in the last verse of the Shema, "I am the Eternal your G–d Who brought you out of the land of Egypt in order to be your G–d", all the days and nights of our lives. And 'Atseret', its concluding Festival of Shavuot, reminds us of commandment 17 and its corollary: that we must *receive* the given Torah, meditating therein by day and by night; and that *you* must now be preparing yourself to fulfil the verse in the Shema from which it is deduced: "And thou shalt teach them diligently unto thy children" when the time comes.

Section 5.   **Sukkot – Tabernacles**

In the calendar this Festival follows very closely on Yom Kippur – only five days after it; and we will later see how the Sages connect the Day of greatest awe to the most joyous of the Three Harvest Festivals. But historically, agriculturally, and by reason of a profound lesson drawn from this Festival's unusual order of sacrifices in Temple times, it has a much closer affinity with Pesach and Shavuot, though they occur some months earlier in the calendar. Let us now consider its special commandments, and see how these conclusions can be reached from them.

85.   LIVE IN A SUKKAH SEVEN DAYS

After ordaining Yom Kippur on the tenth of the seventh month (Tishri), the Eternal instructs Moses: "On the fifteenth day of this seventh month is the Feast of Tabernacles for seven days unto the Eternal . . . Only on the fifteenth day of the seventh month, when you have gathered in the fruits of the land, shall you keep the feast of the Eternal seven days . . . In booths shall you dwell for seven days . . . that your generations may know that I made the children of Israel to dwell in booths when I brought them out of the land of Egypt".

Here we have the statement of the commandment itself, and two reasons for its institution: first as a celebration of the safe ingathering of the fruit harvest – or probably the main part of it; and in commemoration of the miraculous divine sustenance of our ancestors *without* grain and fruit, and the protection He gave them from the desert heat, during forty years of wandering there.

The word *sukkah* literally means a 'covering', and there is a difference of opinion as to what the Eternal was referring when He said "I made the children of Israel to dwell in *sukkot*": R. Eliezer says they were "clouds of glory" which travelled with the Israelites during the day, shading them from the fierce sun; but R. Akiva maintains that "they made real booths for themselves", frail collapsible huts which they could carry with them from place to place.

The Sh.Ar. 'rules' that they were indeed heavenly clouds, and not human structures, then; but *we* erect booths, or 'tabernacles' for ourselves to commemorate that period. There are many laws governing the requirements of a *kasher* sukkah, most of them governing the *sechach*, the covering, which must be sufficiently frail to allow the stars to be seen through it, yet thick enough to provide more shade than sunshine. The walls can be made of any material, just sturdy enough to withstand a normal strong wind. *You* should help father to make your sukkah, even erect it yourself should he be too busy; and you should therefore study all its laws in your CJL.

Section 6.   *Living* In The Sukkah

The sukkah should be your week-long "home-from home", adequately furnished and tastefully decorated. At the very least you should have all your meals there: but ideally you should study and do home-work, relax and play – and even sleep in it, space and weather permitting. Should the weather prove too inclement, however, you are allowed to go indoors, with a show of disappointment, "like a servant who came to fill his master's cup, and the latter pours the pitcher in his face": for rain on *the* Feast – the name of our Sages give to Sukkot, is "a sign of G–d's anger".

"Ladies are free from the obligation of sukkah", because it is a 'fixed-time' commandment – but they *may*, and many do, observe it, at least at meal-times. Children under BM age are also exempt; but the Sages enacted that those of school age should be trained to observe the commandment. Shammai went even further: when his daughter-in-law gave birth to a boy during the Festival, "he made a hole in the roof over its cot and covered it with *sechach*!".

In Israel they bid farewell to the sukkah on the afternoon of the seventh day of the Festival, since the next day is a Festival in its own right – as it is for those outside Israel as well. But to the latter the eighth day is *also* the Diaspora-added last day of Sukkot, which is why they still eat in the sukkah on its Eve and in the morning, and bid it farewell *that* afternoon. However, the blessing 'to dwell in the sukkah', recited at the commencement of meals on all the other days, is not said on the eighth – because it is, after all, another Festival!

Section 7.   'Pesach' And Matza In Sukkah?

Historically, all three events which the Joyous Festivals commemorate – the Exodus, the Giving of the Torah, and the clouds' protection, which presumably was afforded the Israelites from that first event onwards, took place in the wilderness. A very powerful argument, based on the first of R. Ishmael's thirteen principles (SPB 14), is deduced requiring the observance of Pesach in a sukkah, and the eating of matza during Sukkot! But it is refuted by the citing of the phrase in our source text, "only on the fifteenth day of the *seventh* month" must we dwell in Sukkot – but not on the Festival beginning on the fifteenth of the *first* month, Pesach.

But why did not the Eternal institute that Sukkot should coincide with Pesach, which would be very appropriate? Because Pesach is at the beginning of the sunny season "when it is the way of everyone to spend their days out-of-doors, with some shade to protect them from the sun's rays, and therefore it would not be evident that the sukkah has been made to conform with the Blessed One's commandment. Therefore He commanded us to make the sukkah in the rainy season, when most people are going back indoors".

86.   TAKING THE FOUR SPECIES

Section 8. This commandment is in celebration of the agricultural nature of Sukkot, contained in a verse omitted from the source-text of the last commandment. "And you shall take for yourselves on the first day the fruit of a goodly tree, branches of palm trees, boughs of thick trees, and willows of the brook, and you shall rejoice before the Eternal thy G–d seven days".

Not only the 'bread' but also the 'jam' – all the grain and fruits are safely stored by the time that "the Feast of the Ingathering, at the end of the year" – another name given to our Festival. For this reason, and one other to come, "you find the emotion of *simchah* mentioned *three* times in connection with the Chag" – which is why the Sages call it *the Feast* of all feasts.

The fruit of the 'goodly' (Hebrew *hadar*) tree is the citron (*etrog*), "because it stays (*ha-dar*) on its tree from year to year"; the 'thick tree' is the myrtle (*hadass*) "whose branches completely cover its trunk"; and the willows of the brook (*aravot*) and palm branch (*lulav*) just that. Two *aravot* and three *hadassim* are entwined with the *lulav* on either side, and are held in the right hand, with the *etrog* held in the left hand and touching them, when the (SPB 294–295) meditation and the blessing(s) are recited.

After the blessing(s) the *arba minim* (four species) representative of the harvest are, as the *omer* and the 'two loaves' were, waved towards all four compass points and up- and down-wards, "in order to restrain harmful winds and dews" – or rather as a plea to G–d that *He* do so. In Temple times they acted in accordance with the Torah, taking the *arba minim* and *"rejoicing before the Eternal seven days"* in the Temple, while *"you"* – the people elsewhere – "shall take them on the first day" only. But when the Holy House was destroyed, the Sages enacted that Jews everywhere should 'take the lulav', as the ceremony is called, on each of the seven days in its memory.

Section 9. **To Prevent Fighting!**
Actually, it is only on six days everywhere nowadays: for in every seven days there must be a Shabbat – which was *never* the seventh day (see below), and the lulav is not taken on that day, "lest a man carry it through a public domain for four cubits", carrying anything in such a place on that day being forbidden. In Temple times, however, in those years when 'the first day' of the Festival fell on Shabbat, the day on which the Torah explicitly states the *arba minim* must be taken, the people used to bring their lulavim to the Temple the day before, and arranged in order in a covered-in portico normally used for sitting in.

They came back the next morning early, and the attendants threw down their lulavim to them. Just in case anyone should have, by mistake, got hold of someone else's, they had been instructed to say beforehand, "if anyone gets my lulav, I give it to him as a gift": but they nevertheless used to come to blows trying to get their own! And so it was enacted that when that first day fell on Shabbat each should take his own lulav at home. But if any other day of the Festival fell on Shabbat, the lulav was then taken neither in the Temple nor at home. With no Temple now, the lulav is not taken anywhere on Shabbat, even should that day be the first of the Festival.

Section 10. **Your Own – If Possible**
From the source-text phrase "and you shall take *for yourselves* on the first day", it is deduced that the *arba minim* you take on that day must be *yours*, "excluding any borrowed or stolen", i.e. taken without the owner's permission. If you do not have your own, there are two ways in which you can still fulfil the commandment: either by getting someone to give you his *as a gift*, even if it is on the understanding that you return it; or by using one of the sets the congregation to which you belong buys for the use of all its members, with money contributed by them and in which each, therefore, has a share.

But ideally you should have your own, if at all possible, whatever they cost. It is related that of four Sages who were on a sea voyage during the Festival on some urgent mission, only one of them had a lulav (set) for which he had had to pay one thousand silver pieces.

After fulfilling the commandment with it himself, he gifted it in turn to each of his colleagues for that purpose.

Arba minim are quite expensive today – but you can save up to buy your own, and the best obtainable! In the song of Moses and the children of Israel they exclaimed, "This is my G–d, and I will adorn Him", (SPB 36), and R. Ishmael asked: "Is it then possible to adorn one's Creator?"; and he answers, what they meant was, "I will adorn Him with a beautiful lulav, a beautiful sukkah . . ." and all other religious articles. How better can you spend your money?

Section 11.   **The Seventh Day: Hoshana Rabba**
Though not a Yomtov, the seventh day of Sukkot has acquired a mystique of its own through a custom "given to Moses on Sinai", forgotten during the Babylonian Exile, and re-instituted by the last three Prophets on their Return – the custom of beating a small bunch of willows on the floor or some other object three times. So important did this custom become, and that the willows should be as fresh as possible, that when Hillel II. compiled his perpetual calendar, he so arranged it that this day could never be on Shabbat.

It is called Hoshana Rabba, the "Great *Hoshana*" for this reason: on the other days of the Festival when the lulav was taken, after the Musaf Service a Sefer Torah was carried to the *bimah*, deputising for the altar in the Temple, and one circuit of it made by all those carrying the *arba minim*, reciting prayers, frequently interspersed with the plea *Hosha-na*!, "Save, please!", by giving rain in its due season, and fertility and health to cattle, grain and fruit; But on Hoshana Rabba, the *bimah* was circuited seven times, with many more such prayers, after which the willows were beaten.

This is done because "on Sukkot judgment is passed in respect of rain", and Hoshana Rabba is the last day of that Festival. Because it is a day of judgment, and because "the whole life of man depends on water", the Service in the Synagogue that morning is in many ways like that of the "Days of Awe" in content and melodies, with the Cantor robed in white.

Section 12.   **Sukkot's Universal Message**
The sacrifices in the Temple were unusual on Sukkot in that there were thirteen young bullocks offered on the first day, and they decreased by one each day until there were seven on the seventh day, making a total of seventy in all. Now that is the number of basic nations, descended from Noah's sons, into which the Sages divide the whole of humanity; and those Sukkot sacrifices by Israel were intended as atonement for the sins of all of them! This caused R.

Yochanan to exclaim: "Woe to those nations – for they had a loss and do not know what they have lost! When the Temple stood, the altar atoned for them; but now, who shall atone for them?"

This is another connection Sukkot has with Shavuot, apart from the harvest one. The same R. Yochanan interprets the phrase "And all the people heard the voices . . ." to mean: G–d's utterance of the Ten Commandments "split itself into seventy voices, seventy languages, so that all the nations should comprehend His words", thereafter given to Israel in writing in trust for them.

Section 13.   **Eighth Day – Of "Solemn Assembly"!**
The day following the seven of Sukkot, though shown to be "a separate Festival" in its own right in six distinctive ways, is still called "the Eighth Day" in the Torah, which says it "shall be an *atseret* unto you". The English rendering of this is: "On the eighth day ye shall have a 'solemn assembly'" – of the day to which the Sages refer the phrase "and thou shalt be altogether joyful", the day which doubles with Simchat Torah in Israel, the latter being its second day in the Diaspora! Derived from the above verse, the Festival's name is *Shemini Atseret*, and in the Prayer-Book (SPB 312) it is referred to as "the Eighth-day Feast of Solemn Assembly". Solemn indeed!

One meaning of the word *atseret* was given above in explaining why Shavuot is called *the* Atseret by the Sages – because though it occurs six weeks after the end of Pesach, it is, in the agricultural context, the '*closing* day' of the celebration of that earlier Festival. The verb from which it is derived can also mean to 'detain', as in Manoach's request to the angel of the Eternal (HPH 603), "Let us detain (*atsor*) thee, that we may make ready a kid for thee"; and the Midrash understands it in this sense in giving the following parable in explanation of the Festival's institution, connecting it with Sukkot's universal aspect.

A king once made a sumptuous feast lasting seven days for all his people. When it was over, he said to his intimate friend: "Let you and I, now we have done our duty to all the others, have a private get-together, making do with whatever you can find – a little meat, or fish, or even just vegetables", thus explaining why the Shemini Atseret offering was not six, as we might have expected, but only one young bullock! The Jew and his G–d mutually rejoice spiritually, with His Torah, rather than with sumptuous viands!

Another Midrash connects the dating of this closing Festival with the season in which occurs. By right, it says, Shemini Atseret should have been as distant from Sukkot as Shavuot is from Pesach. But the latter pair occur in the sunny season of the year, when it is convenient to travel from all parts of the country to the Temple; while six weeks from Sukkot is in the midst of the rainy season, when it is not. Therefore, says the Almighty, "I will only detain you for our private get-together for one day immediately following Sukkot, so that you can get home before the heavy rains begin!".

Section 14.   Simohat Torah

Need I describe to you how this 'altogether joyful' day is celebrated? You have probably taken part in the celebrations from your tender years, when you ascended the *bimah* "with all the children" and, under the canopy of a big tallit, led by an elder of the congregation, recited the blessings over the Torah in unison, and were thereafter yourselves blessed; and then, after your Barmitzvah, called up by yourself to recite the blessings as a 'man', alone.

We rejoice because on that day we complete the annual cycle of reading the whole Torah; and, not to give Satan the opportunity to say to G–d, "see how they rejoice because they have *finished* with Your Torah!", we start reading it from the very beginning again at once, though we do so again on the following Shabbat.

There must be vivid pictures in your mind of the dancing *hakafot* (circuits) with the Sifre-Torah round the Synagogue evening and morning, and of the parties given by the *chatanim*, the two gentlemen honoured by being called up to the ending and commencement of the Torah's reading. These are given because when G–d gave Solomon "a wise and understanding heart", which was the knowledge of the whole Torah, "he made a feast for all his subjects": and from this "we learn that a feast should be held after the completion of the Torah".

You and I, however, are not given that knowledge as a gift – *we* must "turn the Torah over, again and again, day by day, week by week, year by year, and wax old over it"! And *that*'s the year-round lesson of Simchat Torah.

Section   **Notes**
1 Y. Shimoni Emor 654; Psalms 148.8; Deuter. 8.8; Sotah 9a; Deuter. 16.10–11; Levit. 23.17; R. Hashanah 16a.
2 Deuter. 16.8; Levit. 23.36 & Numbers 29.35; Or. Ch. 494.
3 Shabbat 86b; Exodus chapters 19–20.
4 Exodus 34.3; Or. Ch. 494 with MB; Levit. 23.15; Exodus 19.17 with Malbim; Cant. 4.11.
5 Levit. 23.34–43; Sukkah 11b; Or. Ch. 625 with MB; Ibid. chapters 629 & 630.
6 Or. Ch. 639.1ff; Sukkah 28b; Ta'anit 2b; Sukkah 28a; Or. Ch. 668.1.

7 Sifra Emor 150 & 184; MB. 625. note 1.
8 Levit. 23.40; Exodus 23.16; Ibid. & Deuter. 16.14–15; Sukkah; 35a, 32b, 38a and 41a.
9 Sukkah 42b–43a; Or. Ch. 658.2.
10 Sukkah 41b; Or. Ch. 658.3 & 9; Mechilta on Exodus 15.2.
11 Sukkah 44b; MB. 660. note 1; R. Hashanah 16a; Or. Ch. 664.1, MB. note 7.
12 Numbers 29.12–34; Y. Shimoni on Genesis 9.18; Sukkah 55b; Exodus 20.15; MR. Exodus 5.9.
13 Sukkah 48a; Numbers 29.35; Deuter. 16.15; Judges 13.15; MR. Numbers 21.24; Y. Shimoni on Numbers 29.35.
14 Or. Ch. 669; Ibid. Tur; I. Kings 3. 5–15; MR. Eccles. 1.1; Ethics 5.25.

Twenty-Nine

THE "DAYS OF AWE"

Section 1. It should not have surprised you that, throughout this volume it has been necessary to draw upon explanations of Torah commandments given in the Talmud: for the Mishnah and the Gemara which discusses it and reaches definitive conclusions from it, "are both the words of the living G–d", the Oral Torah divinely conveyed to Moses on Sinai. True, the plain, superficial meaning of many of the Torah commandments can be gathered from the text itself, such as the reasons for, and the manner of observance of Pesach and Sukkot.

But without recourse to the Talmud it would be utterly impossible to understand why the first day of the *seventh* month is New Year, why it is the first of "Ten Days of Penitence" and 'Awe', or how to observe it, so few and difficult to comprehend are the Torah's references to it. Apart from the two comandments it has in common with all the other Festivals, already listed in chapter twenty-six, all the Torah has to say of it is almost the same thing twice: "it shall be a day of blowing the horn unto you", and "it shall be a memorial of the blowing of the horn".

Section 2.   **"Rosh Hashanah"**
That's all! You will remember the Torah gives no explicit date for Shavuot – but it gives that Festival more than one name. The first day of the seventh month is given none, the prayer-book name for it (SPB 329) being adapted from the two above texts, "this Day of Memorial, a day of (remembrance of) blowing the horn". It was the Sages who first declared the first of Tishri to be one of "four *Rashei Shanah*, 'Heads of the year'", and then *the* Rosh Hashanah as we know it today.

Unlike the Shalosh Regalim, Rosh Hashanah is nowhere described as a *chag* (feast-day) in the Torah – but it is elsewhere, according to

258

the Sages. "Blow the horn on the new moon, at the appointed time for the day of our festival (chag)"; and Rosh Hashanah is the only 'appointed time' of the five "appointed seasons of the Eternal" which occurs at the moon's 'covered time' – the rendering which the Talmud gives to the word *bakeseh*, here translated as 'appointed time' – i.e. on the first day of a month. "Which is the feast on which the moon is covered over? You must say that this is Rosh Hashanah".

And it is meant to be observed as such, "half for the Eternal, and half for you". When the Jews came back to Jerusalem from the Babylonian Exile, they were gathered together "on the first day of the seventh month", and had the Torah read to them from dawn to mid-day. When "all the people wept, when they heard the words of the Torah" which they had not kept, Ezra said to them: "Go your way, eat the fat, and drink the sweet, and send portions to him for whom nothing is prepared; for this day is holy unto our Lord; neither be grieved, for the joy of the Eternal is your strength".

We have seen how RM classifies Rosh Hashanah with the Shalosh Regalim as a chag, and not with Yom Kippur. And the Sh.Ar. says of Rosh Hashanah: "Although it is the Day of Judgment, we eat, drink and rejoice on it", the MB commenting on this: "for the command- ment (75) 'thou shalt rejoice on thy festival' applies to Rosh Hashanah also".

Section 3.   **The Other Half: Judgment Day**

But just as in the days of Ezra the people spent the first full half of the day of Rosh Hashanah in hearing the words of G–d, so must we, especially on this day, spend it in His service, praising Him as our Creator, praying to Him for continued life, and reflecting on those of His commandments in whose fulfilment we have been remiss. For just as on Pesach "judgment is passed on the world in respect of grain produce, on Shavuot in respect of fruit, and on Sukkot in respect of rain; so on Rosh Hashanah judgment is passed on all His creatures" according to their acts in the year just ended.

For on that day the calculation of time began with the creation of the goal of the Creation, Man, all the rest of it having preceded him, so that "he might enter the world to enjoy a prepared banquet". In the tenth hour of that day Adam sinned, in the eleventh he was judged, and in the twelfth he was pardoned. "This" said the Holy One, blessed be He, "will be a sign to your descendants: as you stood in judgment before Me this day and emerged with a pardon (from death), so will your descendants in the future stand in judgment and be pardoned on every first day of the seventh month".

Rosh Hashanah, then, is the anniversary of the progenitor of all mankind, and the Mishnah draws the conclusion that all his descendants are annually judged on that day from the verses "The Eternal looketh from heaven, beholdeth all the sons of men . . . He looketh intently upon all the inhabitants of the earth; the Creator seeth their hearts together, and considereth all their doings". And the Gemara deduces the same lesson, that first Israel and then the nations of the world are judged on that day, from the verse following that quoted above, "Blow the horn on the new moon . . . For it is a statute for Israel, a judgment (day) for the G–d of Jacob".

Section 4.	**Trumpets And Horns**

The sound of trumpets (*chatsotsrot*) was a very familiar one to the people of Israel. In the wilderness it served as a rallying-call in preparation for journeying from one encampment to the next; and in the Promised Land both as an alarm-call against an enemy, and as accompanying music over sacrifices "in the day of your gladness, and on your appointed seasons and new moons" – including Rosh Hashanah, at Temple Services.

But on this Festival a ram's horn (*shofar*) took pride of place and sounding: "There were two trumpets, one on each side of it; the shofar gave a long blast and the trumpets a short one – since the proper ceremony of the day was with the shofar". Why particularly a ram's horn? To rouse us to the remembrance of our supreme duty to achieve the love of G–d, and to cleanse ourselves of all the encrustations on heart and soul which impede such attainment.

For the ram's horn recalls the dramatic demonstration of such a would-have-been act of supreme love by the first two fathers of our people, as Abraham and Isaac walked hand-in-hand, the father to sacrifice his beloved son, and the latter to be sacrificed – as they thought, to prove that love. As it happened, just as Abraham took the knife to slay his son, and angel of the Eternal stayed his hand, saying: "Lay not thy hand upon the lad . . . for now I *know* that thou art a G–d-revering man, and that thou wouldst not have withheld thy son, thine only son, from Me".

At that moment G–d showed Abraham a ram "tearing itself free from one thicket, only to entangle itself into another. The Holy One blessed be He, said to Abraham: 'In a similar manner your descendants are destined to be caught by iniquities and entangled in troubles . . . but on Rosh Hashanah let them take their ram's horns and blow them before Me, and I will rise from the Throne of Judgment and move to the Throne of Mercy, and be filled with compassion for them, remembering your binding of Isaac".

87.   TO HEAR THE SHOFAR

Section 5. And so the Merciful One commanded us to observe Rosh Hashanah as 'a day of *teru'ah*' literally 'a day of blowing the alarm note' which was sounded when war threatened, for we should then be alarmed concerning the outcome of the divine judgment on each of us on that day, "be aroused by the sound of the shofar from your slumbers and examine your deeds, and return in repentance" on this first of the Ten Days of Penitence.

The Sages were not sure whether the alarm notes should be nine very short sharp notes called 'a *teru'ah*', or three longer ones, called '*shevarim*', each as long as three teru'ot; and for this reason both kinds are included, sometimes alone and at other times together, in the complete series of one hundred notes which are now usually blown in most Synagogues, the complement consisting of a third note, a '*teki'ah*', a long plain note similar to that used on joyous occasions in the Temple, between two of which the teru'ot and/or shevarim are always sandwiched.

The commandment is, indeed, called "*Teki'at* Shofar", not only because the majority of the notes are teki'ot, but also because its fulfilment is the unique observance of the feast-day of Rosh Hashanah – a joyous day. The series is divided into three sections: one of thirty notes, just before Musaf; a second, also of thirty, but subdivided into three sets of ten, during the course of the repetition of that Amidah; and a third, immediately after that repetition, consisting of forty notes.

"All are under obligation to *blow* the shofar", it was first ruled; and "a man could not hear his own voice for the noise of individuals' shofrot!" Rabban Gamaliel, however, said "the congregation's deputy fulfils the obligation for everybody", and that is the custom today, though individuals may do so for themselves and for others, such as invalids, at home – providing they know how to do so.

Section 6.   **Ladies Exempt, But . . .**
Ladies are not *obligated* to hear the shofar, for it is a 'fixed-time' commandment; but they *may*, and most of them do, come to Synagogue to hear it sounded. They are even permitted to blow the shofar for themselves – but not for any man: since one who is not obligated to fulfil any commandment cannot act as the agent for one who is; and the same law applies as far as minors are concerned, even if they have mastered the art of Teki'at Shofar.

Ideally, you should hear all three parts of the series of one hundred notes, though the last forty are only a custom. You *must* hear at least the blessing recited before the commencement of the first set of thirty, because it is recited for *you*, containing the words "Who has commanded *us* to hear the sound of the shofar"; and the second set of thirty, sounded at intervals during Musaf, for they are the most important.

To our home-going at the end of the Musaf Service, the Midrash refers the verse: "Go thy way, eat thy bread with joy, and drink thy wine with a merry heart; for G–d hath already accepted thy works" – but not with as much joy and merriment as on the three specific Joyous Festivals: for it is still the Day of Judgment, and must therefore "not become light-headed, but have the fear of the Eternal ever before us".

Section 7.   **The "Intermediate" Week**
And of course Rosh Hashanah comprises the first of the opening Ten Days of Penitence, reaching their climax on Yom Kippur, leaving exactly one week intervening, which, it has been suggested, "should be treated like the Intermediate Days of Pesach and Sukkot", as an intermediate week of repentance, all inessential work being avoided on its weekdays, and as much time as possible spent on Torah study, good deeds, and repentance for past sinful acts of commission or omission – particularly those against our fellow-beings for which even Yom Kippur cannot atone, unless we make amends to, and gain the pardon of, those we have offended, before that Day arrives.

It was mentioned in chapter fourteen that ideally every adult Jew from BM onwards should reflect on his (or her) words and actions *every night* before retiring, and immediately put to right and repent of any wrongs committed that day – which is why the Torah command-ment to repent is listed there (no. 27), together with its source-text, and a promise to treat it more fully here. Should you not have adopted this practice, you are urged to do so at least on these penitential days, and to fulfil *all* the commandments which then come your way with more than usual devotion and conscientiousness.

Moses asked which other nation "hath G–d so near unto them as the Eternal our G–d is *whensoever* we call upon Him?", while Isaiah advises us "Seek the Eternal when He may be found, call upon Him *when He is near*", with the implication that there are times when He is *not* near. Harmonising these two tests the Gemara explains: G–d is always near to 'us' – to a congregation at prayer; but the individual will only find Him near "during the ten days from Rosh Hashanah to Yom Kippur".

This should not lead you to the conclusion, however, that prayer at home is of no avail when you cannot join the congregation! First because prayer is, as has been explained, self-inspection which does you good; and secondly, because there is a third text in which king David says: "The Eternal is near to *all* that call upon Him, to all who call upon Him in truth".

Alas there are many who wait until the last of the Ten Days before they repent – not including *you*, I hope; and so further consideration of the important aspects of the commandment to repent is being left over until we have considered the commandments particular to that climactic Day. But first a precautionary note, and a few of the customs which have come to be associated with Rosh Hashanah.

Section 8. **"One Long Day"**

There are some misguided Jews who make light of, and even abrogate, observance of the second day of Rosh Hashanah, on the mistaken assumption that it is 'only' the Diaspora second-day-Yomtov. But, as has been mentioned earlier, this Festival is observed for two days in Israel also, both days "having the same sanctity" and being considered as 'one long day'. Because of this view, doubts were entertained as to whether *shehecheyanu* should be said on the second evening of the Festival in Kiddush (SPB 334–335), since it is then only the second half of 'the long day'!

From this arose the custom on that second evening to put on a new garment before Kiddush, or have on the table a fruit of a species from which you have not eaten that season – for these also require the recital of that blessing, and then the one you recite at Kiddush is no longer doubtful, as it includes the new garment or fruit also. Nevertheless, even if these preliminary measures are not taken, *shehecheyanu* is still said that evening, "for though both days are 'one sanctity', they are, after all, two days"!

Section 9. **Eating Customs**

Instead of, as always, dipping the *Hamotsi*-bread in salt, on Rosh Hashanah we dip it in honey; and then we take a sweet apple and dip it in the same, and after saying the blessing on the fruit, take a bite at it, praying that the year just beginning may be a sweet one for us all. Another custom is to eat as a course in the meal a lamb, chicken or fish *head*, symbolising the divine promise "and the Eternal shall make thee a head, and not a tail"!

It is further customary to include in the meal either raw or cooked vegetables etc. whose Hebrew, or even Yiddish, names have some consonance with the verb in either language meaning to 'increase' – such as carrots, called *merren* in Yiddish, which is also the verb to 'increase' in that language; and uttering the prayer when eating it,

"May it be Thy will that our merits be increased (or outnumber our demerits)".

Both customs, that to eat a 'new' fruit in order to doubly justify the blessing *shehecheyanu*, and to eat something which conveys the idea of 'many', can be fulfilled with just one fruit – a pomegranate, with its numerous seeds, especially since it is one of the "seven species" with which the Land of Israel is blessed – and even more especially if you make a point of seeing to it that it is actually the produce of the Holy Land!

On the other hand, advice is given *not* to eat nuts on Rosh Hashanah, for two reasons: first, because the numerical value of the Hebrew word for 'nut' – *egoz*, is the same as that for the word '*sin*' – *chet*; and secondly because they are said to bring up phlegm and cause coughing which can interfere with one's concentration on his prayers.

But do please bear in mind that these are only customs, not regulations. The eating and drinking you do on this and any other Yomtov or Shabbat are part of the particular day's *enjoyment* – and you therefore do not *have* to eat anything you do not like! The only thing you are *commanded* to eat is a piece of matza made from dough the size of a large olive at the Seder – and you are absolved even from eating that "if you have taken a vow never to eat matza or, presumably, your doctor has diagnosed that any farinaceous food, however much you *do* like it, is harmful to your health.

Section 10.   "Casting Sins Away"

Another custom some observe on Rosh Hashanah is to go to the sea-shore or a river-bank "preferably containing live fish" and say *Tashlich* (SPB 346), a name derived from a word in one of the verses recited there: "He will again have mercy upon us; will subdue our iniquities; and Thou wilt cast (*tashlich*) all their sins into the depths of the sea". For the purpose Hertz cites (HPB 888–889) – to bring to mind an equation between purity of body and soul as the reason for the custom, a *mikveh* would serve just as well as the sea or a river.

The consensus, most literal explanation traditionally given is the best. After long Shacharit and Musaf Services and shofar-sounding to G–d, we go home and feast Jewishly with some restraint, have a short nap – though some say we should not on this day. We then recite Minchah, and then, when the Day of Judgment is almost over towards sunset, confident that the Merciful One has forgiven us our sins, we symbolically do what G–d has promised *He* will do – cast those sins into the running waters, so that they will be carried far and deep away "into a place where they will be no more remembered or visited, or ever again come to mind".

Various explanations are given for the preference that there be fish in the waters: from the fact that their eyes are always open – to remind us of the ever-seeing Eye above, and in future to keep our eyes always open in avoidance of the enticements of sin; to warn us, despite our confidence in the day's outcome, that our fate is still uncertain, "for man also knoweth not his time, as the fishes that are taken in an evil net"; and as a tribute to the Creator, Whose works we commemorate that day, the fish having been the first living creatures to witness them!

Finally, a reason for going to a river to perform Tashlich, which recalls the *Akedah* (binding of Isaac), the leitmotiv of our prayers on that day, and with it the shofar. Even on foot the journey from Beersheba to mount Moriah, traditionally the future Temple site, should not take as long as three days – and Abraham had an ass. What delayed him? It was the ever-inventive Satan, "who transformed himself into a river to impede the Patriarchs' progress to perform G–d's will," a ruse countered by Him only after they had entered the waters to their necks and prayed for deliverance! So we pray daily (SPB 121): "Remove Satan from before us and from behind us!"

But again, bear in mind that Tashlich is a mere custom: it is not with hand or lips that we cast away our sins but with heart, mind and soul – and the Day of Atonement is yet to come!

Section 11. **Rosh Hashanah On Shabbat**

When the first day of Rosh Hashanah falls on Shabbat, Tashlich is postponed to the second day, "because of the possibility that some people might perhaps carry their prayer-books and the like to the river". And not only is this mere custom deferred to the second day in such an event, but also the positive Torah commandment that "the first day of the seventh month shall be a day of blowing the shofar" – whatever day of the week it may happen to fall on.

In the Temple, and after its destruction, as long as and wherever the Great Sanhedrin of seventy-one Sages sat, the shofar *was* sounded even on Shabbat; but thereafter postponement to the second day was observed everywhere, for the same reason – "because there is a danger that perhaps someone will go to an expert to learn (how to blow it), carrying it four cubits in a public place".

Authority for this rabbinic fence preventing a possible, though very unlikely, violation of a Shabbat commandment, is found in the wording of the second source-text for the Torah name of the Festival, a day "of *memorial* of the blowing the horn"; and it is probably for this reason that even in Judea, soon after the dissolution of the Sanhedrin, it became the custom to observe two days Rosh Hashanah, as it is in modern Israel.

Section 12.   **Yom (Ha-)Kippurim**
This is the name given by the Torah to the tenth day of Tishri, sometimes with the prefix *ha-* on the second word, as in the first source-text soon to be cited, and sometimes without it — but invariably in the plural form, a possible reason for which has already been suggested. Its popular name, however, is in the singular, Yom Kippur, which is more often than not used in the Shulchan Aruch. The Talmud uses the Torah name, but the tractate which discusses its laws is called *Yoma*, "The Day". Here, the popular name will be used.

Yom Kippur has two Torah commandments of its own, in addition to the two it has in common with Shabbat, which have already been listed and numbered in chapter twenty-six.

88.   AFFLICT YOURSELF ON YOM KIPPUR

Section 13. Source-text: "'Howbeit' on the tenth day of this seventh month is the Day of Atonement . . . and you shall afflict your souls". The word used for soul here is *nefesh*, the element common and essential to every living creature, which needs food to sustain it. Every animal is afflicted by being deprived of food and drink, which are therefore forbidden on Yom Kippur to animal-man; and the Sages deduce that the human being is also afflicted by not washing, by not annointing with oils, perfumes, etc., by not wearing leather shoes — and one other deprivation which applies to married couples only.

Therefore the Jew must subject him- and herself to these afflictions throughout Yom Kippur from BM onwards — and a year before that as a 'trial run'. For how long? This question has already been answered in chapter twenty-four at length. So I refer you there. The short answer is: about twenty-five hours.

89.   "WHATEVER SOUL THAT SHALL NOT BE AFFLICTED . . ."

The exact wording of this verse which is taken to be a negative commandment is: "For whatsoever soul it be that shall not be afflicted in that same day, he shall be cut off from his people", which means premature death by the 'hand of Heaven' — except for a sick person, who must eat and drink if an expert doctor decides that fasting will make him worse, when disobeying medical orders is accounted as an attempt to commit suicide; or if he himself, knowing the day is Yom Kippur, insists he must eat, even if a hundred doctors say it is not necessary.

(Similarly, a mother must not fast in the first three days after giving birth, should Yom Kippur fall within them; from the fourth to the seventh day she must be given food if she asks for it on The Day; but from the eighth, britmilah, day onwards she must fast like everyone else, unless she is abnormally ill, when she has to be treated like any other sick person).

Section 14.   **Day of "Atonement"**

The verse between these two commandments explains the purpose of The Day: "For it is a day of atonement, to make atonement for you before the Eternal your G–d". Who or what 'makes atonement', purges away your sins of yesteryear, for you? Rabbi Judah the Prince would have had it that it was The Day itself, so potent that it cleansed a person of all but three very grievous ones "whether he repented or not". But his colleagues disagreed with him, maintaining that only after one had repented his sins does Yom Kippur atone for them.

R. Eleazar b. Azariah, citing the clause "from all your sins *before the Eternal* shall you be clean", stresses what has already been said once before: "For transgressions between man and G–d Yom Kippur atones; but for transgressions between man and his fellow it does not atone until he has pacified his fellow". But even after he has done that, he still requires G–d's forgiveness for having wronged that fellow, which He commanded him not to do.

It is G–d Who makes atonement for the repentant sinner. The last-quoted verse begins: "For on that Day shall He make atonement for you . . ."; and on this R. Akiba exclaimed: "Happy are you, Israel! Who is it before Whom you become clean? And Who is it that makes you clean? Your Father in heaven! For He says: 'And *I* will sprinkle clean water over you, and you will be clean'". There is no human mediator between the Jew and his G–d in effecting a reconciliation after man's sinning, but only sincere repentance. That is why we spend all The Day in Synagogue doing just that.

Section 15.   **Sincere Repentance**

It must be sincere! "Should a person say 'I will sin and then repent, I will sin and then repent', no opportunity will be given him to repent". This is repeated twice because "Once a person has committed the same sin twice, it appears to him as if the act is permitted", since Heaven did not immediately punish him! But this is only because "the Eternal is a merciful and gracious G–d, long-suffering . . .". "Have I

at all any pleasure in the death of the wicked, saith the Eternal G–d,
but rather is his return from his ways that he should live!"

And it must be a real 'return' – which is what the word *teshuvah*,
repentance, means. This involves: expressing deep regret for having
sinned; determined resolve never to repeat the sin again; and an
undertaking to make amends for it with good deeds. It is no easy
thing – as the Almighty acknowledges! "My children! Present Me
with an opening to repentance no bigger than that in the eye of a
needle," He pleads, "and I will widen it into openings through which
wagons and carriages can pass!"

"All beginnings are difficult", and true repentance is one of the
most difficult of them; but "he who comes to cleanse himself is helped
by Heaven". So difficult is it, indeed, that "in the place where the
penitents stand, even the consistently righteous cannot stand"! For
having involuntarily succumbed to the wiles of Satan and then
returned to G–d with all your heart, gains you a higher place in His
estimation than that of the cloistered or phlegmatic righteous who
have never been tempted!

The "Days of Awe", like the other Festivals, have their all-the-year-
round lessons. Rosh Hashanah illuminates the supreme duty to love
and revere G–d, and Yom Kippur the warning to fear Him and repent
our sins, *every* day of our lives – indeed every wakeful moment of it;
for these are two of the 'constants' permanently dovetailed into the
uprights of our ladder to Heaven.

Section 16.   **Not Always So Solemn!**

Yom Kippur was not always all-solemnity as it is today. "There were
never in Israel days of greater *joy* than the fifteenth of Av and Yom
ha-Kippurim", on which spinsters and bachelors gathered in the
vineyards, the former urging the latter to choose their partners in life
from amongst them, each extolling her particular outer attractiveness,
or inner virtue, or prestigious family tree! Why on Yom Kippur?
"Because it is a day of forgiveness and pardon, and on it the second
Tablets were given".

We at least treat its termination as "a Yomtov of sorts", eating and
rejoicing – not as ravenous wolves, but as a service to G–d, rendering
thanks to Him on the assumption that "He has already accepted thy
works", i.e. repentance, on returning home after the last, uniquely
extra fifth Service of the Day, *Ne'ilah* (Conclusion), which itself ends
with repeated declarations of our loyalty to G–d, and one long, happy
blast of the shofar (SPB 366).

Even before commencing that so-desired meal, some punctilious
Jews take the first step in preparing their sukkah for the Festival

commencing five days later – so that they might "immediately proceed from the performance of one commandment to that of another", despite their hunger and thirst. That is an *act* which proves their love of G–d and His commandments!

Spend every moment, then, of the ten "Days of Awe" for the purpose they were ordained, to approach nearer and nearer to your G–d. May you be vouchsafed each year a *g'mar chatimah tovah*, a 'final good sealing' in His book for life, with good health and good fortune, so that you can continue to serve Him with all your heart-and-mind, with all your soul, and with all your might!

Section	**Notes**
1	Eruvin 13b; Numbers 29.1; Levit. 23.24.
2	R. Hash. 2a & 16a; Psalms 81.4–5; R. Hash. 8a–b; Nehemiah chapter 8; Or. Ch. 597.1.
3	R. Hash. 16a; MR. Levit. 29.1; Sanhedrin 38a; R. Hash. 18a; Psalms 33. 13–15; R. Hash. 8a; Psalms 81.5.
4	Numbers 10.2–10; R. Hash. 26b; Genesis chapter 22; MR. Levit. 29.10; and R. Hash. 16a.
5	Yad. Teshuva 3.4; R. Hash. 33b; Ibid 29a, 3a and 33b.
6	Or. Ch. 589.3 & 6; Ibid 596.1; Eccles. 9.7; Or. Ch. 597.1.
7	K. Sh.Ar. 130.1; MB. 603.2; Deuter. 4.7. & Isaiah 55.6; R. Hash. 18a; Psalms 145.18.
8	Betsa 3a & 4a; Or. Ch. 600, 223.3 & 225.3.
9	Or. Ch. 583.1–2; Deuter. 25.13; Ibid 8.8; Or. Ch. 485.
10	Micah 7.19; MB. 583 note 8; Enc. Jud. *Tashlich*; Eccles. 9.12; Genesis 1.21; Ibid 22.3–4; Tanchuma *Vayera* 22.
11	MB. 583 note 8; Numbers 29.1; R. Hash. 29b; Levit. 23.24.
12	Levit. 23.27–28; See chapter 27.
13	Levit. 23.27; Yoma 73b & 77a–b; Levit. 23.29; Or. Ch. 618.1; Ibid 617.2.
14	Yoma 85b–86a; Levit. 16.30; Ezekiel 36.25.
15	Yoma 85b & 87a; Exodus 34.6; Ezekiel 18.32; MR. Cant; 5.2.2; Mechilta *Yitro* 5; Shabbat 104a; Berachot 34b.
16	Ta'anit 30a–31b; see Rashi *loc cit*; Or. Ch. 624.5 & MB.; Eccles. 9.7.

Thirty

COMPLETION OF "CROWN" AND CALENDAR

Section 1.   **Sources**

Were we to take 'Torah' in its narrowest sense as referring only to the 'Five Books of Moses', this chapter would have no place in this book: for all the occasions, joyful and sad, described in it occurred long after the death of Moses, and could not therefore be mentioned by him in 'his' Books. But the Tenach which is 'Torah' in a wider sense, contains some of them; and it plus the Mishnah – the 'Oral Torah', 'Torah' in its widest sense, contains them all. Moreover, as we proceed you will see that almost all the occasions are somewhere hinted at, however tenuously, in the Torah proper.

With the enactments as to how .the first two Festivals to be mentioned are to be observed, we have the last two of the 'seven rabbinic jewels' in the crown with which the Sages adorned the Torah (7 plus 613 being the numerical value of *keter*, the Hebrew word for 'crown'); and you must admit, after seeing what they are, that Judaism would have been tremendously poorer without even these two – let alone the others!

Section 2.   **Purim**

Though shorter, and later in the Jewish year, than the Festival which is to follow, I am dealing with Purim first because it has its source in the Tenach, whereas Chanukah has not. As you must know, the event celebrated on Purim is related in the Book of *Esther*, one of the "Five Megillot" contained in the third section of the Tenach, the *Ketuvim*, each of which is read at some time in the Synagogue: *Shir Hashirim* (Song of Songs, or Canticles) on Pesach; *Ruth* on Shavuot; *Kohelet* (Ecclesiastes) on Sukkot; *Eichah* (Lamentations) on the fast of Tisha b'Av; and *Esther* on Purim.

The word *Megillah* means a 'scroll', written by a sofer on parch-

270

ment, just like a Sefer Torah; and, indeed, they are all so written to this day, and read from on those occasions in some Synagogues. But the 'scroll of Esther' popularly known as *the* Megillah, has the distinction of being the only one of them which is so written and so read in *all* Synagogues. I am not going to insult you by relating the story of Purim here! In the extremely unlikely event of your not knowing it, you can read the short Book for yourself in less than half-an-hour!

The dramatic events reached their climax when, "On the thirteenth day of Adar . . . the day that the enemies of the Jews hoped to have rule over them, turned out to the contrary, that the Jews had rule over them that hated them," that "the fourteenth day of the month Adar was declared a day of joy and feasting and a Yomtov, and for sending portions one to another." In the capital Shushan, the fighting continued into the fourteenth day, and therefore its Jewish citizens celebrated on the fifteenth of Adar.

The Festival is called Purim because, to decide on which day to mount his attack on Persian Jewry, Haman "had cast *pur*, that is, the lot, to discomfit and destroy them . . . therefore they called these days Purim . . . and the Jews took upon them and their descendants to keep these two days . . . throughout every generation . . . that these days of Purim should not fail from among the Jews, nor the memorial of them perish from their descendants."

And so have we been doing throughout the two-and-a-half millenia since those events, observing the fourteenth day of Adar as Purim, and the fifteenth, to a lesser degree, as 'Shushan Purim'. In a 'leap' year, when a 'second Adar' is added to the year, the Festival is held in that month, the corresponding days in the 'first Adar' being called *Purim Katan* – minor Purim, on which: "Some say we are obliged to increase our feasting and rejoicing. We are not accustomed so to do, but nevertheless enlarge our meals a little then, in order to conform with the view of those who so require – 'but he who is of happy *mind* has a constant feast,'" i.e. can rejoice without extra food!

Section 3.   **Jerusalem – Joshua – Adam!**

The Or. Ch. section of the Sh.Ar. ends with this last quotation, and all the commentators, in accordance with the oath taken by the exiles as they arrived in Babylon: "If I forget thee, O Jerusalem, let my right hand forget (its cunning)", conclude the volume with their own Messianic hopes; for instance: "May our House of glory be speedily rebuilt, when we will serve Him with reverence there! 'May the mountain of the House be established as the top of the mountains' for ever and ever!"

I mention this because Jerusalem, if not the Temple, is now established as Israel's capital for ever; and its citizens enjoy a rare distinction because it is a city "which has been walled since the days of Joshua the son of Nun;" and all such cities observe Shushan Purim as the main day of the Festival. Why from Joshua's days in particular? On the strength of a textual analogy: *he* captured "a great many unwalled (*perazi*) cities;" and we are told that "the Jews . . . that dwell in the unwalled (*perazot*) towns observed the *fourteenth* of Adar" as Purim. Therefore it is deduced that those who lived in *walled* cities observed it, as in Shushan, on the *fifteenth* – if they are, or were, walled in Joshua's time.

But in one indirect and serious way, and in another direct and light-hearted, the events of Purim are hinted at in the sin of – Adam! R. Shimon b. Yochai, when asked by his disciples why the Jews of Shushan merited the dire threat of extermination replied: "Because they partook of the feast of that wicked man" (Ahazuerus), at which forbidden food must have been served – and Adam's sin was that of eating forbidden food. "Is it from the tree (Hebrew: *hamin ha-ets*) from which I commanded thee not to eat that thou hast eaten?" G–d asked him.

When R. Mattenah was asked: "Where is Haman indicated in the Torah?", he quoted the first two words of this verse which, in the unvowelled Torah script can be read *Haman ha-ets*!, "Haman, the tree!" – on which he was hanged! Most consider he was answering a foolish question in a light vein; but it has also been suggested that he cited those words correctly, and was referring to the above explanation.

Section 4.   **Hearing The Megillah**

This is the most important enactment the Sages legislated to ensure that Purim should ever be remembered. The actual law reads: "Everyone is obliged to *read* the Megillah" from a scroll; but as with most duties which one cannot do for oneself, another can deputise for him or her – as long as he or she listens intently to every word. I say 'he or she' particularly here, because although this is a 'fixed-time' duty coming round but once a year, ladies from BM onwards – and even minors of both sexes, must hear it: for *all* were included in Haman's decree "to destroy, to slay, and to cause to perish all Jews, young and old, little children and women" – and deliverance was wrought through a great lady!

It was the custom in the Rama's day "for children to draw caricatures of Haman on two pieces of wood or stone, or to write his name on them, and bang them together (whenever his name was

mentioned during the reading), and in this way to fulfil the commandment to "blot out the remembrance of Amalek from under the
heaven" – for Haman was his descendant (see commandments 56 and
57 where it is explained why this portion is read as a special Maftir on
the Shabbat before Purim.) They adopt more noisy means of doing so
today, but "we must not annul any custom"!

You know of the Megillah's reading on Purim night; you probably
know that it is read again on Purim morning, after reading of
"Joshua's war against Amalek" from the Torah, but do you know
that the morning Megillah-reading is "the main one"? Well now you
do, and you should make a point of being there – perhaps with your
own *kasher* Megillah! The blessings recited before and after the
reading can be found in SPB 373–375.

Section 5.   **Other Purim Usages**
We fulfil Esther and Mordechai's instructions to make the day one of
feasting by having at least one sumptuous meal, "customarily on the
afternoon of Purim day, between an early Minchah while the day is
still long, and a late Arvit" – most probably: because at that meal "a
man is duty-bound to so 'mellow' himself that he cannot tell the
difference between 'cursed is Haman' and 'blessed is Mordechai'" –
and that involves an awful lot of 'mellowing'! Attempts have been
made to sober up this merry custom – by advising drinking just a little
more than usual so that you fall asleep and in *that* way to 'forget' the
difference; while another ingenious killjoy declares there is *no*
difference between the two phrases since they both add up in *gematria*
to 502!

But Rama has the last word, quoting the saying used more than
once in these pages: "It matters not whether it is much or little,
provided the heart is directed to heaven", i.e. as long as the mellowing
is done in fulfilment of the mitzvah – and you do not forget to *bensch*
after the meal, recite Arvit, and do all else that is necessary before
retiring for the night, and putting on the alarm, if necessary, to wake
you in good time for Shacharit with the congregation!

We also fulfil the instructions to "send portions one to another, and
gifts to the poor" by giving "two ready-to-eat dishes or drinks to at
least one friend – but to the more the better," and by giving gifts,
either direct or through some charitable organisation, to at least two
poor people. *You* also help in the latter way by contributing three
'half-shekels', or halves of the highest coin of the country, to the
collection usually made in the Synagogue just before the reading of
the evening Megillah.

Section 6.   **CHANUKAH**

The events celebrated on Chanukah are nowhere related in the Tenach, though it is not quite certain whether by then (165–162 B.C.E.) it had been finally decided which Books should be included in it. Even the Talmud, which certainly had not yet been committed to writing by then, has very little to say about the Festival. It asks "What is Chanukah?", and briefly tells of the Greeks' defiling the Temple, the Hasmoneans defeat of them, and the well-known miracle of the one-day's undefiled oil which lasted for eight days. "The following year these days were appointed a Festival with Hallel and thanksgiving." The rest deals with the laws regarding the kindling of the lights.

It is to the *I.* and *II. Maccabees*, two books in the Apocrypha, a collection of books which the Sages did not include in the Hebrew Bible, but the Church did in theirs, that we have to turn for the detailed and historic account of the forty-year struggle between Greek Hellenism and Judaism, climaxing in the events of Chanukah and their consequences. Notable is Mattathias' noble declaration refusing to yield to idolatry (see HPH 946–947).

In the first of those two books we are told that, like Mordechai and Esther with regard to Purim, "Judas Maccabeus and his brethren with the whole congregation of Israel, ordained that the days of the dedication of the altar should be kept in their season from year to year for the space of eight days, from the twenty-fifth day of the month of Kislev, with mirth and gladness."

The special Torah readings on the mornings of Chanukah, from "the offerings which the princes of the tribes brought for the dedication of the altar" in the wilderness, to the command to Aaron to "light the lamps in the seven-lamped Menorah", plainly demonstrates the Torah inspiration to Judas for acting as he did, and the institution of Chanukah. But our menorah has eight lights, for the reason mentioned above, and you should know *how* they are lit.

Their kindling is one of the few things which a lady may do on behalf of a man – although the *mitzvah* is a 'fixed time' one, the reason for this being that, according to legend, a woman, Judith the daughter of High Priest Yochanan, "was responsible for the miraculous Jewish victory by giving the commander-in-chief of the Syrian army cheese to eat in order to increase his drunkenness – and then cut off his head, causing his troops to flee." (A very similar story is told in the book of *Judith* in the Apocrypha.)

For this reason, also, "it is customary for women only not to do any work while the candles are burning, and for us to eat cheese dishes." Otherwise work is generally permitted on Chanukah; but we should, when dining, eat something special, and sing praises of G–d, in commemoration of the dedication of the altar *in the wilderness*: for "it was ready to be erected on the twenty-fifth of Kislev, but the Holy One, blessed be He, postponed the ceremony until Nisan, the month in which Isaac was born; and He said: 'it is My duty to repay Kislev' – and He did, with the Hasmonean dedication of the altar"!

Section 7.   **FAST DAYS**

There used to be many more fast-days in the Jewish year than there are today, some individuals going so far as to fast "*every* Monday and Thursday". But only five are public fasts today, soon to be detailed; but it is necessary first to say a word or two on the purpose of fasting, which is not just refraining from food and drink. That abstinence is intended only to induce the frame of mind which will help achieve the inner purpose, which is in essence the same as that of the only Torah fast, Yom Kippur – to repent our sins towards G–d and man, and make amends for them.

It is true that the fast-days about to be listed all commemorate ordeals or tragedies suffered by our nation in the past: but tragedy only befalls Israel when it is deserved, and serves as a warning to us to turn back to our G–d in true repentance. The two Haftarot read on Yom Kippur tell us of the purpose and effect of fasting. Says Isaiah in G–d's Name: "Is not this the fast I have chosen – to loose the fetters of wickedness . . . to let the oppressed go free . . . to deal thy bread to the hungry, and that thou bring the poor that are cast out to thy house, when thou seest the naked that thou cover him . . .?"

That is in the morning Haftarah: and in the afternoon's, which is the cherished Book of Jonah, we are told that the king of Nineveh, in answer to Jonah's call for repentance, proclaimed a fast for both man and beast, and instructed them to be covered in sackcloth, to cry to G–d and turn from their evil ways – and it was their sincere repentance that had the desired effect: for "G–d saw their *actions*, that they *had* returned from their evil ways" – and He forgave them.

The Fast Of Esther. I take this fast first because we have just spoken of Purim, the victory which it celebrates only being vouchsafed the Persian capital's Jews only after they had obeyed Esther's plea that they all "fast for me, and neither eat nor drink three days, night and day," and her undertaking that "I and my maidens will fast in like manner." *That* fast was in Nisan, its last day "coinciding with the first day of Pesach." But *our* fast is on the thirteenth of Adar, the day before Purim on which Haman's evil decree was to have been carried out – or on the previous Thursday, should Purim fall on Sunday.

The other public fasts are connected with the destruction of both

Temples in 586 B.C.E. and 70 C.E.; and I am listing them in the order in which the events they commemorate occurred.

Tenth Of Tevet. On this day the enemies "put Jerusalem under siege," no one and nothing being able to enter or leave the Holy City, which depended so much on outside supplies for its sustenance and the Temple offerings.

Seventeenth Tammuz. This fast commemorates the day on which both Babylonians and Romans breached the walls of Jerusalem and started a carnage of its citizens. They reached the Temple three weeks later, which is why this period is observed as one of mourning, no weddings or joyous occasions, except such as cannot be pre-arranged, like a Brit-Milah, being allowed to be celebrated during their weekdays.

Ninth Of Av. This day saw the climax of Jerusalem's agony on both occasions, with the enemy setting the Temple alight, the fire continuing well into the following day. For this reason, this fast alone of the five lasts, like Yom Kippur, a complete day, from sunset on the eighth of Av to starlight on the ninth – and even then, the custom not to eat meat or drink wine etc., which commences on the first of Av, remains in force until "at least midday on the tenth of the month", because the Temple was then still burning.

Third Of Tishri. This day – the one after Rosh Hashanah – is called the "Fast of Gedaliah". He was the man "whom the king of Babylon made governor over the cities of Judah" after taking the leaders and craftsmen into exile. But Ishmael, a covetous scion of the royal house, assassinated him and his men; and so great was their terror of the vengeance Nebuchadnezzar might take for this act, that the majority of the population, against Jeremiah's advice, fled to Egypt for asylum, thus bringing the State of Judea to an end until seventy years later, as Jeremiah had foretold.

Section 8.   **Torah Origins**

Long before the two great tragedies happened, it was decreed by the Omniscient that when the Temples *were* to be destroyed it would be precisely on the ninth of Av! For it is calculated that when "All the congregation lifted up their voices . . . and wept that night" on hearing the pessimistic report of the ten spies, the date was the ninth of Av; and G–d then said to them: "You have wept without cause, therefore I will set this day aside for a weeping throughout your generations." Thus Tisha b'Av – the Hebrew name of the fast, and its precedents and consequences.

It is also calculated that the day on which Moses descended from mount Sinai and, on seeing the children of Israel worshipping the golden calf "cast the tables (of the "Ten Commandments") out of his hands and broke them beneath the mountain" was the seventeenth of Tammuz. Incidentally, it is also calculated that when he descended "with the *second* tables, it was on Yom Kippur."

There is another fast, much happier in a way, which applies only to a section of the community – which might quite possibly include *you*, if you are a firstborn. It is called the 'Fast of the Firstborns'. It is observed by all firstborn sons, "whether of both parents or only of one of them" on the day before Pesach – or on the Thursday, if the Festival commences on Sunday, in thanksgiving for the firstborn of Israel being 'passed over' during the last plague in Egypt. Some would have it that "even first born daughters should fast" – but fortunately for them the custom was not adopted.

If you *are* a firstborn son, there is a way in which you avoid the need to fast – by attending a *siyyum*. This is an occasion when the conclusion of the study of a tractate of the Talmud is celebrated with a 'feast' which is considered to be a *seudat mitzvah*. The rabbis of most congregations usually arrange such a completion to coincide with the Fast of the Firstborns, and invites all such to join him in participating in the 'feast' – which they may do!

Section 9.   HAPPY DAYS: Ancient and Modern

I want to end this chapter on a cheerful note, so I conclude it with brief paragraphs on two Talmudic minor Festivals, one of which is gradually coming in to its own, and the other a mere memory; and another two which have entered the calendar since the establishment of Israel.

Fifteenth Of Shevat. This day is popularly called 'Tu b'Shevat', the Hebrew letters forming 'tu', *tet* and *vav*, adding up to fifteen. In English it is called "New Year For Trees", that is: fruit whose main growth took place before that date must not be used as tithe for the year commencing on that day. It is the time of year when nature begins to stir after its winter sleep, and is today celebrated by eating 'tu' kinds of fruit – if you can obtain them; and by planting new saplings, particularly in Israel – towards which *you* can contribute by 'buying trees' through the Jewish National Fund.

Fifteenth Of Av. This is the Festival which is a mere memory though, as mentioned at the end of the last chapter, used to be, with Yom Kippur, one of the two most joyous Festivals of the Jewish year. Various reasons are given to explain why it was so considered: it was "the day on which the generation of the wilderness ceased to die;" it was "the day on which the barriers between the divided kingdoms of northern Israel and southern Judah were removed, so that those of the north could again attend the Temple Service" – and others, apart from the one given in the last chapter.

Yom Ha-atsma'ut – Israel Independence Day, which entered the calendar on fourteenth May 1948, when the modern independent State of Israel was dramatically proclaimed, the anniversary of which has been celebrated the Jewish world over ever since.

Yom Yerushalayim. It was on this day, the seventh of June 1967 – but now usually known thereafter by its Jewish date, the twenty-eighth of Iyar, that the soldiers of the Israel Defence Force, after fierce battles, captured the Old and Holy City of Jerusalem from the Jordanian Army. Thousands upon thousands of soldiers and civilian, religious and not, flocked to the Western Wall, the *Kotel HaMa'aravi*, the last remnant of the Temple, and kissed its stones.

The Shofar was triumphantly sounded – Jersualem, *Old* Jerusalem, had at last been re-united with her long-exiled children, never to be driven away again! And in August 1980, in order to ensure that, the Knesset (Israeli Parliament) formally annexed the Old City, and declared it to be the eternal capital of the Jewish State. May the "City of Peace", which is what its name means, ever peacefully remain so!

"Thus saith the Eternal," talking of His Jerusalem which He had chosen: "Yet again shall be heard in this place . . . the voice of joy and the voice of gladness, the voice of the bridegroom and the voice of the bride, the voice of them that say: 'Give thanks to the Lord of Hosts, for the Eternal is good, for His mercy endureth for ever,' even of them that bring offerings of thanksgiving into the House of the Eternal"! May that House be speedily built in our days!

Section	**Notes**
2	Esther 9.1.ff; Ibid v. 24.ff; Or. Ch. 697 end; Proverbs 15.15.
3	Psalms 137.5; Ba'er Hetev; cf. Micah 4.1; Megillah 2a; Deuter. 3.5; Esther 9.19; Megillah 12a; Genesis 3.11; Chullin 139b; Torah Temimah on Gen. 3.11.
4	Arakin 2b & Or. Ch. 689.1; Esther 3.13; Or. Ch. 690.16; Deuter. 25.19; Exodus 17.8–16; MB. 692 note 2.
5	Or. Ch. 695.2; Megillah 7b; Berachot 5b; Esther 9.23; Or. Ch. 695.4 & 694.1.
6	Shabbat 21b; I. Maccabees 4.59; Numbers 7.1 to 8.4; Or. Ch. 670.1–2 and MB. there; Exodus 40.2.
7	Or. Ch. 580; Esther 4.16; Isaiah 58.6–7; Jonah 5.10; MR. Esther 8.6; Ezekiel 24.2; Or. Ch. 558.1; Jeremiah 40.5 & 41.1.ff; Ibid 29.10.
8	Numbers 14.1; Ta'anit 29a; Ibid 28b; Exodus 32.19; Rashi on Exodus 18.13; Or. Ch. 470.
9	Rosh Hashanah 2a & 14a.ff; Ta'anit 30b-31a; Jeremiah 33.10–11.

Thirty-One

PERFECT WITH G–D!

Section 1. **The "Second" Of The "Ten"**

Whenever the Divine Revelation at mount Sinai has hitherto been mentioned in this book, it has been given its popular name – but always in inverted commas: "The Ten Commandments". This has been done for two reasons: first, because its Hebrew name, the *Aseret haDeebrot*, does not mean 'ten commandments', but 'ten utterances'; secondly, and more importantly, many of the codifiers of the 613 commandments, redoubtably led by the great Maimonides (RM), discover *thirteen* commandments in the *Aseret haDeebrot* (while he himself adds a *fourteenth* – as we shall see in the next chapter).

Opposed to RM and his followers, is the no less formidable Nachmanides (RN) and his school, who maintain that there *are* only ten commandments in the ten utterances; and since the popular – though not, by any means, the majority scholarly – opinion accepts this lesser number, it is going to be adopted here, insofar as our numbering of the main hundred rungs of the ladder to the teenager's summit of the mountain of G–d is concerned.

What is the issue between these two giants? It is the contents of the "Second Commandment", which consist of four clauses: (i) thou shalt have no other gods besides Me; (ii) thou shalt not make unto thee any graven image . . .; (iii) thou shalt not bow down to them; and (iv) thou shalt not serve them. RM maintains that each of these is a *separate* commandment, numbering four in all: but RN argues that clauses (ii), (iii) and (iv) are merely subsidiary to (i), exemplifying its meaning.

The three commandments RM adds are: (ii) not to make images of other gods, even not for the purpose of worshipping them; (iii) not to serve other gods in any manner in which G–d is served; and (iv) not to serve such gods in any manner peculiar to *their* service. The consensus of opinion is still with him that these remain Torah commandments –

and rightly so! For though, in Talmudic times, it could be said "the inclination towards idolatry has already been uprooted from the Jewish people"; in *your* days, many queer religious fetishisms, which come close to idolatry, have arisen, against the enticements of which you must constantly guard.

Nevertheless, not only for the reasons mentioned above, but also for another, I am not numbering these three here. It is this: RN *does* include in *his* classification of the 613 a commandment which he says RM 'forgot'! But RM did *not* forget it, say his defenders: he did not include it, they argue, for the same reason that RN did not include RM's three – because it is a summary of other commandments, but not one itself. However, so comprehensive is it, that it can be considered as a heading under which many other Torah commandments can be classified, including RM's three, and I am therefore using my discretion and including it, numbered, here.

90. BE WHOLE-HEARTED WITH THE ETERNAL

Section 2. Just before the Almighty was about to change the name of the first Patriarch of our people from Abram to Abraham – "for thou shalt be the father (*av*) of a multitude (*hamon*) of nations": He said to him "Walk before Me, and be thou whole-hearted (*tamim*)". This Hebrew word, *tamim*, is used commonly of animals for sacrifice, signifying that they should be physically "perfect, without any blemish". In reference to man, says RN:

"It means that we should be wholly at-one with G–d, believing that He alone performs all, that He alone knows the truth about the future, and that from Him alone, through His Prophets and saintly ones, should we enquire about things to come, and not from astrologers and other foretellers of the future. To such and their like we must give no credence, being convinced that 'all is in Heaven's hands'".

Before his death, Moses, after warning the people against adopting any of ten abominable practices which were part of the way of life of the inhabitants of the land of Canaan which they were soon to enter – each one of them reckoned as a separate Torah prohibition – said to *all* the people: "Thou shalt be whole-hearted with the Eternal thy G–d". This, according to RM, summarises all that goes before it; but to RN it is a separate Torah commandment.

The ten 'abominations' include such idolatries and superstitions as "passing one's son or daughter through the fire" as a sacrifice to the gods; believing in lucky or unlucky omens – such as the passage of a black cat or the breaking of a mirror, to give modern examples; and seeking, through one's own manipulations, or through 'professional' fortune-tellers or mediums, to lift the veil over the future, or between the earthly world and the spiritual.

With your heart – which, remember, includes your mind in the Hebrew connotation of the word *lev* – ever wholly at one with G–d, not only will you avoid all three extra commandments in the Second of the Ten – no more inverted commas; but any of the ten practices in the above passage which may now be current – and many others. Such as: "do not turn (your mind) to idols" – i.e. do not ponder over the credibility of other cults; and do not you make idols for others to serve; both of them deduced from the same verse.

Section 3.   **Sculpting And Painting**

Here can be included the commandment forbidding the sculpting of the full human face, deduced from "You shall not make with Me (Heb: itti) gods of silver and gods of gold". By reading oti for itti, the meaning becomes "You shall not make Me as . . ." – and man was "created in the image of G–d"! Of course, the latter refers to His moral qualities, not physical ones – of which He has none! Nevertheless, such a sculpture, though intended by its creator only to express his artistic talent and give aesthetic pleasure to others, can conceivably become, eventually if not immediately, an object of adoration and worship, as history has proven.

One of the reasons given for Jacob's insistence "on being taken from Egypt for burial in the Cave of Machpelah" was in order that the Egyptians should not make of his tomb among them "a place of idolatrous worship," in acknowledgment of the blessings he and his son had brought to their country.

Sculpting of other living creatures, however, or inanimate objects, "is permitted," as is the painting of human beings on a flat surface. The Sh.Ar. finally rules that "it is customary to permit sculpting the human head without its features, or the body without the head". Nevertheless some very observant Jews are averse even to having their photographs taken, unless it is for official purposes such as passes or passports.

So, young gentleman or lady, if you feel you are developing the talent of a Jacob Epstein, and are urged to give it expression, you must take all these limitations into consideration, if you want to comply with this commandment.

Section 4.   **Testing, Questioning And Blaspheming**

Being whole-hearted with G–d will ensure avoidance of three other Torah commandments: (i) not to put G–d's, or His Prophets' powers to the test, and not to question any of their actions; (ii) to accept the decisions of the acknowledged halachic authorities of your time, and (iii) not to disregard these decisions.

There is a place in the wilderness of Sinai which was named "Massah and Merivah" – "Testing and Strife", "because of the striving of the children of Israel, and because they tested the Eternal, saying: 'Is the Eternal among us, or not'?" They were given water, and then given painful proof that G–d *had* been with them – by the attack of the Amalekites, the story of which immediately follows.

The Midrash illustrates this with a parable. What is the connection between the two events? it asks, and answers: It can be compared to a small child who had become so used to the comfort of sitting pickaback on his father's shoulders while passing through a dangerous desert, that he forgot how it was he was travelling! So that when a friend passed by, the son asked him, 'Have you seen my father?' The latter was cross, and said, 'You have been riding on *my* shoulders, yet you ask where I am? I'll put you down, so that the enemy can come and attack you!'

This explains the commandment: "You shall not test the Eternal your G–d as you tested Him at Massah". Thus you must not say: 'I will do such-and-such a good deed – and see whether the Almighty gives me the reward He promises in the Torah for fulfilling it.' There is one exception which G–d Himself makes: "Bring the whole tithe into the store-house . . . and try Me now with this, saith the Lord of hosts – if I will not open you the windows of heaven, and pour you out a blessing that there will be more than sufficiency!" And some say this test may also be made with charity-giving – about which a little more, a little later.

Similarly G–d commands regarding the true Prophets whom, He tells Moses, 'I will raise them up" – after his death – "like unto thee; and I will put My words in his mouth, and he shall speak unto them all that I shall command him", "unto him you shall hearken", and obey, without testing or questioning.

Section 5.   **The Questions of Abraham And Moses**
As for the latter, we do find that both Abraham and Moses *did* question G–d's actions. When G–d was about to destroy the cities of the plain "because their sin was exceedingly grievous", the Patriarch asked in bewilderment: "Wilt Thou indeed sweep away the righteous with the wicked? . . . Be that far from Thee to do after this manner, to slay the righteous with the wicked, so that the righteous should be as the wicked! Be that far from Thee! Shall not the Judge of all the earth do justice?"

But G–d had invited that plea, by telling Abraham in advance what He was going to do – and his words pleased Him! For they proved that Abraham had that compassion for his fellow-men essential in one who was to be the father of G–d's people. Noah, though a "righteous and whole-hearted man in his generations, who walked with G–d", apparently expressed no such compassion for the victims-to-be of the Flood, and was therefore not given that historic role. In the end, G–d made it clear to Abraham that He *was* acting with justice.

Moses' question, however, though it also sprang from *his* compassion for the children of Israel, was not so well received. He had just returned from his first mission to Pharaoh, demanding, in G–d's Name, "Let My people go!"; and that tyrant, instead of showing any sign of obeying, ordered "Let *heavier* work be laid upon the men!" – resulting in the Israelites turning against him. "So Moses returned unto the Eternal, and said: 'My Lord, why hast Thou dealt ill with this people, why is it that Thou hast sent me?'"

And what was G–d's answer? "*Now* shalt thou see what I will do to Pharaoh; for by a Strong Hand he *will* let them go, and by a Strong Hand he will drive them out of his land". From the words "Now" and "what I will do *to Pharaoh*", the Sages deduce that it was *then* first decreed that Moses "shall behold the war against Pharaoh, but *not* the war against the thirty-one kings" – the inhabitants of Canaan. From the trials and tribulations of the Patriarchs, Moses should have realised that 'it is darkest before dawn'!

Section 6.   **The Example Of Job**
Life is rarely all sunshine for anyone: it has its beclouded days, and very often, its storms and even traumatic quakes. If such fall to our lot, and we are whole-hearted with G–d, we accept them with fortitude – while at the same time, of course, making every human effort to alleviate their effects. We accept them, either as retribution for any wrongs we might have done, searching them out and making amends for them; or, in the unlikely event of finding none, in the realisation that "Whom the Eternal loveth, He proveth, even as a father the son in whom he delighteth".

The classical example of these 'chastenings of love', as the Sages call the latter kind of trials, was Job, like Noah "a wholehearted and upright man, and one that revered G–d and shunned evil" – but who *also* manifestly showed his "practical love and sympathy for all his fellow-men, down to the most humble." Yet, despite this exemplary character, he was visited with grievous trials – loss of all his children, all his material possessions, and then loathsome disease.

Though his 'comforters' tried to persuade him, time and again, that his sufferings could only be the result of sin, he stoutly refuted this – but his faith in G–d remained resolute, as his famous utterance, "Though He slay me, yet will I trust in Him" proves. And in the end, G–d attested to Job's righteousness, and doubly blessed him, proving *his* were 'chastenings of love'.

The faith of Job's wife was not so sound, however. When she saw him at the nadir of his misery, despite his life-long loyalty to G–d, and believing that death would be a relief after such horrible suffering, she urged him: "Curse G–d – and die!"; to which Job angrily retorted: "Shall we receive good at the hand of G–d, and shall we not receive evil?", accusing her of speaking like an impious woman!

Had he succumbed to his wife's entreaty, Job would have violated the Torah commandment, "Thou shalt not curse G–d (*Elokim*)" – a terrible sin indeed, to which some less righteous, suffering his ordeals, might possibly have resorted. But some of the Sages were so sure that no Jew, however desperate his situation, would even contemplate doing such a thing, give the bracketed word its occasional "human connotation" – judges, taking the prohibition to mean not to curse the bench of judges after its members have issued a verdict against you! For *elohim* sit in the Name of *Elokim*.

That word, you will remember, has a third meaning, as in the Second Commandment, "the *gods* of others"; and Hertz makes use of it in his commentary on this commandment. "Josephus and Philo explain it thus: 'Let no one blaspheme (curse) those gods which other citizens esteem as such'; that is, do not speak disrespectfully of the religious beliefs of the followers of other faiths".

Section 7.   **Questions Of The Moment**
The other two commandments in the group we are now considering – to accept the decisions of the recognised religious authority of your time, and not to disregard their rulings – have already been shown, in chapter 2, to be included in the widest sense of the meaning of "Torah", from which 'thou shalt turn neither to the right nor to the left". That authority is, in the first instance, the qualified rabbi whom you are advised to provide for yourself – normally the rabbi of the Congregation to which your family is affiliated, whom you should consult on all religious problems.

He may decide it wise, if there is any complexity in the problem, to refer it to the area Bet-Din of three specially qualified *dayanim*, or judges, who, in turn, may consult with other Batei-Din of equal or higher status, until a consensus solution is found. Theirs is Torah authority, and their rulings must therefore be obeyed, once they have been issued. It has been in this way that the continuity and cohesion of Orthodox Jewry has been maintained throughout the generations since the Sanhedrin in Jerusalem ceased to function.

But let me stress: this does *not* mean that you must abrogate all your own thinking, and leave *all* decisions, to them! You must use the mind G–d has given you to solve your own problems. Remember that the Hebrew word for 'heart' includes the mind as well, so that being 'whole-hearted' with G–d means 'whole-minded' also: that is, you have to use all your intelligence to find for yourself the way in which G–d wants you to go; and there are many books which give the answers to everyday problems.

It is only when you cannot solve one yourself that you should consult the above authorities – and you can argue the point with them, if you have amassed sufficient background knowledge with which to do so: in fact, they will relish such arguments, for rabbis and Batei-Din admire the informed layman. When Joshua urged Moses to "shut in two elders who prophesied in the camp", *Moshe Rabbainu*, the Rabbi of all rabbis, replied: "Art thou jealous for *my* sake? would that all the Eternal's people were prophets, that the Eternal would put His spirit upon them!". But once a ruling has been given, it *must* be accepted.

Section 8. **Do Not Take G–d's Name In Vain**

Yes, this *is* the Third of the Ten Commandments – yet I am including it here unnumbered, because no one who is whole-hearted with G–d would, even for one moment, *think* of committing so grave a sin! There are two rather similar Torah commandments, with slightly different wording and meanings. The one mentioned above reads: "Thou shalt not take the Name of the Eternal thy G–d *in vain*" (Hebrew: *la-shav*); and the other: "You shall not swear by My Name *falsely* (Hebrew: *la-sheker*)".

What they both have in common is actually using the sacred Divine Name deliberately in a 'vain' or 'false' oath: and it is because I am so sure that *you* would not do such a thing that I do not number these two commandments, but include them under the positive comprehensive "Be whole-hearted with the Eternal".

The difference between the two is in the kind of oath one swears – a 'false' one, or a 'vain' one. The former is easy to understand: swearing that you did something which you did not do, or you did not do something which you did do; or swearing that you will not do something and then deliberately doing it, or that you will do something, in the full knowledge that you do not intend doing it.

Even worse is to swear to false evidence in court, or denying that you are holding something in trust for another.

But what is a 'vain' oath? Vain means 'useless' or 'superfluous', as when the Prophet accused the people of saying "It is useless (*shav*) to serve the Eternal; for what profit is it that we have kept His charge . . .?" Examples given in the Talmud are: "swearing to that which is contrary to facts known to man," saying a stone pillar is gold, or that a man is a woman; or to an impossibility like having seen a camel flying in the air; or not to fulfil a commandment which the Torah ordains he *should* perform, like not to put on *tephillin*, or not to build a *sukkah*.

The last kind of oath exemplified does not, indeed cannot, take effect, for the interesting reason that we are all already foresworn since the Revelation at mount Sinai to observe the Torah commandments, and "no one can swear to anul any of them." When, on the very last day of his life, "Moses assembled the whole of the people" to re-affirm their obligation to fulfil 'the covenant and the oath' between them and G–d, he declared them to be binding upon "him that standeth here with us this day . . . and also him that is not here with us this day" – i.e. upon all their descendants, for ever.

It follows from this that any punishable false oath can only concern something *permissible* in normal circumstances, like eating and drinking *kasher* foods, etc., and deliberately broken thereafter. And, let me remind you again, they are only breaches of Torah law when one of G–d's Names is included in them to carry conviction. But ideally, it is best never to take an oath – unless the law demands it – just in case, though your intention is good, you may not, due to circumstances beyond your control, be able to keep it.

"Better is it that thou shouldst not vow, than that thou shouldst vow and not fulfil". And while the Torah insists that vows entered into must be fulfilled, it continues: "If thou shalt forbear to vow, it shall be no sin in thee". That is why the Jew who is wholehearted with G–d, whenever he makes a promise to do something, though he sincerely intends honouring it, always adds the proviso "*bli neder*", "without committing myself by a vow". A Jew's mere word is his bond!

Section 9.   **Prayers And Blessings As Well**

There are also such things as vain prayers and purposeless blessings. An example of the former (*tephillat shav*) is: If, on his way home, a person hears a cry of distress coming from the vicinity of his residence, he prays, "G–d grant that it is not coming from *my* home!"

What has happened, has happened, and it is vain to pray that it might not have happened — to 'cry over spilt milk'!

Worse than this, however, is the all-too-prevalent modern habit of using G—d's Name in expletives and exclamations, such as "O my G—d!" — which is the least offensive of them, in the course of general conversation. Such profane utterances, very often in most irreverent context, are often heard on stage or film, or appear in print: so guard against using them yourself, in sheepish imitation!

As has already been mentioned elsewhere, "we must not enjoy any of the pleasures of G—d's world, with any of our senses, without reciting a blessing," a 'thank-You', to Him both before and after having had the pleasure. Most of these blessings have at least two mentions of G—d Names in them, and the whole-hearted Jew who walks continuously in His presence should have in mind Whom it is he is blessing whenever he recites any of them.

Just to gabble the *bracha* off without intent, is bad enough: but to make a 'purposeless' blessing (*bracha le-vatala*) is worse still, as, for instance, reciting a blessing over something which mother says she is going to bring you from the kitchen — where she finds there's none left! That is why you should always actually hold the thing over which you are about to make the blessing in your right hand while making it — or at least see it lying before you on the table.

Just as bad is, through sheer thoughtlessness, to recite the *wrong* blessing over anything, like that for wine over lemonade! In such a case, and after uttering *any* 'vain' blessing, you must immediately thereafter say "Blessed be His Name, Whose glorious kingdom is for ever and ever" — and then make amends by taking hold of the item, and/or reciting the *proper* blessing over it, and again after eating it.

Section 10.   **The Holiest Of Words**

Why all these precautions and this care? Because the Divine Names are the most holy words in the language, and are therefore to be uttered sparingly — except in prayer and blessings, when each mention of any one of them should be with concentrated intent, and in awe of His Majesty. They are also intoned, in their proper pronunciation, when the Torah is read in congregation: but when revising the Sidra at home, practising your Barmitzvah or any other Haftarah anywhere; or even when studying Torah, it is customary to alter the pronunciation of G—d's Names slightly, in order to preserve the real Names for those special occasions.

The Prophet Micah is said to have 'epitomised' all the 613 commandments of the Torah into three: "To do justice, to love kindness, and to *walk humbly* with thy G—d". This 'walking', as in the 'walking by the way' in the Shema, and in G–d's command to Abram, "walk before Me, and be whole-hearted", refers to our going about our daily affairs, whatever they may be: and one of the ways in which we practise such humility is to be sparing in the use of His Holy Names in general conversation.

Yet we must also always remember that we are constantly in His Presence – all the hundred-and-more blessings we make throughout the course of each day being very useful aids to such remembrance: and we must thankfully ascribe to Him all the happenings of the day. Thus, should anyone ask you the usual question, "How are you?", and – as I hope you always will be – you are well, your answer should be, "I'm fine, *baruch haShem*!" – "blessed be 'the Name'", without actually mentioning it.

Similarly, should you be invited to some forthcoming event, and you accept, you should say, "I *hope* to be there, *b'ezrat haShem*!" (with the help of 'the Name'). And we extend this ascription of all our talents to G–d by heading all letters etc. we write with the first characters of those two words, *bet* and *heh*, conveying the idea, "I could not write this letter were it not for G–d's help".

Section 11.   **"Destroying" G–d's Names**
I come now to the last of the unnumbered Torah commandments which I am including under RN's comprehensive "Be whole-hearted with the Eternal thy G–d". One who is that, in action and both the spoken and the written word, will also take great care not to erase or destroy anything with which His Names are associated. This prohibition is deduced from the warning ". . . You shall not do so to the Eternal your G–d" (read the verse in its context).

You are not, of course, going to demolish any part of G–d's House, or take a chisel or brush-and-paint and erase His Name from any inscription therein – though I have seen many a carelessly broken window! Neither are you, I feel sure, going to show disrespect to His Names – scores of them, probably, by throwing away any loose pages from a Siddur or Chumash into the waste-paper receptacle. However, if you use such sacred books without the care and respect due to them, and put them aside higgledy-piggledy, instead of rightway-up in their shelves, you are indirectly 'destroying' them by rendering them unserviceable before their due time.

When that due time comes round, with regard to *tephillin, mezuzot* and *Siphre-Torah*, as well as Chumashim and Siddurim, their having become unserviceable through constant, respectful use – or by unfortunate accidents like fire or flood: they are reverently collected and stored away, and eventually buried, with due ceremony, in a Jewish cemetery – just as if they were cherished, departed humans!

I mentioned above that we ascribe our ability to write to the grace of G–d, by heading letters etc. with *bet'heh*. Since most letters are destined to be thrown away, sooner or later, we therefore never write out G–d's Names in full in them, substituting for it either just a capital G, or replacing the middle letter with a dash, thus: G–d. In Hebrew, either the letter *dalet* or *heh*, each followed by an acute accent, is used to represent the divine Name.

Section 12.   **King David's 'Paraphrase'**

King David paraphrased the comprehensive commandment with which this chapter has been concerned, when he said: "I set the Eternal always before me: when He is at my right hand, I shall not be moved" – from walking ever in His ways. It is with the opening words of this verse, in large type, that every copy of the *Kitsur Shulchan Aruch* – the concise compendium of all-the-year-round practical Jewish living, commences. With it, or one of the English versions of it, as your vade-mecum, you will be able to walk whole-heartedly with G–d at all times, observing all the unnumbered commandments included in this chapter – which are all, remember, Torah commandments.

Section	Notes
1	Exodus 20.3–5; MR. Cant. 7.8.
2	Genesis 17.1 and 5; Deuter. 18.13; Levit. 19.4.
3	A. Zarak 43b; Exodus 20.20; Genesis 47.29; MR. Genesis 95.5; Yad. A. Zarah 3.10–11; Y. De'ah 141.7.
4	Exodus 17.7; Deuter. 6.16; Malachi 3.10; Deuter. 18.18 & 16.
5	Genesis 18.23 & 25; Ibid 6.9; Exodus 5.22; Ibid. 6.1; Sandhedrin 111a.
6	Proverbs 3.12; Job 1.1; Ibid chapter 31; Ibid 13.15; Ibid 2.9–10; Exodus 22.27; see chapter 3.
7	Ethics 1.6; Numbers 11.28–29.
8	Exodus 20.7; Levit. 19.12; Malachi 3.14; Shevuot 29a; Ibid 27a; Deuter. 29.9–13; Eccles. 5.4; Deuter. 23.23.
9	Berachot 54a; chapter 13; K. Sh.Ar. 50.3; Y. Berachot 39b (6.1).
10	Makkot 24a; Micah 6.8.
11	Deuter. 12.4.
12	Psalms 16.8.

Thirty-Two

LIFE AND PROPERTY

Section 1.   **Introduction**

It would appear, from only a superficial reading of the Torah text, that G–d regards the life He gave us rather cheaply, decreeing the death penalty not only for grave criminal acts, but also for moral sins, many of which are nowadays considered mere peccadillos, deserving only a slap, a tut-tut, or just a raised eyebrow. But a little surface knowledge is dangerous! The Torah is not man's word, but G–d's, not disjointed bits and pieces, but an integrated whole. To understand His words, so far as is humanly possible, we have to delve carefully, patiently and deep; and we have to dovetail the pieces neatly together, to make them into a harmonious whole.

It is because they read the Torah in such a cursory manner, stressing isolated chapters and verses here and there, that the two daughter-religions of Judaism reached false conclusions about the nature of Judaism. On the one hand, Christianity views the G–d of Israel as a stern, revengeful G–d – despite the fact that He declares that He is "merciful and gracious, long-suffering and abounding in true kindness, preserving kindness to the two-thousandth generation, forgiving iniquity and transgression and sin, and clearing the guilty" – should they repent! While on the other hand, Islam takes most of the death-incurring crimes and sins literally, at surface meaning, without qualification.

Section 2.   **The Sanctity Of Life**

But qualification, which deep study and cross-reference render essential, must be made; and the result is truly amazing! In Temple times, when a Jewish court was empowered to inflict the death penalty, "Any court which carried out the death penalty once in seven – and, some say, seventy – years, was branded a 'destructive court'": and R. Tarfon and R. Akiva, usually at loggerheads on most matters legal

290

and moral, agreed that had they lived in those times – when they would undoubtedly have been members of such tribunals – "no person would *ever* have been put to death"!

Does this mean they would have ignored, or circumvented, the Torah's patent decrees of stoning, burning, decapitation, and strangulation for this, that or the other crime or immorality? They – doctors and ardent lovers of every letter of the Torah? Not *they*, but the Torah itself assuages the sternness of its own capital punishment sentences, by qualifying their applicability through other commandments, so demanding and intricate that the death sentence became virtually impossible. You must study, at the very least, the *mishnayot* of tractate Sanhedrin to gain a reasonable appreciation of this fact: here I give just one facet.

To be convicted of a capital offence, such as murder or adultery, evidence had to be given verbally and directly, without aid of counsel, by two or more – but not just one – *eye*-witnesses of stainless moral character: "By the *mouth* of two witness, or three witnesses shall the condemned be put to death"; and that evidence was given in the knowledge that "The hand of the witnesses shall be the first against him to put him to death . . ."!

But that is not by any means all! Even before they began to give evidence, "the fear of Heaven was put into them with the warning that they would be responsible for taking not only the life of the accused, but also those of his never-to-be-born descendants until the end of time!" If this did not deter them, they were then separately vigorously questioned and exhaustively cross-examined, to make sure that their testimony concurred on every point. When asked how they would have eliminated the death sentence altogether, R. Tarfon and R. Akiva replied that they would have asked the witnesses questions so intimate and intricate that they would not possibly have been able to answer them!

When the first murder trial was held after the modern State of Israel was established, "*the two Chief Rabbis* cabled the Minister of Justice urging the immediate abolition of the death penalty, and warning the court that pronouncing a capital sentence would be incompatible with, and *a sin against Jewish law*." And it was eventually abolished, in 1954, except for the crimes of treason and genocide, its only victim being Butcher Eichmann.

91.   SAVE LIFE!

Section 3. Another caution administered by the examining judges to would-be witness in capital cases was: "At the Creation, one man only was created, to teach us that whosoever destroys a single life is considered as if he had destroyed a whole world; and whosoever saves a single life is as if he had saved a whole world." This demonstrates how preciously life is regarded in Judaism, and how we must strive to preserve it, in others as well as ourselves.

"Whence to we know that if a man sees his fellow drowning, or being mauled by wild beasts, or attacked by robbers, he is duty-bound to attempt to save him! From the verse "(Thou shalt not go about as a tale-bearer among thy people); neither shalt thou *stand idly by* the blood of thy neighbour'." Of course this depends on whether you have the ability to save him – "if you are a good swimmer," as RM instances in the case of the drowning man. If you cannot, you should rather swiftly find someone who can, than risk your own life as well. It is interesting to note here that one of the things which some Sages maintain a father must teach his child – or have him taught – is swimming, "because his life may sometimes depend on it" – or that of others.

The Torah here speaks of saving life from actual death: but rescuing another in less dramatic circumstances must also be included. Thus, from the phrase "and thou shalt cut off her hand" (not to be taken literally: the whole context should be studied:) the commandment is deduced that it is your duty "to help save anyone being pursued with muderous intent," like the luckless victim of a bully – if you think you can beat him! And to have no pity on such a strong-arm person is another commandment!

The fact that the commandment to save life is coupled in one verse with the prohibition against tale-bearing can teach us that it is wrong to remain silent when you have the ability to prove that the reputation-destroying tales and gossip being spread around about another are false. The Sifra deduces from this juxtaposition that it is not tale-bearing to give evidence in court against anyone, provided there is another witness to support you, but, on the contrary, it is your *duty* to do so.

Section 4.   **Saving "Souls" And Property**
But perhaps the most constructive act of saving you can perform is saving other Jewish souls, encouraging friends to be loyal to Jewish observance by your personal example and gentle persuasion: by encouraging them to go to Synagogue with you, to eat kasher, to keep Shabbat, and the like; to be honest, kind and considerate to others. For you should remember that it is your duty not only to learn Torah, but to ṭeach it; and the best teaching is achieved by personal example.

The duty of saving extends to the property of another: "Let the property of thy friend be as dear to you as thine own." If, then, you see someone trying to steal or destroy someone else's property, it is your duty to confront him and rescue it, if you can, or inform the owner or the police. For very often, a person's possessions are as precious to him as life itself – "and sometimes even more so!"

92.   DO NOT MURDER!

Section 5. After all that has gone before, the realisation of the sanctity of life, and your duty to save it whenever you can, this Sixth of the Ten Commandments, "Thous shalt not murder", comes as somewhat of an anti-climax! What civilised, let alone religious, person, when the stern warning was given to all mankind, almost at the beginning of time: "He who sheds man's blood, by man shall his blood be shed; for in the image of G–d made He man" – would even contemplate taking a human life?

True it is that the Giver of life here demands its forfeiture for taking that of another – if, as we have seen, stringently-sieved, utterly trustworthy evidence proves murder has been done. But in most civilised countries today, "judicial murder" has been severely restricted, or even abolished – as it was among Jews long long ago. So how can 'thou', i.e. any individual, even contemplate shedding another's blood?

Nevertheless it *is* shed, and, alas, all too freely, to this day. Quite apart from unnecessary wars, cruel pogroms, massacres and acts of genocide committed by whole nations or large sections of them, no one day goes by without reports of dozens of murders the world over. What greater proof can we have that it is not material wealth, intellectual sophistication, or advanced technology, that civilises man, but only the disciplines of religion and morality?

You, most assuredly, are not going to kill anybody with cold premeditation. But the Torah here, as in all the other Ten Commandments, cites extremes of human conduct, towards which we should aspire, or from which we should distance ourselves, under which all the other 603 commandments can be classified. And there are lesser degrees of murder which, even though the victim may live on after it has been perpetrated, are still morally included under this heading.

Section 6.   **Degrees Of Homicide**

There is only one circumstance in which the individual is permitted – indeed commanded, to take the life of another human being: as a last resort in *self* defence, or that of a third party. The general law is deduced from the particular one: "If the thief is found breaking in,

and be smitten so that he dieth, there is no bloodguiltiness for him" –
i.e. the owner is guiltless of murder. Why? "Because it is certain that
no man will stand passively by where his property is concerned.
Therefore the burglar must have reasoned: 'If I go there (and am
discovered), the owner will defend himself, and I will have to kill
him.' So the Torah decrees: If he comes with the intention of killing
you, anticipate his act and kill him first."

And so in the case of saving the pursued from his pursuer, referred
to above – and "in saving a young lady from a would-be rapist in a
lonely place". But, I repeat, *only* as a last resort, and after the
perpetrator has been warned, as in all criminal cases, of the legal
consequences of his intended action. If one could have saved himself
or another just by inflicting a non-fatal wound, yet killed him, his act
is considered as murder.

Nor may one kill at the behest of a third party, however serious the
threatened consequences may be for himself. A man came to Raba
and said: "The governor of my town has ordered me, 'Go and kill
so-and-so; if you do not, *I* will kill *you*!'" To which Raba replied:
"Let him kill you, rather than you should commit murder. Who can
say that *your* blood is redder? Perhaps *his* blood is redder!" – i.e. his
life may be more valuable than yours. You might think such a
possibility unlikely and far-fetched: but many a Jewish 'councillor' in
Hitler's concentration camps was faced with just this awesome
dilemma when ordered to select fellow-Jews for the extermination
chambers.

Section 7.   **Manslaughter And "Accidental" Killing**
In biblical times, everyone who had taken another's life, whatever the
circumstances, had, in the first place, to flee to a "city of refuge",
where he was given sanctuary from the next-of-kin of his victim,
whose wrath might urge him to take immediate vengeance. The
manslayer would then be brought before a court of at least twenty-
three learned judges and tried: if he were found guilty of premeditated
murder, he was handed over to the next-of-kin, who, in those days,
had the right and duty to exact the ultimate penalty; or executed by
the court itself, if the latter declined to claim his right.

If, however, the death proved to be a case of manslaughter – i.e.
occasioned not by malice aforethought, but due to carelessness or
neglect: like, for instance, as a result of driving under the influence of
drink, or in a faulty car; the slayer, in those days, would have had to
remain confined in a city of refuge until the death of the then
incumbent High Priest. Nowadays prison, more-or-less, takes the
place of a city of refuge – though the next-of-kin no longer has first

claim to wreaking vengeance! No man has the right today to 'take the law into his own hands'.

When death had been brought about by 'pure accident', the killer, after his original contemplative stay in the city of refuge, was acquitted by the court, and he was free to go where he wished. A modern instance of such an 'accident' would be if someone suddenly rushed from behind a stationary vehicle into the path of a car travelling within the legal limit. A biblical example is: "A man is chopping wood in a public place, and the axe-head, on hitting the branch, flies off the handle and kills a by-stander." In such cases, the driver of the car or the hewer of wood would leave court as a free man – but not, according to Judaism, "without a stain on his character".

Why not? Because Judaism does not accept *any* happening as a 'pure accident': "No one (even) bruises his finger here on earth unless it was decreed against him from Above," R. Chanina deduced from Holy Writ. Everything that happens to us is 'an act of G–d', Who also "brings about reward through a person of merit, and punishment through a guilty person." This is inferred from the verses: "He that smiteth a man so that he dieth, shall surely be put to death. And if he did not lie in wait (i.e. it was an 'accident'), but G–d caused it to happen, I will appoint thee a place whither he may flee."

It was to these verses, say the Sages, "that the future king David was referring" when, having proved to his pursuer, King Saul, that he could easily have killed him had he wished, said: "The Eternal shall judge between me and thee, and the Eternal avenge me of thee – but my hand shall not kill thee. As the proveb of the ancients (scan: the Torah) saith: out of the wicked cometh forth wickedness . . .". And they give an illustration of what it means:

"Two people have killed, one accidentally, and the other with premeditation, without there having been witnesses in either case. The Holy One, blessed be He, arranges for them to meet at the same inn: the deliberate murderer walks under a step-ladder, and the other, coming down the ladder, falls on him and kills him. Thus the intentional killer is killed, while the 'accidental' slayer goes into banishment" – there being witnesses at the inn.

Had the unintentional slayer been going up the ladder when he fell and killed the other, the Talmud points out, "he would not have been sent to a city of refuge," and would have been acquitted, since the Torah only holds one guilty when he, or something of his, kills in the course of a *downward* movement. Nevertheless, he *was* used as G–d's instrument in meting out punishment to the other – which means that he had committed some wrong in the past, for which he will receive his deserts in G–d's own time – now!

It is for this reason that the Supreme Judge warns human judges to be scrupulously fair and law-abiding in their verdicts, and not to worry when they have to acquit what appears to be an obvious homicide, owing to the lack of adequate evidence. "For I will not acquit the wicked," says G–d: and Rashi paraphrases it: "If he emerges innocent from *your* court, I have many messengers to punish him in the manner to which he has rendered himself liable."

Section 8.   **A Lesser Degree Of "Murder"**

And so, young reader – and older – take care, and avoid 'accidents'! If you *are* involved in any, think back! It may very well be that you are being given a reminder that there is something you have done in the past which requires recalling and rectifying or eliminating, so that you can put your life on an even tenor again. There is, however, one kind of 'murder' to which many of us are often prone. "He who shames his neighbour publicly is as though he sheds blood," asserted a Mishnaic teacher; whereupon R. Nachman remarked: "You speak well, for I have seen such (an instance), when the redness of the shamed person's face turned to white" – i.e. the blood rushed from his face. The opposite also happens, blood rushing *to* a shamed person's face: and in both cases that person's life may thereby be shortened, if only by a few minutes, making it a degree of murder.

The Talmud there proceeds to cite the story of "Judah and Tamar", to illustrate the opinion of R. Shimon ben Yochai that "a person should rather throw him- or herself into a fiery furnace, than put another to shame in public" – as Tamar was prepared to have done to her, rather than put Judah publicly to shame, by revealing that her twin sons were his. To his credit, he admitted the fact, and avoided the horrendous fate which he himself had pronounced on Tamar – and was rewarded therefor, by having one of those sons become the ancestor of Israel's royal dynasty.

There are other ways of murdering-by-degree – by causing another physical harm or mental anxiety to the detriment of his or her health and possible length of life. The person who "desires life, and loves days, that he may see good therein" – for himself, has to desire it for everyone else as well; and has to "depart from evil and do good, seek peace and pursue it," the very opposite of murder, manslaughter, careless 'accidents' and talk to the harm of others.

93.   DO NOT STEAL

Section 9. This commandment apparently occurs in two places: as the Eighth of the Ten Commandments, "Thou shalt not steal", and

"You shall not steal" – but neither is superfluous. By means of the twelfth of R. Yishmael's Thirteen Principles (SPB p. 15) the Sages show that the first of them, because it is sandwiched between two other commandments for the violation of which the extreme penalty is death, refers, like them, to an extreme kind of violation, which can incur the death penalty – the stealing of a human being, or kidnapping.

Though the incidence of kidnapping is alarmingly increasing in our times, *you* are certainly not going to indulge in this most heinous of crimes. Neither, I trust, are you going to commit the ordinary crime of stealing, of another's property, however trifling its value, to which the other "You shall not steal" refers. "Let the property of thy fellowman be as dear to you as your own," counsels R. Yose. Nor may you even "steal" innocently, as a practical joke, with the intention of returning the object eventually, because such a joke 'tastes' of stealing.

For the same reason you must not steal even with the intention of doing positive good! How is this possible? According to Torah law, if a thief is caught red-handed, he has, in most cases, "to pay back double." So someone, wanting to do a friend down on his luck a good turn, could steal something belonging to him, invite discovery by the police, and pay back double!

Finally, with regard to property, you must not even stealthily re-possess your *own* goods from the thief's premises, because such action *looks* like stealing. You must take recourse to the law, and let it regain your property for you.

Section 10.   **"Stealing Hearts"**

There is yet another way of stealing – not human beings, not even property, but 'hearts'! That is, to withhold information reasonably expected, or to make promises without any intention of fulfilling them, to anybody; or to issue invitations, which you know will not be accepted, in order to curry favour, and the like. Laban *accused* Jacob of such action, when he complained, "Why did you steal my heart (AJV: outwit me), and carry away my daughters . . . why did you flee secretly . . .?" Jacob, however, was guiltless, knowing that Laban would have tried to prevent him and his family and possessions from leaving.

Absalom *did* act in this way when, in an attempt to ensure the succession for himself, after David's death, by popular acclaim, he promised everybody everything – just like politicians in the run-up to an election! "Let every man who has any suit or cause come to me, and I will give him justice," Absalom promised: "And when any man approached to bow before him, he took hold of him and kissed him . . . thus did Absalom steal the hearts of the men of Israel."

Examples of 'heart-stealing' given in the Mechilta are: to invite someone to be your guest, knowing that he will not accept; and to offer presents to someone in the knowledge that he will not, or cannot, receive them. And you can probably think of many instances on your own.

94.   DO NOT ROB

Section 11. "Thou shalt not rob" differs from stealing in that, whereas the latter is carried out with secrecy, usually in the still of the night, robbery is committed even in broad daylight, with no fear of onlookers. The Sages add to this lesser degrees of robbery, such as those whose sole income derives from gambling, like dice-throwing and card-playing; and even anyone who partakes by invitation of a meal which he knows is not sufficient for his host, excusing his action by saying to himself: "I have done nothing wrong! Did I eat without his permission?"

In the main, the laws governing robbery are the same as those concerning stealing, incuding buying stolen or illegally seized property, "which is a grave sin, since it strengthens the hands of evil-doers, and encourages them to commit further thefts: for if there were no receivers, they would not steal."

But there is one difference between the thief and the robber – the relative gravity of their respective offences. Which, do you think, is the worse offender? Instinctively one would plump for the robber, for to seize with violence and without fear for any man, seems worse than to steal in secret. However we find that whereas the robber only has to return the seized item plus a *fifth* of its value, when caught, the thief has to pay *double*! Which means that the latter is the worse offender. Why is this?

The answer is a moral one. When his disciples put the question to R. Yochanan b. Zakkai, he replied: "because the robber at least shows he has no fear at all, either for man or G–d; whereas the thief evinces fear of 'the servant' (man) but none for 'the Master' (G–d)" – Who sees in secret as well!

95.   DO NOT COVET

Section 12. The last of the Ten Commandments forbids us to 'covet': "Thou shalt not covet thy neighbour's house . . .". What is covetousness (*chemdah*, from *lo tachmod*)? Surprisingly, Rashi does not define it: but the consensus of the commentators who do, is well summed up by Hertz who observes: to covet is "to long for the possession of anything we cannot get in an honest or legal manner."

RM, however, follows the Mechilta in maintaining that one is not guilty of covetousness until he has not only longed for, but successfully schemed to obtain the desired object, whether by foul means *or* '*fair*', citing the verse "and they coveted fields, *and seized* them." The verse "And the woman saw that the tree was to be desired (*nechmad*) ... so *she took* of the fruit thereof . . ." might also have been cited in support.

But from the verse "thou shalt not covet the silver and the gold upon them, and take it unto thee . . ." they deduce that even to *buy* the coveted article legally – for the Hebrew verb to 'take' is the same as that to 'buy' (lako'ach) – by persuading the reluctant owner to part with it by paying much more than its actual value, is to be guilty of *lo tachmod*.

96. DO NOT (EVEN) DESIRE

Section 13. Do you remember my saying, at the beginning of the last chapter, that RM found *fourteen* commandments in the *Aseret Hadeebrot* (popularly called "The Ten Commandments")? Well, this is the fourteenth: for, when re-stating them in Deuteronomy, after declaring "Thou shalt not *covet* (lo tachmod) thy neighbour's wife," it continues "thou shalt not *desire* (lo titaveh) thy neighbour's house. . .." Rashi *does* comment on the latter phrase, merely to agree with the Targum that to covet and to desire are more-or-less the same thing – and most of the commentators follow him.

Not so RM, however, who sees and numbers "thou shalt not covet" and "thou shalt not desire" as two separate and distinct commandments: and RN presumably agrees with him, since he does not express any disagreement! Not to desire, RM maintains, means not even to *want* anything not yours: what G–d gives you, after you have exerted all possible effort, if necessary on all six working days of the week – that is your lot; and "Who is rich? He who rejoices in his lot, as it is said: 'When thou eatest the labour of thy hands, happy art thou, and it shall be well with thee.'"

Why *did* Moses make this 'addition' to the Ten Utterances? I have opined that it was because he was then addressing his flock after their forty years' wandering in the wilderness, throughout which they had experienced that the very food they ate, the very water they drank, came to them miraculously and directly from G–d: how "the greedy got no more than others," and "the power-seekers were swallowed

up with their wealth." By then they must have realised that even to
harbour a passing desire to have more than one's rightful lot, more
than G–d wanted them to have, was a vain and useless thought. And
you and I, and all their descendants should realise this as well – only
more so!

The above reflections really belong in the volume which, it is
hoped, will follow this one, for the particular guidance of the
livelihood-earning and home-building married person. But, in a way,
they are relevant to the teenager as well, and especially the student:
for the career you will eventually choose, and its success, will largely
depend on your studies today, which can ensure an on-going intellectual interest, more fulfilling than mere pursuit of wealth – as most
ageing adults find out, only too late! It is the real knowledge you
acquire now which will shape you into the man or woman you will be
tomorrow; and, like ill-gotten material wealth, cribbing and overnight cramming for a one-time exam, are mere whiffs of knowledge,
which soon fly away. You must constantly, and patiently persevere in
building up a vast store of sound knowledge, moral and secular.

97.   RETURN LOST PROPERTY

Section 14. To such an extent must we respect our neighbour's
property that, if you should come across an obviously lost and
identifiable article or animal – like a wallet or a name-tagged cat, in a
public place "thou mayest not hide thyself," i.e. pass by and ignore
them, but "thou shalt surely return them to thy brother." However, if
"thy brother be not nigh unto thee, or thou know him not, then thou
shalt bring it to thy house, and it shall be with thee until thy brother
seek it, then shalt thou restore it."

There are two Torah commandments here: (i) not to pass by and
ignore a lost article, and (ii) to restore it to its owner. In former times,
if the owner lived far away or was not known, announcement of the
find was made in the Temple precincts during the Three Foot
Festivals, when *everyone* was gathered in Jerusalem; or later, in the
Synagogues, where everyone assembled every Shabbat, if not every
day. Nowadays, we have telephones and police-stations at our
service, which serve the same purpose, more speedily and effectively.

Sometimes we might take a strong fancy to the object or animal
found, and, though it is identifiable, decide to keep it, and even deny
having found it. This, of course, "is a sin," and is treated as robbery, a
fifth of the article's value having to be added when restitution is
forcibly made. But as for unidentifiable objects, such as scattered

money or fruit – they are cases of "finders – keepers", according to Jewish law.

Section	**Notes**
1	Exodus 34.6.
2	Makkot 7a; Deuter. 17.6; Sanhedrin 37a; Encyc. Judaica 5. 145.
3	Sanhedrin 37a; Ibid 73a; Levit. 19.16; SM. N. 297; Kiddushin 29a; Deuter. 25.11–12; see B. Kama 28a; on third note here.
4	Ethics 2.17; Sanhedrin 74a.
5	Genesis 9.6.
6	Exodus 22.1; Sanhedrin 72a; Deuter. 22.25–26; Sanhedrin 74a; Ibid.
7	Numbers 35.11–32 and Deuter. 19.2–13; Numbers 35.25 (see HPH); Deuter. 19.5; Chullin 7b; Shabbat 32a; Exodus 21.12–13; Makkot 10b; I. Samuel 24.13–14; Makkot 7b; Exodus 23.7.
8	B. Metsia 58b–59a; Genesis chapter 38; Psalms 34.15.
9	Exodus 20.13; Levit. 19.11; Sanhedrin 85b–86a; Exodus 21.16; Ethics 2.17; Sifra second note here; Exodus 22.3; Y. Sanhedrin 30b (8.5).
10	Genesis 31.26–27; II. Samuel 15.4–6.
11	Levit. 19.13; Sanhedrin 24b; Ch.M. 356.1; Levit. 5.24; B. Kama 79b.
12	Exodus 20.14; SM. N. 265; Micah 2.2; Gen. 3.6; Deuter. 7.25.
13	Deuter. 5.18; Ethics 4.1; Psalms 128.2; Exodus 16.20; Numbers 16.32.
14	Deuter. 22.1–3; Levit. 5.21 & 24; B. Metsia 21a.

Thirty-Three

THE COMPLETE JEW

Section 1.   **Your Life Comes First!**

In our detailed discussion of commandment 36, we saw that the literal meaning of the golden social rule is 'Thou shalt love *for* thy neighbour as for thyself'; and that R. Akiva declared it to be "a great comprehensive principle of the Torah." That this was the interpretation he gave it – and not the popular translation 'And thou shalt love thy neighbour *as thyself*", is proven by his contribution to an interesting hypothetical question raised in the rabbinic academy.

"Two men are travelling on a journey far from civilisation, and only one of them has a canteen of water. Should they share its contents, both would die; but if only one drinks all the water, *he* will be able to reach civilisation", but the other would die of thirst. What should be done? Ben Patura opined that both should drink and die, rather than the one should be responsible, if only indirectly, for the death of his companion. But R. Akiva declared "Thy life takes precedence over that of thy neighbour," proving his contention from a Torah text.

From another such text it is deduced that a person has the right to kill in self-defence – if that is the only way in which he can save his own life. "The Torah states: If one comes to kill you, anticipate his act by killing him first." (However, if the threatened life could have been saved by just maiming the attacker, killing him would be considered as a case of murder.)

G–d is the Giver of precious life: only He can take it back, command a judicial court to take it, or demand of an individual that he surrender it back to Him in any of "three dire situations" he might find himself, happily very rare in our times.

It goes without saying, of course, that you yourself must protect your G–d-given life. A Roman officer, considering himself to have been treated discourteously by a pious Jew who, engrossed in reciting

302

the Amidah by the roadside, did not immediately return his greeting, waited until the *chassid* had completed his prayer, and then asked angrily: "Does it not say in your Torah, 'Only take heed to thyself, and guard thy life (*nefesh*) diligently'? Why did you not return my greeting? If I had cut off your head with my sword, who would have demanded satisfaction for your blood from me?", all-powerful that he was!

That Roman officer was appeased – but he was right in his choice of proof-text! You *do* have to guard your life diligently by living cleanly and taking adequate physical exercise; by avoiding risks to your health like under-, or more likely over-eating, and failing to protect yourself against the elements; and by not endangering yourself by jay-walking, amber-gambling, drug-taking, immoderate smoking – if any at all, and the like.

"An important principle in health-preservation," states Dr. RM, "is the prompt and easy answering of nature's calls; and whenever we do that, after washing our hands we thank our Creator (SPB 5) "Who healest all flesh and doest wondrously" – but we do not believe in faith-healing alone when illness overtakes us, for "the Torah authorises the medical man to heal" – and "Is it not common sense that if a man has a pain he visits the healer?"

Section 2.   **Healthy Service!**
I pray that you may always maintain good health, but that should you be unlucky enough to contract any illness, you will immediately consult a doctor divinely endowed with the gift of healing, and also pray to Him for a speedy recovery, so that you can, as soon as is advisable, return with full vigour to your full-time occupation as a Jew: "Acknowledgeing Him in all your ways – then He will direct your paths."

In what directions will those paths take you? Upwards, towards Him, in prayer and thanksgiving; inwards, to your own mind and heart, in the search for intellectual and spiritual advancement; and outwards, 'on the way', in striving for the good and the welfare of all your fellow-men. When R. Akiva declared 'Love for thy *neighbour* as for thyself' as being a comprehensive principle of conduct, Ben Azzai suggested that there was one which embraced even more than did R. Akiva'a choice: "This Book is the generations of *man*: in the day of G–d's creation of man, in the likeness of G–d did He make him."

All men, of all races colours and creeds, are the descendants of one human father, and inspirited by the One Heavenly Father. All are brothers, all His creation: "Have we not all one Father," asked the last of the Prophets, "hath not One G–d created us? Why should we

deal treacherously every man against his brother?" On the contrary!
The Jew must always manifestly act with faithfulness in his associations with all his fellow-men, whether he personally likes them or not
– but eventually learning to love them as his brothers under G–d.

Section 3.   **The Real 'Neighbour'**

In the commandment just mentioned, and in many other places in the
Tenach, the Hebrew word translated 'neighbour' (*raya*) is used in a
much wider sense than the literal meaning of that English word which
is 'a person who dwells near another', the Hebrew word for which is
shachen. (See chapter eighteen for the exact connotation of the two
terms.) Among the bad influences from which every individual asks
G–d to deliver him is a 'bad *shachen*'; for the environment in which
you live can have a very great effect upon the moulding of your
character.

You, however, should always be a *good shachen* to you next-door
neighbour and those beyond, not disturbing their privacy and rest,
and helping them in any way you can, especially if they are old and
alone or incapable of leaving home. And you should also be a *shachen
tov* to your neighbourhood Synagogue, which is your Father's House
in which He is always delighted to see you – on weekdays as well as
Shabbatot and Festivals.

The great Hillel urges you: "do not separate yourself from the
congregation"; and the best place in which to join it, demonstrating
and fortifying your Jewish identity, and your solidarity with the
whole house of Israel – is in the Synagogue.

Said Resh Lakish: "Anyone who has a Synagogue within his area
and does not go there to pray, is called a bad *neighbour*". Note that
description well: he is not called a bad *son* to his Father Whose Home
he does not visit when He announces a holy convocation – though he
is that; but a bad neighbour to his congregation. For the Synagogue
is, or should be, not only a House of Prayer, but the centre of all local
social activity, and a link with the wider Jewish community, both of
which have many ancillary organisations; and by actively sharing in
their work would give practical expression to your good neighbour-
liness.

In its widest connotation, which consenus of opinion accepts, the
biblical *raya* is 'all the world and his wife' – every human being, and
involvement in muncipal, national and even international welfare is a
mark of the best neighbour. But for the present, you should be
primarily occupied in studying, preparing to make your contribution
in any of those spheres, well-versed in the Jewish attitude to the
particular sphere in which you choose to interest yourself.

Section 4. **Our Other Neighbours**

But you cannot be a complete Jew unless you extend your love and devotion into even wider fields. Among the many qualifications acquired by "everyone who occupies himself in the practice of Torah for its own sake," says R. Meir, "and to whom, moreover, the whole world is indebted," is that he becomes 'a lover of the *briyyot*'. This Hebrew word is commonly translated (SPB 276, HPM 704) 'mankind'; but, derived from the verb 'to create', it means *all* living creatures.

Thus we are told that "When R. Akiva read the words 'the great lizard after its kind', he used to exclaim: 'How manifold are Thy works, O Eternal! in wisdom hast Thou made them all . . .': Thou hast creatures (*briyyot*) that live in the sea and Thou hast creatures that live on dry land . . . creatures that live in fire and creatures that live in the air . . . 'How manifold are Thy works, O Eternal!'." And, together with humans high and low, "sea-monsters . . . beasts and all cattle, creeping things and winged birds" are called upon to praise the Name of the Eternal.

True it is that they are all subservient to man, the goal of the whole creation: "Thou hast given him dominion over all the works of Thy hands . . . sheep and oxen, all of them, and also the beasts of the field, the fowl of the air, and the fish of the sea, whatsoever passeth through the paths of the sea." But they are still *His* creatures, *our* fellow-beings and neighbours on earth; and we must respect and love them as such.

"To cause living creatures suffering is a Torah prohibition," the Sages point out; and there are no less than seven Torah commandments enjoining the avoidance of acts of cruelty towards them. They are not being detailed or numbered here, because they are mainly concerned with agriculture, a field in which few readers of this book are likely to be occupied – with one exception, and for two reasons: because some people still pursue it as a hobby; and because it is concerned with protecting a creature even against emotional distress.

98. DO NOT TAKE A BROODING BIRD

Section 5. Here is the literal translation of the commandment: "If a bird's nest chance to be before thee in the way, in any tree or on the ground, prefledglings or eggs, and the mother is brooding on the pre-fledglings or on the eggs, thou shalt not take the mother on the offspring." That is the negative commandment. What then should one do if his dubious hobby is bird-nesting, which the dictionary defines as 'seeking and robbing birds' nests'? He must first fulfil the accompanying positive commandment:

99.   FIRST SEND AWAY THE MOTHER

"Send thou shalt send away the mother, then thou mayest take the offspring for thyself – that it may go well with thee, and thou wilt prolong thy days."

The Midrash gives us the reason for these commandments – to show that G–d has compassion upon cattle, just as He has upon man. "Just as He has compassion on a male child in delaying his circumcision 'until the eighth day' when he should have gained some strength; so He commanded that only 'from the eighth day and thenceforth may an animal be accepted for an offering, and whether it be cow or ewe, you shall not slaughter it and its young in one day'. And in the same way that He has compassion upon cattle, so is G–d filled with mercy for birds," citing our commandments as illustration.

A whole chapter of the Talmud, actually named after these commandments, discusses at very great length all the laws their fulfilment entails; and the Sh.Ar. summarises them in a short chapter with the same name "*Shilu'ach hakkan*" – 'sending the nesting bird away'. Here only two possibly relevant ones are being mentioned: the commandment only applies to *kasher* birds; and does *not* apply to domesticated farm or back-yard fowls. Nevertheless, since the purpose of the commandments is to teach us not to cause *any* living thing distress, it would be an equitable act 'beyond the requirement of the law' to shoo the hen away before taking her eggs to eat!

Section 6.   **No Contradiction**

Not only does the consumption of kasher meat not contradict this ethical command to show compassion towards all G–d's creatures, but it actually accentuates it. I am not going to iterate the arguments on this subject already expounded in chapter thirteen, but only remind you that the eating of such meat was "divinely sanctioned", and the detailed laws of *shechita*, the Jewish method of slaughter, were "divinely communicated to Moses orally on mount Sinai," by Him "Whose tender mercies are over all His works," and must therefore be the *least* painful method of all. But even so, we should have compassion on the animals chosen for this purpose.

The great Rabbi Judah the Prince once lapsed in this respect: a calf being led to the slaughter broke away from the drove and hid its head under his cloak, lowing in terror. "Go!" he said to it, "for it was for this you were created!". Thereupon it was decreed on High- "Since he

showed no pity, let us bring suffering on him" – and he was afflicted
with various illnesses for thirteen years, until he *did* show compassion
on some weasels his daughter was about to sweep out of the house,
instructing her to leave them alone, citing the above-quoted verse
from Psalms to her; whereupon it was decreed on High: "Since *he* has
shown compassion, let us be compassionate towards him" – and he
was healed.

Vegetarians may disagree with RM's opinion that "the killing of
animals is necessary, because the natural food of man consists of
vegetables and animal flesh . . . and no doctor has any doubts about
this." But none will disagree with his general conclusion that: "If the
Torah provides that grief should not be caused to cattle and birds,
how much more careful must we but not to cause grief to our
fellow-men!"

But let me repeat a brief summary of what was said in that earlier
chapter: it is no *mitzvah* to eat meat – in fact, since Temple days
vegetarianism has been commendable; but it is *wrong* to refrain from
meat on the score of its provision involving cruelty to animals. For it
is the Giver of all life who permits that of *kasher* animals to be used
for food, and He ordained the method of slaughter. Rabbi Judah was
right in telling that calf that it was created as food for man: it was for
the brusque manner in which he said it that he was punished so
severely. For he was the Prince of the Holy Land's Jewry, otherwise
called 'our holy teacher'; and G–d "is meticulously exacting towards
the righteous, even (when they err) to the extent of a hair's breadth!"

Section 7.   **The Comprehensive Lesson**
You will remember that the Sages considered the respect and
reverence due to parents (commandments 19 and 20) to be the most
difficult commandments to fulfil, since their obligation lasts for a
life-time. At the end of the scale, they assess *shilu'ach hakkan* as the
easiest, for all you have to do is to shoo the bird away, which takes a
second. Yet the *same* rich reward is held out for each – "that thy days
may be long, and that it may go well with thee." Why is this?

"G–d did not reveal to His creatures the reward for every separate
commandment, so that they may perform *all* of them without being
tempted to say: 'Seeing that this commandment is a great one, I will
perform it because its reward is great; and seeing that the other is a
minor one, I will not perform it'." And to discourage us from
'weighing' the commandments in order to estimate their relative
importance and measure of reward, He allocated the same reward to
the hardest and the easiest of them.

Thus, from *shilu'ach hakkan*, in conjunction with *kibbud av va-em*, you have a comprehensive guide regarding the fulfilment of all the commandments that come your way, advice which Rabbi Judah puts succinctly in other words: "Be heedful of a light commandment as of a grave one, for you do not know the grant of reward for each commandment."

Better still, perform them all – your duties to G–d, and your duties towards your fellow-men and your fellow-creatures out of love! Be guided by the maxim of Antignos: "Be not like servants who minister to their master upon the condition of receiving a reward; but be like servants who minister to their master without the condition of receiving a reward" – and then you will be pleasantly surprised how big it is when it does come!

There is one medium through which friendship, kindness and compassion can be shown – money. But consideration of the important commandments which can be fulfilled in this way has been held over to the next volume, since the average teenager has just about enough 'pocket-money' with which to satisfy his or her own needs. Nevertheless, whatever you can do in this sphere, do: and your mite will be as weighty in the divine scales as the rich man's million!

Section	Notes
1	Y. Nedarim 9.4; B. Metsia 62a; Sanhedrin 72a & 74a; Ibid 74a; Berachot 32b; Deuter. 4.9; Yad. De'ot 4.1 & 13; B. Kama 85a and 46b.
2	Proverbs 3.6; Genesis 5.1; Malachi 2.10.
3	Ethics 2.5; Berachot 8a.
4	Ethics 6.1; Chullin 127a; Levit. 11.29; Psalms 104.24; Ibid 148.7 & 10; Ibid 8.7–9; Shabbat 128b.
5	Deuter. 22.6–7; MR. Deuter. 6.1; Levit. 12.3; Ibid 22.27–28; Chullin, last chapter; summarised in Y. De'ah 293; B. Metsia 30b.
6	Levit. chapter 11; Chullin 42a; Psalms 145.9; B. Metsia 85a; Guide 3.48; MR. Numbers 20.24.
7	Deuter. 5.16 and 22.7; MR. Deuter. 6.2; Ethics 2.1; Ibid 1.3.

Thirty-Four

GROWING UP

Section 1. Life can be compared to the re-winding spools of a tape-recorder: at first, the full spool appears to revolve only very slowly, but as the process continues, it gathers momentum until, towards the end, it rolls very fast, clicking into stillness. So is life: our earliest years appear to pass so slowly, that we wish they would 'get a move on'; but as the end draws nigh, the years roll away so swiftly that we want to command them 'Halt! slow down a little!' But *all* our days are equally precious if wisely lived. "So teach us to number our days," we should all pray to G–d with Moses, "that we may get us a heart of wisdom"!

Life does not stand still, needless to say: it rolls on. And the years of adolescence, approximately from Bar-Bat-Mitzvah to marriage, should be the most enjoyable, until that latter fruitful stage of real fulfilment is reached – if a wise heart directs them. "Rejoice, young man, in the days of thy youth, and let thy heart cheer thee in the days of thy youth . . .", advises *Kohelet* (the author of *Ecclesiastes*, reputed, by Jewish tradition, to have been king Solomon).

But the way in which that verse continues is given as one of the reasons why the Sages, when they were considering which books should be included in the Jewish Bible, wanted to exclude this one! For he goes on to say: ". . . and walk in the ways of thy heart, and in the sight of thine eyes . . ." – which is totally opposed to the Torah commandment "and you shall *not* stray after your hearts and after your eyes"! "Is restraint to be abolished?" they asked: "is there no judgment and no Judge?"

It was only because the verse concludes with "but know thou, that for all these things G–d will bring thee into judgment" that they relented, and exclaimed "Well has Solomon spoken!". Kohelet also begins the next and last chapter of his Book (or *megillah*, for it is one of the five such) with "Remember then thy Creator in the days of thy youth"; and ends it with "For G–d shall bring every act into judgment, concerning every hidden thing, whether it be good or whether it be evil".

Section 2.   **The Battle Commences!**

You will remember the reason given for the choice of the Bar-Bat-Mitzvah age – because about then a *physical* change, puberty, takes place in the average person: or, in rabbinic terms, the *yetzer hara*, the lower, animal instinct in man (and woman), which enters the child as it emerges from its mother's womb, really begins to assert itself. To combat it, however, the *yetzer hatov* is 'born' concomitant with the BM-age: man becomes aware of the spiritual and intellectual powers instilled into him by G–d to take up the challenge of its wily antagonist of thirteen-years' or so seniority.

Not only is the *yetzer hara* senior, but it grows stronger every day, seeking to animalise its host-body; and "were it not for the help of the Holy One, blessed be He – the gift of the *yetzer hatov* – he would not be able to withstand it". Therefore, the school of R. Yishmael taught: "If this repulsive wretch challenges thee, drag him to the Torah study-house" – i.e. disarm him with a rich dose of moral medicine, which he hates!

That is the battle which, with ever-growing intensity will be waged within you daily from BM-age onwards and throughout life – or until "the evil days – old age – come, when thou wilt say, 'I have no pleasure in them'". Animal or human? "without understanding, like the beasts that perish", or "but little lower than the angels, crowned with glory and honour"? That is what you have to decide *now*, at the earliest stage of the struggle, when the combatants within you are raring to go – the older one most certainly!

Now – because "The *yetzer hara* is at first like the thread of a spider's-web, but ultimately (if allowed free rein) becomes like a tow-rope. . . . At first, he is a passer-by, then he becomes a guest, and finally he becomes the occupier of the house" – if you let him! "If one indulges his animal passions in his youth, they will eventually rule over him in old age". Therefore "a man should ever incite the *yetzer hatov* to fight against the *yetzer hara*". I think that it sufficient moral exhoration for the present.

Section 3.   **Adam And Eve Onwards**

Adam and Eve were the only two humans fashioned by G–d Alone: from them onwards, man, like the rest of the animate world, was self-reproducing, implanted with seed "bearing fruit after its kind, wherein is the seed thereof" – with this difference: only in the reproduction of the human kind did G–d deign to become a Partner. When R. Simlai was asked to explain the reason for the change from the plural in "Let *us* make man in *our* image", to the singular "and G–d made man in *His* image", he thus expounded:

"In the beginning, Adam was created from the earth, and Eve from Adam. From then onwards, man will be created in *our* image and likeness – not by man alone, or by woman alone, or by them both together alone, but by the Divine Presence also. And so 'G–d created man in *His* image' *as well*" – that 'image' being His contribution of "the spirit and the breath, dignity of apperance, the ability to see and hear, to speak and to walk, to understand and discern".

The first fruit of Adam's seed, fructified within Eve, was Cain (Hebrew: *Kayin*), after whose birth his mother so named him, saying: "I have gotten (*kaniti*) a man *et ha-Shem*." JAV translates these last two words "with the help of the Eternal", rendering *et* as 'with the help of' – a meaning it has nowhere else; while the CAV renders it 'from', which it also does not mean. But if we give *et* the meaning it very often does, and sometimes *must*, have, the translation becomes "I have gotten a man *with* the Eternal" as one of the three partners in the child, which corresponds with R. Simlai's explanation above.

G–d's contribution to the children you may have in due course is perforce limited by the nature of the seed, and the nursery for it, you and your human partner contribute. He wants it to be perfect fruit of "a noble vine, wholly of right seed" – but, as stated there, He is only *One* of the partners, and the rest will depend on you.

I shall develop this theme at length in the next volume, *b'ezrat ha-Shem*: what is pertinent to *you, now*, is that that seed is already stirring within you, young man, and its nursery is in preparation within you, young lady; and both must be preserved in purity to produce luscious fruit!

Section 4.   **Defy "Satan"!**

When the Sages were discussing "the proper age for marriage," some suggested between eighteen and twenty-four, and others between sixteen and twenty. In his 'calendar for life', R. Yehudah b. Tema sets the age at eighteen, and Rava, supported by the school of R. Yishmael, said: "Until the age of twenty, the Holy One, blessed be He, sits and waits (saying), '*when* will he take a wife?'

As soon as he attains twenty, and has *not* married, He exclaims, 'May he be blasted!'". Sharp words, indeed, not to be taken too

literally: but they do follow upon the understandable view of R.
Huna, as regards the average young man: "He who is twenty years of
age and not yet married, spends all his days in sinful thoughts"!

And R. Chisda was very self-revealing when he added to the
discussion: "The reason why I am superior to my colleagues is that I
married at sixteen: and had I married at fourteen, I would have said
to Satan, 'An arrow in your eye!' – i.e. 'I defy you to tempt me!'".
From which it may be inferred (a) that 'Satan', the *yetser hara,* did
tempt him between fourteen and sixteen; and (b) that he was superior
in knowledge because, after marriage, he was able to put his mind
completely to his studies, without 'sinful thoughts'!

"Satan" means 'adversary' or 'enemy' – of the *yetzer hatov,* and his
ruses and enticements are countless and persistent. He will tirelessly
urge you not to preserve seed or nursery in all their strength and
purity until the due planting season, but either to follow the "example
of Onan," employing more 'modern' methods, or actually to sow – or
be the recipient of – 'wild oats', with all the consequences of such an
act.

And he has so many aids at hand today! I wonder whether R.
Ammi was a prophet, looking ahead to our times, when he said: "The
Tempter does not lurk at the side of the street, but walks in the broad
highway; and when he sees a person rolling his eyes, smoothing his
hair, and proudly strutting along, he exclaims, 'This one belongs to
me'!" There are plenty of aids to hand for him to manipulate on the
highway of today – posters, sleezy shop-windows, rolling eyes and
strutting feet of members of the opposite sex, also after 'a little bit of
fun' – or worse! Do *I* have to tell *you*?

Our father Jacob "did not marry until he was eighty-four!" Yet
when, on his death-bed, he blessed his children, he could say to
Reuben: "Thou art my firstborn, my vigour, and the beginning of my
manhood", which latter phrase our Sages take to mean that Reuben
was conceived of the very first seed to issue from his father.

You will duly marry – because it is a Torah commandment – long
before that, perhaps at the ideal age of eighteen, which is now the
legal age at which you can marry without parental consent – or you
might even follow R. Chisda's example, which you can do *with* your
parents' consent! But it will probably be later – by twenty perhaps,
remembering that the eye of your Father in Heaven is upon you; but
in any case not later than twenty-four, the rabbinic limit! It is with
how you conduct yourself until you come to that important decision,
which will affect the whole of your life, that the last of our hundred
commandments is concerned, acting as a bridge between this volume
and the next.

100.   NO SEX BEFORE MARRIAGE!

Section 5. As explained in the last chapter, Jews are strongly advised not to "wash their dirty linen in public" – not to submit disputes, and especially such as would bring discredit upon the community as a whole, thus 'desecrating the Name', before a civil court. They should be kept within the community, by being submitted to a Bet-Din, whose verdict, should both parties consent in writing to accept it, is recognised by the law of the country.

There are certain Torah commandments which are applicable today in this respect: that is, if disputes concerning them were submitted to a Bet-Din for adjudication by both parties, a binding verdict, in accordance with Jewish law, could be given. But since many of these commandments are grave *moral* offences, they are not all considered to be criminal by the secular law, some of them not only being connived at by it, but even legally sanctioned in today's permissive society. It would seldom happen, then, that *both* sides involved in such cases would submit them to a Bet-Din.

The comandment under review is, as it were, the ideal one towards which all related Torah commandments aim. It is formally stated, and is inherent in: "There shall be none devoted to sexual immorality of the daughers of Israel, neither shall there be anyone devoted to sexual immorality of the sons of Israel". (I use the term 'sexual immorality', rather loosely, somewhat euphemistically, in preference to the harsher 'harlot' and 'sodomite'.) But the extension of this commandment to include any such *single* act, depends on deductions from two other Torah prohibitions with which 'the Satan' will tempt you, with increasing vigour, to breach as your teenage years progress.

To be able to follow the argument, you should know that, according to *Jewish* law, so far as marriage is concerned, you reach your majority at BM-age, from which time onwards a contract of marriage may be entered into without parental consent; and, I would opine, the only reason why the most liberally-minded of the Sages advised 'delay' until sixteen was because "a husband-to-be must first provide a home and a livelihood for his future dependants." Until BM-age one is a minor, and during the years of minority a child is wholly under parental control and care, any of his or her earnings, etc. belonging to the father.

Should any man commit the heinous crime of rape against a minor girl, "he has to pay the father a fine *and* marry the girl," without the right ever to divorce her. In a case of seduction – glibly talking a minor girl into committing an immoral act, he also "has to pay the fine, and *should* marry her": but if the father refuses his consent, he only has to pay the fine.

But what if a heartless brute of a father wants to exploit his minor daughter, and make financial gain by encouraging such conduct on a regular basis? The Torah sternly warns against such a fiendish thought! "Do not degrade thy daughter, to make her an addict to sexual immorality . . .". And what if the girl herself, after reaching her majority, consents to such acts? That verse continues, "lest the land fall into sexual immorality, and the land become full of unchastity", which is taken to mean: such conduct must be avoided, lest it become general, the whole of society thereby becoming corrupt.

Hence "There shall be *none* devoted to sexual immorality of the daughters of Israel, neither shall there be *anyone* devoted to sexual immorality of the sons of Israel". It only takes one to initiate an animalish and pleasurable corrupt practice, and other weak characters will sheepishly follow suit. *You* cannot initiate such general misbehaviour – it is, alas, rampant all around you! And you will find it hard enough to avoid slipping into the drove of silly sheep leading themselves into the spiritual slaughterhouse!

Section 6.   **The Rabbinic "Fence"**
Yes, you will find it very, very hard, not only on account of the permissive society in which you probably reside, and by your contemporaries among whom you will be considered 'square' if you do not conform; but also by the incessant urgings of the Tempter within. That is why R. Yehuda b. Pazzi said: "Whoever fences himself against the temptation of sexual immorality is called 'holy' – a term which means morally separated from, and superior to, one's environment. The Talmudic Sages, in accordance with the instruction handed down to them by the "Men of the Great Assembly", who included a few of the latter Prophets, "made a fence around the Torah" to guard it from violation, and especially around those "for which man's soul has a craving and longing" – like immorality and non-*kasher* food, he who refrains from the latter also being called "holy".

The many stakes in the rabbinic fence around the Torah commandments regarding immortality are summarised in the Sh.Ar. and they include: not to gesticulate to, wink at, or indulge in jesting and banter with, one of the opposite sex; not to gaze at a lady's attire, even when she is not wearing it (unless you are in that kind of business!); not to walk behind a lady, or look at "even her little finger", let alone other limbs, for sensual gratification. For her part, a lady must not dress or walk in a provocative manner in public in order to rouse the interest of the opposite sex.

After even just these few excerpts from the many precautionary measures, I can hear you protest: We're living in the twentieth century, not in the Middle Ages! *Our* emancipated generation takes a much more liberal view on association between the sexes: we have co-ed schools and colleges, mixed Youth Clubs, and are accustomed to mixed dancing, dating girls – and lots more!

And I would answer you: Have you ever considered that *your* generation may be more lax and permissive in these matters than any that have gone before, just *because* of its breaking down the fence – and "Whoso breaketh through a fence, a serpent may bite him"? Are we not urged "Remove not the ancient landmark, which thy fathers have set"? It may well be that technologically we have become much more advanced than those 'ancients' were – but human nature has not changed, unless it is for the worse!

Nor can you deny that *your* generation has provided 'the Satan' with many more 'sophisticated' tools and artifices with which to entice and entrap the unwary than he had when *I* was at your age! Need I detail them? Pornographic 'literature', 'artistic' photographs no longer secreted under the counter or sold at the back door, but gaudily displayed in the front window; the unacceptable screen of film and TV – I don't have to go on! That's enough!

Section 7.   **But What If . . .?**

Yes, the animal impulse is a doughty challenger, and has powerful and entrancing agents! To prevail against it, your *yetser hatov*, your heart, mind and soul must do constant, unflagging battle; and the Jew has an advantage in this inward arena, for his heavenly-implanted higher nature can summon up the most devastating ammunition ever created; the most potent spiritual bomb!

In the course of his lengthy debate with his 'comforters', Job says to G–d: "Thou knowest that I will not be condemned, for there is none that can deliver out of Thy hand"; to which, a little later, Eliphaz replies, "Thou doest away with fear, diminishest (the power of) prayer before G–d".

Rava interprets this verbal cut-and-thrust as follows: Job says to G–d: 'You can condemn no one for his sins, since You created the *yetser hara* within man, against which no one can deliver himself'; to which Eliphaz replies: 'True it is that He created the *yetser hara* – but he also created in advance an antidote against it, the Torah, which teaches fear of G–d, and the power of prayer and good deeds'. "Therefore the advice of the School of R. Yishmael."

But while some do not even need that advice, with others it can fail to achieve the desired end even when taken, since the nature of one is different to that of his fellow. "There are many moral characteristics inherent in every human being, one being different and very divergent from the other . . . there is the sensual man, whose lust is never fully satisfied, and there is the pure of heart who does not even desire the few things that the body needs!"

Both extremes are bad, and RM advises those in whom they are innate to search for, and traverse, the medial path between them, upon which the feet of the majority are destined from birth to tread. And on that path the *yetser hatov* may sometimes come off worse in the never-ending struggle – and the Sages recognised this! What if it does?

"If a man sees his animal impulse prevailing over him, let him go to a place where he is not known, put on black (mourning) garments, and do what his heart desires – but let him not desecrate the Name of Heaven publicly" (i.e. do so in a place where he is known, and will probably be found out, and thus bring disgrace upon himself and his community).

Many of the commentators are so astounded that a Mishna Sage, R. Ilai the Elder, should condone such sinful action, whatever the pressure, that they suggest that he meant that the exhaustion of a journey to a far away place in those days, together with the sight of his dreary attire throughout it, would cause a change of mind, a cooling of his passion on arrival at his destination – if not before; and that he would then turn back home, repentant and unscathed. Others, on the other hand, accept that R. Ilai literally meant what he said, but given only to "one who is incapable of overcoming the *yetser hara*", try as he may.

But of anyone who has the moral stamina to wrestle on, but yields to temptation before it has been fully spent, R. Yitschak said: "When anyone commits a transgression in secret, it is as though he thrust aside the feet of the Divine Presence, for "Thus saith the Eternal: The Heavens are My throne, and the earth is My *foot*-stool" which the sinner, even in privacy *and alone*, brushes aside. "Can any hide himself in secret places that I shall not see him? saith the Eternal: Do I not fill heaven and earth?"

Section 8.   **You Too, Young Lady!**

All the above texts and quotations refer to the male, only because "It is the way of a man to go in search of a woman, but it is not the way of a woman to go in search of a man. This may be compared to someone who has lost an article: who goes in search of whom? The loser goes in search of the lost article" – and man goes in search of his lost rib! (I wonder whether R. Shimon would be of the same mind as to which sex does the searching were he alive in our age!)

But the use of the masculine in all these places is of common gender, and applies to you, young lady, as well – and perhaps even more so: for it is realistically stated, the author having wisely not put his name to the saying, that "More than a man desires to marry, a woman desires to be taken in marriage". Even that, with 'Women's Lib', is not as true and as general as it used to be – not quite!: but there are still girls who do silly things in attempts to secure husbands, and belittle themselves thereby.

Section 9. **Other Associations**
Though they are most definitely "Torah prohibitions," I had thought of not even mentioning either homosexuality or bestiality here, the first being termed an 'abomination' and the second a 'perversion' – my reason being that the Sages said, in Talmudic times, "Israel is suspected of neither". As to the latter, I think their conviction still holds good; but there have been rapid changes in the public attitude towards the former in the last half century, from Hertz's description of it in 1936, as "the abyss of depravity from which the Torah saved the Israelite", through legal permit for consenting adults by the British Parliament in the 70's, to the establishment of 'Gay' congregations in the 80's.

As for lesbianism, RM includes it among "the forbidden practices of the land of Egypt" where, he says, "man used to marry man, woman used to marry woman, and one woman was married to two men". While he admits lesbianism is not a direct Torah prohibition, it is still a rabbinic one, and should be prevented.

Within the human family as a whole, which is by-and-large heterosexual, those with homosexual tendencies of both sexes are an abnormal minority, towards whom, if they do not repel it, we must evince every consideration and sympathy. But, as Jews, we cannot permit or condone violations of an explicit Torah prohibition by males, and a rabbinic one by females. Perhaps their nature will change; perhaps medical science may find a way – if they want it.

They are as precious to the general Jewish community as any others, and can be of valuable service to it, without forming separate congregations. Of another somewhat similar minority section of the community, specifically those who have been rendered childless, but applicable to the childless generally, the Prophet declares: "Let not the childless say, 'Behold I am a dry tree'! For thus saith the Eternal concerning the childless that keep My Shabbatot, and choose the things that please Me and hold fast by my covenant: even unto them will I give *in My house* and within My walls, a monument and a memorial better than sons and daughters. . . ."

There is room and a welcome for everyone who holds fast to His covenant in the Orthodox community. And if those sections which differ from the majority, *do* consider their difference a disability, and accept them as "chastenings of love", great will be their reward. More on this subject in the next volume, where it really belongs; but I felt a need to mention it here because you might have an incipient inclination towards a homosexual association which can probably be nipped in the bud. If it can be, nip it! – however difficult it proves to be.

Section 10.   **An Exhortation!**

In order to demonstrate its moral justification, the Sages give various non-literal meanings to the divine warning, given in the Second Commandment, that He "visits the sins of parents upon their children . . . to the fourth generation" (see HPH 296). But in one sense it can carry its literal meaning: Being a Partner in their creation, G–d earnestly desires that all His children should be born perfect in every way; but He predominantly acts through Nature, and He can therefore only pass on to children the genes which their parents have cultivated before their children's conception.

This is what R. Chanina b. Papa was undoubtedly referring to when he says that at the time a child is conceived, the 'angel of conception' produces the conjoint seed before the Holy One, and asks, among other questions: "What shall be the fate of this seed – shall it grow into a strong person or a weak one, a wise one or a foolish one, short or tall, ugly or good-looking, fat or slim . . .?" (to be continued anon).

Again, a full discussion of this literally vital theme must await the next volume: I mention it here only to caution you against even having one brief association with one of the opposite sex who, unknown to you, might have contracted some horrid disease and pass it on to you with the possibility – nay the probability – of impairing your offspring even to the fourth generation! Very apt in this connection is the general conclusion reached by Resh Lakish that "no person commits a transgression unless a spirit of folly enters him (or her)". What greater folly can there be than, in return for gratifying a moment of passion, you endanger the physical and/or mental well-being of your offspring to the fourth generation even!

Resh Lakish was speaking specifically of adultery – an illicit association with a married woman, one of the prohibitions in the Ten Commandments, the consequences of which can be so grave and, theoretically at least, fatal. So even if, Heaven forbid, the Satan does prevail over you, and you take R. Ilai's advice literally – let not the other party be a married woman!

I say 'Heaven forbid!' because in a prayer we daily recite (SPB 8) – which is couched in the singular in the Talmud – we ask G–d "to subdue our inclination that it may submit itself unto Thee": yet the battle between the two inclinations is the *one* issue on which G–d does not pronounce in advance, since freedom of will and action is fundamental to Judaism! "Everything is in the power of Heaven (to grant) – except the fear of Heaven itself!".

R. Chanina deduces this from "and now, Israel, what does the Eternal ask of thee? Only to fear (and revere, and stand in awe of) the Eternal thy G–d . . .". Once you have voluntarily chosen between the wrong and the right, and the latter is your option, *then* "He will assist you" – or if you select the former, "He will reluctantly open the door to you." But your moral make-up is in *your* hands!

Section 11.   **The Moral**

So, my dear reader, I earnestly beg of you: defy the Satan for the devil he is: neither pay any heed to his aides-de-camp, those doctors, psychologists, psychiatrists and their ilk who advise you that the royal physician, Maimonides, did not know what he was talking about when he said: "Indulgence in self-abuse and excessive sexual activity, cause physical weakness, premature ageing, loss of hair . . . and many other ailments". Even if these knowalls are right when they maintain that restraint is physically harmful, morally they have not a toe to stand on! Remember the warning in the Second Commandment!

To summarise: avoid all the manifold modern temptations which entice your heart, eyes and body! Cling firmly to the highest morality of the fruits of "the vine Thou didst pluck up out of Egypt . . .", its seed wholly pure seed, its nursery virginal to receive it, that it may bring forth new fruit in its due season – children healthy in body and mind! It depends tremendously on how you conduct yourself between now and marriage.

Section   **Notes**

1   Psalms 90.12; Eccles. 11. 9–12; MR. on previous note.
2   ADRN chap. 16; Sukkah 52a-b; Eccles. 12.1; Psalms 49.21; Ibid 8.6; MR. Genesis 22.6; Berachot 5a.
3   Genesis 1.11; Y. Berachot 56a (9.1); Genesis 1.26–27; Niddah 31a; Genesis 4.1; Jeremiah 2.21.
4   Kiddushin 29b–30a & Ethics 5.24; Genesis 38.9; MR. Genesis 22.6; Ibid 70.18; Genesis 49.3.
5   Deuter. 23.18; Sotah 44a; Deuter. 22.28–29; Exodus 22.15–16; Levit. 19.29.

6   MR. Levit. 24.6; Ethics 1.1; Makkot 23b; Levit. 11.45–46; E.H. chaps. 21–22; Eccles 10.8; Proverbs 22.28.

7   Job 10.7; Ibid 15.4; B. Batra 16a; Sukkah 52a; Yad. De'ot 1.1; Chagigah 16a; Isaiah 66.1; Jeremiah 23.24.

8   Kiddushin 2b; Yevamot 113a.

9   Levit. 18.22–23; Kiddushin 82a; HPH 492; Levit. 18.3; Yad. Is-Biah 21.8; Isaiah 56.3–4.

10   Exodus 20.5; Tanchuma. Pikuday 3, cf. Niddah 16b; Sotah 3a; Berachot 60b; Ibid 33b; Deuter. 10.12; Shabbat 104a.

11   Yad. De'ot 2.19; Psalms 80.9.

Thirty-Five

MINORITIES AND RARITIES

All the commandments hitherto listed have general application, both to gentlemen and ladies, unless the latter are explicitly excluded: and even then, it is nearly always from the 'must' that they are excluded, rather than the 'may'. However, there are minority sections of the community who are obliged to perform certain additional duties, and some rare situations in which individuals may find themselves, which merit attention; and it is to them that this chapter is devoted.

Section 1.   The *Kohanim*
The largest minority group comprises the *Kohanim*, the priests, those reputedly descended from Aaron, the first High Priest, and only to the male descendants: for Moses is instructed to convey the laws applying to the priesthood to "*bnei Aharon*," which *can* be common gender meaning "the children of Aaron", but in this instance is confined to its literal and limited meaning, "the *sons* of Aaron – and not the daughters", the Sages conclude.

   In Temple times, of course, the *kohanim* had many scores of commandments which were theirs alone to perform, the vast majority of them associated with the proper maintenance of the Temple and offering the sacrifices there. It is interesting to note that the *Chafetz Chayyim*, who was a *kohen*, made a special study of these commandments, revising them frequently – just in case the Messiah came, and the Temple was miraculously built, in the twinkling of an eye, and officiating priests would be immediately required! And he urged all his fellow-priests to follow his example.

   In order to be prepared at all times to serve in the Temple, the priests had to be in a state of ritual purity: and since the father of all sources of impurity is the dead human body, which could only be finally removed "by a seven-day sprinkling rite with the waters of the red heifer solution," the priests were warned not to come in close contact with death – except in the case of one of their seven nearest relatives; and even this exemption was not allowed the High Priest.

There is no Temple and no red-heifer solution today, so the laws of ritual purity and impurity are generally in abeyance – though there are important exceptions. Nevertheless, the prohibition against *kohanim* coming in contact with death – not only by touching a dead body, but also by being under one roof with it, or within close proximity of one in the open air, are still in force. And so, if you are a *kohen*, and wish to fulfil the two-worlds-reward *mitzvah* (SPB 6) of "attending the dead to the grave", you must keep well away from the coffin, and outside the prayer-hall while it is inside.

If you really want, as a *kohen*, to satisfy all opinions, you will take these laws into consideration when contemplating the career you are going to follow – and decide against becoming a doctor! For medical training inevitably involves dissecting corpses: and while some authorities appear to grant dispensation in such a case, since it can lead to the saving of life, and today's *kohanim* are only presumed to be such; others frown at the violation of explicit Torah commandments. There are many other careers from which to choose.

Section 2.   Bless Israel!

To the *kohanim* was given the privilege to be the medium through whom (SPB 324–325) G–d bestows His blessings upon His people Israel. Said the Eternal to Moses: "Speak unto Aaron and unto his sons saying: 'In this way shall you bless the children of Israel, saying unto them: 'The Eternal bless thee, and keep thee; the Eternal make His face to shine upon thee, and be gracious unto thee; the Eternal lift up His countenance unto thee, and give thee peace'. So they shall put My Name upon the children of Israel, and *I* will bless them'".

The plain meaning of this text is that through the priests' pronouncement of this formula, in a manner handed down from generation to generation amongst them, G–d will bless the people of Israel, they being only the channel through which He does so. But R. Yehoshua b. Levi saw that the last word can refer to the *priests*, thus: "when they, the priests, put My Name upon the children of Israel, I (in return) will bless *them* (the priests)." And he supports this view with G–d's promise to Abraham "And I will bless those that bless thee".

So, when the *kohen* fulfils his duty in bringing G–d's blessing upon Israel, G–d rewards him by blessing *him*. But conversely, R. Yehoshua warns, any kohen who does *not* fulfil this duty with which he is especially privileged, and withholds the threefold blessings from the congregation, commits a threefold transgression! Therefore every post-Barmitzvah, having been trained by his father, other *kohanim* or the rabbi, must perform this commandment.

The ceremony has two names: it is called either *nesi'at kapayim* – 'the lifting of the hands', for that is the stance the *kohanim* take up when they pronounce the priestly benediction; or *alot laduchan* – 'ascending the platform', the steps that usually lead up to the Holy Ark, from the top of which the blessing is pronounced. If, then, *you* are a privileged *kohen*, ascend, lift your hands, and bless the Levites and Israelites of your Congregation!

Section 3. **Only One Debarment**
Remembering that the kohen is, by mere birth, the channel through which G–d blesses His people, it is not surprising that *every kohen*, however unworthy he may consider himself to act in that capacity, must nevertheless 'duchan', as the ceremony is briefly called – though, of course, he must always strive to make himself as worthy as possible to merit that privilege.

The only crime which debars him from duchaning is that of having taken another's life, either by deliberate murder or manslaughter – though custom permits one who has committed the latter to ascend, "after he has repented." The ban is deduced from the Prophet's words in the Name of G–d: "When you spread your hands out, I will hide My face from you . . . for your hands are full of blood".

There are a few sins which involve temporary debarment, like compromising one's priesthood by deliberately flouting the prohibition against defiling oneself by contact with death of others than those permitted, the ban not being removed until one promises not to repeat the offence. It could go without saying, but it is still formally enacted that anyone who is even slightly drunk should not duchan.

As for any other sins, it was G–d Who chose the priests as the medium through which to bless His people: the medium may be imperfect, but His perfect blessing nevertheless passes through them.

Section 4. **When To Bless**
In Israel today, the kohanim bless the congregation once every day, during the repetition of the Shacharit Amidah, and a second time whenever there is a Musaph Service. But outside the Holy Land, they do so only to Musaph on Festivals – because then the congregation "are in a joyous frame of mind", and Rosh Hashanah and even Yom Kippur are included, the confidence in G–d's gracious forgiveness of our sins being the source of that joy. But not Shabbatot – "because they are then concerned about their livelihood and cessation from work".

(Nowadays, when so many enjoy a five-day working week, one of the two others usually being Shabbat, I should imagine that such concern is more likely on Festivals falling on weekdays! But the custom prevails, for "custom at times supersedes the law".)

The abbreviated "Order of Lifting the Hands" in SPB does not include the beautiful introductory prayer and plea made by the *kohanim* just before descending from the duchan — so I give it here: "Lord of the universe! We have fulfilled that which You decreed we should do. Do You now fulfil *Your* promise to 'Look down from Thy holy habitation, from heaven, and bless Thy people Israel, and the Land which Thou hast given us, as Thou didst swear unto our fathers — a land flowing with milk and honey'."

Section 5.   **For Levites — Or Firstborns!**
The Levites, also, both in the wilderness and in the Temple, had many special duties as assistants to the *kohanim*; but with the destruction of the Temple, they all disappeared. Yet there is still one custom reserved for the Levites, perhaps to remind them that they were once assistants to the priests — "to pour the water over the hands of the *kohanim*" when they prepare to bless the congregation, in accordance with the verse "Lift up your hands, towards the sanctuary, and bless the Eternal", interpreted: "When you are about to lift your hands, sanctify them first, i.e. with washing, and thereafter bless the blessing of the Eternal, which is the priestly benediction".

But what if there *are* no Levites in the congregation? Who should then pour the water? The answer, very logically though surprisingly, is "any firstborns" in the congregation! For after all, it was from them that the Levites took over the duties in the sanctuary: indeed, before it was erected, "the firstborns performed the whole of the sacrificial service"; and it was only taken away from them because they worshipped the Golden Calf while the Levites — of which tribe the priests are part — did not.

So if *you* are a firstborn, and there are no Levites in the congregation when the priests are about to duchan, you can perform this service. This is a *mitzvah*, not a commandment — but still worth looking out for!

Section 6.   **Rare — But Possible**
For the sake of completeness, I am mentioning two Torah commandments here, the first of which is extremely unlikely to apply to you, young man, and the second slightly less unlikely; because both of them were, in the first instance, duties which your father had to perform with regard to your person, which he almost certainly

fulfilled – unless the circumstances of your birth were very exception-al in the case of the first one. I refer to circumcision and the redemption of the firstborn.

Circumcision, as you probably know, is a sign of "everlasting covenant" which G–d made with the father of our people, binding upon all his descendants, to be performed when the child is eight days old. That it is the father's duty to perform it, is understood from the verse "And Abraham circumcised his son Isaac when he was eight days old, as G–d had commanded him".

However, unless he is one himself, the father usually engages the services of an expert and experienced *mohel*, 'circumciser', to act on his behalf, since "a man's agent is equivalent to himself" in the performance of commandments – *if* that man cannot fulfil them himself, as in this case, in which the very life of his precious son is involved.

For this same reason, if the baby shows the slightest signs of weakness or illness, the *milah* (circumcision) must be postponed until he is stronger and healthy, because "danger to life thrusts aside all other considerations". There are occasions, indeed, when a child *must not* be circumcised: when two of his brothers, or his own brother and a son of his mother's sister, unfortunately died after the *milah* – in which latter case none of the other sisters, when they have male children, may circumcise them.

In all these cases and the like, the rite has to be postponed until expert medical opinion positively declares that there can be no possible danger from the performance of the *brit milah* (the "cove-nant of circumcision"), as the rite is more fully termed. But otherwise, if the baby is in perfect health and weight on birth, and his father neglects to fulfil his duty, then "the Beth-Din has to step in and perform it"; and if they do not, the boy has to have the omission rectified as soon as he becomes a Barmitzvah.

It is extremely unlikely that you should find yourself in such a situation – but it can happen! In brutal Hitler's days, when the sign of the covenant of Abraham – even borne by non-Jews for health reasons – was almost a certain passport to the gas-chamber, many a Jewish parent in Germany did not have their sons circumcised, considering the situation a matter of life-or-death. And then, after escaping, with G–d's help, from that fiery furnace, neglected to rectify the omission.

I have come across a few such cases, and recall one in particular. Two swimming-mates of a boy soon to become Barmitzvah informed me that he had not had a *brit milah*, and subsequent enquiries from the father, who had been a refugee from Germany, verified the fact.

The boy was an understanding and brave lad, and willingly agreed to have himself entered into the covenant less than a month before his Barmitzvah!

More recently, many young, and not so young immigrants to Israel from Russia participated in a mass *brit milah* ceremony, either because of prior ignorance – since religion may not be taught, under the atheistic law of that country until one is eighteen; or because of the lack of trained *mohelim*. I have also met with Jewish mothers whose non-Jewish husbands have refused to allow their sons to be circumcised.

Section 7.   **Mother's Firstborn**
The second rarity, even more rare because it involves even a smaller number of men than the last, is still nevertheless slightly more likely to occur, since some fathers consider its performance less essential and important than a *brit milah*. It is "The redemption of the son" (*Pidyon Habben*), i.e. the first child of a mother, if it is a male, and born naturally – but not by caesarean section.

If you are such a firstborn, then it was your father's duty "to redeem you from the priest" as soon as possible after the thirtieth day from your birth. You can read for yourself "the reason for this redemption": I mention it here just in case, on enquiry, you discover that the ceremony was not performed *for* you, you will be able to put the matter right yourself, "as you must." You may be a *kohen* or a Levite yourself, in which case you did not have to be redeemed. Furthermore, if your mother is the daughter of a *kohen* or Levite, "redemption is also not necessary."

A more detailed account of the Pidyon Habben ceremony will be given in the next volume, and numbered there, since that is where it rightly belongs, it being almost certain that your father, whose duty it initially was, performed it.

Section 8.   **For the Young Lady**
None of the laws or customs regarding the firstborn apply to you: but there is one rabbinic enactment which, though not exclusively applicable to ladies, generally falls within their sphere in the home. And if you desire to become a really good housewife when that stage in your life comes round – as I am sure you do, you will already be training yourself in the art in which the enactment calls for fulfilment.

The children of Israel were commanded in the wilderness: "When you come into the Land whither I bring you, then it shall be that when you eat of the bread of the Land, you shall set apart a portion as a gift unto the Eternal. Of the first of your dough you shall set apart challah as a gift . . . throughout your generations."

From the unusual form of the word translated 'when you come', which literally means 'in your coming' and is addressed to all the people, the Sages understand the commandment to have application only in "the coming of all of you, and not of the coming of a portion of you" i.e. the Jewish people, to settle in the Land of Israel; and therefore it did not apply Torah-wise even when the exiles returned from the Babylonian exile, because "when Ezra brought them up, not all of them went up" – and not even a majority of them.

Nevertheless, the Sages enacted that the commandment of *challah*, as this setting apart of part of the dough is called, should be observed not only in Israel, though only a minority of the Jewish people live there, but also outside Israel, wherever Jews live, "so that the torah (law) of challah should not be forgotten." But with this difference: whereas in Temple times the private, home-baker had to give one twenty-fourth of the dough to a priest, a minister of the Eternal; today she only "separates a symbolic olive-size portion, and burns it."

Section 9. **Ascend!**

By rights, this volume should have ended here: our ladder of two five-fold uprights and ninety rungs, together with almost half as many again underpinning Torah brackets, has been built and erected, ready to be scaled by every BM from the great day onwards. All together, they comprise more than half of the 270 Torah commandments *any* Diaspora Jew can observe. But the reason for the enactment of the above custom – 'so that the *torah* of challah may not be forgotten', should remind every Jew that *the Torah* as a whole not only must not be forgotten, but must be made to be fulfilled, by whatever contribution he or she can make.

The Tenach ends with the famous "Cyrus Declaration inviting "Whosoever there is among you (in Babylon) of all His people – may the Eternal his G–d be with him! – let him go up!" to Jerusalem which is in Judah. But just as Ezra only led a minority of the Jews from exile to Jerusalem, so today, some forty years after the modern State of Israel opened its arms wide to embrace all newcomers, the majority of Jews still live in the Diaspora, most of them of their own free will.

Every soul counts! And if you go up on Aliyah, you will bring your own, and the whole Torah's, fulfilment that little bit nearer. To encourage you to do so is the reason for the additional and final chapter which will explain itself.

Section	**Notes**
1	Levit. 21.1.ff; Sotah 23b; Numbers 19.12.
2	Numbers 6.23–27; Sotah 38b; Genesis 12.3; Megillah 23b; Shabbat 118b.
3	Berachot 32b; Or. Ch. 128.35; Isaiah 1.15.
4	Or. Ch. 128.44; Y. Yevamot 57a (12.1); Deuter. 26.15.
5	Numbers chap. 8; I. Chron. 23.6–32; Or. Ch. 128.6; Psalms 134.2; MB. 128 note 19; Ibid note 22; Numbers 3.45 and Zevachim 112b.
6	Genesis 17.9–14; Ibid 21.4; Berachot 34b; Y. De'ah 263.1.ff; Kiddushin 29a.
7	Numbers 18.15–16; Exodus 13.13–15 & Numbers 3.12–13; Kiddushin 29a; Y. De'ah 305.18.
8	Numbers 15.18–21; Ketubot 25a; Bechorot 27a. Y. De'ah 322.5, Rama.
9	II. Chron. 36.23.

Thirty-Six

ONE-HUNDRED-AND-ONE?

Section 1. **The Elusive Fulfilment**

The purpose of this chapter is not to prove the obvious – that the divine experiment which the creation of man was (see chapter four) is still on-going; but to show that there never was a better opportunity for the Jewish people to help realise it than today, you included!

Israel was forged into a people in the iron furnace of Egypt, as G–d had "forewarned their founder father" that they would be. Many nations have since then learnt to their cost, as did the Egyptians – though many more have not yet taken the lesson to heart – that bondage and persecution of a minority only result in the fusion and refinement of the oppressed. Indeed, it was Pharaoh himself who first referred to the Israelites as "the *people* of the children of Israel"; and it was during their affliction that G–d first called them "My *people*" – in His dialogue with Moses at the vision of the Burning Bush at mount Sinai.

It was there and then that He promised to deliver His people, and "to bring them up . . . into a good and ample land, unto a land flowing with milk and honey". And when Moses expressed doubt as to the likelihood of the Israelites accepting him as G–d's emissary, he was given a sign that his mission *would* succeed: "When thou bringest forth the people from Egypt, you will serve G–d at this mountain" – and that 'service' included the Divine Revelation and the acceptance of the Torah.

It was "a mere eleven-day journey from there to the Promised Land," and they could have made it, and entered upon their inheritance, under the leadership of Moses! But even *he* had freedom of will; and despite an indication that "his action would displease G–d," he sent spies to reconnoitre the land, at the people's request. Yet he himself had just told them: "Behold, the Eternal thy G–d hath set the land before thee! Go up, take possession, as the Eternal, the

329

G–d of thy fathers, hath spoken unto thee: fear not, neither be dismayed." So he and they forfeited that option.

You know what happened: ten of the spies reported adversely, the people were alarmed and sentenced to forty years wandering in the wilderness, during which time Moses got himself debarred from entering the Holy Land – explicitly for striking the rock, instead of speaking to it, that it should bring forth water for the thirsty people; but for other reasons as well, implicit in various texts. But one lesson the Torah quite often teaches us is that when man errs, his mistakes are frequently incorporated into G–d's own plan to good purpose: and so it was in this case.

"As for me," Moses informs the people, "the Eternal did command at that time to teach you statutes and judgments (*chukkim u'mish-patim*) that you may do them *in the land* whither you go over to possess it". This does *not* mean, as has before been stressed, that *none* of the commandments are applicable *outside* the Land, but that there are many whose fulfilment is tied up with the land. And that is how Moses spent those forty years – teaching the Torah, Written and Oral, to the people, particularly to the younger generation who were the ones who were to enter the Land.

Section 2.   **Moses' Anguish!**
It should not be difficult to imagine Moses' anguish at not being permitted to oversee the implementation of all he had been striving to achieve all those forty hard years, against much opposition: and the Midrash "poignantly relates the many pleas he made to have the decree annulled". We have already had one illustration of how he "performed half-a-commandment which could only be completed in the Land of Israel," no doubt hoping that "to anyone who commences to do a *mitzvah* we say 'Finish it'."

And here is another: While all the Israelites, presumably including Joseph's descendants, "were busy collecting gold and silver prior to their departure from Egypt," Moses was occupied in finding the remains of Joseph, in order to re-bury them in the soil of the Holy Land, as his brothers had sworn they or their descendants would do when the time of redemption came. Yet he was not allowed to complete either: the three other Cities of Refuge "*were* established on the other side of the Jordan"; and Joseph's remains "*were* buried in Shechem (Nablus)" – but by others!

Section 3.   **The Plan Completed?**
But the divine plan proceeded under the leadership of Joshua who, towards the end of his life could say: "So the Eternal has given to

Israel all the land which He swore to give unto their fathers. . . . There
failed not aught of any good thing which the Eternal has spoken unto
the house of Israel; all has come to pass". And we are further told:
"And Israel served the Eternal all the days of Joshua, and all the days
of the elders that outlived Joshua, and had known all the work of the
Eternal that He had wrought for Israel". Was then the divine plan
complete? Had G–d's promise to Abraham on his arrival in Israel:
"Lift up thine eyes, and look from the place where thou art,
northward and southward, and eastward and westward; for all the
land which thou seest, to thee will I give it, and to thy descendants for
ever" been fulfilled?

Alas, No! Joshua had been too premature and optimistic: throughout the period of the Judges who succeeded the elders, there were
wars with the inhabitants of Canaan and its neighbours whenever the
people strayed from the service of the Eternal, as they frequently did;
and the first king, Saul, who followed them, had his problems. It
seemed that the promise was to be fulfilled in the golden reigns of
David and Solomon: but after the latter's death, the united kingdom
was divided into two, which often warred one with the other, and
eventually both went into exile, ten of the tribes to Assyria – and 'lost'
there, and the other two, Judah and Benjamin, to Babylon.

But even this tragedy, "against which the Almighty had also
forewarned", and Moses had foreseen and prescribed the antidote
against; was used to good purpose within the grand divine design. In
Babylon, soon thereafter to come under the benign rule of Cyrus and
the Persians (now Iranians), "the passion for idolatry", one of the
prime reasons for the Exile, was uprooted, the Torah, both Written
and Oral, was studied in depth and observed, the latter eventually
being put into writing in the Talmud; and the Synagogue came into
being.

The majority of the Jews, as we must now call our people – an
abbreviation of 'Judah-ites', the larger of the two tribes – remained
snugly ensconced under Persia's tolerant rule, even after the "Cyrus
Declaration", which gave them permission, nay encouraged them, to
return to Jerusalem and rebuild the Temple – though many of them
undoubtedly changed their minds after the trauma of Haman's
near-successful attempt to exterminate them! But a patriotic minority
did take advantage of the royal pronouncement.

In a much truncated State, inspired and urged on by the Prophets,
Chaggai, Zechariah and Malachi, they *did* build "a much more
modest Temple than Solomon's"; and under Ezra who, some say,
"*was* Malachi", and "would have been worthy of receiving the
Torah, had not Moses anticipated him", assiduously studied the

Torah and put its commandments into practice. These Prophets were the leaders of the first "Great Assembly", the supreme religious body which administered the Torah down to "the time of Simon the Just, who was one of its last survivors" (c. 200 B.C.E.). It was they who introduced the easier Assyrian script for Hebrew, "formulated our main prayer and blessings", instituted the Festival of Purim – and other vital practices which have survived to this day.

Section 4.   Another Near-Completion – But . . .

During the near two-and-a-half centuries from Ezra to Mattathias (c. 450–200 B.C.E.), so firmly rooted had the Jewish people become in Jewish living, greatly helped by no hostile distractions from outside, that when the next mighty confrontation came with the Syrians and the cult of Hellenism, the Maccabees, with their battle-cry 'Who is like unto Thee among the mighty, O Eternal!' were able to rout their overwhelmingly superior forces, re-dedicate the dese-crated Temple, and institute the Festival of Chanukah.

That epochal event could have ushered in the Messianic Era – and almost did. The great-grandson of Mattathias and the Hasmonean, Alexander Yannai, had restored to Jewish rule all the territory of Israel by 80 B.C.E.; and after his death his Queen's brother, R. Simeon b. Shetach, "restored the Torah to its pristine glory"; and she, Alexandra Salome, ascended the throne as the first Jewish Queen in her own right – apart from "the usurping Athaliah, daughter of Jezebel."

So healing and benevolent was the reign of Shelom-Tsiyyon (76–67 B.C.E.), to give her her Hebrew name, that the Sages say that "the land showed all the signs foretold of the Messianic Era" – but it was short-lived, a blissful calm before the oncoming storm. Internecine strife between her sons for the succession, resulting in an invitation to Pompey to intervene, brought Rome on to the scene, ending the independence of Judea, and culminating in the destruction of State and Second Temple in 70 C.E., a last heroic stand by Bar-Kochba in 135 being of no avail.

During the eighteen-or-so intervening centuries, somewhere or other, at some time or other, the gloomy predictions of Moses "Thou shalt become an astonishment, a taunt, and an object of biting remarks among all the nations whither the Eternal shall lead thee away", and "among these nations thou shalt have no repose, and there shall be no rest for the sole of thy foot . . . and thou wilt fear night and day, and wilt have no assurance of thy life . . ." and so on and so forth, have been the fate of the scattered segments of the Jewish people, reaching its horrible climax in the bestial German

Holocaust which burnt away a third of them. But even that nadir in man's inhumanity towards man, had its compensation, took its place in the inscrutable divine plan: for it led, in 1947, to the two-thirds majority of the United Nations recognising that the Jews *were* a people, and *were* entitled to an independent homeland in at least part of the Promised Land; while in 1967, in a defensive war, He led his People to gain possession of all of it.

Section 5. **It Can Happen – NOW!**

Why do I mention all this here, and now? To make you realise that G–d's promise to the father of our people, reiterated again and again to the other Patriarchs and by all the Prophets, never yet brought to fulfilment by their descendants, *now can be* – and *you* are a most important particle in the element most likely to bring this dream to reality!

It was the older generation, the over-20's, who, even while still in Egypt, begged of Moses "Leave us alone, and let us serve Egypt!"; who, once in the wilderness, hankered after the time when "we sat by the fleshpots of Egypt, when we ate bread to the full", and recalled with slavish nostalgia, "the fish, which we were wont to eat in Egypt for nought; the cucumbers and the melons, and the leeks, the onions and the garlic!" as they ate the monotonous manna; and who prayed "would that we had died in Egypt, or would that we had died in this wilderness!"

That death-wish was granted them! After they had cowardly yielded to the adverse report of the ten spies, "The Eternal had said of them, 'they shall certainly die in the wilderness'; and there was not a man left of them, except Calev the son of Yephunneh, and Joshua the son of Nun" – the two courageous spies. All the other over-20's of the *men* died during the next forty years as they reached the age of sixty – "but not the women", young lady, for they refused to follow the advice of the ten, since the ladies *loved* the Holy Land!

It was their *children*, the under 20's, many of them born in the wilderness, all of them not contaminated with the Egyptian way of life, all of them "taught of the Eternal" through His faithful servant and their devoted teacher, Moses. Their parents had complained that they would become prey to the wilderness: but of *them* G–d said: "But your little ones, that you said would be a prey, *them* will I bring in, and *they* shall know the land which you have rejected"! *They* surmounted all the hardships, *they* learnt the arts of war from Joshua, and *they* eventually entered the Promised Land under his leadership!

Though it is nowhere explicitly stated, it was undoubtedly also the younger generation of Persian Jewry who must largely have comprised the minority who responded to the "Cyrus Declaration" and went up to rebuild Jerusalem and the Second Temple, "half of them holding spears from dawn to nightfall . . . that in the night they may be a guard to us, and may labour in the day".

True, the older generation, and generations after them, remained under Persian rule − not without occasional scares and alarums, particularly that contrived by Haman; and that, at their zenith, they produced the Babylonian Talmud. But when the Muslim Arabs conquered Persia, the Jews, like all non-Moslems, became second-class citizens, discriminatory laws being enacted against them, with the result that many had to flee to other countries − where the same pattern repeated itself time and time again through the centuries.

Section 6.   **It Is Up To You Now!**

And, insofar as voluntary return to modern Israel in concerned, and the up-building of the State from the desert in which its temporary Arab tenants left it, it has been primarily *young* Jews from scores of countries who have undertaken the arduous task, and have also had to learn the arts of war, however much they are against the Jew's love and yearning for peace, *and* stand on guard, by day as well as by night, against enemies round about and within.

The older generation, for the most part, comprising the majority of the Jewish people, having become thoroughly acclimatised to the comforts and relative affluence of the Galut, prefer to live out their days there − the swift-changing vagaries of political and economic conditions permitting; but progressively being decimated through assimilation, inter-marriage, and even conversions to other religions and cults.

But *you* are an alert and growingly-knowledgeable young Jew or Jewess! *You* are aware of the numerous pitfalls which the *yetzer hara* has put in your path! *You* are beginning to realise how much superior is the Torah way of life, even its *mishpatim* − its 'between-man-and-his-neighbour' laws, to the environment in which you live; and *you* must appreciate by now that it is only by putting these into general practice by a Jewish nation, living independently in its own Land, that Judaism can have any real impact for good on the other nations of the world, thus fulfilling its divinely-ordained mission.

As explained, not all the Torah commandments, even those not dependent upon the re-building of the Temple, can come into full force until at least the majority of our people are resident in our Land. Therefore you should go up there, as soon as you can, perhaps pursuing your higher academic studies in the excellent Universities,

Technical Colleges, and even Yeshivot, there; working on the land itself, helping to produce its bounteous and variegated harvest – or doing one of the hundred-and-one other things the old-young Land needs to bring it to the pitch of perfection in all spheres.

In fact, it is only because of two very weak reasons that I do not make this *duty* to settle in Israel not only the hundred-and-first Torah commandment in this book, but the eleventh of them, after the ten 'constants', or even the very first of them – for reasons that will emerge as we go along. The paper-thin excuses I have given myself for not doing so are: because I wanted to limit the number of commandments to a nice round hundred; and the fact that, although, having become a BM, you are technically 'your own boss', you are nevertheless most probably wholly dependent upon your parents for board, lodging, schooling, etc., and cannot therefore make your own decisions as to what to do and where to go!

According to RN, *dirat Eretz-Yisrael*, residing in the Land of Israel, has always been one of the 613 commandments – one of those which, he claims, RM 'forgot'! The latter's champions dutifully defend him against this charge of amnesia; but most of their arguments, as we shall see, today hold no water; and I am thoroughly convinced that were RM among us now, he would unequivocally agree with RN! Let me explain.

Section 7. **The View of Nachmanides (RN)**

I quote RN's opinion at some length, because of its importance. He states: "We are commanded to take possession of the Land which G–d, blessed be He, gave to our fathers Abraham, Isaac and Jacob, and not to abandon it to other nations or to desolation. This is ordained in His saying: 'And you shall take possession of the Land, and dwell therein; for unto *you* have I given the Land to possess it. And you shall cause the Land to be inherited by lot according to your families . . .'." He then details all the boundaries of the Promised Land as part of this commandment, and continues:

"Under certain conditions, peace may be made with the erstwhile inhabitants, but once land is Jewish, it must not be sold back to them or anyone else in any generation. . . . And I maintain that our Sages esteemed this commandment so highly that they said: 'Anyone who leaves it, to reside outside the Land of Israel may be regarded as one who has no G–d'. Therefore it is a positive commandment, in all generations, upon every one of us to possess the Land and dwell there".

RN actually tones down that Talmudic saying, for the text there is: "Whoever lives outside the Land of Israel may be regarded as one who has no G–d", it being deduced from the verse: "I am the Eternal your G–d Who brought you forth out of the land of Egypt, *to give you the land of Canaan to be your G–d*": i.e. there you will be under My protection, but elsewhere you will be subject to natural forces and local political circumstances. But even RN's text is a denunciation of those who leave Israel for other lands, thus casting off, as it were, G–d's protection.

Section 8.   Maimonides (RM) Defenders

A story told there, illustrates one of the arguments used by RM's apologists to explain why he did not include *dirat Eretz-Yisrael* as one of his 613 commandments. R. Zera wanted to go up to Israel to study, but feared earning the displeasure of his teacher Rav (not the famous Rabbi) Yehudah, who considered anyone who left Babylon, even for Israel, to be violating a command that "'They' shall be carried to Babylon, and there they shall be, until the time I remember them, saith the Eternal".

When R. Zera respectfully pointed out that that verse refers to the vessels of the Temple and the royal palaces, and not to the exiles themselves, Rav Yehudah cited another rather tenuous verse in support of his contention: "I adjure you, O daughters of Jerusalem . . . not to awaken or stir up love until it pleases" – taken to mean, not to yearn to return to Jerusalem until it pleases G–d to bring them back.

But it is on "a deduction from repetitions of this verse" that RM's defenders base their main refutation of RN's accusation. R. Yose reads into these verses a warning given by G–d that Jews should not go up to Israel *en masse* ('like a wall'), and that they should not rebel against the nations of the world. But our present occupation of the Land of Israel violates neither of these warnings! At first our people went up under the terms of the Balfour Declaration, and later to an independent State sanctioned by the United Nations!

The only action that can in any sense be termed an act of 'rebellion' was Israel's occupation of Judea and Samaria in the Six-Day War of 1967 in the course of a defensive war, thus taking under its administration the most venerated area of biblical Israel first trodden by our Patriarchs, which Jordan had illegally annexed in 1948, with the acquiescence of only Britain among the nations of the world.

Most certainly according to RN, and almost as certainly even to RM, this action was *"milchemet mitzvah"* – a war, albeit forced upon Israel, in fulfilment of the Torah commandment to occupy the G–d-given Land within all its biblical borders, concerning which RN cites the verse, "Every place upon which the sole of thy foot shall tread shall be yours" – and must never be relinquished. Most nations regard territory captured in defence of their country as legitimate 'spoils of war'. Judea and Samaria and certainly the Old City of Jerusalem, are not spoils of war, but part and parcel of our people's heritage, ancient and modern, and will not easily be relinquished, though an accommodation with their non-Jewish occupants, willing to live in peace and goodwill, can be made.

The last argument of RM's protagonists is that the precious evaluation by the Sages of *dirat Eretz-Yisrael* only applies when the Temple is standing, "but today there is no such *mitzvah*". Were we able to ask them: How can the Temple conceivably be built without Jews living in Israel?, the answer would most probably be: With the coming of the Messiah, who will take us all there *en masse*, and miraculously rebuild it!

(Before I deal with this argument, I must inform you that R. Zera did chance his master's displeasure, *did* go up to Israel, and it is related: "When he could not find a ferry to take him over the river Jordan, he crossed it by means of a rope-bridge and retorted to a bystander who mocked his eagerness: How can I delay a crossing which even Moses and Aaron did not merit to make?")

Section 9.   **Who, What Is "The Messiah"?**
No Jew knows precisely what 'the coming of the Messiah' really means. The word 'Messiah' is merely a transliteration of the Hebrew *mashi'ach*, which means 'an annointed one', and is used to describe "the High Priest", the first two kings of Israel, "Saul and David", the last king of Judah, "Zedekiah"; and, so far as identifiable individuals are concerned, to "king Cyrus of Persia"! (It could well be applied, also, to Lord Balfour, of Declaration fame!)

Daniel "uses the term twice" enigmatically, the first traditionally also taken to refer to Cyrus, and the second, either to Onias III, the High Priest in the time of Antiochus Epiphanes (the villain of the Chanukah story), or to Agrippa II, the last king of Judea who was "cut off", and during whose reign "the City (of Jerusalem) and the Sanctuary were destroyed".

The only other occurrence of the term is in the verse "Thou art gone forth for the deliverance of Thy people, for the deliverance of Thy annointed", in which the 'Messiah' is equated with the people of Israel. In other words, provided that they are worthy of G–d's help in their deliverance, *the Jewish people are their own 'Messiah'*! And 'his footsteps', harbingers of which were the Balfour Declaration, the United Nations vote, and the Six-Day War, are the footsteps of every Jew and Jewess the sole of whose foot regularly treads the soil of the Holy Land anywhere!

When Joab, king David's nephew and Commander-in-Chief of his army, saw that the war against Syria was going against him, "He selected the choice young men of Israel" and urged them: "Be of good courage and let us prove strong, for our people, and for the cities of our G–d; *then* the Eternal will do what is good in His eyes". On this Ralbag comments: "We learn from this that a man should not depend on miracles, but should strive as far as he can to save himself, and *then* rely on G–d's help".

Section 10.   **What About *The* "Messiah"?**
Will then there never be what is popularly called a "Messiah", an individual human, a super man, a perfect person, who will bring the whole of mankind into a harmonious brotherhood under the Father-hood of G–d Alone? There most decidedly will be, is the consensus opinion. Much to the consternation of at least one of his colleagues, Hillel II (fourth century) asserted "There will be no Messiah for Israel, because they have already enjoyed him in the days of Heze-kiah". What he meant was that when Isaiah prophesied "A child has been born to us, a son has been given unto us", he was speaking at the birth of that royal infant, of whom, he predicted, "the ministry (Of G–d) shall be upon his shoulders; and He Who is wonderful in counsel, the Mighty G–d, the Everlasting Father, will name him 'the prince of peace! . . .'". And "that prophecy was wholly fulfilled" throughout the twenty-nine years of that righteous king's reign.

Nevertheless, Hillel's colleague, R. Yosef, prayed that G–d might forgive him for making such a statement! For another Prophet, who spoke at least two centuries after Hezekiah's death, foretold to Zion and Jerusalem: "Behold, thy king cometh unto thee; he is righteous and victorious . . ."! Various conjectures have been made to identify this king in the days of the Second Temple, about which Zechariah mainly prophesied; and Ibn Ezra suggests it is a reference to Judas Maccabeus.

However, that text continues: "And I will break off the chariot from Ephraim, and the horse from Jerusalem, and the battle bow shall be cut off" – i.e. wars will no longer be waged – "and he will speak peace unto the nations, and his dominion shall be from sea to sea, and from the river to the ends of the earth". *That* was not fulfilled in Judas Maccabeus' time – nor in *any* age, by *anyone*, thereafter, to this war-ridden, armaments-proliferating, hate-soaked era.

Therefore many look forward still to an individual Messiah, a scion of the royal house of David, who will achieve all this. When Samuel said, then, that "There is no difference between this world and the days of the Messiah, except (absence of) bondage to foreign powers" – i.e. the people of Israel will live in freedom in an independent Land of Israel; the rest of the Sages disagreed with him, looking forward to much grander times – but they, also, only speak of *the days* of the Messiah, i.e. an era, not necessarily an individual.

Section 11. **The Ideal Messianic Era**

The ideal vision of that era was written in almost identical, beautiful language by both Isaiah and Micah in memorable, justifiably famous words, in which they see the "Messiah" neither as king or prince – but as *G–d Himself*! It worthily merits full quotation:

"And it shall come to pass in the end of days, that the mountain of the Eternal's house shall be established as the top of the mountains, and shall be exalted above the hills, and all nations shall flow unto it. And many peoples shall shall go and say: 'Come, and let us go to the mountain of the Eternal, to the house of the G–d of Jacob; and He will teach us His ways, and we will walk in His paths'. For out of Zion shall go forth the Torah, and the word of the Eternal from Jerusalem. And He shall judge between the nations, and shall decide concerning mighty nations afar off; and they shall beat their swords into plowshares, and their spears into pruning-hooks: nation shall not lift up sword against nation, neither shall they learn war any more".

To achieve this is the mission of the Jewish people – of every son and daughter among them! "To raise up the tribes of Jacob, and to restore the preserved ones of Israel! Then will I make thee a light to the nations, that My salvation may be unto the end of the earth", says G–d. But it can only be realised "When all thy people will be righteous, when they will inherit the Land for ever, as a branch of My planting, the work of My hands that I may be glorified!"

And you can assist in bringing about this goal for which the very universe was created, by becoming one of those righteous ones inheriting the Land. Should you ask: what value the aliyah of one individual like me?, that text goes on to say: "The smallest shall become a thousand, and the youngest into a mighty nation" – which can, perhaps, be taken to mean: you, and thousands of youngsters of like mind and determination, can make Israel into a mighty nation!

To a further possible question: if it has of necessity to come about, why not let me just wait for it to happen?: the verse continues with the paradoxical statement, "I, the Eternal, will *hasten* it in *its time*"! If the Messianic Era is to come in its time, the Sages ask, how can its advent be *hastened*? And they answer: If Israel is unworthy, it will come when it must; but if they are worthy, G–d will hasten its coming *before* the appointed time!

Be you worthy! Be you righteous and inherit the Land! Ascend!

Section	Notes
1	Genesis 15.11; Exodus 1.9; Ibid 3.7.ff; Sifre on Deuter. 1.2 and Rashi there; MR. Deuter. 16.7; Deuter. 1.21; Ibid 4.14.
2	MR. Deuter. 11.8–11; Deuter. 4.41–49; Y. Megillah 21b (2.7); MR. Exodus 20.19; Joshua 20.7; Ibid 24.12.
3	Joshua 21.41–43; Ibid 24.31; Genesis 13.14; Deuter. 31.14ff; MR. Cant. 7.,8.1; 11. Chron. 36.23; Haggai 2.3; Megillah 15a; Tosefta Sanhedrin 7.8; Ethics 1.2; Megillah 17b.
4	Kiddushin 66a; II. Kings 11.3; Ta'anit 23a; Deuter. 28.37; Ibiv vv. 65–66.
5	Exodus 14.12; Ibid 16.3; Numbers 11.5; Ibid 14.2; Ibid 26.65; Rashi on last note; Isaiah 54.13; Numbers 14.31; Nehemiah 4.15–16.
7	Numbers 33.53; Ketubot 110b; Levit. 25.38.
8	Ketubot 110b; Jeremiah 27.22; Cant. 2.7; Ketubot 111a; Sotah 44b; Deuter. 11.24; Ketubot 112a.
9	Levit. 4.3; I. Samuel 12.12 & II. Samuel 23.1; Lament. 4.20; Isaiah 45.1; Daniel 9.25–26; Habbakuk 4.13; II. Samuel 10.9–12; see SBB. comment. on last note.
10	Sanhedrin 99a; Isaiah 9.5–6; Ibid 32.1.ff; Zechariah 9.9–10; Berachot 34b.
11	Isaiah 2.2–4 and Micah 4.1–3; Isaiah 49.6; Ibid 60.21–22; Sanhedrin 98a.

ABBREVIATIONS

ADRN	Avot d'Rabbi Natan, a minor Talmud tractate
A. Zarah	Talmud tractate, and section in Yad.
B. Batra	Baba Batra, Talmud tractate
B. Kama	Baba Kama, Talmud tractate
B. Metsia	Baba Metsia, Talmud tractate
Cant.	Canticles, or Song of Songs
CAV.	Church Authorised Version of Bible
Chron.	(Books of) Chronicles
Deuter.	Deuteronomy
Eccles.	Ecclesiastes
HPB.	Authorised Daily Prayer Book with Hertz commentary
HPH.	Pentateuch and Haftarot with Hertz commentary
JAV.	Jewish Publication Society of America's English translation of Bible, taken as "Jewish Authorised Version")
K. Sh.Ar.	Abridged version of Shulchan Aruch
Lament.	Book of Lamentations
Levit.	Book of Leviticus
M. Asurot	Maachalot Asurot, section in Yad.
MB.	Mishnah Berurah, commentary on Orach Chayim
M. Katan	Moed Katan, Talmud tractate
MR.	Midrash Rabba on the Torah and Five Megillot
Or. Ch.	Orach Chayim, first of four sections of Sh. Ar.
PRE.	Pirke d'Rabbi Eliezer, Midrash on Tenach parts
P. Teshuva	Responsa on Yoreh De'ah
Rama	Rabbi Moshe Isserlis, co-author of Shulchan Aruch
Rashi	Rabbi Shlomo Yitschaki, Tenach and Talmud most popular commentator
R. Hash(anah)	Rosh Hashanah, Talmud tractate
RM.	RambaM – Maimonides (R. Moshe b. Maimon)
RN.	RambaN – Nachmanides (R. Moshe b. Nachman)
SBB.	Soncino Books of the Bible

Shach.	Sifse Chohen, commentator on Yoreh De'ah
SM.	Maimonides' Sefer haMitzvot: followed by P. or N., section on positive or negative commandments.
Sh.Ar.	Caro-Isserlis Code of Jewish Law, Shulchan Aruch
SPB.	Authorised Daily Prayer Book, Singer's translation
Tenach	The Hebrew Bible, Genesis to Malachi
Y.	Preceding tractate name: Jerusalem Talmud
Yad.	Maimonides' Yad Hachazakah or Mishne-Torah
Y. De'ah.	Yoreh De'ah, section of Shulchan Aruch
Y. Sh(imoni).	Yalkut Shimoni, Midrash on Tenach

SCRIPTURAL REFERENCES

References are to chapters and their sections.

343

INDEX

The first number in each reference is chapter; the second, the section in that chapter.